BROTHERS IN ARMS

Koufax, Kershaw, and the Dodgers' Extraordinary Pitching Tradition

Jon Weisman

Copyright © 2018 by Jon Weisman

No part of this publication may be reproduced, stored in a retrieval system, or transmitted in any form by any means, electronic, mechanical, photocopying, or otherwise, without the prior written permission of the publisher, Triumph Books LLC, 814 North Franklin, Chicago, Illinois 60610.

Library of Congress Cataloging-in-Publication Data

Names: Weisman, Jon, 1967– author.
Title: Brothers in arms : Koufax, Kershaw, and the Dodgers' extraordinary pitching tradition / Jon Weisman.
Description: Chicago, Illinois : Triumph Books, 2018.
Identifiers: LCCN 2017043254 | ISBN 9781629374673 (paperback)
Subjects: LCSH: Los Angeles Dodgers (Baseball team)—History. | Pitchers (Baseball)—California—Los Angeles—Biography. | BISAC: SPORTS & RECREATION / Baseball / General. | TRAVEL / United States / West / Pacific (AK, CA, HI, NV, OR, WA).
Classification: LCC GV875.L6 W37 2018 | DDC 796.357/640979494—dc23
LC record available at https://lccn.loc.gov/2017043254

This book is available in quantity at special discounts for your group or organization. For further information, contact:

Triumph Books LLC
814 North Franklin
Chicago, Illinois 60610
(312) 337-0747
www.triumphbooks.com

Printed in U.S.A.
ISBN: 978-1-62937-467-3
Design by Patricia Frey

To Dashiell, Casey, Lilah, Dana, and all of my family. I've written this book in part to honor special people, to lasso their memories and preserve them forever. I only wish I could do the same for you. It goes by too fast, but please know from this dedication how dedicated I am to you. You are everything that matters.

Contents

FOREWORD *by Joe Davis*   7

INTRODUCTION   9

QUICK NOTES ON SOURCING AND STATISTICS   11

ALL-TIME DODGER PITCHING LEADERS
   IN WINS ABOVE REPLACEMENT   13

PREGAME: THE ANCESTORS   17

PART ONE: THE KINGS OF BROOKLYN   37
Ralph Branca   38
Preacher Roe   46
Carl Erskine   51
Don Newcombe   58
Johnny Podres   77

PART TWO: THE TWO EMPERORS   87
Sandy Koufax   89
Don Drysdale   117

PART THREE: THE POST-KOUFAX GENERATION   131
Bill Singer   134
Claude Osteen   136
Don Sutton   141

PART FOUR: THE MODERN CLASSICISTS	169
Tommy John	172
Andy Messersmith	180
Burt Hooton	185
Bob Welch	193
Jerry Reuss	201
PART FIVE: EL TORO AND THE BULLDOG	211
Fernando Valenzuela	212
Orel Hershiser	234
PART SIX: THE INTERNATIONAL ROTATION	255
Ramón Martínez	258
Chan Ho Park	269
Ismael Valdez	279
Hideo Nomo	289
PART SEVEN: THE HIRED HANDS	301
Kevin Brown	302
Zack Greinke	307
PART EIGHT: THE BULLPEN ACES	315
PART NINE: THE MAGNIFICENT	343
Clayton Kershaw	345
ACKNOWLEDGMENTS	371
BIBLIOGRAPHY	375

Foreword

WHEN I TOOK THE DODGERS TV JOB, I did so understanding how important the franchise's history was to its identity. I knew I couldn't do the job justice without having an advanced degree in the names, the games, and the moments that define the Dodgers. But I wasn't around when the team was in Brooklyn. I didn't grow up in Los Angeles. The "impossible" happened three months before my first birthday. So I dived in.

What began as work quickly became a passion. I read everything Blue I could get my hands on. Lasorda led me to Alston, and together they led me to McGunnigle. Seager, I found, was a hop, skip, Russell, Wills, and Reese from World War II. The euphoria of '55 began to make sense when I learned about the tears of '51. (And '49. And '47. And '41. And...) And those ever-present Koufax comparisons gave me a new appreciation for what I'm watching every fifth day when Kershaw takes it.

Speaking of those two…

There have been so many great books written about the Dodgers. But with the foundational role pitchers hold in this franchise's glorious history, doesn't it seem like there's been an empty spot on the Dodger shelf that needed filling? With *Brothers in Arms*, Jon Weisman slides a must-have into that void. This book instantly becomes one that I'll always have handy while prepping for broadcasts, and one that I know Dodger fans and history buffs won't be able to put down.

I write this while sitting on the Dodgers' charter plane, a row behind Hershiser and a few in front of Kershaw. They're connected in the same way Grimes and Roe and Drysdale and Sutton and Valenzuela are. Between these covers, Jon gives color and context to those links. The Dodgers' men on the mound now have their own storybook, their own encyclopedia, their own definitive guide.

I hope you enjoy it as much as I do. Off we go.

Joe Davis *is the play-by-play broadcast announcer for the Los Angeles Dodgers on SportsNet LA. He also broadcasts college football, college basketball, and Major League Baseball on Fox Sports.*

Introduction

THE FIRST IDEA WAS TO WRITE a biography of a Dodger, a pitcher in particular. Don Newcombe or Fernando Valenzuela, Orel Hershiser or Clayton Kershaw.

The second idea was, why not do them all?

The Dodgers are the team of Jackie Robinson, of Vin Scully, of the Boys of Summer, and the improbable, impossible home run. They play in one of baseball's most idyllic ballparks, wearing one of its most iconic uniforms, and whether you're their fan or they're your foe, they stand as a tentpole not only in baseball, but all of sports.

And yet, through the years, if anything defines one of baseball's flagship franchises on the field, it's been the Dodgers' ability to continually, almost relentlessly, produce greatness atop that humble rise of dirt in the middle of the diamond. The Dodger pitching tradition is like no other.

It's a pantheon filled with towering figures, any one of whom could be the defining pitcher for a franchise: Newcombe. Koufax. Drysdale. Sutton. Valenzuela. Hershiser. Kershaw.

In the deep supporting cast, you'll find the troops that tie the tradition together: the Knights of the Round Mound. Preacher Roe, Carl Erskine, and Johnny Podres weren't mere men of character—they were characters, perfectly cast in the longest-running show on the Great Blue Way. Since World War II, when the Dodger pitching tradition tiptoed into life, decade after decade has costarred underrated pitchers who deserve the light of a better sun, from those harshly torched by singular moments, such as Ralph Branca, to steady aces lost in the shadow of flashier ones, like Claude Osteen or Burt Hooton. Their stories fascinate with their joy, their poignancy, even their agony.

The Dodger pitching tradition also hosts the origins of some of the most significant developments in baseball history. The Dodgers led baseball in diversifying the men on the mound by recruiting pitchers from untapped leagues, whether Negro, Mexican, Korean, or Japanese. They practically redefined the medical treatment of pitchers, most notably with Tommy John (and a leading assist from Dr. Frank Jobe) but also on several quiet but significant levels. The Dodgers even played important roles in the intersection of pitching and free agency, whether as antagonists to Andy Messersmith or deep divers into the enticing but dangerous waters for Kevin Brown and Zack Greinke.

The attention to scouting and development, the broad-based talent-hunting and high-end fine-tuning, was passed from the past to the present. Executives like Branch Rickey and Peter O'Malley, managers like Walter Alston and Tommy Lasorda, coaches like Red Adams, Ron Perranoski, and Rick Honeycutt, men with generations of service, students who grew up to teach, honed and preserved the Dodger pitching tradition, to the benefit of Los Angeles in particular and baseball in general.

Like the sunsets and San Gabriel Mountains underpinning the skyline behind Dodger Stadium, like the Three Sisters gazing kindly over the left-field bullpen, pitching excellence now seems organic to Dodger life. And yet, we know pitching doesn't grow on trees (not even palm trees). The Dodger pitching tradition came not from nowhere, but from somewhere. In many ways, it's an incredible journey, and in every way, a fascinating one.

Here is the history of that tradition, and the people upon whose shoulders it was built. Time to toe the rubber, stare in for the sign, and read on.

Quick Notes on Sourcing and Statistics

MORE THAN 25 INTERVIEWS were conducted for *Brothers in Arms*. When quoted, the references will be in present tense (e.g., Erskine says, Hershiser recalls). All remaining quotes, derived from books, periodicals, websites, and video recordings, will be in past tense (Newcombe said, Drysdale recalled) and are sourced in the bibliography at the end of the book.

Frequently, you will see **ERA+** referenced in the narrative. This refers to adjusted ERA, which frames a pitcher's ERA with adjustments for the ballparks and the era in which he played. Higher is better, with 100 being average.

Wins Above Replacement (WAR) is a cumulative assessment of value that takes a player's statistics and calculates the number of additional wins he contributed to his team above the number expected from a replacement-level player (that is, a minimum-level major-leaguer). WAR is also adjusted to enable comparisons across time.

Less frequently in the book, you'll see **fielding-independent pitching (FIP)**, which approximates ERA based on statistics that do not involve fielders (except the catcher), ideally to give a valuation to a pitcher that isn't dependent on factors he can't control. FIP is also adjusted for time period.

WHIP (the combination of walks and hits, divided by innings pitched) is not adjusted for ballpark or time period, but does provide a quick-and-dirty indication of baserunners per inning.

Except where otherwise indicated, Baseball-Reference.com is this book's source for statistics.

All-Time Dodger Pitching Leaders in Wins Above Replacement

Rank	Player	WAR	ERA+	ERA	W–L	G	GS	CG	SHO	IP	SO	K%	Years
1	Dazzy Vance	61.8	129	3.17	190–131	378	328	213	29	2,757⅔	1,918	16.8	1922–35
2	Don Drysdale	61.3	121	2.95	209–166	518	465	167	49	3,432	2,486	17.6	1956–69
3	Clayton Kershaw*	57.4	161	2.36	144–64	292	290	25	15	1,935	2,120	27.9	2008–
4	Sandy Koufax	53.2	131	2.76	165–87	397	314	137	40	2,324⅓	2,396	25.2	1955–66
5	Don Sutton	50.8	110	3.09	233–181	550	533	156	52	3,816⅓	2,696	17.3	1966–88
6	Nap Rucker	47.9	119	2.42	134–134	336	274	186	38	2,375⅓	1,217	12.9	1907–16
7	Orel Hershiser	39.9	116	3.12	135–107	353	309	65	24	2,180⅔	1,456	16.1	1983–2000
8	Fernando Valenzuela	33.0	107	3.31	141–116	331	320	107	29	2,348⅔	1,759	17.9	1980–90
9	Jeff Pfeffer	32.8	125	2.31	113–80	226	200	157	25	1,748⅓	656	9.2	1913–21
10	Bob Welch	32.7	114	3.14	115–86	292	267	47	23	1,820⅔	1,292	17.2	1978–87
11	Brickyard Kennedy	31.7	102	3.98	177–149	382	333	280	11	2,866	751	6.0	1892–1901
12	Burleigh Grimes	28.7	105	3.46	158–121	318	287	205	20	2,426	952	9.1	1918–26
13	Watty Clark	27.8	117	3.55	106–88	322	199	90	14	1,659	620	8.8	1927–37
14	Johnny Podres	27.6	107	3.66	136–104	366	310	74	23	2,029⅓	1,331	15.5	1953–66
15	Van Lingle Mungo	26.8	114	3.41	102–99	284	215	114	16	1,739⅓	1,031	13.9	1931–41
16	Claude Osteen	26.3	106	3.09	147–126	339	335	100	34	2,397	1,162	11.8	1965–73
17	Ramón Martínez	26.1	109	3.45	123–77	266	262	37	20	1,731⅔	1,314	17.9	1988–98
18	Burt Hooton	26.1	113	3.14	112–84	322	265	61	22	1,861⅓	1,042	13.7	1975–84
19	Preacher Roe	25.4	124	3.26	93–37	201	173	74	12	1,277⅓	632	12.1	1948–54
20	Don Newcombe	22.7	116	3.51	123–66	258	230	111	22	1,662⅔	913	13.3	1949–58
21	Kevin Brown	20.6	147	2.83	58–32	137	129	11	2	872⅔	784	22.2	1999–2003
22	Whit Wyatt	20.1	128	2.86	80–45	157	148	75	17	1,072⅓	540	12.3	1939–44
23	Ismael Valdez	19.1	115	3.48	61–57	185	158	10	5	1,065	785	17.6	1994–2000
24	Leon Cadore	19.1	107	3.11	68–71	189	146	83	10	1,251	440	8.5	1915–23
25	Jerry Reuss	18.4	113	3.11	86–69	253	201	44	16	1,407⅔	685	11.7	1979–87
26	Chan Ho Park	18.2	108	3.77	84–58	275	181	9	2	1,279	1,177	21.4	1994–2008
27	Bob Caruthers	18.1	113	2.92	110–51	175	158	147	14	1,433⅔	391	6.5	1888–91

Rank	Player	WAR	ERA+	ERA	W-L	G	GS	CG	SHO	IP	SO	K%	Years
28	Zack Greinke	17.5	156	2.30	51–15	92	92	2	1	602⅔	555	23.3	2013–15
29	Ed Stein	17.3	104	4.01	90–66	181	155	135	10	1,394⅓	432	7.0	1892–98
30	Chad Billingsley	16.9	110	3.65	81–61	219	190	4	2	1,175⅔	1,037	20.6	2006–13
31	Carl Erskine	16.6	101	4.00	122–78	335	216	71	14	1,718⅔	981	13.5	1948–59
32	Adonis Terry	16.6	102	3.42	126–139	290	275	255	14	2,376⅓	1,200	11.7	1884–91
33	Ralph Branca	16.3	107	3.70	80–58	283	166	64	12	1,324	757	13.4	1944–56
34	Pedro Astacio	15.8	104	3.68	48–47	174	132	13	9	886⅔	598	16.1	1992–97
35	Andy Messersmith	15.6	129	2.67	55–34	125	123	43	13	926	637	17.1	1973–79
36	Jim Brewer	15.6	127	2.62	61–51	474	18	1	1	822	672	20.2	1964–75
37	Tommy John	15.1	118	2.97	87–42	182	174	37	11	1,198	649	13.1	1972–78
38	Hideo Nomo	15.0	104	3.74	81–66	191	191	12	7	1,217⅓	1,200	23.4	1995–2004
39	Ron Perranoski	14.9	132	2.56	54–41	457	1	0	0	766⅔	461	14.2	1961–72
40	Tom Candiotti	14.8	106	3.57	52–64	187	159	15	3	1,048	718	16.2	1992–97
41	Luke Hamlin	14.8	110	3.61	60–57	186	136	54	9	1,011	427	10.1	1937–41
42	Kenley Jansen*	14.7	183	2.08	24–13	474	0	0	0	477	741	40.1	2010–
43	Jesse Petty	14.7	112	3.52	54–59	148	118	64	5	934⅓	315	7.9	1925–28
44	Derek Lowe	13.2	120	3.59	54–48	137	135	7	2	850⅓	563	16.0	2005–08
45	Tim Belcher	13.1	118	2.99	50–38	138	119	21	12	806	633	19.2	1987–91
46	Rube Marquard	13.1	111	2.58	56–48	149	115	61	9	950	444	11.6	1915–20
47	Doc Scanlan	13.0	94	2.96	64–67	176	145	100	15	1,221	574	11.4	1904–11
48	Doug Rau	12.9	106	3.30	80–58	219	184	33	11	1,250⅔	694	13.2	1972–79
49	Hugh Casey	12.9	115	3.34	70–41	293	56	24	3	867⅔	325	8.8	1939–48
50	Curt Davis	12.9	111	3.23	66–54	169	122	62	13	1,007⅓	291	6.9	1940–46

Statistics through 2017 season.
*Active with Dodgers in 2017.

Pregame: The Ancestors

NO LIGHTNING BOLT SHOT FROM THE SKY, no command came from on high. Nothing was preordained to dictate the flow of great pitching that the Dodgers have known since the end of World War II.

Before then, the Dodgers were scavengers, occasionally stumbling upon a prize arm without paying any mind to how it got there. There was no apparatus to generate a pitching staff, and no one prioritized making one.

As a result, in the early years of Brooklyn baseball history, there are names worth remembering—even a few Hall of Famers passing through—but they fall haphazardly into the pre–Boys of Summer era. The whole was not greater than the sum of its parts, as the franchise's frequent struggles back then illustrate. But even if those parts predate the Dodger pitching tradition, they still deserve a small float at the start of the parade.

Jim Creighton

Organized baseball in Brooklyn, New York, began in the 1850s, and within its first 10 years gave birth to arguably the sport's first ace, teenage phenom, two-way star, and tragic legend all in one: Jim Creighton, who took flight from 1860 to 1862 with the Brooklyn Excelsiors.

In 1859, the 18-year-old Creighton had been playing second base for another Brooklyn squad, the Niagras, when he ambled to the mound in a mop-up relief role and made an immediate impression.

"When Creighton got to work," a rival player observed, "something new was seen in baseball—a low, swift delivery, the ball rising from the ground past the shoulder to the catcher."

Working within (or perhaps just outside) the era's rules requiring a pitcher to throw underhanded without break in the elbow or wrist, Creighton quickly became a pioneer and a star.

"Some deplored this uncharacteristic aggressiveness from a pitcher—it was still technically supposed to be his job to help the batter, not to hinder him," noted Geoffrey C. Ward and Ken Burns, writers of the documentary *Baseball*, "but Creighton won game after game." And, by season's end, he was his own boss. Before baseball had evolved such encumbrances as the reserve clause or service time, Creighton effectively became the equivalent of the first big-name free agent.

After three years of brilliance, in a twist robbed from the world of fiction, Creighton suffered a fatal injury on the field—while hitting a home run. "Creighton had swung so mighty a blow—in the manner of the day, with hands separated on the bat, little or no turn of the wrists, and incredible torque applied by the twisting motion of the upper body—that it was reported he ruptured his bladder," wrote John Thorn, the official historian of Major League Baseball. (Researchers deduced that Creighton had suffered a ruptured inguinal hernia.) After four days, he died, just 21 years old.

Creighton would have been the perfect player to inspire generations of pitching stars to follow, but when he passed away, he left no bridge to the future. Neither Creighton nor any of the other players from the first quarter-century of Brooklyn baseball had any connection to the future Boys of Summer, other than geographic.

Adonis Terry, Bob Caruthers, and Brickyard Kennedy

The next teenager to debut memorably in Brooklyn, William H. "Adonis" Terry, was the first to do so for the actual franchise we know today as the Dodgers. Terry won 19 games at age 19 (though he did lose 35) in 1884, the year ownership took Brooklyn from the minor-league Interstate Association into the more respected American Association. Terry was solid (3.42 ERA, 102 ERA+ in 2,376⅓ innings) and occasionally spectacular, throwing the first of his two career no-hitters in 1886.

In 1888, the year of Terry's second no-hitter, a frail-looking pitcher also born in the Civil War era ascended. Official records list Bob Caruthers at 5-foot-7 and 138 pounds. "The lad took up baseball, despite the objections of his overprotective mother," wrote Charles F. Faber. "He developed a muscular physique and compensated with his brain for what he lacked in brawn." Purchased by Brooklyn from the St. Louis Browns—after a lengthy conversation to obtain Mom's approval—Caruthers averaged 358⅓ innings over four seasons. He also married that off-season, becoming one of the players who inspired Brooklyn's latest team nickname, the Bridegrooms.

Caruthers' best ERA came in his first season with the Bridegrooms: 2.39 (126 ERA+), but it was the 40–11, 445-inning campaign with a league-high seven shutouts in 1889 that sparked Brooklyn to its first official pennant and a postseason appearance against the National League champion New York Giants—as well as the historic transfer of Brooklyn to the NL itself in 1890. That year, with Caruthers, Terry, and Tom Lovett starting 118 of the team's 129 games, Brooklyn won the NL pennant in its debut season, splitting a seven-game "World's Series" (three wins apiece, one tie, in a low-level precursor to the modern-day World Series) with its former AA rivals from Louisville.

If a pattern for Brooklyn's aces developed, it's that their success was too fleeting. Caruthers pitched only one more season for the Grooms, finishing his four years there with a 2.92 ERA (113 ERA+) in 1,433⅔ innings. From 1891 to 1898, Brooklyn lagged an average of 25½ games out of first place and never placed higher than third.

Brooklyn's top pitcher of the century's final decade was William "Brickyard" Kennedy, who threw several innings-heavy if statistically mediocre seasons. His best-known nickname came from his onetime off-season workplace, though he also went by "Roaring Bill," as David Nemec wrote, "for his foghorn voice and the way he incessantly ran his mouth at the top of his lungs while ragging umpires, opposing batters, and even his own teammates."

Kennedy's control could be as unsteady as his temperament, but in 1899, his finest season (277⅓ innings, 2.79 ERA, 139 ERA+) propelled the squad—now known as the Superbas—to its second NL pennant with a 101–47–2 record (.682), to this day the franchise's best winning percentage. (It helped that during the 1898–99 off-season, a transaction that would never pass muster in the present brought on shared ownership between Brooklyn and the Baltimore Orioles, with Baltimore's top players, including pitcher Jay Hughes and Hall of Fame hitter Wee Willie Keeler, heading to the borough.) Though Kennedy's ERA rose by more than a run the following year, signaling the beginning of the end of his pitching career, Brooklyn repeated as champions, winning the first NL flag of the 1900s.

Kennedy pitched 2,866 innings for Brooklyn (3.98 ERA, 102 ERA+) with 31.7 wins above replacement, fourth among pre–World War II pitchers for Brooklyn. As Nemec noted, his 174 wins from 1891 to 1900 trailed only three pitchers—Kid Nichols, Cy Young, and Amos Rusie, all Hall of Famers.

"That Kennedy never quite achieved enough to join them may be largely attributable to his greatest failing as a pitcher: an utter inability to cover first base," Nemec wrote. "He simply could never master the task and kept vainly trying to persuade his managers that it wasn't part of a pitcher's job description."

Neither Terry, Caruthers, nor Kennedy lived to see Brooklyn win another pennant. Like Caruthers, Kennedy died at the age of 47, while Terry (along with Hughes) died at 50.

Ned Garvin, Kaiser Wilhelm, and Nap Rucker

From 1901 to 1915, Brooklyn's baseball fortunes deteriorated, the franchise finishing a combined 537½ games out of first place, an average of nearly 36 games out per season. It was an era that gave Brooklyn such pitchers as Ned Garvin, who combined a 1.68 ERA with a 5–15 record for the 1904 team that went 56–97. (Four years later, Garvin, whom Bill James once labeled "probably the unluckiest pitcher in major-league history," died at age 34 of consumption.)

In 1908, three years after going 3–23 for Boston (a .115 winning percentage that would be the worst by an NL starting pitcher for another 80 years), the college-educated Irvin "Kaiser" Wilhelm used a spitball for a career year with the Superbas, moistening his way to a 1.87 ERA and 33 complete games, second in the NL. Wilhelm, who hated the nickname that linked him with the German emperor antagonizing multiple countries in the years leading up to World War I, improved to 16–22 but progressed no further with the Superbas, though more than a century later, he still held the professional minor-league record for consecutive scoreless innings with 72.

In those 15 seasons, only one Brooklyn pitcher won more than 70 games, and it's telling that at the end of it all, he was a .500 pitcher. Nevertheless, Nap Rucker stands as the most underappreciated Brooklyn pitcher of the time.

"No one talks about Nap Rucker," John Thorn says. "Rucker was the great star."

Spending his entire major-league career in Brooklyn, Rucker threw 2,375⅓ innings with a 2.42 ERA (119 ERA+). His 47.9 wins above replacement rank sixth in franchise history and second among Brooklyn arms.

Born in 1884 to a former Confederate soldier in Crabapple, Georgia, George Napoleon Rucker was a 20-year-old teammate of future legend Ty Cobb and Black Sox star Eddie Cicotte on the 1905 Augusta Tourists of the Class C South Atlantic League. "As a red-headed youth," wrote historian Eric Enders, "he worked as a printer's apprentice, and one day he was given a headline to set in type: '$10,000 for Pitching a Baseball.' That moment, Rucker always claimed, was when he decided to become a pitcher."

Acquired by Brooklyn before the 1907 season for $500, Rucker delivered above-average ERAs in his first seven years. In 1908, he became the franchise's first left-hander to throw a no-hitter, and a year later, he matched the record for strikeouts in a game with 16. In 1910, he led the NL with 39 starts, 27 complete games, 320⅓ innings, and six shutouts, and two years later he was a career-best third in the NL in ERA at 2.21 (151 ERA+). He went 18–21 for a 58–95 Brooklyn team that finished 46 games out of first.

Rucker fully embraced Brooklyn and took the Dodgers' struggles with the kind of grace and good feeling that heroes on bad teams such as Ernie Banks and Tony Gwynn embodied decades later.

"It's got New York beaten by three bases," he told a reporter in 1912. "You can get a good night's rest in Brooklyn. You meet more real human beings in Brooklyn. Your life is safer in Brooklyn."

Not unlike others of the time, Rucker took the "off" in "off-season" to heart, and whether it was his lack of conditioning or the 2,111⅔ innings he threw in those first seven years, he evolved from a fastball pitcher compared with Walter Johnson to a veritable junkballer. "He started throwing a strange, particularly effective slow curve—called 'the slowest ball in the history of the majors' by one reporter," Enders wrote. "Nap claimed he learned the pitch with Augusta when he accidentally gripped the ball the wrong way, but another story attributes its origin to a 1913 thumb injury that forced him to change his grip. Others, meanwhile, claimed that the pitch was an early version of the knuckleball. Whatever it was, reporter Dan Daniel called it 'one of the amazing phenomena of baseball history.'"

Pitching intermittently over his final three seasons while serving as a mentor to both pitchers and such position players as Casey Stengel (who credited him for keeping his career in baseball alive), Rucker hung on long enough to give Brooklyn, then known as the Robins, a 1.69 ERA in 37⅓ innings in 1916, the year the team went to its first modern-day World Series. His final professional appearance came in Game 4 of the 1916 Fall Classic, when he retired seven of the eight batters he faced.

Jeff Pfeffer and Rube Marquard

As Rucker's workload declined, 26-year-old Jeff Pfeffer emerged for Brooklyn. The 6-foot-3 righty threw 1,201⅓ innings from 1914 to 1917, with a 3.01 ERA (136 ERA+), completing 107 of his 134 starts. To show how different times were, Pfeffer averaged only 3½ strikeouts per nine innings, but his 50 hit batters from 1915 to 1917 demonstrated the level of aggressiveness this proto-Drysdale brought to the mound.

Fun with Pfeffer first arrived in 1914 with a 1.97 ERA (144 ERA+) that was third in the NL, along with 27 complete games. This was Brooklyn's 11th consecutive losing season, but that streak ended in 1915, thanks to Pfeffer (2.10 ERA, 134 ERA+) and the arrival of Sherry Smith, whom Pfeffer had pushed Brooklyn to acquire. Among Pfeffer's achievements that year was the longest outing ever by a Dodger pitcher in defeat, enduring 18⅔ innings on June 17 in a complete-game loss to the Chicago Cubs.

In 1916, Pfeffer's third consecutive superb season (1.92 ERA, 141 ERA+), augmented by Smith (2.34 ERA, 115 ERA+) and two relative newcomers, Larry Cheney (1.92 ERA, 140 ERA+) and former Giants great Rube Marquard (1.58 ERA, 171 ERA+), gave the Robins a league-leading 2.12 ERA and ultimately their first World Series matchup against the American League.

Marquard's performance was a major story, and his ERA that year remained a franchise record more than 100 years later, withstanding challenges from Sandy Koufax in the 1960s as well as Clayton Kershaw and Zack Greinke in the 2010s. (In adjusted ERA, Marquard's season ranks 11th in Dodger history.)

That being said, when Marquard was inducted into the Hall of Fame in 1971, his plaque was devoted entirely to his years with the Giants. The résumé is at once impressive and thin: three pennant-winning seasons (1911–13) in which he averaged 24 wins with a 2.52 ERA, including an NL strikeout title in 1911 and a 19-game winning streak in 1912. The left-hander threw "a wicked curveball to complement his blazing fastball," wrote Larry Mansch, "and a fine screwball learned from his friend and roommate Christy Mathewson."

Marquard was a true celebrity, in and out of the game, appearing in Vaudeville on Broadway with costar Blossom Seeley, who divorced her husband to marry Marquard in 1913, electrifying the gossip appetites of the day. But amid a subpar 1914 and 1915 (with a no-hitter against the Robins in his first start of the '15 season belying his inconsistency), Marquard was on the verge of becoming a 28-year-old has-been when he was all but donated to Brooklyn in August 1915. Over the next month, he reached his nadir, allowing 17 runs in 24⅔ innings.

Marquard's 1916 rebirth changed all that, launching him anew as a mesmerizing figure on what had, for a rare season, become the best pitching staff in the league. Even so, Pfeffer remained the dominant one. In an era of iron-man starters, Pfeffer pitched nearly 25 percent of Brooklyn's innings that season—75⅔ more than any of his teammates—and he allowed two runs or fewer in 26 of 36 starts.

In an unusual way, Pfeffer was the hero of the clinching game. With three games left in the season, the Robins had a one-game lead over

Philadelphia. Playing the fourth-place Giants, who earlier that year had an MLB-record 26-game winning streak, Smith was taken out after falling behind 4–1 in the third inning on Nap Rucker Day at Ebbets Field, but Brooklyn rallied with four runs in the bottom of the third to take the lead. Three days after his 30th complete game of the season, Pfeffer pitched the final six innings in relief in a win that, combined with the Boston Braves' doubleheader sweep of the Philadelphia Phillies, wrapped up the NL title.

However, when it came time for the World Series against the Boston Red Sox, Brooklyn manager Wilbert Robinson steered away from Pfeffer, partly to avoid using the right-hander against a lefty-heavy lineup, though the *Brooklyn Daily Eagle* also wrote that his "inexperience in the biggest of the big shows is held up against him." Pfeffer began Game 1 in the bullpen behind Marquard. Once again, Pfeffer pitched in relief after the Robins fell behind, once again the Robins rallied, but this time they fell short in a 6–5 nailbiter. Pfeffer was then on the sidelines as Smith and Boston's star pitcher, 21-year-old Babe Ruth (who led the AL in ERA and didn't allow a home run in 323⅔ innings), each went to the 14th inning before the Sox won Game 2, 2–1.

When Game 3 arrived for Ebbets Field's World Series debut, it had been 10 days since Pfeffer had started a game for Brooklyn, but Robinson turned to 33-year-old veteran Jack Coombs, who had thrown half as many innings as Pfeffer in 1916. Pfeffer came out of the bullpen for the save (as Eric Enders notes, the first and only in Brooklyn postseason history until 1947). Only after Marquard then took his second loss in Game 4 did Pfeffer receive his first World Series start, in Game 5, when he suffered a Series-ending 4–1 defeat.

Though his best days were past, Pfeffer remained with Brooklyn until 1921, hurling 1,748⅓ innings with a 2.31 ERA (125 ERA+) and 32.8 wins above replacement, ninth in franchise history and third among the Brooklyn set.

Burleigh Grimes

After the 1917 season, Brooklyn spitballed in its search for starting pitching.

The Dodgers traded two of their eight primary starting position players from the previous five seasons—second baseman George Cutshaw and outfielder Casey Stengel—to Pittsburgh, gambling on 24-year-old Burleigh Grimes and 23-year-old Al Mamaux. Mamaux pitched adequately for the Robins, but Grimes, who had gone 3–16 with Pittsburgh the year before with a 3.53 ERA (81 ERA+—hello, Deadball Era) was the huge, sticky find.

Grimes spent the meat of his career with Brooklyn, throwing 2,426 innings from 1918 to 1926 with a 3.46 ERA (1.05 ERA+), leading the league in complete games three times. But what Grimes accomplished tends to be overshadowed by how he accomplished it, as one of baseball's finest practitioners of the spitball.

"I used to chew slippery elm—the bark, right off the tree," he said. "Come spring the bark would get nice and loose, and you could slice it free without any trouble. What I chewed was the fiber from inside, and that's what I put on the ball. The ball would break like hell, away from right-handers and in on lefties."

When the spitball ban arrived, it was originally supposed to be universal, but a campaign began to grandfather existing spitballers.

"Grimes became one of the more eloquent spokesmen for the proposed modification," wrote Charles F. Faber. "He maintained that it took him 10 to 15 years to develop a big-league-caliber spitter. The muscles in a pitcher's arms develop according to the way the arm is used, Burleigh claimed, and it is physiologically impossible for a mature adult to change from his customary style of delivery."

At the same time, "Ol' Stubblebeard" (he didn't shave on days he was scheduled to pitch) wanted fans to know that he was more than just a wet-and-wild wonder.

"It wasn't necessarily my No. 1 pitch—the fastball generally was," he said. "People meet me today and they say, 'Oh, Burleigh Grimes? You were the spitball pitcher.' Well, hell, I threw a fastball, curve, slider, change, screwball. One time I pitched [16] innings against the Cubs, beating Hippo Vaughn 3–2, and I threw only three slow spitballs in the ballgame. The rest were all fastballs."

Grimes' top season—2.22 ERA (144 ERA+) in 303⅔ innings—came in 1920, and not coincidentally, Brooklyn returned to the World Series, winning the pennant by seven games over the Giants. Leon Cadore, a relatively anonymous starter, made history May 1 with the Braves' Joe Oeschger when each went 26 innings in the longest major-league game ever, called because of darkness with the score still tied 1–1. But Grimes was the difference maker, and though he—like Pfeffer four years prior—was a postseason rookie, this time Wilbert Robinson didn't shy away from the new blood when the World Series came.

Grimes pitched three times in the best-of-nine Series, beginning with a seven-hit shutout in Game 2. After Sherry Smith's three-hit masterpiece in a 2–1 Game 3 victory, the Robins were three wins away from glory. And then things went decidedly sour.

Rube Marquard, the Game 1 starter scheduled to start Game 4, was arrested by an undercover Cleveland detective for scalping his box seats for the game (though he was released from jail, Cadore got the start), leaving Grimes to start Game 5 with the Series tied. That game was historic, for all the wrong reasons for Brooklyn fans.

In the first inning, the Cleveland Indians' Elmer Smith faced Grimes with the bases loaded and hit the first grand slam in World Series history. (Later, it was learned that Grimes' own teammate, second baseman Pete Kilduff, was unconsciously tipping the spitball by scooping up a small handful of dirt to dry his hands each time the pitch was signaled.) Grimes yielded the mound to another spitballer, Clarence Mitchell, who not only gave up the first World Series homer hit by a pitcher (Jim Bagby), but in the bottom of the fifth lined to Bill Wambsganss for the World Series' unprecedented unassisted triple play.

Sherry Smith, whose 0.89 postseason ERA is the best in Dodger history, lost a 1–0 nailbiter in Game 6. With Grimes on the mound, a rival spitballer, Stan Coveleski, shut out Brooklyn 3–0 in the clinching Game 7.

Grimes went 22–13 with a 2.83 ERA (139 ERA+) in 1921—after a holdout that went to the eve of Opening Day, before manager Wilbert Robinson pleaded for owner Charles Ebbets to yield—but Grimes' final five seasons with the Robins hovered around average. Still, in 1964, Cooperstown welcomed him into its place of honor.

"I think Grimes was a journeyman and not an outstanding pitcher, and he kind of forms the baseline of the Hall of Fame," John Thorn says. "He won the Good Attendance award."

Dazzy Vance

The top Dodger pitcher of the pre–World War II era had the goofiest name and the latest start. Put it this way: when he won his first major-league game, he was 31 years old—older than Sandy Koufax was when he retired.

But when Bill James named the three top right-handed pitchers of the 1920s, Dazzy Vance was one of them.

Charles Arthur Vance was born in Orient, Iowa, in 1891, and his early professional record wasn't that of a slow starter. At age 23, he won 26 games in two leagues in 1914, with a 2.96 ERA for Class-A St. Joseph. He debuted with the Pittsburgh Pirates in 1915 and then pitched eight games for the New York Yankees. But plagued by a sore arm, he pitched in only two more major-league games from 1916 to 1921.

Then, playing poker one night and reaching out to rake in a pot—in a cinematic twist—Vance knocked his arm against the edge of the table, generating unbearable pain. He submitted to surgery, which revealed a previously undiscovered injury. (James speculated that bone chips were removed). The operation was beyond successful.

Turning 30 in 1921, Vance had the arm of someone years younger, throwing 253 innings for the New Orleans Pelicans of the Southern Association, with a 3.52 ERA. In an echo of the Burleigh Grimes–Al Mamaux pickup, the Dodgers lucked out. When they acquired him before the 1922 season, Vance was the sidecar in a $10,000 deal primarily designed for 27-year-old catcher Hank DeBerry.

The intended target was a success: DeBerry had a .354 on-base percentage for the Dodgers in 1922 and finished a nine-year run as Brooklyn's part-time catcher with a .322 OBP in nearly 2,000 plate appearances. But Vance proved remarkable, levels ahead of any other NL pitcher, complementing his fastball with a killer curve.

"Dazzy's pitching style was simple," wrote Jack Kavanaugh and Norman L. Macht. "He reared back, kicked his left foot high, and catapulted the ball overhand. It exploded past the batter or swerved away. Although his speed excited the fans, it was his control of the curve that delighted his manager."

Moment in the Sun: Watty Clark

- Ranked 13th in Dodger history with 27.8 wins above replacement from 1927 to 1937
- In 1929, led NL in both losses (19) and fielding-independent ERA (3.61)
- Only Dazzy Vance, Nap Rucker, and Van Lingle Mungo had more above-average ERA+ seasons in Brooklyn than Clark

Vance led the NL in strikeouts and strikeouts per nine innings in each of his first seven seasons with Brooklyn. In those years, from 1922 to 1928, Vance had nearly twice as many strikeouts as any other major-league pitcher—1,338, compared with 689 by the runner-up, Grimes.

"At a time when pitchers were not routinely throwing six or seven strikeouts per nine innings, Vance was," Thorn says, noting that putting fewer balls in play was a valuable trait at a hitters' park like Ebbets Field.

Vance's adjusted ERA for those years was better than any other big-league starting pitcher except Lefty Grove. Only Grover Cleveland Alexander had a lower WHIP than Vance's 1.20. He won three ERA titles, and ranked first in fielding-independent pitching four additional times.

"Dazzy Vance could throw a cream puff through a battleship," said former Brooklyn Dodgers teammate Johnny Frederick.

Vance's 1924 season was a stunner: 28–6 with 30 complete games—he *averaged* 8.94 innings per start—and a 2.16 ERA (174 ERA+) while striking out 262, a total exceeded in franchise history by only Koufax and Clayton Kershaw. Until 1961, only Christy Mathewson (267 in 1903) had more strikeouts in an NL season than Vance, and no one older than Vance fanned that many until Jim Bunning in 1965.

Vance did everything he could to lift Brooklyn back into the World Series in 1924. From July 11 to September 18, Vance won 15 consecutive decisions (in 16 appearances) with 14 complete games, a 1.92 ERA, and 120 strikeouts in 131 innings. His streak ended with consecutive starts in which he gave up the winning run in extra innings—two losses that were the difference for the 92–62 Robins, who finished 1½ games behind the Giants and were eliminated from the pennant race on the season's penultimate day.

"When the greatest of all Brooklyn pitchers was fogging them over for the Dodgers, the right sleeve of his sweatshirt was an unsightly rag, a flapping thing of shreds and tatters," wrote Red Smith. "Daz would hide the ball until the last instant and then if the batter was lucky, he would see something white rocketing toward him out of a distracting flutter of dry goods."

In September 1925, Vance pitched Brooklyn's first no-hitter since Rucker, capping a 22–9 season. Against increasingly hostile offensive environments, he had a 2.09 ERA (190 ERA+) in 1928, and at age 39 in 1930—a year in which NL teams averaged 5.7 runs per game—Vance had a 2.61 ERA (189 ERA+). At age 40, Vance led the NL in FIP, strikeout-walk ratio, and strikeouts per nine innings.

The only missing link for Vance and the Dodgers was the postseason. Not until he was 43, in a short stint with the 1934 St. Louis Cardinals, did he make his one and only World Series appearance, throwing 1⅓ innings of relief with an unearned run in a 10–4 loss to the Tigers. When Vance finished his career back with Brooklyn in 1935, pitching 51 innings in relief with a 4.41 ERA (91 ERA+), the Dodgers were 15 years into their latest postseason drought and six years away from its end.

"During the late '20s and early '30s, they definitely had the reputation of a team that was basically squandering a good opportunity," Eric Enders says. "It was a team that was still trying to find itself really all the way up until 1941."

Vance's election to the Hall of Fame came in 1955, the year of the Dodgers' first World Series title. Vance became the first player to wear a Brooklyn cap on a Hall of Fame plaque—cementing himself as a unique figure in the Bums' history. More than a century after his MLB debut, Vance ranked first all-time among Dodger pitchers with 61.8 wins above replacement, having thrown 2,757⅔ innings for Brooklyn with a 3.17 ERA (129 ERA+) and 2,045 strikeouts.

"So you've got Dazzy Vance," says Mark Langill, the Dodgers' official team historian, "and you've got the 1916 team with Rube Marquard and Nap Rucker. But you didn't necessarily have that long-established pitcher like you'd have with a Zack Wheat—a pitcher who had been there for 20 years. You'd have guys who sporadically were okay, but not a 300-game winner or anything like that, somebody like the Washington Senators having Walter Johnson and all those wins or Christy Mathewson [on the Giants]."

Van Lingle Mungo and Whit Wyatt (and Larry MacPhail)

In 1925, dysfunction had arrived in Brooklyn when owners Charles Ebbets and Ed McKeever died 11 days apart. McKeever's brother, Steve, became the majority owner, but he was overruled as Wilbert Robinson became president/manager. In 1928, McKeever was trying to starve Robinson out, refusing to provide him with the means for success.

"Charles Ebbets and his heirs did not have good estate planning," Mark Langill says. "Between the Ebbets clan and the McKeever clan, they couldn't agree on anything. And by the '30s, you've also got the Depression. They're not making capital improvements to Ebbets Field and they're not investing in ballplayers. And so they're a second-division team in a crumbling ballpark."

In the 1930s, a decade in which the team never finished higher than third place and Dazzy Vance was a fading memory, Brooklyn's top pitcher was Van Lingle Mungo (1,659 innings, 3.55 ERA, 117 ERA+), known in his time for having the top fastball in the NL but most remembered for his weirdly melodic name that emerged as the title of Dave Frishberg's 1969 song. Mungo, a much-buzzed-about prospect whom Wilbert Robinson had said would be a harder-throwing Rube Marquard, was more steady than sensational (except when it came to off-field incidents, the most noteworthy of which included a jealousy-induced brawl with a matador-turned-dancer in Havana).

To illustrate his extremes, Mungo led the league in strikeouts per nine innings in three different seasons—and in walks in three different seasons as well. Using Bill James' Game Score method, Mungo pitched the single-greatest nine-inning game in Brooklyn history, striking out 15 and walking none in a two-hit shutout of the Phillies on September 29, 1935. Three years earlier, also against Philadelphia, he set a Brooklyn record in a June 5, 1932, start by walking 11.

"There was just enough success sprinkled with colorful tales to make it an interesting ballclub," Langill says. "But by the mid-'30s, they're at a crossroads."

The first step of a turnaround in Brooklyn came three years later, when a desperate ownership turned to former Cincinnati Reds vice president and general manager Larry MacPhail, who understood how much out-of-the-box thinking on generating revenue streams meant for eventual success.

MacPhail, who brought night baseball to the majors in Cincinnati, did the same as team president in Brooklyn, while also breaking the citywide ban on home radio broadcasts that had served to inhibit the growth of fan interest. Hiring Red Barber to do play-by-play didn't hurt either.

"Financially, if MacPhail doesn't step in, I don't know what the future of the franchise would have been, because they were in dire straits," Langill says. "It was just the Dark Ages in the early decade. They have no games on the radio. The ballpark's crumbling and MacPhail comes in like a hurricane—and within three years they're in the World Series."

Dodger attendance, which was less than 500,000 for the 1937 season, was nearly 1 million two years later. Despite finishing the decade with their 19th consecutive season as an also-ran, Brooklyn outdrew the Yankees (who went 106–45 and swept the World Series) by nearly 100,000.

Whit Wyatt, a nine-year AL vet who at age 30 had given up baseball for farming after the 1937 season, became the latest reclamation project to excel on the mound for the Dodgers, following in the footsteps of Vance to emerge as the Dodgers' top pitcher of the World War II era. Wyatt made every NL All-Star team from 1939 to 1942.

"The has-been pitcher with the big windup and kick had been picked up on a whim from a minor-league club in St. Paul, Minnesota, which was about to retire him in 1938," wrote Bruce Chadwick. "Wyatt's fastball had died in St. Paul, but he somehow managed to develop an exceedingly slow and torturous curveball that gave him new life."

In 1941, Wyatt had a 2.34 ERA (159 ERA+) and led the NL in wins and the majors in shutouts and WHIP, and the Dodgers, after a 21-year drought, made it back to the World Series. Brooklyn won 100 games for the first time since 1899, and three Dodgers—Dolph Camilli, Pete Reiser, and Wyatt—topped the NL Most Valuable Player vote. All three were MacPhail acquisitions, as were four of the Dodgers' five top pitchers (Wyatt, Kirby Higbe, Hugh Casey, and Curt Davis).

In his only career postseason, Wyatt pitched two complete games, including a 3–2 win in Game 2—the Dodgers' lone victory in a World Series that featured Casey's infamous uncaught third strike in the ninth inning of Game 4, which led to a four-run Yankees rally.

At this point, on the eve of World War II, the Dodgers still had no farm system to celebrate, nor any special attention to pitching to distinguish the Dodgers from other teams. But MacPhail was the thunder. Soon came the lightning.

Branch Rickey

Branch Rickey had no greater impact on the Dodgers—much less baseball and the United States—than his efforts to integrate the game, beginning with the signing of Jackie Robinson to a minor-league contract in 1945.

But Rickey did much more than that. In essence, the most important executive in baseball history also could be considered the godfather of the Dodger pitching tradition.

"I think it started with Branch Rickey," Tommy Lasorda says. "For many, many years, the Dodgers always had really top pitchers, because they concentrated on control and the ability to master certain pitches."

Before joining the Dodgers, Rickey was a successful general manager for St. Louis, which won five NL pennants and three World Series between 1926 and 1934. With the Cardinals, Rickey developed the modern farm system, with a chain of teams that enabled the franchise to stockpile potential.

"When the Cardinals were fighting for their life in the National League, I found that we were at a disadvantage in obtaining players of merit from the minors," Rickey said. "Other clubs could outbid. They had money. They had superior scouting machinery. In short, we had to take what was left or nothing at all...I do not feel that the farming system we have established is the result of any inventive genius—it is the result of stark necessity."

Moment in the Sun: Dan Bankhead

- The first black pitcher in MLB history, debuting at 27, four months after Jackie Robinson in 1947
- Homered in first big-league at-bat and pitched 153⅓ innings for Brooklyn from 1947 to 1951, with a 6.52 ERA (63 ERA+)
- Played in Negro and Mexican Leagues in pro career lasting from age 20 to age 46, retiring in 1966

Rickey succeeded MacPhail as Dodger team president after the 1942 season. With World War II in full swing, he immediately put into practice the best of his lessons from St. Louis to address the aging and depleted Dodger roster. Rather than focus on proven major-league talent, Rickey invested in player development.

"Find a whole lot of them and throw them at the wall and see what sticks," says Eric Enders. "Just sign as many guys as you can, set up as many minor-league teams as you can, and see who works out, basically as survival of the fittest...The pitchers that came up in the late '40s, like Carl Erskine and Ralph Branca, came to be a result of this philosophy."

Even the discards were part of Rickey's process.

"He'd have these auctions of these players that he didn't want at the end of spring training—$50,000 for this guy, $70,000 for this guy," Mark Langill says. "And that was just as important as making a trade, because that was how he would get the capital to keep the machine going."

Rickey didn't abandon trades—after all, it was he who famously suggested it was better to trade someone a year too early than a year too late. But he prized acquisition and development—of players of all colors.

"I went to spring training my first year—I was a hot-shot high school pitcher, striking out a bunch of guys," Carl Erskine says. "I went down there, and there's 200 just like me."

In addition, Rickey also created Dodgertown, as legendary a spring training complex as has ever existed. Making a deal for a former Navy training base in Vero Beach, Florida, Rickey created a home—an academy, really—for the more than 700 players in the Dodger system, augmented by simple but useful innovations, such as the pitching strings.

"They were just strings with slipknots that you threw at to work on throwing to spots," Don Drysdale explained. "You could adjust the strings to approximate the exact width of home plate and the strike zone, or you could narrow the strings if you wanted to zero in on the outside of the plate or the inside."

With Rickey's influence, Dodger pitching was no longer dependent on wishing upon some stars. It had a focus, a philosophy—and a future.

PART ONE

THE KINGS OF BROOKLYN

BACK IN 1932, the time had come to quit dodging the issue of Brooklyn's baseball nickname. After years volleying between Bridegrooms, Superbas, and Robins—and less formally, Bums—the official choice had come down to two: Dodgers (the shorthand version of the Trolley Dodgers of lore) or Kings, a new choice harkening back to Kings County, as Brooklyn was the seat of the borough.

Dodgers won out, and happily so, giving the team and its fans a name rooted firmly in franchise history and unique in sports culture.

But in what turned out to be the final decade of Major League Baseball in Brooklyn, in the nascent days of the Dodger pitching tradition, kings did emerge, with the mound their throne. Their memories linger, flickering in black and white, in stories too often summed up in shorthand but that are, as you'll see, much more complex.

Ralph Branca

For the first five years of the 1940s, the United States was a country in search of victory and peace. In Brooklyn, World War II had been an encompassing distraction from the struggles of a team that had won only two NL pennants since World War I. As the latest conflict ended and the soldiers who survived were coming home, Brooklyn refocused as a city firmly in search of a title.

The first key Dodger pitcher to emerge from that era was Ralph Branca, in some ways a guinea pig for a team turning its emphasis to developing a tradition of arms. He made his major-league debut on June 12, 1944, five months after his 18th birthday and six days after D-Day. Branca embodied the internal, infernal contradiction of the postwar Bums, achieving regular-season greatness punctuated by postseason heartbreak. His name has long since become branded by devastating disappointment, but that acid link diminishes how much Branca meant to the Dodgers.

Born in 1926 in Mount Vernon, New York, Branca came into MLB service like a sailor handed a mop. The Dodgers were down by six runs when he entered his debut game, down nine in his next. In his first 17 career appearances, the Dodgers neither led when he entered nor won when he exited, and his ERA for the season in 44⅔ innings was an immature 7.05.

As a 19-year-old, Branca was shipped out to St. Paul for the first half of the 1945 season before returning to the Dodgers in July. He was predictably uneven, pitching 2⅓ shutout innings in his season debut July 18 in the second game of a doubleheader for what we would now call a save, before allowing five runs in 1⅔ innings of his first start four days later. Taking the mound again on July 27, Branca won his first big-league game with eight innings of two-run ball against the Braves, only to get knocked out by the same team with none out in the third inning on August 3.

Branca announced himself as a pitcher to be reckoned with in the second game of an August 9 doubleheader against the Reds, the day Fat Man was dropped on Nagasaki. Branca allowed a run in the first inning, then two unearned runs in the third. But he stayed in the game, throwing shutout ball—nine innings of it—all the way through the 12th, when an RBI single by Babe Herman finally made him a winner. While no pitch count is available for the game, based on the 49 batters Branca faced (six hits, seven walks, 11 strikeouts), the 19-year-old likely threw at least 150 pitches, if not closer to 200. The 12 innings remain the second-most by a teenager in Dodger history, trailing only Rex Barney's 14 innings in 1943.

This was the first of four consecutive complete games for Branca, who split the decisions despite a 1.38 ERA. In fact, the young right-hander started 12 of the Dodgers' final 52 games in 1945 and finished with a 2.45 ERA. At times it was a wild ride—including 10 walks in six innings September 1 at the Giants—but he finished the year with a 1–0 victory at Philadelphia and an 8–1 complete-game victory at the Polo Grounds. Branca remains the all-time leader among teenage Dodger pitchers in games, starts, complete games, innings, and strikeouts, throwing twice as many innings before turning 20 as latter-day Dodger phenom Julio Urías.

Despite an 87–67 record, the '45 Dodgers finished 11 games out of first place in the NL, but starting the following year, Brooklyn would be in every pennant race for the next 10 years. Branca played an important role many times over.

Leading the NL in 1946 by as many as 7½ games on July 2, the Dodgers found themselves in a dogfight throughout the second half of the season. Branca was kept on a leash until September 14, when he was scheduled for a one-batter start—yes, that's right—against the Cardinals. After Branca faced switch-hitting leadoff man Red Schoendienst, Dodger manager Leo Durocher planned to counter the Cardinals' lefty-heavy lineup by flipping to southpaw Vic Lombardi beginning with the second batter.

"I turned to [coach] Charlie Dressen and said, 'Are my eyes fooling me, or is that ball really jumping?'" Durocher said. "Charlie said it was jumping all right, and when [catcher] Bruce Edwards turned to me and motioned that Branca was really tearing his glove off with each pitch, I told Lombardi to sit down and forget about everything."

Moment in the Sun: Ed Head

- A natural southpaw, he became a right-hander as a teenager after a car accident nearly cost him his left arm
- No-hit the Braves on April 23, 1946, in his first start in 21 months because of military service
- Never pitched in big leagues again after that season, finishing career at age 28 with a 3.48 ERA (98 ERA+) in 465 innings

Branca pitched a shutout that day and again September 18 against the Pirates. Brooklyn and the Cardinals finished the season tied at 96–58, and the Dodgers joined in the first of two best-of-three playoffs during Branca's career—the 20-year-old starting the first game at Sportsman's Park. With the score tied 1–1 in the bottom of the third inning, Branca gave up two runs. He was replaced with two out, but the Dodgers never claimed the lead or the pennant.

In 1947, the year of Jackie Robinson's breakthrough, Branca broke out at age 21 as a premier pitcher. Making a league-high 36 starts and throwing 280 innings (second in the NL)—163 after July 1—Branca went 21–12 with a 2.67 ERA (154 ERA+) and was on the NL All-Star team. Only Ewell Blackwell and Warren Spahn had more wins above replacement that year. On July 18, the two-year anniversary of his big-league debut, the high-flying Branca retired the first 21 batters he faced before Enos

Slaughter's eighth-inning single left him to settle for a 29-batter one-hitter against the Cardinals.

"I had a good curveball," Branca said. "I could throw the ball 95 miles an hour, I had control and I was coachable…As a kid I would dream about playing in the big leagues, and here I was, 21 years old, a Dodger and an All-Star."

Clinching the pennant 10 days before the end of the season, Brooklyn reached the World Series for only the second time since 1920, inaugurating the Boys of Summer era.

Branca started Game 1 of the World Series at Yankee Stadium and was perfect for four innings, preserving a 1–0 Dodger lead. In the fifth, however, Joe DiMaggio's infield single not only gave New York its first baserunner, it set off a cascade of six straight Yankees to reach base, five of them scoring.

"Looking back, my inexperience hurt me," Branca said, "because I started pitching in a hurry. I was grabbing the ball and throwing it and not taking my time, pressing, and I ended up wild."

Branca came back in relief during a Game 3 Dodger victory and once more in Game 6, when he was the winning pitcher in a wild, 8–6 triumph that set up the first winner-take-all championship game in Dodger history, one that the Dodgers lost, 5–2.

For the next two seasons, Branca repeated as an All-Star, though again occasionally riding out bucking broncos at the ballpark—on June 25, 1949, Branca pitched a complete-game, 17–10 victory at Pittsburgh in which he allowed five runs before he got an out and 17 baserunners in all. That October brought another disappointment. After the Dodgers and Yankees split 1–0 games at Yankee Stadium, Branca started Game 3 at Ebbets Field, pitching in a 1–1 tie with two out in the ninth inning, when Johnny Mize singled home two runs. After the Dodgers' Luis Olmo and Roy Campanella hit cork-but-no-champagne solo homers off Joe Page in the bottom of the ninth to take it to extra innings, Jerry Coleman's RBI single off Brooklyn reliever Jack Banta proved the difference. The Yankees won the Series in five games.

Once 1950 arrived, Branca—still only 24 but passing the 1,000-inning mark in his career—was increasingly relegated to the bullpen, his ERA soaring to 4.69 (88 ERA+). But the less rigorous schedule seemed to serve him well, and he had something of a renaissance in 1951. Branca delivered a 1.40 ERA in nine relief appearances to start the season before jumping into the rotation on May 28, with the first of four consecutive complete games. On August 11, it was his go-the-distance, 10-strikeout, 8–1 victory over the Braves that put the Dodgers a season-high, ostensibly insurmountable 13 games ahead of the Giants with 49 to play.

Branca finished August with back-to-back shutouts. On the second of those games, on August 27, he hadn't allowed a hit heading into the ninth inning.

"I knew I had the no-hitter so I was really busting it, and I strained my arm," Branca said. "And subsequently, I pitched effectively enough, but I didn't throw as hard."

Though his ERA was still below 3.00 as late as September 21, Branca, like other Dodgers, grew more inconsistent—yet the team couldn't afford to use him any less. After allowing four runs in three innings on September 15, he was asked to start again on two days' rest; in that outing, he allowed 13 baserunners in 5⅔ innings. He pitched three more innings out of the bullpen on two days' rest September 21, then started on three days' rest September 25 and didn't record an out.

When Branca opened the first game of the best-of-three tiebreaker playoff against the Giants at Ebbets Field, it was a day after he pitched 1⅓ innings in the all-hands-on-deck, 9–8, 14-inning, season-saving victory at Philadelphia. Branca pitched admirably against New York, allowing three runs in eight innings. None other than Bobby Thomson hit the game-winning home run in *this* game, a two-run drive in the fourth inning into the first row of the seats in left-center—a ball that would have been an out, perversely enough, at the Polo Grounds—that put the Giants ahead to stay in a 3–1 victory.

After the Dodgers won the second game behind Clem Labine's shutout, Don Newcombe took the mound in the winner-take-all NL finale and pitched into the ninth inning, leading 4–1. Carl Erskine and Branca were throwing in the bullpen behind Newk, who allowed a one-out, RBI double that put the tying run on base and the winning run at the plate in Thomson.

"It [had] looked like to the world and everybody else that we're going to clinch this pennant finally," Erskine recalls. "But the phone rings, and I couldn't hear [manager Charlie] Dressen, but I could hear Sukeforth—Clyde Sukeforth was our bullpen coach, and he was a former catcher himself. And I heard him say to Dressen, 'They're both ready.' [Dressen] must've asked him which one has got the best stuff or looks the best or something, and Suky said, 'Erskine's bouncing his overhand curveball.'

"On that day, Campy was hurt, and Rube Walker was the catcher. And the Polo Grounds had the longest distance to the screen behind home plate—there was a big area back there. Rube Walker was, as the old Texas guy told me once, 'slower than pond water.' He was an outstanding catcher and outstanding hitter—good power, but he was slow as molasses. So now, try to piece together: Did Dressen say, 'We don't want any wild pitches with Walker catching'?... That's the only clue I have of how he made the choice between me and Ralph."

Branca, who had thrown 201 innings since May 1, made his way into the game. The first pitch was a get-ahead pitch, down the middle and dangerous, but Thomson took it for strike one. The next pitch had been meant to be wasted, but Branca aimed it. Thomson swung.

"He hit it with an uppercut," Branca said. "It had overspin, and he hit it down the line, and it was sinking, and all I could remember saying was, 'Sink, sink, sink,' and it just did go in. It went in like six inches over the wall. Probably went over the wall at 300 feet.

"And from there to the locker room, I don't remember. I remember getting in the locker room and sitting on the steps, and I remember [Dodger team photographer] Barney Stein taking pictures, and I think it was [Associated Press sportswriter] Will Grimsley who gave me a hard time, wanted to talk to me, and I said, 'Just leave me alone, just leave me alone.' And that's about what I remember. I sat there a long time, and the guys drifted out, and finally I went up and took a shower and got out of there."

Branca left Ebbets Field with his fiancée, whom he was set to marry in 17 days.

"When I finally got out to the car, Ann started to cry," he said. "And she had a cousin who's a priest, Father Pat Rowley, and I said to him, 'Why me?' He said, 'God chose you because he knew your faith would be strong enough to bear this cross.'

"And I accepted that."

His teammates did likewise. There was internal scuttlebutt at the time, documented decades later by Joshua Prager in the *Wall Street Journal*, that the Giants had set up an elaborate scheme in '51 to steal signs, though Thomson forever denied being tipped off on the pitch. Either way, according to John Thorn, Branca wasn't considered a villain inside the Dodger organization, partly because everyone knew how hard he had been worked.

"Somebody was gonna throw that pitch," Thorn says, "and everybody knew that the Giants had that extra help. It was unstated at the time, but everybody knew it then. It was common knowledge. The fans knew nothing about it."

But Branca didn't have much left in him to change the post-homer narrative. Having thrown 1,250 big-league innings by age 25, Branca threw only 234 after turning 26. The easy story was that the Shot Heard 'Round the World did him in, but the reality was that his arm had already been through a grinder, and a spring training injury in 1952—when he slipped on a waxy floor and his pelvis landed on top of a Coke bottle—all but ruined him. He pitched eight shutout innings on June 27 that year, but made only one start for the Dodgers the rest of the season.

After Branca allowed six runs in the fifth inning of a 20–6 loss to the Giants on July 5, 1953, the Dodgers bid Branca farewell. He pitched scattered innings for the Detroit Tigers and Yankees in 1953 and 1954; spent the Dodgers' World Series title year of 1955 in the Giants' farm system, of all places; then made a brief comeback attempt with Brooklyn in '56, pitching two shutout innings that September, but he was done.

With 16.3 wins above replacement, Branca ranked 33rd in Dodger history, 16th among Brooklyn arms. To say the least, Branca would have preferred that for the rest of his life, 99 percent of the baseball-loving world didn't reduce his career to a single pitch. But he always kept perspective.

"Life has been good," he said early in 2013. "I'm healthy outside of walking slowly. My brain works, and in January I finished my 87th year. That's how the Italians put it. The Italians have it right."

Branca's connection to the Dodgers spanned generations. His wife, Ann, was the daughter of former Dodger co-owners James and Dearie Mulvey. Dearie herself was the daughter of Stephen McKeever, co-owner of the Dodgers with Charles Ebbets when Ebbets Field was built. The Brancas' daughter Mary married Bobby Valentine, the onetime hot Dodger prospect who later embarked upon a memorable managerial career.

"I was closer to Ralph than to any other Dodger," Vin Scully said after Branca passed away at age 90 in 2016. "We traveled around the world and became very good friends. He carried the cross of the Thomson home run with dignity and grace. I was grateful for his friendship and I grieve at his death. He was a great man."

Preacher Roe

If Ralph Branca's reputation has wrongly been reduced to a moment, perhaps Preacher Roe's has been overdubbed by a name.

To be fair, Elwin Charles Roe (born in 1916 in the Arkansas town of Ash Flat, whose population didn't break 500 until the 1980 census) had one of the better nicknames in baseball history. In his SABR biography of Roe, Warren Corbett rounded up the explanation—sorry, explanations:

> Well, it was like this: "One day when I was three years old my Uncle Bathis—my daddy's only brother—asked me what my name was. I said to him, 'Preacher.' Don't know why I said that, but it's stuck with me ever since."
>
> Or maybe like this: "It came from his grandma," a longtime friend, Kay Matthews, said. "As a child, Preacher was a nasty little cuss, and she called him that hoping he would grow up to be a preacher."
>
> Or maybe it was because of the Methodist minister with his horse and buggy: "He and his wife didn't have any children, and everywhere they went they took me with them in that buggy. My mother thought I associated liking the preacher with what I'd like to be called."

However it happened, the Preacher could deliver a heck of a sermon on the mound. In franchise history, Roe is 19th in wins above replacement—even though he didn't put on a Dodger uniform until he was 32.

Signed to the Cardinals organization by Branch Rickey out of Harding College, Roe pitched in his first MLB game before the war in 1938, but didn't enter his second for six more years, when at age 28, he was finally peeled from the Cardinals' farm system and began the 1944 season in the Pirates rotation. He had two fine seasons with the Pirates, leading the NL in strikeouts in his second full year with a 2.87 ERA (138 ERA+).

His career-changing moment actually came before spring training began in 1946, when he was working his off-season job, teaching and coaching at Hardy High School in Arkansas.

> **Moment in the Sun: Vic Lombardi**
> - A 5-foot-7, 158-pound left-hander, the shortest Dodger pitcher of the postwar era
> - Had a 3.07 ERA (122 ERA+) with Brooklyn from 1945 to 1947
> - In first 14 games vs. Giants, went 9–0 with a 2.21 ERA

"At one game I didn't like a referee's call and I shouted something," Roe said. "He shouted, 'Shut up.' I thought he shouted, 'Stand up.' He decked me. My head hit the gym floor. I got a skull fracture and a lacerated brain. The fracture ran eight inches long."

Roe struggled for the next two years, going 7–23 with a 5.21 ERA (77 ERA+), though he didn't take the hardships lying down, making the transition from a fireballing thrower into a precision pitcher. "He credited catcher Al Lopez with giving him a makeover, changing his position on the rubber and shortening his delivery," Corbett wrote.

That December, two months after the Dodgers had started Hal Gregg (5.87 ERA in the regular season) in Game 7 of the World Series, Rickey made a big move, packaging Gregg, Dixie Walker (the erstwhile "People's Cherce," who had become an antagonist in Jackie Robinson's integration that year), and Vic Lombardi to Pittsburgh for Roe, Billy Cox, and Gene Mauch.

Though Walker, nearing the end of the line at age 37, did have a .387 on-base percentage for the Pirates over 677 plate appearances in 1948 and

1949, Roe was a steal, one of the greatest trade acquisitions the Dodgers have ever made. He was superb over the next five seasons (four of them All-Star campaigns), pitching more than 1,000 innings with a 3.00 ERA (2.996, to be precise), leading the NL with a 133 ERA+ over that span.

"Campy [Roy Campanella] used to say, 'Who's pitching today?'" Erskine recalls. "'Preacher.' 'Well, you could take the middle of the plate out and throw it away—he's not going to be using it.' He never threw a ball down the middle.

"Preacher had a good reputation with control, so he got a lot of close pitches always. But he had two or three good curveballs. He threw offspeed. He didn't throw his fastball a lot. He had a pretty good fastball, which he called his 'birder,' but he was crafty. He was excellent setting up a hitter. Today, you wouldn't like Preacher—he was too slow. But he kind of psyched the hitters out."

Campanella believed that Roe was the best pitcher he ever caught, saying that "he was a guy who knew what he was doing every second of every minute." Roe's value enhanced the rest of the staff in a particularly important way.

"This is something that historians don't mention much—none of the broadcasters seem to know about it," Erskine says. "Before about the mid-1950s, all the pitching coaches on pitching staffs were catchers. There were no former pitchers in my early years of baseball. I had four pitching coaches in my baseball career—they were all four catchers. I never had a pitching coach who was a pitcher. The young pitchers would actually go to the older pitchers for advice, and Preacher Roe was the [one] on this staff."

A longstanding question remains about whether Roe had more going for him than people even realized. In a much-scrutinized story in *Sports Illustrated*, he dropped a bombshell.

"Lots of people have asked me what I used to throw," he said. "I like to tell 'em it was my sinker. Well, you know, the ball did drop real pretty, but it was more than a little ol' sinker. I guess it won't hurt anybody to tell the truth now. I threw spitballs the whole time I was with the Dodgers. Seven years in all."

Roe's description of his illicit endeavors occupied six full pages in the magazine, and he went so far as to pose in a series of photos for the issue demonstrating his various techniques, which began with chewing a stick of Beech-Nut gum to give him "slick" saliva.

"I'll tell you another little secret," Roe said. "I wasn't always the one to load up the splitter. Once in a while, after the ball had been tossed around the infield, Pee Wee [Reese] or my buddy, Cox, would come up to the mound, drop the ball easy in my glove, and say: 'There it is if you want it.' That meant they already had the ball wet for me. If I wanted to throw it, I could. If not, I'd just wipe it off."

It was the cheating controversy of its day, mitigated by the assumption Roe wasn't the only one doing it—just that he was the only one talking about it. Then there were those who felt the whole confession, for which he received $2,000, was a charade.

"He never threw one against me in batting practice," said Reese, "so I take it he never threw one in the game." Carl Furillo countered that "when Preach went to his cap with two pitching fingers together, that was our signal."

Roe's first Dodger season in 1948 ended with a 2.63 ERA (152 ERA+, third in the NL) in 177⅔ innings, and he came back to go 212⅔ innings with a 2.79 ERA (148 ERA+, fourth in the NL) in 1949. In his World Series debut—Game 2 of 1949 Fall Classic—Roe pitched the Dodgers' first postseason shutout since Burleigh Grimes in 1920, a six-hit, 1–0 win over the Yankees, walking none, despite taking a line drive that broke the tip of his finger in the fourth inning. (The injury sidelined him the rest of the postseason.)

"That boy is an artist—a supreme artist," Rickey said of Roe, who then kicked off the new decade with a 3.30 ERA (124 ERA+) over 257⅔ innings in 1950.

But Roe's most awe-inspiring year was 1951, when he went 22–3 with a 3.04 ERA (129 ERA+) in a career-high 257⅔ innings. Five years before the creation of the Cy Young Award, Roe was named NL Pitcher of the Year by *The Sporting News*. Even as the Dodgers were faltering, Roe was doing his part holding things together, with three consecutive complete-game victories from September 14 to 23 in which he allowed three runs total.

"Down the stretch, there were three of us—[Don] Newcombe, Preacher Roe, and I—that pitched with short rest several times, just trying to stem this craziness that was happening with the Giants," Erskine says.

However, Roe was knocked out in the second inning of the scheduled regular-season finale, and though the Dodgers rallied for their 14-inning win to reach the tiebreaker series with the Giants, he didn't pitch again that year. Chuck Dressen said that Roe just wasn't ready to come back.

After the horror-show ending of 1951, Roe returned effectively in 1952 (3.12 ERA, 118 ERA+), albeit with nearly 100 fewer innings—by this time he was 36 years old, after all. Rising to yet another occasion, he pitched another complete-game victory in Game 3 of the World Series, as well as in relief in Games 6 and 7, as the Dodgers tried but failed in two chances to clinch the Series at home.

In 1953, Roe went 11–3 with a 4.36 ERA (99 ERA+)—and his only career home run, a shot so improbable that teammates sprung out to lay a carpet of towels for his return to the dugout.

"You got a secret weapon like that, you don't want to go showing it around," Roe quipped.

In his final World Series game, Game 2 of the '53 Classic, the 37-year-old Roe went the distance but gave up a game-tying homer to Billy Martin in the seventh inning and a mammoth, tiebreaking homer to Mickey Mantle in the bottom of the eighth.

Roe's Dodger career ended after the 1954 season, when he was traded (once again with Cox) to Baltimore. In February 1955, before the season got under way, Roe officially retired. For Brooklyn, he pitched 1,277⅓ innings with a 3.26 ERA, and his 124 ERA+ trails only Clayton Kershaw, Sandy Koufax, Dazzy Vance, Whit Wyatt, and Jeff Pfeffer among Dodger pitchers with at least 1,000 innings.

When Roger Kahn caught up with Roe for *The Boys of Summer*, he had moved across the Arkansas border to Missouri, and they drove the distance back to where Roe spent his childhood. The ride revealed what Roe, who died in 2008 at age 92, fundamentally saw as the core of his own story.

"Heck, we can talk about any of it, then, now, the spitter, but I'll bet you one thing," Roe said. "After you see how it was where I started out, you won't believe the feller riding you went from there to being a major-league pitcher."

Carl Erskine

Speaking shortly before his 90th Thanksgiving, in 2016, Carl Erskine could still recall when any kind of Dodger success was rare.

"Well, you know, their reputation was not a winning team," Erskine says. "Because I got to personally go to Ebbets Field and practice as a kid, that to me was the ultimate place to be. But their team had been very mediocre. In fact, the old days, the reputation of the Dodgers were a bunch of clowns."

As one of the postwar pitchers working to change the perception of the franchise, Erskine holds a special place in Dodger history. He wasn't the most dominant pitcher, but few embraced and epitomized the Dodger ethos more than the cheerful righty from Anderson, Indiana.

Erskine is a true appreciator of origin stories, telling one after another of how his youth informed his future.

"My early recollection of baseball was my dad and two older brothers, who used to play catch at the side of the house in the summertime a lot," Erskine says. "I was a little guy, so we used to play 'burnout,' and that was kind of stacked against me. They were just teasing me, but they would throw nice and soft, and they would just gradually get a little harder and a little harder. And we had an old barn, and I'd keep backing up, and they'd try to come forward, so they'd get me against the old barn.

"And I think that's how I learned to throw straight overhand, because in order to try to get more on the return to them, I kept reaching higher and higher. [Sandy] Koufax threw straight overhand, and [Warren] Spahn—but I saw very few right-handers ever throw straight, really direct overhand."

Striking out "about 20" in an American Legion game while he was a 16-year-old sophomore in high school, Erskine was offered his first contract by the Cubs, who were willing to start him high in the minor leagues, Class-A. "That was a pretty amazing thing, for me to be offered that," Erskine says. But wanting to stay eligible in sports for the remainder of high school, he didn't sign. After all, this was Indiana.

"During the baseball season, we didn't draw many big crowds," he says. "Our high school basketball gym, the old Wigwam, held about 9,000—in Indiana, they packed it for games. So people still to this day say, 'Carl, I remember seeing you play'—I think they're going to talk about baseball. 'No, no, you played basketball against Kokomo—I remember you guys.'"

In his remaining prep years, Erskine and a catcher named Jack Rector were scouted by an Indianapolis legend, Stanley Feezle, a Big 10 basketball official from 1920 to 1941 who then became one of baseball's treasure hunters. Gil Hodges was among his finds.

"Mr. Feezle was so nice to Jack and me," Erskine says. "Treated us so well, didn't put any pressure on us. But when we graduated from high school, Mr. Feezle came over to my house, and I remember him on the front porch of my house. Jack Rector was there, and my parents, and he said, 'Boys, I've got a graduation present for you. Here's a first-class ticket'—that meant a Pullman on the train—'here's a first-class ticket to New York. You guys are going to go to New York and stay in the New Yorker Hotel for a week, and you're gonna work out with the Dodgers every day.' No kidding. And he said, 'By the way, here's a hundred-dollar bill for each of you.'

"Gee whiz. Now, just think about that. Do you think I would ever want to play for another team besides the Dodgers? He put the fix in real fast. We went there, and every night, Branch Rickey Jr. would host us to Radio City or some other nice restaurant or Madison Square Garden, and they treated us like royalty."

The military delayed Erskine's Dodger destiny—and nearly derailed it. Drafted into the Navy at age 18 as the war was ending, Erskine was stationed at the Boston Navy Yard, where he attracted the attention of the Braves while pitching for a semipro team. But the courtship experience with the Dodgers had won his heart.

The Dodgers had good reason to be thankful. Years after Erskine's retirement, Dodger historian Mark Langill found the original scouting report on him, and the most important thing on it, according to Erskine, was that it said "fastball A+ with movement." For an organization that was beginning to flex its pitching might, Erskine offered some muscle ready for development.

"You don't hear much people talk about a four-seam curve," he says. "But the Dodgers taught a four-seam curveball. It's the same principle as the four-seam fastball. If you throw a fastball with four-seams and tight rotation and you've got velocity, you get movement…And when you rotate a curveball with velocity, you get a tight rotation and a sharp break. So when I learned to throw the Dodgers' four-seam curveball, the scouts jumped out of their skin."

"Then Mr. Rickey showed me an off-speed pitch, a four-seamer—think of that. All four [of my] pitches were four-seam and had good tight rotation, so you didn't see any seams. You know, a lot of times you can pick out the slider because you can see the spiral, but with a full rotation on a fastball, curveball, change, they all looked alike."

> ### Moment in the Sun: Rex Barney
> - Made Dodger debut with eight starts at age 18 in 1943
> - At age 22, allowed two runs in 6⅔ innings in 1947 World Series, including bases-loaded strikeout of Joe DiMaggio
> - No-hit the Giants on September 9, 1948, on his way to a 3.10 ERA (129 ERA+) in 246⅔ innings
> - Wild righty walked 410 batters in 597⅔ career innings with 336 strikeouts and 4.31 ERA (92 ERA+)
> - Served as public-address announcer for Baltimore Orioles from 1973 to 1997

When Erskine made his major-league debut on July 25, 1948, he was still only 21 years old. After three shutout relief appearances, Erskine entered the rotation August 5 for his first career start. It was a milestone, and a millstone.

"They gave me a start against the Cubs," Erskine remembers, "and I was pitching well, into the seventh inning, and I threw a fastball to Bill Nicholson, a big, left-handed hitter, called 'Swish' Nicholson. I threw him a high fastball, and I pulled a muscle in the back of my shoulder.

"Well, I finished the game, so now I've got a complete game and three wins. Four days later, with my arm really hurting bad—killing me—I started against the Phillies. And by the sixth inning, I was hurting so bad that I told the manager—that was Burt Shotton by that time—I said, 'Mr. Shotton, I hurt my shoulder the other day against the Cubs, and boy, I can't hardly lift it.' He looked at me with big surprise on his face and he said, 'Well, son, you're pitching [well]. Now you just go right ahead and do your job, and if you get in trouble, we'll get somebody in there.'"

Erskine never got in trouble—he didn't even allow a runner past first base after the fourth inning—and finished the victory. The next week, despite struggling to get loose, he allowed no earned runs in a 10–1 romp at Philadelphia.

"Boy, I had such a hard time warming up," Erskine says. "But…I'm 5–0 with three complete games in a row, and if I'd have told somebody I had a sore arm, nobody'd have believed it."

When he allowed 21 runs in his final 34 innings that raised his rookie ERA from 0.61 to 3.23, Erskine's ailment became apparent, but nothing was done about it.

"In those days when the season ended, they'd say, 'Good-bye, we'll see you in the spring.' There was no off-season program," Erskine recalls. "Nobody knew about anybody's shoulder. So I came home, and four months later we go back to spring training, and believe me, I couldn't have hardly blacked your eye if I hit you with my fastball, because of my bad shoulder."

As a result, despite his finishing his rookie campaign with a 3.23 ERA (124 ERA+) in 64 innings, Erskine shuttled between the majors and minors for nearly two seasons, until he was brought back from Montreal to stay in August 1950, forced to grow up in a hurry as a pitcher. His big-league ERA for those two seasons was 4.68 (88 ERA+).

"I never had quite the magic on that fastball that I'd had as a kid," he says. "Never quite had as much movement. Campy, he used to say, 'Erskine throws hard'—but I never had the ease. I lost a little of that edge, starting my first game in the big leagues. Can you beat that?"

Persevering, he worked his way back from the precipice of the discard pile into a role that would make him an all-time beloved Dodger.

In the indescribable 1951 season that ended with him watching Ralph Branca enter the final inning from the bullpen, Erskine made 19 starts and 27 relief appearances with a 4.46 ERA (88 ERA+). Then in 1952, the adjustments he had been making since his rookie season began to pay off. In 206⅔ innings, he had a 2.70 ERA (136 ERA+). On June 19 against the Cubs, he pitched the first of two career no-hitters, with only a walk to pitcher Willie Ramsdell standing between him and a perfect game. (Throwing 103 pitches, Erskine struck out only one but recorded 18 groundball outs, and only five batters hit the ball out of the infield.) On September 20, his 10-inning, 1–0 complete-game victory over Spahn and the Braves gave the Dodgers a commanding five-game lead in the NL with a week to play.

That October, Erskine made two World Series starts, losing the first after being charged with four earned runs in five innings. The second was epic. After allowing five runs in the fifth inning of Game 5 to surrender a 4–0 Dodger lead, Erskine was visited by Charlie Dressen, who held a lengthy, *Bull Durham*–style discussion at the mound about how Erskine and his wife would be celebrating their fifth wedding anniversary that night. Dressen left the mound, and Erskine stayed in to pitch perfect ball—19 up, 19 down—for the remainder of the day, finishing the 11-inning, 6–5 victory with a strikeout of the 41st batter he faced, Yogi Berra, just as a blister on his finger was tearing open.

"I get the count to 2-2, and by now this blister has broken completely, and the skin has rolled up. It stings; I can feel it. I took a look at Dressen and thought, *Should I say anything?*" Erskine said. "[But] Campanella gives me a curveball sign, and I threw one of the best curveballs I ever threw for strike three. When I did, that blister tore completely off, and I couldn't have thrown another pitch. That blister was down to the red meat.

"That was an amazing thing. I never had a blister before or since."

Baseball has hardly seen a postseason effort like that before or since. Working on only two days' rest, Erskine was the first pitcher to throw at least 11 innings in a World Series game since Schoolboy Rowe in 1934, and no NL pitcher has thrown that many innings in any playoff game in the aftermath. Erskine even came back to relieve Preacher Roe and pitch two shutout innings in another heartbreaking Game 7 defeat.

In 1953, Erskine set a career best with a 20–6 record (3.54 ERA, 121 ERA+), becoming the team's unquestioned ace that year. After allowing four runs in one inning of the World Series opener, Erskine brushed it off like a sprinkle of dirt from his trousers, returning 48 hours later in Game 3 to set a new World Series record with 14 strikeouts in a 3–2 victory.

"That had to be my best day ever in baseball, to do it against a team like the Yankees," Erskine says. "But then, 10 years to the day, I was in the stands at Yankee Stadium as a retired player and watched Koufax, a teammate, get 15. So he took my record, but that wasn't so bad because he was my teammate. And then I was in the stands in '68 in Detroit when [Bob] Gibson got 17. So I got a baseball signed by Sandy with his record and Gibson on the other side with his record and me on the backside with my record. And the odd part about that was that all three of those dates are October 2: '53, '63, and '68."

Erskine threw a career-high 260⅓ innings in 1954—80 more than any teammate—and made his only All-Star team while the Dodgers finished in second place. In 1955, the return of Newcombe from military service took pressure off "Oisk," who, even with a 12-inning shutout that May against the now-Milwaukee Braves, was dialed back to 194⅔ innings. His ERA was 1.73 at the end of May but 5.32 thereafter, leaving him at 3.79 (108 ERA+) by season's end and a nonfactor in the Series when Brooklyn finally brought its title home.

He threw his second no-hitter against the Giants on May 12, 1956, during a season with a 4.25 ERA (94 ERA+), but was again mostly ineffective in Brooklyn's last World Series. In his final three years, though he pitched mostly out of the bullpen, Erskine started the Dodgers' first game in Los Angeles at the Memorial Coliseum, on April 18, 1958, going eight innings in a 6–5 victory before a crowd of 78,672. He made his final appearance in June 1959, at age 32.

Erskine moved back home to Indiana but remained a popular figure for decades after his playing days were over, particularly active in the Special Olympics while working with his son Jimmy, who was born with Down syndrome. Memorably, Erskine played the national anthem on harmonica before the Dodgers' final spring training game at Vero Beach, Florida, on March 17, 2008.

Nearing the end of his sixth decade since retirement diminished none of the pride and joy of his playing days.

"To have been a Dodger, only a Dodger—and how I got to be a Dodger—is such a remarkable thing for me," Erskine says. "And boy, what team could you have picked to have pitched for? They could get runs, they could play defense. Boy, I played with some of the great players—we were close friends, we would raise our kids together—and I couldn't have drawn it up in Fantasyland better than how it actually happened. I thank the Good Lord every morning and night, and then I wake up sometimes and I say, 'Did that really happen?' I mean, that's too much. That's beyond…being a kid and dreaming of being a big-leaguer. That was too big a dream, to think that would ever happen that way."

Don Newcombe

The agony. The terror. The hopelessness. The tears. The pain.

At the climax of his incredible career, these were the feelings that consumed Don Newcombe.

It's all hard to imagine, hard to reconcile with the image that remains of the burly 6-foot-4 right-hander, pitching like the side of a mountain coming at you from 60 feet, 6 inches away, or with his regal presence at Dodger Stadium in the 21st century, floating into the stands during batting practice in a suit and hat past his 90th birthday, with present-day members of the team lining up to spend time.

But Newcombe's sublime legacy has masked the heartache that came along the way.

Surely it should have been enough, more than enough, just to endure, just to survive, as an African American pitcher in the opening decade of Major League Baseball's integration. The attacks and the indignities, big and small, on and off the field, could have broken Newcombe, who wasn't the first player to sever the color line like Jackie Robinson, nor the first pitcher like Don Bankhead, but who was years younger than either—a mere 23—when he took the stage for Brooklyn in 1949.

But on top of it all, like a fusillade of fastballs to the gut, Newcombe was repeatedly drilled during his big-league career—by fans, by the media, even by managers and teammates. Some of the damage was self-inflicted, brought on by his own behavior. Much, however, was superfluous, misguided, and even cruel, judging Newcombe by his shortcomings—real or imagined—no matter how numerous his successes.

The pressure and expectations crescendoed into a collapse, a breakdown of a vulnerable soul that few understood. That he eventually recovered to give the rest of his life back to the game and its players is as important as the story that preceded.

His journey, as much as that of any pitcher in Dodger history, is profound.

Like Ralph Branca and Carl Erskine, Newcombe was born three years before the Great Depression. His father was a chauffeur who had a steady job working for the same family, and the skinny youngster, who dropped out of high school, adjusted his ambitions accordingly. "He had grown up in New Jersey a gifted athlete who wanted above all to be a truck driver," Michael Shapiro wrote. "He played baseball well, but not seriously, assuming that if he did not make a living driving trucks he might become a drummer instead."

"I was going from pillar to post," Newcombe said, "and I was sitting in the poolroom one day, and I was playing checkers with this guy, and he says, 'How would you like to play professional baseball, or at least try out?' I said, 'Man, that would be fine.'"

It was the height of World War II, with the military depleting the ranks of ballplayers, so just like in the major leagues, the Negro Leagues were taking practically all comers. Newcombe's first encounter with future teammate Roy Campanella (five years his senior) came as an opponent in 1944, when Newcombe's manager, Mule Suttles, told him to knock Campanella down with a pitch. Newcombe fired the ball up but not in, and Campy slammed it out of the park.

On the cusp of adulthood, Newcombe was questioned, maybe for the first time but far from the last, if he was man enough for this life.

"Suttles came out to the mound to take me out of the ballgame," Newcombe recalled. "He said, 'You'll never make a big-league pitcher because you're too goddamn dumb.' I always remembered that. I had to learn to become a big-league pitcher—big-league, that is, as far as Negro baseball was concerned."

The next year, a new manager, Willie Wells, gave Newcombe a less eviscerating but wholly useful instruction.

"He said, 'I don't want you to throw a baseball for the first two weeks you're in spring training. All I want you to do is run, just run,'" said Newcombe. "Your legs are your most important part of your body, and the more you run, the stronger your arm will be. You never have to fear injury."

"Newcombe running is an awesome sight," a beguiled Robert Creamer wrote years later. "He looks taller than his 6-feet-4, heavier than his 240 pounds. He starts slowly, lumbering at first, but then gradually picking up speed like a Mack truck or an elephant, until with heavy, ground-shaking steps he pounds over the grass. A teammate has observed, 'When Newk runs it's like the wall of a building falling down. He's not very fast, but once he gets going he can't stop, and ain't nobody going to get in his way.'"

Clyde Sukeforth, the scout who had brought in Robinson to be signed by Branch Rickey, did likewise for Newcombe. For the 1946 season, Newk and Campy went to Nashua, two levels below the majors, where they were managed by Walter Alston. The following year, while Campanella moved up to Montreal, Newcombe returned to Nashua and pitched 223 innings with a 2.91 ERA, then 189 innings with a 3.14 ERA in '48 for Montreal after Campanella matriculated to Brooklyn. On May 20, 1949, Newcombe's turn arrived.

Less than a month shy of his 23rd birthday, Newcombe made his major-league debut at St Louis in the seventh inning, the Dodgers trailing 3–2. With three fastballs, he struck out the first batter he faced, Chuck Diering, but then gave up three straight singles to Red Schoendienst, Stan Musial, and Eddie Kazak and a bases-clearing double to Enos Slaughter. Dodger manager Burt Shotton pulled Newcombe and his 81.00 ERA from the game.

"Well, I got my dauber down, and I thought I was on my way back to Montreal," Newcombe said. "And I recall sitting down at the end of the dugout by myself and feeling damn dejected, I'll tell ya. Burt Shotton came over—he was an old man who always wore civilian clothes and a damn nice man—but I didn't know him. I didn't know anything about him. He came over, and I thought, *Uh oh. Here it comes. I'm going back to Montreal.*"

Remarkably, Shotton told Newcombe he'd be starting the second game of a doubleheader in Cincinnati—in 48 hours. More remarkably, Newcombe pitched a five-hit shutout, walking none.

"Newcombe was just a hard thrower," Erskine says. "What you want to be is a pitcher. He didn't have a very big curveball. He had a small, sharp—actually, it was a slider. But he had excellent control. Campanella took him as a young pitcher, and he actually made Newk. And if you talk to Newcombe, I think he'll tell you that without Campanella's early coaching and encouragement, he might never have been the outstanding pitcher he was."

Despite making his first start with 121 games left in the regular season, Newcombe led the NL with five shutouts and 5.5 strikeouts per nine innings and the Dodgers with 244⅓ innings and 19 complete games, finishing with a 3.17 ERA (130 ERA+) while averaging 7⅔ innings per start. He won the NL Rookie of the Year Award, finishing eighth in the MVP voting that was topped by Robinson—a just result not only for Robinson's performance on the field, but Robinson's role in Newcombe's success.

"Robinson, who saw true ability in the youngster, was determined to teach him how to win," wrote Arnold Rampersad. "Off the field, he could be cuddly with Newcombe. 'This kid's going to be a great pitcher,' he assured a reporter as Newcombe stood bashfully by. 'All he needs to be sensational is a little more experience. He can win the pennant for us.' On the field, however, Jack was often brutal. 'I cuss him out from the beginning to the end,' Robinson wrote. 'I call him all the bad things I can think of. I got to, to keep him interested in the game.'"

Not only had the questions about Newcombe's character that had sprouted when he was still a Negro League teenager never gone away, they seemed to multiply. Newcombe's temperament was an issue from the start.

"If they took a popularity poll, I sure as hell wouldn't win," Newcombe told Roger Kahn. "Lots of guys don't like my attitude. Can't blame 'em. I don't like it myself."

"How so?" asked Kahn.

"I say things I shouldn't."

But he also faced torment that few understood. *Forever Blue* author Michael D'Antonio describes an incident from spring training in 1949, when Newcombe and Philadelphia A's catcher Fermin Guerra renewed a winter-league beef that had begun months before.

"This time," wrote D'Antonio, "Guerra crossed some verbal line, and Newcombe responded by ripping a slat off a fence and using it to hit him. As a black sportswriter named Sam Lacy intervened, a white spectator began screaming about how (as Newcombe recalled), 'a n——r can't go after a white man that way.'

"The next morning, the camp was alarmed by a rumor that a mob was coming to lynch Newcombe. While an airplane was readied to take him away, the local sheriff arrived with the word that no one had to worry because tempers had cooled when locals realized Guerra was Cuban."

Newcombe could never pretend that any of his actions wouldn't be judged through a prism of racism.

"He couldn't stay in the hotel with us either, in those early years," Erskine says. "He was a little defensive with the press, and I think it was just because it was such a new experience for Newk."

At the same time, some Dodgers didn't think Newcombe got angry enough, or at least at the right things—that he needed to channel his anger into the game. "Trouble with Newk is he doesn't push himself," Campanella told Roscoe McGowen of *The New York Times*.

"The story was told again and again," McGowen added. "And though the sight of Newcombe lumbering across the outfield between starts was a familiar one, Campanella's words stuck. They offered what seemed the only plausible explanation for why a man of such promise and accomplishment could fail to be wonderful at the very moments when everyone needed him to be nothing less."

While Campanella would be the nurturer, Robinson challenged him to the point of fury.

"In later years he told me, 'I knew that you could be a better pitcher when I made you mad, and I made you mad on purpose,'" Newcombe said.

If that weren't enough to bear, Newcombe's love for playoff baseball was utterly unrequited.

As a rookie, Newcombe started Game 1 of the 1949 World Series, the first African American to make a start in baseball's biggest showcase. Other than Ralph Branca, Newcombe was the youngest pitcher to start a World Series opener since Babe Ruth—and it was Newcombe's third start in a week's time.

For eight innings, the 23-year-old matched zeroes with 32-year-old Yankee veteran Allie Reynolds. Newcombe walked none, struck out 11, and allowed only two runners past first base, stranding them both at second. He called it the best game he pitched in his life.

But in the bottom of the ninth, Tommy Henrich came to the plate. Newcombe fell behind 2-0, then threw a curveball.

"I'd throw the same pitch to him today and dare him to hit it again," Newcombe said. "I'd like to see him hit it again. And he hit it over the right-field fence."

Said Henrich: "Heck, I don't even know what I hit."

"'It was a low curve," said Newcombe, making no effort to hide his disgust and despair. "It was also one of the biggest disappointments of my life. I knew when he hit it that it was gone. I never saw where it landed. I just put my glove in my pocket and walked off the goddamn field."

It was Newcombe's first big game—if you subtract all the other big games he pitched in a season when the Dodgers won the pennant by a single victory. And the aftermath set a harsh tone that accounted not at all for his youth or the obstacles he faced, much less the eccentricities of the sport.

"Dodger fans never warmed up to Newcombe," said Larry King, the broadcaster whose roots in rooting for Brooklyn are well documented. "We liked him, and we didn't like him. We didn't think he was a clutch pitcher. For some strange reason…even though he pitched better than Reynolds, we said he choked."

Well then.

Newcombe, who gave up three runs in a Game 4 defeat (the Dodgers lost the Series in five), continued to pitch exceptionally in high-stakes regular-season games, but he never found postseason redemption. His career had barely begun by the time he was cursed with sky-high expectations that never yielded the crowning victory.

In 1950, Newcombe's first full calendar year in the majors, he wasn't quite as consistent (3.70 ERA, 111 ERA+), though he finished 19–11. But with the season coming down to a fierce race with the Phillies, Newcombe shouldered the team.

On August 21, he went the distance in a 3–2 win over the Pirates. On three days' rest, he shut out the Reds, and after three more days' rest, he pitched another complete game, allowing only two unearned runs at Wrigley Field. In his next start, he blanked the Giants, and in the first game of a doubleheader at Philadelphia, whom the Dodgers trailed by 7½ games, he whitewashed the Phillies, extending his streak of innings without allowing an earned run to 41.

"I won the first game, 2–0, and I remember Mr. Shotton standing on the top step of the dugout and he puts his arms around me," Newcombe said. "He said, 'You're a big young guy. Why don't you take the second game, too?' Allan Roth, our statistician, said I only made 83 pitches."

"I said to him, 'Are you serious?' He said, 'I'm serious if you are.' I went into the clubhouse and changed my shirt, and [Dodger trainer] Doc Wendler gave me a rubdown. When I went out to the warmup area to get ready for the second game, I'll never forget the Phillie fans as a murmur went through the stands, and when they announced my name as starter for the second game there was loud applause."

Newcombe's scoreless streak ended with a first-inning run, but he still nabbed 21 outs in a game the Dodgers won with three runs in the ninth, 3–2. In 17 days, Newcombe threw a monstrous 52 innings—capped by the unreal 16 innings on September 6—averaging essentially a complete game every 72 hours with a 0.69 ERA.

Thanks largely to Newk, the Dodgers nearly made a comeback that itself would have been an all-timer. Trailing by nine games with 17 remaining, they had pulled within one of Philadelphia on the final day of the season, when they hosted the Phillies at Ebbets Field. After nine innings, Newcombe and Robin Roberts were tied 1–1. (Cal Abrams, trying to score the winning run for Newcombe and Brooklyn from second on a Duke Snider single in the bottom of the ninth, was thrown out at the plate, an event so thoroughly dissected after the game that third-base coach Milt Stock was fired days later.)

With Newcombe returning to the mound in the top of the 10th, Eddie Waitkus followed a Roberts single with a bloop hit of his own to shallow center. One out later, Dick Sisler, son of Hall of Fame first baseman and Dodger head scout George Sisler, hit an opposite-field, three-run home run.

"Abrams stood for a split second, then ran madly toward the wall," Roscoe McGowan wrote in *The New York Times*. "But it was no use. The biggest home run—and possibly one of the shortest—the stands are only 348 feet from home plate—that young Sisler ever hit, was on the records."

The blow, hit by the 1,099th batter Newcombe faced that season, denied him a reprieve from the Henrich homer. Come the late summer and great fall of 1951, when the Dodgers suffered their most infamous collapse in their history, knives were out for Newcombe everywhere.

Understand that Newcombe was a superstar. In his third big-league season, he went 20–9 with a 3.28 ERA (120 ERA+) in 272 innings, leading the majors with 164 strikeouts and completing 19 of 36 starts. Brooklyn—the team and the city—leaned relentlessly on him, then with almost willful ignorance wondered why he seemed tired.

On September 14, six days after Newcombe pitched a two-hit shutout against the Giants, Tommy Holmes of the *Brooklyn Eagle* wound up and delivered a haymaker of a column, topped by this headline:

IS NEWCOMBE AILMENT CASE OF IMAGINITIS?

In the second paragraph, Holmes began dressing down Newcombe by pointing out that the 25-year-old, third-year major-league pitcher had yet to win 20 games, though he was 18–8 with 16 days left in the season. In fact, Holmes noted with a straight face (or a straight razor), "experts had predicted he would win 30 games in 1950," and when Newcombe failed to do so, Holmes laid the blame on Newcombe, rather than the pundits who expected him to reach a win total unachieved in baseball since Dizzy Dean in 1934.

Holmes pointed out that after Newcombe complained of a sore arm following several spring training outings in 1950, manager Shotton had flat-out told reporters that Newcombe was "jaking it" and said he had no sympathy for pitchers who didn't want to pitch.

"Newcombe claims he is also prone to sore arms, but nobody has ever found anything wrong with his arm," Holmes wrote unironically. "They say that if you want to find out where the trouble is, you should look in his head and they are probably right."

When the Dodgers found Newcombe five years earlier, "he was just a big Negro kid of tremendous natural talent and modest future." Now, Holmes complained, here was the gratitude he was showing them.

Undaunted by the previous failed predictions, Holmes reminded his readers that the "experts" once more insisted Newcombe would win 30. "But again, with the beginning of the 1951 season, Newcombe complained of a sore arm, and then in July he asked to be taken out of a game in which he held an 8–2 lead," Holmes wrote. Newcombe, by the way, was 12–4 with a 3.16 ERA at the time.

The Dodgers lost their next four games—all Newcombe's fault, no doubt, even if he didn't play in any of them—before new manager Dressen "blew up and repeated all the unkind things Shotton has said about Newcombe," according to Holmes.

"Actually, of course, it is a case of a young man who knows he has a chance to make a small fortune out of baseball and who has read how sore arms ruined the careers of other great stars," Holmes enlightened the public. "He is desperately attempting to avoid doing anything that would ruin that career, and in his desperation he does not realize that he is doing the one thing that could ruin it.

"Don's chronic case of imaginitis is getting under the skin of the top brass, and his fellow players don't like it a bit, either."

That last line, taken at face value, makes the case that Holmes wasn't coming up with this preemptive autopsy of Newcombe's failings alone. The blows were also being struck from inside the clubhouse. But regardless of the pummeling he took—royal cynicism on the left, impossible expectations on the right—Newcombe had to soldier on, in a fashion that could have inspired the baseball version of Joseph Heller's *Catch-22*.

On September 26, with the lead over the Giants down to one game and five left on the schedule, Brooklyn scored four runs in the first and four more in the fifth to take an 8–0 lead against the non-contending Boston Braves. Newcombe allowed three runs in the bottom of the fifth, but stayed in the game. He stayed in the game in the sixth and seventh. Even after the Dodgers added seven runs in the top of the eighth for a 15–3 lead, Newcombe trudged out to pitch the bottom of the eighth. He allowed two solo home runs, yet batted for himself in the top of the ninth, reached on a fielder's choice, stayed on base through three more batters, and in the bottom of the ninth, with a 10-run lead, came back to the mound to face his 34th, 35th, and 36th batters of a game in which he threw in the neighborhood of 150 pitches. He struck out the final two.

At this point, one might have suggested that the shortsighted Dodgers weren't building a pitching tradition as much as they were force-feeding it.

Unable to shake the Giants, the Dodgers then sent Newcombe out for his next start on two days' rest. He pitched superbly, shutting out the Phillies on seven hits to help Brooklyn maintain a first-place tie with New York with one game remaining.

The next day, the scheduled season finale, the Giants edged the Braves 3–2, and Brooklyn needed a win to stay alive. Trailing 8–5 in the top of the eighth, the Dodgers scored three to tie the game, but pinch-hit for Erskine in the process. From their entire pitching staff, they chose as their next pitcher the guy who had thrown nine innings the day before, the guy with the chronic case of "imaginitis."

"All through my career, my arm was such that it didn't get stiff until the second day after I pitched, not the first day," Newcombe said. "The first day was fine. This was the first day after pitching."

Out of the bullpen, Newcombe pitched 5⅔ innings as the game staggered to the 14th inning. He wobbled, walking six, and benefited from Robinson making one of the most stunning catches in Dodger history, snagging a bases-loaded, two-out liner up the middle by Waitkus to end the 12th, but Newcombe kept runs off the board.

"I left the mound, and the Dodger fans and the Phillie fans gave me a great ovation," Newcombe said. "I won't soon forget that, and it's been a lot of years now. Even though the Philadelphia fans didn't like the Dodgers, they appreciated the effort."

In the top of the 14th, the desperately exhausted Robinson homered to win it, and the Dodgers and Giants were set for their three-game playoff. After the split of the first two games, it was up to Newcombe again to save the season, pitching once more on two days' rest. When he reached the ninth inning with a 4–1 lead over Sal Maglie, Mr. Imaginitis had thrown 31⅔ innings in eight days.

Even Holmes was impressed. "Surprisingly," he wrote, "at least to this observer, was that Newcombe's pitching poise seemed to hold up better than the more mature, more phlegmatic and methodical Maglie."

But that ninth inning was going to be a mountain.

"When Newk returned to the bench in the eighth with the score 1–1, I asked him how he felt," Campanella said.

"Tired," Newcombe grunted.

On an 0-2 pitch, Al Dark hit a little bouncer to the right side for a single. Don Mueller followed by grounding one to the right of Hodges, who inexplicably had been instructed by the Dodgers to hold Dark at first despite the three-run lead. Monte Irvin fouled out, but then Whitey Lockman doubled, driving in one with the tying runs now on base.

Dressen came to get Newcombe, bringing in Branca. Without a doubt, Branca is the one associated with the final defeat. But the moment also cemented Newcombe's unfortunate reputation as a small-timer in big games.

"Everybody talked about my getting taken out of the final game in 1951 in the ninth inning, but nobody said one thing about what I did for the two weeks leading up to that playoff game," Newcombe said. "I gave the Dodgers everything I had. I was leading 4–1 in the ninth. And they say I choked up because I left in the ninth inning? Other pitchers get in trouble…Why is it they concentrated on me and said I choked up in 1951? Why? I don't know, but they did.

"If I was gonna choke up, I would have choked up in the second or third inning. If I was afraid of the Giants, I wouldn't have pitched the game that I pitched. Nobody gave me credit for it at all, especially in the press. They tore my ass up."

Moment in the Sun: Billy Loes

- As a 22-year-old rookie in 1952, posted a 2.69 ERA (136 ERA+) in 187⅓ innings
- Suffered heartbreaking 3–2 loss in Game 6 of the 1952 World Series, but came back to win Game 4 of the '53 Series
- Famously explained key hit in '52 loss by saying he lost ground ball in the sun, which Carl Erskine later validated by saying that the setting sun did sneak through the lower levels of Ebbets Field
- Spent majority of 11-year MLB career with Dodgers, with a 3.86 ERA (105 ERA+) in 639⅔ innings

For all the faults so many wanted to lay at his feet from 1949 to 1951, Newcombe was 56–28 with a 3.39 ERA (120 ERA+), 57 complete games, and 12 shutouts. During those three seasons, Newcombe's first years in the majors, only 30-year-old Warren Spahn had more complete games or strikeouts. Roberts and Newcombe, both born in 1926, were the premier right-handers of the next generation.

"Newcombe came in and just tore up the league from the beginning," John Thorn says. "He was a fully formed pitcher—he could have come to the majors earlier, but he was probably held back at Nashua with Roy Campanella so there would be two blacks on that team."

In 1952, Roberts went 28–7 with a 2.59 ERA. Newcombe went into the military, losing his age-26 and age-27 seasons to the Army Medical Corps, "most of the time as a part of a special demonstration unit," according to Creamer. Newcombe returned to Brooklyn in 1954, a season that amounted to shaking off the rust (144⅓ innings, 4.55 ERA, 91 ERA+).

Of the diversion into the military, Thorn says plainly, "I think it cost him a position in the Hall of Fame."

Even in his absence, the Dodgers ping-ponged between appreciation and aversion to Newcombe. "Losing Newcombe is worse than losing [Willie] Mays," Dressen said. "Where can you get a pitcher like that? Let the Giants have Mays back. Let 'em have two Mays. It's okay with me, so long as the Army gives me back Newcombe." But when Dressen was fired at the end of the year, he sniped in *Look* magazine that Newcombe "missed repeatedly in the crucial low-run games."

Newcombe couldn't walk away, wouldn't walk away. If it wasn't clear how much the game meant to Newcombe before his forced sabbatical, it was unmistakable upon his return, which began with a complete-game, 6–4 victory against the Giants at the Polo Grounds.

"We go in the clubhouse," Erskine recalls, "and everybody's happy and everybody's hitting around, having a good time. So I go over to Newk's locker in the Polo Grounds to congratulate him, and he kind of jerks away from me and turns his back on me. 'Oh, what's this about?'—that was my first reaction. But I didn't leave. I stayed there, and finally Newk turned around a little bit. I could see he was crying. And I said, 'Newk, are you okay?' And he kind of swallowed hard—you could see tears in his eyes. He said, 'Carl, I didn't know if I could pitch again in the big leagues.' His emotions…"

As time has passed, Robinson's pioneering status has made it all too easy to dismiss Newcombe's place on the front lines of transcending the color line in baseball, but that outsider status—the racism both explicit and implicit—is inseparable from his story.

"It should be noted that the belief that African Americans lacked fortitude was an important component of the psychology of race prejudice," wrote Carl E. Prince. "It was this deeply rooted bias that Dixie Walker reflected in his 1946 statement that blacks didn't have what it took to play major-league ball. This was a view prevalent among a large number of major-leaguers, especially those who were southerners, in that post–World War II era.

"Neither Robinson nor Campanella would ever qualify as race-tainted gutless wonders, but as is always the case with deeply embedded prejudice, the arrival of one possible victim would erase for many all other evidence."

The 1955 season, of course, was a triumph for Brooklyn. The race ended almost as soon as it began, the Dodgers taking a double-digit lead in the NL by June and, unlike '51, never giving it back. Ascending again as the unquestioned ace of the staff, Newcombe opened the season 10–0 in his first 11 starts (with a 2.44 ERA) and was 18–1 by the end of July.

Not for nothing, Newcombe was also a tremendous hitting pitcher at the peak of his skill. Bill James, who called Newcombe the best hitting pitcher of the 1950s, said that Newcombe's 1955 season at the plate was "with the exception of one Wes Ferrell season and Babe Ruth, the best-hitting season by a pitcher in the 20th century." Newcombe posted a .395 on-base percentage and .632 slugging percentage, thanks to an NL-record seven home runs, a triple, and nine doubles—and added a cherry on top with a steal of home. Newcombe even had a .435 OBP in 23 pinch-hitting appearances.

In August, he pitched complete games in three consecutive losses in which the high-powered Brooklyn offense was held to a combined four runs. But Newcombe won his 20th game on September 5, and Brooklyn clinched the pennant on September 8, leading the league at the time by 17 games. That September, in contrast to previous years, Newcombe pitched only 20⅔ innings, finishing the regular season with a 20–5 record and 3.20 ERA (128 ERA+), leading the league in WHIP, walks per nine innings, and strikeout-walk ratio, but also evincing renewed concerns about his health.

In their most memorable World Series, the Dodgers played seven games, and Newcombe won none. Set up to start Game 1, Newcombe surrendered leads of 2–0 in the second inning and 3–2 in the third, ultimately allowing six runs in 5⅔ innings of a 6–5 loss.

McGowen wrote that Newcombe, who "didn't linger around the clubhouse" to meet the press, "wasn't happy about his showing and neither, for that matter, was Alston and the rest of the boys."

"No, I don't think he was as fast as I've seen him," Alston said. "He wasn't overpowering."

Billy Loes started Game 2 (also a defeat), followed by Johnny Podres in Game 3 and Erskine in Game 4 (both wins). But when Newcombe could have started Game 5 on three days' rest, Alston went with rookie Roger Craig, who had made 10 starts all year and was pitching in the Piedmont League a year earlier. When Newcombe could have started Game 6 on four days' rest, Alston went with Karl Spooner, who hadn't finished the fourth inning in a start in nearly four weeks. And for Game 7, it was the 23-year-old Podres, not Newcombe. Alston told reporters before Game 6 that "Newk has had the flu, a sore arm, and a sore back."

Deprived of individual glory in the World Series, Newcombe wasn't denied his place in the celebration. "Newcombe, so fastidious that he once threatened violence if a pennant celebration left beer on his clothes, allowed Duke Snider to fill his hat with Schaefer and then press it down on his head," wrote D'Antonio.

Newcombe came back in 1956 to achieve the pièce de résistance of his career, winning baseball's inaugural Cy Young Award and in turn becoming the first in history to win Cy Young and MVP honors in the same season. He even almost fulfilled those outrageous predictions of a 30-win season, finishing 27–7 with a career-best 3.06 ERA (131 ERA+), and an MLB-leading 0.99 WHIP. Again, he was the Dodgers' iron man and then some (18 complete games, including six consecutive starts from

July 20 to August 11 with a 0.67 ERA), beginning his September with an 11-inning, 3–1 victory over the Giants and climaxing with 20⅓ innings in the season's final eight days, capped by 7⅓ innings in the 8–6 victory over the Pirates that clinched the defending World Series champions' fourth NL pennant in five years.

Once more, it might have been overwork that deprived Newcombe of his crowning moment. This time, it set the stage for his biggest downfall.

Starting Game 2 of the World Series at home against the Yankees, Newcombe gave up a run in the first inning and was KO'd in a five-run second, crowned by Yogi Berra's grand slam. That the Dodgers actually rallied from the 6–0 deficit for a 13–8 victory might as well have been an event from another universe for Newcombe, who, upon exiting Ebbets Field, was confronted by a heckler—a Brooklyn parking lot attendant, no less—named Mike Brown. A frayed Newcombe punched the man in the gut, and charges (ultimately dismissed) were brought against him for simple assault.

A last chance at redemption evaporated in the Dodgers' fourth Game 7 in a decade. Berra took Newcombe deep again—not once but twice, with two-run homers in the first and third innings. A leadoff homer by Elston Howard in the fourth ended Newcombe's season and soon that of the Dodgers, who lost 9–0.

"He drove his Ford station wagon with his right hand, and with his left he held a handkerchief to his face," wrote *New York Post* columnist Milton Gross, who accompanied him after the game with Newcombe's father, James. "Sometimes he put it to his mouth, sometimes to his eyes, and sometimes he dropped it on the seat between his legs. He balled it into his fist or he rolled it between his fingers and always he stared straight ahead, almost unseeing, because there was a mist before his eyes and memories he cannot erase."

"I was thinking about what I do wrong," Newcombe said. "But I can't put my finger on why I do it." He paused, and then went on. "I was running in the outfield at the stadium the other day and a guy called me a yellow-bellied slob. How do you take things like that?"

Newcombe played 1957 in Brooklyn and part of 1958 in Los Angeles, then spent his remaining two and a half big-league years with the two Ohio teams, Cincinnati and Cleveland. There was even a stint for Japan's Chunichi Dragons as a first baseman/outfielder (12 homers in 81 games). But Newcombe's recovery came years after he was done putting on a uniform.

"In 1956," he said, "I won 27 games. I was 27–7! We win the pennant, and because in the World Series Yogi Berra hits a couple of home runs off me, they say I choke up. You know, that knocked the hell out of me that year.

"That's when I started drinking. That's where my whole career came to an end. Really to an end…Then I began to say, 'The hell with it,' and then my career started down, and four years later I was out of the major leagues.

"I went over to New Jersey and crawled into a shell and stayed there. I couldn't go stand up in front of a bunch of kids and have them ask me, 'What does it mean, Mr. Newcombe, when they say you choke up?' How can I explain that to kids? So I said to myself, 'I'm not even going to go out and speak to any of them. I'm not going to do anything.' I went out, and I played golf, and I got drunk. Gained a lot of weight. 'The hell with it.' That's where my head went…Because I didn't give a goddamn. And I think it helped destroy my baseball career."

Newcombe, who reigns in the 21st century as one of most glorious Dodgers—one of the earliest pillars of the Dodger pitching tradition as we know it today—was a beaten man.

"Whatever the realities of Newcombe's contributions in his first three years in the majors, and despite his magnificent years in 1955 and 1956, his reputation was fixed forever by the combination of Giants' jockeying, racist stereotyping, and even the Dodgers' misguided efforts to provoke him into baseball's version of manhood," Prince pointedly stated. "It was the Dodger management and a few players who really did Newcombe in, for they should have known better."

Newcombe was a sad byproduct of the sporting world's primal impulse to tear down those it doesn't quite understand. The fixation on his failings cruelly denied how often he carried the Dodgers on his broad shoulders.

From the moment Newcombe made his Brooklyn debut until the team's move west, no Dodger threw more innings—even though Newcombe spent two full seasons in Army green. He had nearly twice as many complete games, 110, as any other hurler. Despite only eight seasons in a Dodger uniform, he ranked 20th in team history with 22.7 wins above replacement. Podres, as we'll see, was the hero of the '55 World Series. But without Newcombe, there is no Podres.

That all those pressures drove Newcombe down would have been enough, but there was also a Damoclean sword hovering over his entire life, that came down on the Dodgers' 1956 postseason goodwill tour of Japan, a voyage that came and went in a haze for Newcombe.

"It was only years later, when he elevated his story to the realm of tragedy, when he admitted to the alcoholism Labine had seen on sorry display on the flight from New York," wrote Shapiro. "He told of starting to drink beer when he was eight years old: His father, his greatest fan and booster, thought it would help him grow up big and strong. He never pitched drunk, but he did pitch hungover. Schaefer Beer, the team's sponsor, kept the clubhouse stocked. He would drink a six-pack and then stop and buy another for the drive home. By 1956 he was mixing liquor with grapefruit or grape juice."

"On December 7, 1941," Newcombe said, "I was sitting in a Staten Island bar. The Japanese were bombing Pearl Harbor, and I was getting bombed on a barstool." He was 15.

According to Shapiro, Newcombe "stopped drinking in 1965, when his family found him passed out on the floor." He turned his life around, becoming an alcoholism counselor. In 1970, Dodger president Peter O'Malley hired him as the Dodgers' director of community relations.

Newcombe was instrumental in saving the career of Bob Welch, a Dodger pitcher born 24 days after the '56 World Series ended.

"I wasn't going to let that boy go down the drain," Newcombe said. "I know what happened to my career, and it wasn't going to happen to Bob Welch."

In his later years, Newcombe became a super-generational figure at the ballpark, a mentor to so many, particularly Dodger closer Kenley Jansen. He won the level of appreciation, the unequivocal love, that was withheld from him at the height of his prowess. Newcombe rehabilitated himself, and time rehabilitated the rest of us. No great Dodger was less understood in his prime, but no one will ever question him again.

Johnny Podres

So we come to Johnny Podres, and a big question.

How, after 53 years of baseball in Brooklyn in the World Series era, did Podres end up on the mound for the team's first moment of triumph?

How was it Podres and not any of the great names that preceded him: Nap Rucker, Burleigh Grimes, Dazzy Vance?

How was it Podres and not any of the other legendary Boys of Summer: Ralph Branca, Preacher Roe, Carl Erskine, Don Newcombe?

Some of it was pure timing. Some of it was pure stamina.

The rest of it was pure Podres.

In their hot-footed pursuit of an elusive championship, the Dodgers acquired and developed elite talent, but burned through it almost as fast as they gathered it.

"They didn't know a lot about arms," Erskine says. "They never would coddle an arm. I get questions today like, 'There seems like there are so many injuries today. You didn't have that many injuries. How's come?'

Oh yeah, we had 'em. But nobody knew it, because you're not gonna tell somebody, you're not going to the trainer's room as a rookie and complain about your arm. They would've sent you to the minors and bring up a fresh arm. So, yeah, there were a lot of arm injuries.

"I could name you guys that should've been superstars: Rex Barney—he threw so hard, Joe DiMaggio said at the '49 World Series, 'He threw harder than [Bob] Feller.' Karl Spooner—Campy said, 'Of all the pitchers I ever caught, Spooner was the fastest.' And I could give you a list of guys. Erv Palica. Jack Banta. All great prospects with super, super abilities, but they hurt their shoulders and they never made it, or at least never made it significantly."

By 1955, the Dodgers even ambled into statistical analysis, as Dick Young noted in his *Sports Illustrated* article, "Walter Alston's School for Boys." On their off days, different hurlers regularly tracked pitches.

"It wasn't always the same man, but he was always busy on the same job," Young wrote. "He was keeping a chart, on a large, yellow piece of paper. The paper, strangely checkered, was attached to a conventional clipboard the man kept in his lap. One day he was Carl Erskine; the next, Russ Meyer; then maybe Billy Loes, or Clem Labine; or Carl Erskine again. Whoever he was, this was not his day to pitch. This was his day to watch intently every pitch made by his teammate and to record it on the chart. Fastball…curve…changeup…slider…screwball. High, low, inside, outside, foul. And at the end of the 10 games, there, on the clipboard hanging in the office of Dodger manager Walter Alston, was a record of every pitch thrown by a Brooklyn pitcher during that opening rush.

"What purpose does all this serve? Says Alston, a former schoolteacher who has not lost his faith in instruction: 'It will show me when a pitcher's curve is hanging too often, or when he's not getting his change over. And it'll help me show it to him, because he won't be taking my word for it; it'll all be there, in black and white, and I won't have written it down.'"

All quite precocious, but it's apparent what all that nascent data was not used for: to gauge rest.

Podres was not immune. But he did recover at the right time.

He knew tales of true hardship from his grandfather, an immigrant miner from czarist Russia. "In America," wrote Robert Creamer of the man known as Barney Podres, "he found his way to an iron-mining community in upstate New York in the rough foothills of the Adirondacks near Lake Champlain, married a Lithuanian girl, and took his broad back and big hands down into the mines again. Forty-six years, two wives, and eight children later, he came out of the mines for the last time."

One of those eight kids was Joseph Podres, who also grew up to be a miner but in his spare time was a semipro pitcher from ages 18 to 43. And from Joe Podres came young John.

"When I was a kid in school, I wanted to be a Dodger," said the native of the hamlet of Witherbee, near the northeastern edge of New York state. "I was a Dodger fan, loved the Dodgers, always listened to the Dodgers on the radio, and when I had a chance to sign with them, that's what I wanted to do. I always, always wanted to be a Dodger."

Podres hit the mound running as an 18-year-old immediately after signing with the Dodgers, going 21–9 with a 1.66 ERA in 200 innings for the 1951 Hazard Bombers of the Class-D States League. The next year, Podres jumped all the way to Montreal, one rung shy of the majors, where his ERA was 3.27 in an abbreviated 88 innings.

His big-league dream came true on April 17, 1953, in the Dodgers' third game of the season, allowing two earned runs in seven innings of a loss to the Giants. He was 20 years old, swinging between the rotation and the bullpen in his rookie year, finishing with a 4.23 ERA (102 ERA+) in 115 innings. He also made his World Series debut, starting Game 5, though a costly Gil Hodges error hastened his exit before the third inning was over.

Podres continued developing in 1954, with a 4.27 ERA (97 ERA+) in 151⅔ innings, starting 21 times in 29 appearances with two shutouts. He began the 1955 season with a complete-game win and had back-to-back shutouts in June to lower his ERA to 3.14.

"Podres had three pitches," Erskine says. "I don't think I ever saw him throw a slider. But he had an outstanding off-speed pitch, and good control. He had very good control. He seldom got himself in trouble, and he had a little moxie. He had a little bit of spirit about him."

If any thought surfaced that Podres would be a postseason hero in '55, it came before a series of maladies, including a midseason appendectomy, threatened to derail what was left of his season. He had a 4.96 ERA from July 1 on, and his September consisted of 12 innings with eight runs allowed. In the Dodgers' final dozen games, Podres got six outs.

"For a while, my shoulder was so sore I couldn't sleep," he said. "Then, when I was okay again and getting back into the groove, I got slammed on the foot by a line drive and had a swollen left instep. Then I had a freak accident in September, at Ebbets Field. Batting practice was over, and we were getting set to take infield. I had a fungo bat and was going to hit balls to the outfielders. Well, in Ebbets Field they used to wheel the batting cage across the diamond and out through a gate in center field. They started wheeling that thing and they hit me right in the side with it. Banged up my ribs pretty good, plus a severe muscle pull. For two or three weeks I could hardly breathe.

"After the season ended, I had no idea I'd be starting in the Series… Sometimes when I think about how close I came to not playing in the '55 Series, I break out in a cold sweat."

On his 23rd birthday, Podres started Game 3 of the fifth World Series between the Dodgers and Yankees in nine years. Brooklyn had lost the first two games, and when Podres took the Ebbets Field mound, he hadn't pitched into the eighth inning in more than three months. Roy Campanella gave Podres two runs on a homer with Pee Wee Reese aboard in the first, but Podres gave the runs right back in the top of the second. However, Brooklyn tallied two more in the bottom of the second and again in the fourth, and thus buoyed, Podres cruised to an 8–3, complete-game victory.

After the starts by Erskine and Roger Craig in the victories of Games 4 and 5, and Spooner (who lasted one-third of an inning) in the Game 6 loss, the Dodgers conceivably had a choice for Game 7. Loes, the righty who had pitched Game 2, could have gone on four days' rest, or Podres the lefty could go on three. Alston let Podres know before Game 6 that if there was a Game 7, it would be his.

"Podres was so young," John Thorn says. "He would not have been the Dodgers' ideal candidate to start Game 7—you would want a veteran instead. And I'm sure that some consideration was given to others, but a lot of pitchers got their ears pinned back. The Dodgers had a starting pitching staff that year that did not perform very well…Podres would have been something of a crapshoot choice."

When Podres got the nod, his pregame determination was mythic—but true all the same, as multiple sources recount. "Give me one fellas," Podres said. "That's all I need. Give me one today."

Said Podres later: "The guys were down after that sixth game, especially Reese. I had to say something, so I told them not to worry, I'd shut them out tomorrow. What the hell? You've got to say something at a time like that."

Hodges' RBI single in the fourth and sacrifice fly in the sixth handed Podres his requested run plus a bonus. The incredible catch by defensive replacement Sandy Amoros of a Yogi Berra drive to the left-field corner in the bottom of sixth preserved the lead. In the bottom of the eighth, with runners at the corners, Podres got Berra to fly out to right before striking out Hank Bauer. There was one inning to go.

Moose Skowron slammed a comebacker at Podres, who bobbed and weaved from the blow before throwing to first for the first out. Bob Cerv popped to left.

The final at-bat lasted 10 pitches. Elston Howard fouled off five 2-2 fastballs. Campanella called for another but Podres shook him off, throwing what Creamer called "a big, fat, arrogant changeup." Howard grounded to short, Reese threw wide—but Hodges snagged it with a toe on the bag.

A hurricane touched down in Brooklyn, with Podres the eye.

"Podres is the street-smart Eddie Haskell," Mark Langill says. "He's only 23 years old in Game 7 of the World Series, but he's already got a big number on the odometer in terms of the type of guts he has. His line to me was, 'When you're that young, you think you can do anything.' In his mind, he was not nervous at all. It was something that he knew he could do in his mind."

"I won the car, the Corvette, after they voted me Most Valuable Player in the World Series," Podres said. "I was flying for days. I didn't really come down until a few weeks later. I was at a deer camp in the Adirondacks, walking in the woods by myself. It was silent. You couldn't hear a thing except the rustle of the leaves. All of a sudden I stopped and said to myself, 'Hey, Podres, you beat the Yankees in the World Series!'"

Moment in the Sun: Karl Spooner

- Set record with 15 strikeouts in MLB debut, September 22, 1954, shutout vs. Giants. Four days later, struck out 12 in shutout of Pirates
- Injured arm during spring training before 1955 season, which turned out to be his last
- Pitched 5⅔ innings of shutout relief to finish 10–2 victory over Braves that clinched '55 NL pennant on September 8
- Finished big-league career with a 3.09 ERA (133 ERA+) and 105 strikeouts in 116⅔ innings

What do you do when your crowning achievement comes at the age of 23? Next for Podres was a year away in the military, but when he was discharged in 1957, for what turned out to be the Dodgers' farewell to Brooklyn, he led the NL with six shutouts, a 2.66 ERA, 155 ERA+, and a 1.08 WHIP, the first of five consecutive above-average seasons. After two solid years in 1958 and '59 following the Dodgers' move to Los Angeles, Podres' next-best year came in 1960, with a 3.08 ERA (128 ERA+) in 227⅔ innings.

"Podres threw the most effective circle change, and it still serves as the prototype," Tim McCarver said in 1998. "He gripped the ball with only his last three fingers, while his thumb and index finger formed a circle halfway up on the ball. It was a changeup that he could throw on any count."

Even in 1961, when his ERA rose to 3.74 (114 ERA+), it was at 2.95 as late as August 12. That summer, Podres' father, Joe, only 52 years old, fell ill. The miner died September 25, of lung cancer.

The 1962 season was Podres' most challenging since arriving in Los Angeles. On the mound for the grand opening of Dodger Stadium on April 10, Podres gave up five runs in 7⅓ innings, and spent the rest of the year battling back and other physical issues while trying to get his ERA below 4.00. He accomplished that mission, and nearly, nearly, so much more.

Pitching three times in the final eight scheduled games of the regular season, the 29-year-old Podres held opponents to three runs in 22⅓ innings. On September 22, his 4–1 victory lifted Los Angeles to its 100th win of the season and a four-game lead over the Giants with seven remaining. Four days later, Podres won the Dodgers' 101st game, 13–1 over Houston, preserving the team's lead in the NL at two games.

The Dodgers lost their next three games, taking them to September 30, the final day on the schedule, with a one-game lead, the most precarious of their 85 consecutive days in sole possession of first place. Podres dueled St. Louis lefty Curt Simmons into the eighth inning, the score refusing to budge from 0–0. From San Francisco, news came over the wire: Willie Mays' tiebreaking eighth-inning homer had given the Giants a victory over Houston. Moments later in Los Angeles, with one out in the top of the eighth, Cardinals catcher Gene Oliver sent a 1-2 pitch from Podres down the left-field line, landing it in the seats to the right of the foul pole.

Podres finished the game, allowing five hits, no walks, and the one unmatched run. It was his 30th birthday.

"I pitched the best game of my life," Podres declared, seven years after bathing himself in World Series glory. "Even the pitch to Oliver was a good one, a curve in tight." But adhering to his well-established upbeat demeanor, Podres then mused: "We won it in a playoff [in 1959], so why in the hell can't we again?"

In the season's 165th game, the rubber match of the tiebreaker series against San Francisco, Podres made his career-high 40th start, approximately 72 hours after the loss to the Cardinals. He allowed two runs, one unearned (he made one of the Dodgers' three third-inning errors) in five innings, leaving before the Dodger bullpen allowed a pennant-losing four in the ninth. Podres was powerless to stop the bitter end.

Whatever grim reapings 1962 left behind vanished a year later. One day shy of the eighth anniversary of his 1955 Game 7 victory, Podres took the mound at Yankee Stadium. Cucumber cool for that '55 start at age 23, he was more anxious at age 31, but there turned out to be no need for worry.

"The celebrated bon vivant, marriage counselor (he counsels against it), and woodcraft instructor," Jim Murray wrote, "expertly stuffed the Yankee bats into their hip pockets."

When Podres began the ninth inning with a shutout and 4–0 lead intact, it was nearly poetic that the third batter due up was Elston Howard, the final batter from '55. However, after allowing a one-out double to Hector Lopez, a tiring Podres yielded the stage to Ron Perranoski, who allowed Howard to hit an RBI single that made the score 4–1, before getting the save in Game 2 of the Dodgers' World Series sweep.

"I didn't have real good rhythm at the start," Podres said. "And I was probably a little nervous. But after a while, I got my feet on the ground."

Of all pitchers to face the Yankees at least three times in World Series play, Podres has the lowest all-time ERA: 1.24 in 29 innings.

Podres remained a Dodger all the way into the 1966 season, recording a 3.66 ERA (107 ERA+) in 2,029⅓ innings—plus a 2.11 ERA in 38⅓ World Series frames. His 27.6 wins above replacement in Brooklyn and Los Angeles placed him 14th in franchise history. He wound up his playing days with Detroit and the expansion San Diego Padres, retiring in 1969 before becoming a pitching coach.

"He was a free spirit who could cure another guy's bad mood in two minutes," Don Drysdale said. "We've all known people who make you crack up just by looking at them. Johnny was one of them. He'd give you his last dollar if you needed it."

No Dodger pitcher formed a better bridge between Brooklyn and Los Angeles. No one else pitched in the last victory by the Brooklyn Dodgers and the first victory by the Los Angeles Dodgers. No other pitcher started at least 40 games each at Ebbets Field, the Los Angeles Memorial Coliseum, and Dodger Stadium. No pitcher won World Series games for both Brooklyn and Los Angeles.

"I'm fortunate I've been able to play at all as long as I have," said Podres, who passed away in 2008 at age 75. "Sometimes my back has been so bad that getting up was all I could do. But I've been fortunate in a lot of ways."

The New York Times' October 4, 1963, editorial page noted during the World Series that "there is joy in Flatbush that the Dodgers have been behaving beautifully just a couple of rivers and one subway token away. It's as if they never tore down Ebbets Field."

That might have been a bit Panglossian, but memories of kings remained vibrant in Brooklyn, even as two emperors were ascendant in Los Angeles.

PART TWO

THE TWO EMPERORS

DRYSDALE AND KOUFAX, KOUFAX AND DRYSDALE. From their kingdom, you could rule the world.

They were the glory, the dream come true, the ideal becoming the actual. If you were designing the two parts of a pitching duo that would excel individually while complementing each other seamlessly, these two were the everything. Don Drysdale and Sandy Koufax ascended side by side, at different speeds, meeting at their peak, in the stars.

"For the longest time, Drysdale was the better pitcher—and then Sandy sort of blows past him in a way. But I don't think there was a competition," Mark Langill says. "I just don't ever sense there was any jealousy or anything, because Sandy wasn't the type that wanted the spotlight, and Don wasn't the type—even though he was an extrovert—who would talk about himself. Don was the type of guy who could throw at somebody and then have had beers with him after the game. Very interesting personalities. Neither one craved to have all the attention, because that was not in either of their natures. And so it was the perfect match."

At their combined height, from 1962 to 1966, the Dodgers averaged 95 victories per season, enjoying three NL pennants and two World Series championships. Winning was a way of life, winning was breathing. If they didn't pitch a shutout, it was news. If they didn't win a title, it was an earthquake.

Together, the pair of Hall of Famers struck out 4,882 batters, pitched 304 complete games, and spun 89 shutouts. At their new playground of Dodger Stadium, their ERA was 1.87. In the postseason, their ERA was 1.77.

Drysdale and Koufax, Koufax and Drysdale. Making the mound their throne, they—more than anyone else—are responsible for bringing the glow to the Dodger pitching tradition.

Sandy Koufax

Sandy Koufax loved baseball.

Is this the most important point to make about the legendary left-hander? Maybe not, but it might be the most revelatory about a man often portrayed mistakenly as aloof from the sport in which he defined greatness.

He was not a reluctant warrior who ran away from his success. He was an impassioned student of his profession who waited and waited years, patiently then impatiently, just for the chance to play on a regular basis, and once achieved, to play it at his highest capacity. His potential was prodigious, but his skill was hard won.

Koufax didn't grow up wanting to be a pitcher, but in the 1960s, it was his refuge and his paradise. In many ways, he found no better place of comfort—mentally and even physically—than the pitcher's mound.

During the 1965–66 off-season, before his retirement was announced but certainly with the knowledge that it was coming, Koufax worked with sportswriter Ed Linn to produce his autobiography. While the spine of the book was a chronological recap of his life and baseball career, its prime objective can be found in the opening chapter.

"I have nothing against myths," Koufax began. "But there is one myth that has been building through the years that I would just as soon bury without any particular honors: the myth of Sandy Koufax, the anti-athlete. The way this fantasy goes, I am really a sort of dreamy intellectual who was lured out of college by a bonus in the flush of my youth and have forever after regretted—and even resented—the life of fame and fortune that has been forced upon me."

Anybody at Game 7 of the 1965 World Series, Koufax added sarcastically, "could see how I leaped up at the final out, throwing my arms out in pure boredom, beaming in sheer distaste."

Humor aside, Koufax's passion for pitching cannot be stressed enough.

"What offends me about the myth, aside from its sheer falsehood, is that it makes me sound as if I feel I'm above what I'm doing, which is an insult not to me but to all ballplayers," he said. "I *like* what I'm doing. I find that pitching, both as an art and a craft, is endlessly demanding and endlessly fascinating.

"There were times in the early years when I wondered whether I was ever going to make it. At one period of my career I was so discouraged that I was ready to give it all up. But never for a moment did I regret having given myself the chance."

Mark Langill emphasizes that "it wasn't inevitable for Koufax that he would succeed." Like a sculptor working on a masterpiece for years, Koufax slowly chipped away at all that didn't serve the ideal, ultimately mastering two pitches that enabled him to dominate the sport like no other.

"Physically, it was not easy catching Sandy, because he had the biggest, best curveball I've ever seen in my life," adds Jeff Torborg, who came up as a Dodger catcher in the 1960s. "Early in the count, he could drop a bigger, slower one over, or with two strikes he would really pull one down and the bottom would fall out of it. You had to catch up close to the hitter because it was such a big breaking ball that it could almost hit behind the point of the plate and be a strike and bounce if you don't get up there and reach in toward it—which is uncomfortable as a catcher, because you've got that bat whizzing around your head."

If you tried to time the curve, you risked getting absolutely getting burned alive by Koufax's sizzling, head-scratching fastball, which not only handcuffed catchers but confounded hitters—and umpires.

"In 31 years, I've never seen anybody else that could do that," umpire Doug Harvey told author Jane Leavy for her biography of Koufax. "Nolan Ryan's ball did not do it. Jim Maloney's ball did not do it. I'm talking hard throwers—[Bob] Gibson, [Tom] Seaver. Nobody's ball did what Koufax's ball did."

It was the definitive mirage—a rising fastball that seemingly violated the laws of nature. "Physicists insist that the hop on Koufax's fastball was an optical illusion created by the expectation that it would drop more than it did," Leavy wrote. She interviewed Dr. Marilyn Pink (a colleague of innovative Tommy John surgeon Dr. Frank Jobe), who performed a qualitative visual analysis of Koufax and "discovered what batters already knew: He was biomechanically perfect," with no wasted energy, no extraneous movement.

"The beauty of his delivery was a function of his mechanics, and his mechanics were a function of obeying the laws of nature," wrote Leavy. "Every pitch came over the top. He didn't drop down. He didn't come sidearm. He didn't fool around. His fluidity lulled minds and dulled reflexes. *Let the body put you to sleep and let the arm get you out,* he would say. No matter how many times a batter saw it, the ball's arrival at home plate always came as a shock. It was a humbling, disorienting sensation. In the immortal words of Willie Stargell, trying to hit Koufax was like 'trying to drink coffee with a fork.' Hitters talk about it all the time and invariably in the same words. The ball presented itself as an offering. *It was right there. I was right on it.* And then, nope, good-bye, it was gone."

Listed at 6-foot-2 and 210 pounds, Koufax was neither wallflower nor mountain, but one attribute shouldn't go unnoticed. At a public appearance in 2010, Koufax put his hand against that of the Dodgers' prodigy Clayton Kershaw (himself 6-foot-4). Koufax's paw dominated that of Kershaw, who said Koufax had the biggest hands he had ever seen.

Still, if Koufax was born to be a major-league pitcher, a Hall of Fame pitcher, the greatest left-hander of his era if not all eras, it was not immediately apparent in his childhood.

Quiet, focused on sports, and close to his sister, mother, and the stepdad he unequivocally considered his true father, Koufax was an athlete from the start in his native Brooklyn, though more than anything, he was a basketball player. His first mention in the *Brooklyn Eagle* came as a 15-year-old on February 13, 1951: "Sandy Koufax, the Tomahawks' top scorer, again paced his team's scoring with 19 tallies in a 39–22 victory over the Knights in the Community Center P.S. 200 Basketball League." Two years later, Koufax played in an exhibition game against the New York Knicks and so impressed pro center Harry Gallatin that he told the *New York Post*, "We'll be coming back for this kid someday."

Koufax didn't start pitching until he was 15, in Pop Secol's Ice Cream League—far more prestigious at the time than it might sound today—and, much like Drysdale, didn't do so on a regular basis until he was 17. The best hint of his future, Koufax once told Orel Hershiser: "I was the best snowball fighter on the block."

By the summer of 1954, he was lighting up the baseball scouting radar.

"Fourteen of the 16 major-league clubs, including all three metropolitan teams (Dodgers, Yankees, and Giants) are vastly interested in Sanford (Sandy) Koufax," wrote the *Eagle*, "well-put-together southpaw, owner of two no-hitters, who helped spin the Parkviews to the Senior Division title of the Coney Island League this season.

"The 18-year-old Koufax fires a sizzling fastball, mixes up a fine repertoire of sharp-breaking curves, a tantalizing change of pace, and has good control. As one political admirer of Sandy put it, the portsider has a Democratic delivery with Republican twists and Socialist tendencies."

A May 1954 scouting report by the Dodgers' Bill Zinser was a rave, calling him an A+ arm with A– accuracy and describing Koufax as "tall, muscular, quick reflexes, well-coordinated."

Not even at this point was it clear that Koufax's destiny was in baseball. Koufax said he knew enough about the sport to worry that he would be mere fodder for some team's farm system—one of many organizational darts that would either hit its target or clank to the ground, forgotten. Once Cincinnati had offered him a basketball scholarship, Koufax clarified that, to guard against washing out, he required a signing bonus from any baseball team to cover his college costs.

Koufax had a successful freshman year on the court at Cincinnati in 1953–54, including a high-scoring game against Miami of Ohio attended by school alum Walter Alston, soon to begin his first year as manager of the Dodgers. In his only college baseball season, Koufax struck out 52 and allowed only 16 hits, but he walked 32 in his 32 innings.

All three New York teams checked in. Koufax nearly became a Giant, but in his 1954 workout for the team, he was nervous and unconscionably wild. "I was scared to death," he remembered. "Did I get 'em over the plate? Gee, I got 'em over the wall." The Yankees took a glance, but more indifferently (no bonus, for one thing), and when they sent a Jewish scout specifically to offer the contract, the Koufaxes were offended.

The closest call was with the Pirates, run by Branch Rickey, with Ed McCarrick the chief area scout. Their interest was unmistakable, but two events derailed it. At a critical moment when they could have jumped the queue and landed Koufax before the Dodgers fully understood what had been growing in their own backyard, the Pirates were short of spending money. Then, in a summer game attended by Branch Rickey Jr., a Pirates executive underneath his father, Koufax pitched despite nursing a bad ankle injury and got clobbered.

That opened the door for the Dodgers. On a drizzly day in Brooklyn with batting practice canceled, everyone watched Koufax work out. "As soon as I saw that fastball, the hair raised up on my arms," Dodger scout Al Campanis said memorably. "The only other time the hair ever raised up was in Rome when I saw Michelangelo's paintings on the ceiling of the Sistine Chapel." Rube Walker, who caught Koufax, later told the pitcher what he advised Dodger management that day: "Whatever he wants, give it to him. I wouldn't let him get out of the clubhouse."

Koufax's father, Irving, negotiated directly with Dodger owner Walter O'Malley, lawyer to lawyer, and they agreed to a $14,000 bonus plus $6,000 in salary each of the first two seasons. For procedural reasons, Koufax couldn't sign at that moment but heeded the handshake agreement even after the Milwaukee Braves dangled $30,000 and the Pirates, having sold their farm team in New Orleans, came back suddenly flush with cash and prepared to top any offer by $5,000.

On December 14, 1954, the Dodgers traded Preacher Roe and Billy Cox to the newly relocated Baltimore Orioles (fresh from their previous incarnation as the St. Louis Browns) to open up their roster, and then officially signed Sanford Koufax. When the *Eagle* announced the news, Koufax was pictured in his Lafayette High School basketball uniform from two years prior.

"What had started so casually, almost as a lark, had become a career," Koufax said in his autobiography. "The feeling that had come over me at that moment, to my own astonishment, was the sense of sheer pleasure that comes when you have set off on some impossible course and have unexpectedly brought it off. *I got away with it*, I thought."

Though he understood it intellectually, Koufax couldn't fully appreciate the quandary he soon found himself in. Under the current rules of the time, a "bonus baby" such as Koufax would be bound to the Dodgers' major-league roster for a minimum two full years.

"It was a way of providing some measure of competitive balance," John Thorn explains, "in that the clubs that were doing better at the gate would tend to win every year, and they would restock by paying the most for amateur talent. You wanted to penalize them by forcing them to give up a roster spot by paying too much. It was, in effect, a salary cap on amateurs."

Says Carl Erskine: "Here's a kid that has leapfrogged 200 minor-league pitchers and gets a Dodger uniform, never having thrown a pitch in the minors. Now I know Sandy well enough to know that looking back, that that bothered him. He missed all of the great teaching that goes on in the minor leagues that you almost can't play in the big leagues without. The proof of this is to me in football and basketball, a first-round draft choice comes right into the top and plays in the starting lineup. You never, ever see that in baseball."

And yet, that's what you saw with Koufax, who took a jersey with No. 32 because it was available and because it fit, and got to work.

"I was easily the most inexperienced kid ever to come to a major-league camp," Koufax said. "But I was not—repeat, not—as green, as wild, or as awkward as some of the taller tales make me out to have been."

His first step in joining the new Dodger pitching tradition was to follow in the figurative and literal footsteps of Don Newcombe. Koufax began to run every day, to prepare himself for the shock to the system of throwing every day. "It's important now," Newcombe told him, "and it will be more important later. It just never stops."

But more than anyone, pitching coach Joe Becker was a major figure in Koufax's on-the-job development, keeping him sane and supported through the difficult process of becoming a big-leaguer on the fly.

"Joe commanded that kind of loyalty because he treated everybody the same whether he had won 25 games or none," Koufax said. "You were one of his boys, you belonged to him. He was like the shepherd of the flock. If you were going badly, he worried with you, and if you were going well, he rejoiced with you.

"Joe helped me where he could. For one thing, he told me, I was leaning back too far in my windup. The farther I leaned back, he said, the more room I was giving myself to make a mistake and the tougher it was to keep the ball low. To put it the other way, the less you do before you throw the ball, the less trouble you can get yourself into."

Koufax's first year on the Dodger roster (or on any professional roster) began in 1955 with his dominant teammates blistering the NL with 10 straight wins out of the game and a 22–2 start. For better or worse, the presence of Koufax didn't slow them down—ankle and arm issues before the season began put him on the disabled list. On June 9, the Dodgers outrighted another left-hander, Tom Lasorda, to Montreal to activate Koufax.

For two additional weeks, Koufax sat and watched. On June 24, he made his professional and MLB debut, starting the bottom of the fifth inning against the Braves with a 7–1 lead. He gave up a single to Johnny Logan, made a throwing error on an Eddie Matthews comebacker, and walked Hank Aaron to load the bases before he got his first out—a strikeout, of Dodger nemesis Bobby Thomson. Joe Adcock then grounded into a Pee Wee Reese–Jim Gilliam–Gil Hodges double play, and Koufax was on his way to two shutout innings.

In his next relief appearance five days later, Koufax loaded the bases with none out again, and escaped again. That paved the way for his first start, on July 6, in which he struck out four and allowed one run in 4⅔ innings—but walked eight. "Koufax, the 19-year-old Brooklyn bonus southpaw…did some stout hurling to overcome a grievous lack of control," wrote John Drebinger of *The New York Times*. Over the next seven weeks, Koufax pitched only four innings, before he was put back on the mound to start against the Reds.

Those who caught a glimpse saw rock-and-roll future.

"Sandy Koufax, the Brooklyn club's bonus baby, wrote a new chapter in the annals of baseball at Ebbets Field yesterday," declared the *Times*' Roscoe McGowen. "Ted Kluszewski, the majors' home run leader, singled through the hole to right in the first inning. The next hit off Sandy didn't come until two out in the ninth and was the hardest-hit ball off the youngster."

Koufax struck out 14, setting an NL record at the time for a teenage pitcher. He walked five, but Campanella said he "didn't ever miss the plate by much," and when he issued back-to-back free passes in the sixth inning with Kluszewski coming up, Alston ran out to the mound not with a hook, but with encouragement.

"I thought maybe he was trying to aim the ball," said Alston. "I just wanted to tell him to keep throwing it as he had been doing. Sandy said he was all right, and Roy Campanella told me the same thing."

After allowing four runs in one inning of a relief appearance that came four days after he had faced the 34 batters and thrown approximately 150 pitches, Koufax threw his second shutout September 3 against the Pirates. Given his age and lack of apprenticeship, his rookie season was successful and promising: a 3.02 ERA (136 ERA+) with 30 strikeouts and 28 walks in 41⅔ innings. Solve those control issues and you've got yourself a pitcher.

It took five more seasons.

"Koufax in the '50s as a pitcher was somebody who was ready to break out at any minute and never quite did," Eric Enders says. "And from his statements, you get the impression that he was very frustrated with Walter Alston for not giving him more of a chance to pitch in those years… Koufax could strike out 16 batters in a given day, was very likely to pitch the best game of your season, but wasn't likely to have the best season of anyone on the pitching staff."

In 1956, Koufax only pitched 58⅔ innings, and his ERA shot up to 4.91 (82 ERA+). He threw 9⅓ innings before June 3, when he went into the rotation for five consecutive starts that ranged from 2⅔ to 8 innings. He started thrice more the next month, striking out a season-high seven on July 17, then pitched in one inning the entire month of August and made one final start in September. "I was the Great Unwanted," he said.

With the Dodgers falling out of contention in 1957, their final season in Brooklyn, his innings increased to 104⅓, but his performance and usage was still sporadic. Still only 21, he struck out 13 and walked seven in a 39-batter, no-earned-run complete game May 16, his first start after the Bonus Baby requirement had expired, making him eligible for the minors. If it was a test, he passed, and after fanning 12 on June 4, he was actually leading the NL in whiffs despite having thrown barely 50 innings. But the Dodgers still didn't seem sure what to do with him. Despite his 2.90 ERA, Koufax pitched just 2⅔ innings over the next month and a half. Though he finished the season with a 3.88 ERA (106 ERA+) and 10.5 strikeouts per nine innings (inducing the final out as a reliever in the top of the ninth on September 29, becoming the last Dodger pitcher ever to take the mound at Ebbets Field), it's all but certain Koufax could have benefited from some minor-league tutelage.

When the Dodgers moved to Los Angeles and the Memorial Coliseum, the short distance to a tall fence in left field got all the attention, but a low mound troubled Koufax more at the start of the season—that is, when he pitched. At the outset, his use was irregular as ever: nine innings in the Dodgers' first 32 games, then 11 innings on May 20 in the 33rd. In the month of June, Koufax started five times and relieved five times. His ERA was 3.54 before the All-Star break and 5.36 after, and he led the league with a Dodger-record 17 wild pitches.

In 1959, Koufax made four April starts for the first time in his career, but he didn't make it out of the fourth inning in any of them, baffling the Dodgers and Alston. After allowing five runs in a two-out relief appearance May 2, the 23-year-old's ERA nearly matched his December 30 birthdate: 12.27.

"You can teach a kid to throw a curve or a changeup, but I never felt that you could help his control," Alston said. "The day Sandy pitched his first major-league game, he beat Cincy with 14 strikeouts. He was only 19 then, and he wasn't as wild as he is now."

Koufax neared a crossroads. One rumor had the lefty going to the Kansas City A's in exchange for Roger Maris, who instead was dealt that December to the Yankees. Years later, Al Wolf of the *Los Angeles Times* reported that Alston and Bavasi had decided to trade Koufax to the Phillies for two players, before Walter O'Malley invoked a rare veto, saying that Koufax might yet come around.

"The ballclub, I suspect, was very close to getting rid of me," Koufax said, noting that even Becker, his one-man support system, believed Koufax had lost all confidence and mechanics. "I was only hoping that if they did ask waivers, somebody would claim me and keep me in the big leagues."

He was as beguiling and mysterious as ever. With his ERA at 5.71, Koufax pitched two shutout innings at the end of a doubleheader on June 14. Three days later, he pitched a complete-game victory over the Braves, and zipping right back on June 22, he struck out a career-high 16 against the Phillies, then punched in June 27 with a shutout of the Pirates.

By July 5, he had whittled his ERA down to 3.33 with 90 strikeouts in 80⅔ innings, only for his ankle to get spiked and sprained by a baserunner at first base. The injury stunted Koufax's momentum for about a month but only that, before a breathtaking sequence of three consecutive complete games with 41 strikeouts in 28 innings.

On the final day of August, against the rival Giants, Koufax struck out 18, tying Bob Feller's 21-year-old big-league record, breaking Dizzy Dean's 26-year-old NL record, and enchanting the city of Los Angeles. In the Fairfax neighborhood where Koufax kept his bachelor pad, wrote Mal Florence of the *Times*, "the natives are thinking of changing the intersection name to Beverly and Kou-fax."

The roller coaster of 1959 wasn't done looping. To the surprise of the baseball world, the Dodgers reached the 1959 World Series after sweeping a tiebreaker playoff for the NL title from the Braves, but the achievement seemed to come despite Koufax instead of because of him. After allowing five runs in 7⅓ innings on September 16, Koufax faced only 16 batters in the regular season's final 23 games—and walked eight, loading the bases on free passes in a nearly disastrous ninth inning of the clinching game, which the Dodgers rallied to win.

Still, the cyclone nearly landed Koufax in glory. After throwing two perfect innings of relief in his Game 1 World Series debut, Alston gave Koufax the start in Game 5 with a chance to pitch the Dodgers to the title before a Coliseum crowd of 92,706. Only one run came across the plate, on a double-play grounder in the fourth, but it was enough to saddle Koufax with a 1–0 loss that forestalled Los Angeles' first title for 48 hours. "The lone run arrived in a routine manner," wrote Braven Dyer of the *Los Angeles Times*, "and it is doubtful if anybody in the park thought it would stand up as the game decider."

> **Moment in the Sun: Roger Craig**
>
> - As a 25-year-old rookie, right-hander won Game 5 of the 1955 World Series with six innings of two-run ball
> - In 1959, had a 2.06 ERA (205 ERA+) in 152⅔ innings and led NL with four shutouts despite starting only 17 games
> - Pitched 814 innings for Dodgers from 1955 to 1961 with a 3.83 ERA (104 ERA+)
> - Lost 46 games in two years (1962–63) with New York Mets after being selected in expansion draft

For all his setbacks, a big-league strikeout record and a 1.00 postseason ERA should have primed Koufax for the long-awaited breakout season in 1960. But doubts still remained, and among those holding them was Koufax.

"He told me midseason that he was going to quit at the end of the season, that he had a chance to buy into a radio station in Los Angeles," Erskine says. "But before the season ended, he said to me, 'Carl, I was thinking about that. You know, the Dodgers paid me a bonus. Now they've paid me for five seasons, and I've really never produced the way they think I should or could. So I've got to go back to spring training one more time and pull out all the stops, and if I still feel the same way at the end of the season, I think I'm gonna go do something else.'"

Koufax's rough-and-tumble career was entering its sixth year, and perhaps no single month captured the yin-yang frustration like May 1960. He made five starts, pitched 48 innings (13 on May 28, a game in which he threw 193 pitches), struck out 55, had a 2.81 ERA, came within an opposing pitcher's single of a no-hitter on May 23—but walked 30 and took four losses. Halfway into a rocky June, Koufax was 1–8 with a 4.64 ERA. Four complete games with 10 or more strikeouts in the second half, leaving him with a 3.91 ERA (101 ERA+), did little to ease the Brobdingnagian burden weighing upon Koufax at the end of the year.

"Having given myself six years, a full apprenticeship, I was convinced that the time had come to admit to myself that I wasn't going to make it," Koufax said. "It wasn't that I hadn't gotten my chance to pitch in 1960, either. I had been given more chance than ever. Nor did I feel that I hadn't learned anything about pitching...The most frustrating thing in the world, I had discovered, was to feel that you knew what you were doing and were doing it about as well as you could, and find that you were still losing."

He had pitched in 174 games, starting 103, and his lifetime record was 36–40 with a 4.10 ERA. He was, for all his extremes, average. (His career ERA+ at the time, later generations can now see, was exactly 100.) He had struck out 683 batters in 691⅔ innings, but he had walked 405.

As he tended to do, the 25-year-old Koufax tried to suss out the future.

"I knew I wanted to stay in Los Angeles," he said. "I had just bought a home that summer. I liked the climate. I liked the people. I had already gone into business, with a partner, as a manufacturer's representative for several electrical lines. It seemed to me that I might be far better off devoting the next few years to building up that business or some other one so that I would not be starting out, at the age of 35, from scratch."

By his own account, at the end of the 1960 season, Koufax tossed his baseball gear in the trash. But over the winter, his second thoughts returned. He still wasn't ready to leave the game without being pushed out of it.

"It isn't that easy to walk away," he said. "To leave at the end of a successful career is one thing; the time that it's tough is when you haven't made it, when you've done nothing, when it's an admission—no matter how graciously you chose to explain it to yourself—that you've been licked.

"I had to ask myself whether I had really worked as hard as I could have, absorbed as much as I should have, given myself every possible chance. Once you are thinking along those lines, the answers are probably inevitable. I decided I would give it one more year, one last, all-out effort."

When he arrived at Vero Beach for spring training in 1961, Dodger clubhouse manager Nobe Kawano handed Koufax the gear he had rescued from the garbage months before.

It was the first of many auspicious moments, but not the most unusual. That might have been the positive effects of an off-season tonsillectomy that sent him to spring training 21 pounds underweight. The upside was that as he worked himself into shape, instead of simply burning off fat, he was building up muscle.

Koufax also spent extra time studying the charts and reports of team statistician Allan Roth, who was doing pioneering work long before sabermetrics was even a term. For most of his career (though not in 1960), the typical platoon advantage worked against Koufax, and left-handed hitters actually hit better against the southpaw than righties did. Koufax realized his curveball wasn't breaking away from the lefty hitters enough, so he moved his fingers slightly on the ball to make that happen. Koufax also further tightened his windup, making it as compact as he could while, in his words, "still building up the body motion I needed for my momentum."

But the most significant, transformative moment came at a spring training game—a B game in which the shorthanded Dodger split squad needed Koufax to provide some innings. Norm Sherry, the catcher, practically begged Koufax to turn down his intensity on the mound.

"Sandy, we only got one other pitcher here," Sherry recalled saying. "And at this rate, you're gonna be out here all day. Why don't you take something off the ball? Don't even try and strike these next guys out. Just throw it over the plate and let them hit it.

"So I go back behind the plate," Sherry said, "and lo and behold, he did it. He wound up nice and easy, like he was saying, 'Here, hit it.'...And I guess the light bulb just went off in his head."

Koufax described it as "taking the grunt" out of his pitching. "I had heard it all before. Only, for once, it wasn't blahblahblah," he said. "There comes a time and place where you are ready to listen."

It would be false to imply that Koufax avoided his typical sketchy start in 1961, but starting in mid-May, in the year of the first manned spaceflight, this Hall of Fame career at last found its orbit. In 42 games (35 starts), he pitched 255⅓ innings with a 3.52 ERA (122 ERA+), allowed an MLB-low 7.5 hits per nine innings (a title he kept for five years), and, in a telling landmark, also led the NL in strikeout-walk ratio. The control issues hadn't quite been eliminated, but clearly he was on the right track.

In the Dodgers' final official game at the Coliseum, just as he had for the Ebbets Field finale, Koufax stood on the mound, this time as the starting pitcher. Thirteen innings later, before a remaining crowd of 12,068, Koufax had gone the distance, facing 50 batters and striking out 15 in a 3–2 victory, throwing *205* pitches. A week later, in his final two innings of the year, Koufax fanned his 268th and 269th batters, breaking Christy Mathewson's NL record for strikeouts in a season that was set in 1903.

The following spring, the Dodgers moved into their new stadium, the most beautiful in baseball, and Koufax became the symbol of its grandeur.

There was no messing around. In his first start of the season, Koufax went the distance. In his fourth start, Koufax struck out 18 Cubs. On June 18, he pitched his first career no-walker, and on June 30, he pitched his first career no-hitter, stifling the expansion New York Mets with 13 strikeouts, 5–0, with one of Dodger Stadium's first promotional giveaway nights becoming part of the scene.

"The joint blew as Sandy's teammates and box-seat rooters swarmed onto the field amid a shower of cushions from the stands," wrote Frank Finch of the *Los Angeles Times*.

By mid-July, Koufax's ERA was down to 2.06, and he already had 208 strikeouts in 174⅔ innings. During the All-Star break, Warren Spahn, 41 years old and with more than 300 victories, asked Koufax to teach him his curveball. (A month earlier, Spahn had allowed the first home run Koufax had ever hit as a professional and nearly chewed the whippersnapper's head off in anger as he rounded the bases.)

And then, fortune played yet another trick on Koufax.

Months passed before he pieced together what had happened. Back in April, while attempting to bunt, Koufax attempted to fight off a pitch and jammed the bat into the palm of his left hand, unknowingly developing a blood clot that decreased the flow of blood to his left index finger. Over time, the condition became progressively worse.

"The fact that Koufax got hurt was a case of backfiring strategy," Finch wrote. "Ordinarily, he bats right-handed, but he figured there would be less chance of getting hit by a ball on his pitching arm if he batted left-handed, so he made the switch just in time to get jammed."

He kept pitching, because he was pitching so well, because, as he said, "I had spent too much of my life *not* pitching to think about missing any turns."

"Each morning when Sandy woke up, his finger hurt more—as if he kept slamming a door on it," Jim Murray wrote. In effect, he was. Nature had thrown up a roadblock to that extremity, and almost no blood was getting through to the end of it.

Finally, Koufax left his July 17 start after one inning. His entire season was in jeopardy, perhaps his entire career. The threat of amputation, because of infection, hung in the air.

"It's sort of useless right now," Koufax told reporters. "The finger is raw, and I can hardly put any pressure on the ball. I have no idea when I'll be able to pitch."

The Dodgers, meanwhile, were fighting for a pennant, and Koufax couldn't come back soon enough. On September 21, he tried, but he gave up four runs in his first inning and was a nonfactor the rest of the year in the most painful way for the Dodgers, who fell into a first-place tie with the Giants on the last day of the regular season and collapsed in the ninth inning of the three-game playoff's finale.

Would Koufax's problems carry over into 1963? That was the question on everyone's mind at spring training...and the answer was a resounding no. His finger was great, his arm was great, his first start (10 strikeouts in a 2–1 complete-game win at Wrigley Field) was great. He struck out 14 Houston Colt .45s on April 19, retired the first 22 batters on his way to, ho hum, his second career no-hitter on May 11 against the Giants—then, perhaps more impressively, came back to throw 12 innings in his next start on three days' rest, striking out 12 in a 3–2 win over the Phillies.

Year after year, Koufax had contemplated quitting. From 1955 to 1961, he hadn't come near the kind of year that would define him. In 1963, at age 27, he said hello to his destiny. He pitched 311 innings, became the first NL pitcher ever to break the 300-strikeout barrier, turned in a 1.88 ERA (159 ERA+), lowered his once-massive walk rate to 1.7 per nine innings, went 25–5 (with the Dodgers 34–6 in his 40 starts), and won both the Cy Young—the first to do so unanimously—and NL MVP awards. Nothing slowed Koufax on the mound in '63, though he had begun having a pregame rub of Capsolin, an ointment that was almost literally the equivalent of playing with fire, but served the purpose of increasing circulation in his arm through the necessary evil of irritating his skin.

The 1963 World Series lasted 36 innings. Koufax pitched 18 of them, winning the first and final games. "I threw nice and easy, and I knew I had great stuff," he said. "Not good stuff, *great* stuff."

To start Game 1, Koufax fanned the first five Yankees: Tony Kubek, Bobby Richardson, Tom Tresh, Mickey Mantle, and Roger Maris. The tell was his disposal of Richardson, who in 668 regular-season plate appearances struck out only 22 times. Against Koufax, he went down on strikes three different times.

"The scouting report on him was don't throw him a high fastball," wrote Roger Kahn. "So Koufax threw Richardson three high fastballs. Three pitches, three strikes, sit down. Then Koufax looked straight into the Yankee dugout. I could see Sandy saying in that look, 'I can pitch it to your power and I'll still strike you out.'"

Though Tresh hit a two-run homer in the eighth inning to make the score 5–2, Koufax finished the game by whiffing pinch hitter Harry Bright for his 15th strikeout, breaking the World Series record Erskine set 10 years earlier to the day. As Finch pointed out, not until the penultimate batter of the game, Clete Boyer, flied to Willie Davis did a Dodger outfielder make a putout. Catcher John Roseboro had 18, including three foul-outs.

"With his long legs, his loose hips, his ropelike motion, and his lean, intelligent face, he looked his part elegantly," wrote Roger Angell of *The New Yorker*, "a magnificent young pitcher at an early and absolute peak of confidence, knowledge, and ability."

"I wonder," waxed Yogi Berra, expressing a similar sentiment more bluntly, "how come he lost five games this year."

Pitching four days later in Game 4, Koufax surrendered a tender 1–0 Dodger lead when Mantle homered in the seventh. The Dodgers came back to score an unearned run in the bottom of the inning when Joe Pepitone lost a throw from third to first in the sun, but Koufax had to protect the lead in the ninth after allowing a leadoff single to Richardson.

When Mantle came up with one out, Koufax wanted to make an unexpected but risky choice, taking something off his curveball. He wasn't sure Roseboro would endorse it. But when he looked in at his catcher, Koufax said, "Roseboro put down a sign with an extended wiggle of the fingers, as if he were saying to me, 'Sandy, baby, you don't know how glad I am that you see it this way too.'" Mantle took the pitch for a called third strike, and despite one more Yankee reaching base on an error, Koufax closed out the inning, the game, and the Series when Hector Lopez grounded to Maury Wills for a forceout.

In every sense of the word, Koufax was a champion.

"In the Dodger dressing room everyone wanted Koufax—radio, television, photographers, the press," wrote William Leggett of *Sports Illustrated*. "Tommy Davis stood with tears in his eyes deep inside his dressing cubicle...Finally, Koufax walked away from his pursuers and into Davis' cubicle. He threw his arms around Tommy, and Davis blurted out: 'Sandy, you are the greatest pitcher that ever lived!'"

Coming back in 1964, Koufax started on Opening Day for, rather unbelievably, the only time in his career, shutting out the Cardinals at Dodger Stadium on six hits, and (no longer surprisingly) zero walks. By this time, Koufax had become a perfectionist—one who could realistically aspire for flawlessness. As June arrived, Koufax saw pictures of himself in an issue of *Sport* magazine and, he said, "suddenly realized that I had been stepping too far to the left with the right foot across my body." Soon after, on June 4, he pitched his third no-hitter and first on the road, smothering Philadelphia on 12 strikeouts and allowing one baserunner, a walk to Dick Allen, who was caught stealing moments later. (That was the night that Don Drysdale, who had been traveling ahead during the game, was listening to the radio and heard so much about Koufax's no-hitter and so little about the actual score that he finally shouted, "Who *won?*")

For the second time in three years, Koufax's season was cut short by an injury suffered while on offense. On August 8, he landed on his elbow diving back into second base on a pickoff attempt, waking up the next morning with a lump on his elbow. Over the next week, Koufax pitched two complete games with a combined 23 strikeouts and only one run allowed, but on August 17, the situation had become untenable.

"I had to drag my arm out of bed like a log. That's what it looked like, a log. A waterlogged log," Koufax said. "The elbow was so swollen that the whole arm was locked in a sort of hooked position."

The sliding injury both revealed and accelerated an arthritic condition for Koufax. Fluid drained, pills consumed, throwing attempted, and the arm just blew up again.

"The blow to the elbow in Milwaukee may have been the final traumatizing incident, but the condition...had been developing for as long as I had been pitching," Koufax said. "This had to be the most discouraging time of all, the one time when it did seem as if my pitching career might be at an end."

Koufax was able to throw a bit of batting practice in a couple of weeks, but by that point, the Dodgers were well out of the race, and Koufax was shut down for the year. It was still a magnificent one: a 1.74 ERA (186 ERA+) with 223 strikeouts in 223 innings, though in an era of only one Cy Young Award winner for the two leagues, Koufax couldn't outpoll the Los Angeles Angels' Dean Chance, who had a 1.65 ERA (200 ERA+) in 278⅓ innings while pitching his home games in the same ballpark.

But unlike the case with his finger the year before, off-season rest hadn't seemed to help Koufax before the 1965 season—not that he or the Dodgers were exactly careful. Illustrating the Old School at the height of its Old Schoolness, Koufax pitched consecutive complete games in March, in the middle of spring training, nearly two weeks before Opening Day.

"The Dodgers didn't back off," wrote Bill James. "Their attitude was, 'We don't need Sandy to be a spot starter. We don't need Sandy Koufax to be a seven-inning pitcher. We need him to take his turn every fourth day and win, and we need to find out whether he can do that or not.'"

In no time, Koufax, now 29, was on a plane to see Dr. Robert Kerlan, and the following day, headlines shouted fears about arthritis and his entire future being in doubt.

Koufax adjusted to accommodate his arthritic rifle. His slider usage dipped from little to none. He curtailed side activities, such as throwing on the second day after the start. The chief irony remained: nothing made Koufax feel better about the pain from taking the mound than actually taking the mound.

"Years of pitching had brought on the traumatic arthritis," he said, "and yet the act of pitching in itself lessened the effects, even while—and there is no reason to doubt this—it was also irritating the joint further."

It was a sight. "Gosh, it looked like an inflated tire," says Torborg of Koufax's elbow.

"We were well aware of what Sandy was going through," adds rotation-mate Claude Osteen, "and if you didn't know it, all you had to do was watch him."

Incredibly, Koufax didn't miss a start in a fantastic 1965 season, pitching a career-high 335⅔ innings and 27 complete games with a 2.04 ERA (160 ERA+)—and setting a new MLB record with 382 strikeouts.

"When he was warming up and would say, 'I don't have it tonight,' we'd laugh because we knew he was going to have a good game," Roseboro said. "But he got to the point where he always had good games. Some were just better than others. At his best, he seemed unbeatable."

September 9, to be sure, was one of those nights: Koufax's fourth no-hitter, the perfect game, etched in history as his pinnacle performance. The Dodgers themselves had only one walk, one hit, and one run. On a night when Koufax needed to be untouchable, he was immaculate.

"You could see it in his eyes," says Torborg, who was behind the plate that night at Dodger Stadium. "His eyes are really intense. And by near the end of a game, you could see his eyes were almost tired because he was so intense."

Thanks to Vin Scully's memorable call, we know the celebration began at 9:46 PM, but Koufax's first pitch wasn't thrown until 8:03 PM, a scant 103 minutes earlier. In front of 29,139 ticketed fans (not to mention third-base umpire Paul Pryor, who had flown in from San Francisco after working a Juan Marichal shutout of Houston at Candlestick Park earlier in the day), the first 15 Cubs toppled like dominoes before the Dodgers squeaked across their run in the bottom of the fifth, when Lou Johnson walked, went to second on a Ron Fairly bunt, stole third, and came home on a bad throw by Chicago catcher Chris Krug.

Billy Williams' full-count fly to left field, ending the top of the seventh, was the last ball anyone put into play against Koufax. He needed only 26 pitches to strike out the final six Cubs, with Scully's symphony of words at the microphone augmenting the grand finale.

"One and one to Harvey Kuenn," Scully said, studying Koufax. "Now he's ready: fastball, high, ball two. You can't blame a man for pushing just a little bit now. Sandy backs off, mops his forehead, runs his left index finger along his forehead, dries it off on his left pants leg. All the while Kuenn just waiting. Now Sandy looks in. Into his windup, and the 2-1 pitch to Kuenn: swung on and missed, strike two!"

Kuenn, the 1959 AL batting champion who had a .303 lifetime average, had made the final out in Koufax's 28-batter no-hitter in 1963 while hitting leadoff for the Giants. Now he was the Cubs' last chance, pinch-hitting for pitcher Bob Hendley (who in eight innings allowed only one hit himself). Koufax fired his 101st pitch of the night—a fastball.

"Swung on and missed—a perfect game!" exclaimed Scully, and the Dodgers engulfed their ace.

"There are times when everything is right," Koufax said. "I don't know if I've ever had better stuff or better control than I did in the final two innings of that game."

Los Angeles needed every pitch it could get from Koufax that year. With 16 games left in the season, the Dodgers were 4½ games out of first place. But they won 13 straight games to take the lead, then hung on for dear life. On October 2, the penultimate day of the season, Koufax pitched a complete game for the clincher. In the final 32 calendar days of the 1965 regular season, the arthritic Koufax threw an unimaginable 71⅔ innings with 79 strikeouts and a 1.51 ERA. In the pennant race's final *week*, he pitched 27 innings, allowed one run, and struck out 38.

"Koufax won 26 games pitching for the Dodgers," an unknown wag said, according to the *Los Angeles Times*. "Can you imagine what he would have done pitching against them?"

Having made the much-discussed decision to observe Yom Kippur rather than pitch the opener of the 1965 World Series, Koufax's arm enjoyed a luxurious fourth day of rest before he took the mound in Game 2, his biggest sabbatical since the perfect game. It was of no help, as the Minnesota Twins broke a scoreless tie with two runs (one unearned) in the sixth inning on their way to their second straight victory. Not that there was despair in the Dodger clubhouse.

"After I visited the clubhouse and heard Sandy Koufax's precise, unapologetic, and totally unruffled analysis of the game," wrote Angell, "I came away with the curious impression that the Twins, after two straight victories, were only slightly behind in the World Series.

With the Dodgers winning the next two games in Los Angeles, Koufax came back to dominate Minnesota in Game 5 with a 10-strikeout shutout, but when Los Angeles dropped Game 6, a winner-take-all Game 7 awaited. Koufax skipped ahead of his turn to take the start, with Drysdale and Perranoski set to relieve him, in part to potentially hit the Twins with a left-right-left combo, in part simply because he was Koufax.

"Some say Drysdale was embarrassed, but I think even he understood," Roseboro said. "He never bitched about it. I think Don would have won. I was sure Sandy would."

When Koufax walked two batters in the first inning, Drysdale began to throw in the bullpen. But Earl Battey struck out, and Koufax didn't allow a runner past second base the rest of the game, though he was compelled to abandon his curve midway through the contest.

"I didn't have a curveball at all," Koufax said. "When I threw it I couldn't get it over. And those first few innings I really didn't know how long I was going to last."

A spectacular defensive play by Jim Gilliam at third base with runners on first and second in the bottom of the fifth helped preserve the shutout, but otherwise Koufax simply owned the day. The final two batters summed up his dominance. After swinging at his first two pitches, Battey was helpless in taking a called strike three. Bob Allison, whose two-run homer in Game 6 had kept the Twins alive, worked a 2-1 count, then swung and missed at the final two pitches of the season.

"The perfect game," Torborg says, "was really something, but what he did in that seventh game in the '65 World Series was an incredible thing, without a curveball on two days' rest with an arthritic elbow."

With "Sweet Lou" Johnson providing the offense he needed on a fourth-inning homer, Koufax's 2–0 shutout gave the Dodgers their fourth World Series championship in 11 seasons. In the World Series, he pitched 24 innings, struck out 29, and allowed one earned run.

"If you want a conductor, try Leonard Bernstein. Heifetz will do on the violin," wrote Murray. "If you want to dance, see if Fred Astaire is busy. Want someone to sing nice, just hand the music to Andy Williams.

"But if you want to win a pennant or a World Series, just hand the ball to Sanford Koufax. He gave a performance here Thursday afternoon that should go to Carnegie Hall."

The 1966 season began, famously or infamously, with the dual holdout by Koufax and Drysdale. The roots of the disagreement with the front office went back years, to other forced contract renewals and incidents that offended Koufax, most notoriously a 1964 dispute in which Koufax accused general manager Buzzie Bavasi of planting false stories in the press. With Koufax secretly eyeing retirement at the end of the year, his threat not to play was real, though his desire to pitch in '66 hadn't abated.

After the holdout ended days before the season began, Koufax's performance bore no consequences. He took a 1.75 ERA into May—and then he got hot. From May 10 through July 5, he completed 12 of 14 starts with a 1.16 ERA and 126 strikeouts in 124 innings. As summer ceded to fall and the season wound to a close, "Koufax went to Alston and told him, 'Use me any way you want, as often as you want,'" Leavy wrote.

"Well, he was stoic," Torborg says. "That's a good way to describe it. His elbow was so inflated, so bloated, so swollen that you wondered how in heaven's name is he ever going to pitch another game."

The Dodgers were in yet another tough pennant race. Forced to play a doubleheader on the final day of the season, their lead was reduced to a single game over the Giants after a 4–3 loss to start the day. Koufax, once again working on two days' rest, took a 6–0 lead into the ninth inning at Philadelphia, but gave up three runs (two earned) before an out was recorded. Summoning his supernatural strength once more, he struck out two of the final three batters for the triumph.

"We were a team, and every player played a part in our victories," Roseboro said, "but he was our top gun and we all knew it. The guts of that guy really got to us. We not only loved him, we really respected him.

"We did not know that he had just won his last game."

Koufax's final regular season might have been his finest, with a 1.73 ERA (190 ERA+) and 317 strikeouts in 323 innings. Over his final four years, he went 97–27, throwing 1,192⅔ innings and striking out 1,228 with a 1.86 ERA (172 ERA+), a 0.91 WHIP, and 4.7 strikeouts per walk.

"I remember he pitched well at the '59 World Series," Erskine says, "but he wasn't really in command of himself as a pitcher yet. But when he came back the following five or six years, after I retired, Sandy became the most dominant pitcher—I don't know if you can say in history—but he goes at the top of the list of dominant pitchers to ever play the game. He made the Hall of Fame in five years—who does that?"

Koufax's final appearance on the mound for the Dodgers was not the perfect capstone, though far from inadequate (six innings, one earned run). Pretty much everything in the 1966 World Series, after all, went wrong for the Dodgers, who scored a total of two runs in four games while making six errors in Game 2, leading to three unearned runs against their ace left-hander. Still, the celebration of Koufax's third unanimous Cy Young selection remained, and he hadn't let on what was impending.

"My arm's feeling pretty good," he said publicly. "I haven't had any trouble with it, and I'm not taking any treatments for it now. I'm resting a lot and playing golf in the high 80s."

But Koufax knew he wasn't being forthright, and he would not avoid the truth much longer. While the Dodgers were on a postseason goodwill tour of Japan, he called a press conference. The living legend was retiring.

"My health is something that means too much to me," he told the stunned press. "I decided I had a lot of years left after baseball, and I want to live them with the full use of my body."

Wrote Charles Maher of the *Los Angeles Times*: "On the face of it, this may appear to put the Dodgers in terrible trouble. But it is actually a little worse than that."

Word filtered to his Dodger teammates, who hadn't known what was coming. "It surprised me," Drysdale said. "It leaves you with kind of an empty feeling. It's been a real privilege to have played ball with Sandy. I just thank him for everything he's done for me and my family."

Said 21-year-old rookie Don Sutton, who was taking off-season college classes: "I was living in a dorm, and there were some guys who couldn't understand why I was standing there with tears in my eyes."

Koufax's final career totals all but wiped out any memory of his struggles: a 2.76 ERA (131 ERA+) with 2,396 strikeouts in 2,324⅓ innings. His 53.2 wins above replacement leave Koufax behind only Dazzy Vance and Drysdale among 20th century Dodger pitchers. In that group, Koufax's ratio of WAR to innings pitched—in short, pure production—ranks first.

"Baseball lost its left arm because Sandy Koufax didn't want to lose his," Murray concluded. "In a way, I'm glad Sandy isn't going to 'cute' his way through five more seasons or so. In the first place, I want to see him with both arms in place and equidistant from his shoulder[s]. But mostly, I wouldn't want to see Rembrandt doing billboards. I hated to hear Tibbett reduced to yodeling 'Accentuate the Positive.' I wouldn't want to see Dickens doing soup copy.

"Watch Koufax trying to get Willie Mays out with 'junk?' Watch Joe Louis try to win a flight by clinching? Never! Go, Sandy. And thanks for the memory. This way, it remains the one I want."

In 1972, Koufax entered the Hall of Fame, the youngest player ever elected. Asked if he ever second-guessed himself, if he thought he might have retired too soon, Koufax told Ross Newhan of the *Los Angeles Times*, "I started to second-guess myself the very next day. I wasn't so much the feeling that I had retired too soon, but that I just wished I hadn't had to make the decision. I wish I could have played longer."

Over the next half century, Koufax was often portrayed as an elusive, mythic figure—and certainly, his accomplishments were worthy of Mount Olympus. According to the narrative, Koufax retired from atop the baseball world at the end of the 1966 season, levitated into the stratosphere, and returned only grudgingly when dragged down by us mortals. He didn't develop a taste for sportscasting after signing a multiyear contract with NBC, and he didn't seek out attention.

The world concluded he was a recluse, for little reason more than he didn't make himself available at the drop of a hat. Yet among those with whom he is comfortable, he remained a frequent, smiling presence.

"I think he only really relaxed among his teammates," Roseboro said. "He treated them all as equals and he wanted to be just one of the guys. Sometimes he was like a big kid, kidding around with them."

Many of his springs were spent as a special instructor, and he has been a pivotal mentor for pitchers, most notably Kershaw. "Some Hall of Fame baseball players that I have met, I don't want to say they weren't approachable, but you're more in awe of them almost," Kershaw said in 2010. "But he makes it really easy to talk to him. It's almost like he is another coach that you're talking to about pitching."

Rick Honeycutt, who first joined the Dodgers as a pitcher in 1983 and later became a long-serving pitching coach in the Kershaw era, says Koufax's thoughts and expertise have helped shaped him and others in the organization, keeping him part of their tradition.

"Some of the things that I heard in the first few weeks of spring training were things that nobody had ever focused on or even talked about," said Honeycutt, "which I thought was extremely unusual. He just had a simple way of explaining the delivery—just really the fundamentals—of what he felt was important. Working from the ground up instead of thinking about your arm, just to work on having a powerful strong base and understanding how your lower half became interactive with the ground. So it was very, very enlightening to me. Nobody ever told it to me that way."

For years, Koufax could show as well as tell. In 1985, at age 49, he took a turn throwing batting practice at spring training to Dodger outfielder Ken Landreaux. Koufax signaled that a curveball was coming.

"The pitch was coming in on the left-handed batter, chest-high and over the plate," wrote Claire Smith of *The New York Times*. "But at the last split second, the ball snapped viciously, landing almost at the catcher's foot.

"Landreaux, the batter, fell back laughing. Then, as if describing the most incredible phenomenon he had ever seen, Landreaux showed his teammates where he thought the curveball was going—and where it ended up."

At an onstage interview with columnist T.J. Simers, Koufax busted any illusion that he was baseball's J.D. Salinger, parrying Simers' teasing repartee in the most lighthearted manner.

"I don't know that I've dropped out of sight," Koufax said. "I go to the Final Four year after year…I go to golf tournaments. I've been to Super Bowls. I've been to Dodger Stadium. I go to dinner every night; I go to movies."

It is true, or at least Koufax's own spun legend, that when he told his mother about the autobiography he would be producing in 1966, she asked for an early copy. "You never told me anything," she said.

As it turned out, there was much to learn. But perhaps, amid all the highs and lows, the impossible struggles and successes, the biggest nugget of all is still just how much Sandy Koufax loved playing baseball.

"If it were only the baseball, I'd enjoy playing for the rest of my life," he said. "The actual pitching—I love it. I love it when it's going good, when the rhythm is with you and you're doing everything you want out there. And I love it when I've got nothing and I'm struggling to survive. Because that's exactly what it becomes—survival.

"When you have your stuff, you should win. But when you can end up winning, not on the strength of your arm, which is after all a gift from the heavens, but on the strength of your brains and your experience and your knowledge, it is a victory that you feel belongs peculiarly to yourself."

Don Drysdale

"As far back as I can remember, I always had a bat and a ball in my hand," his story began.

Some children are born to play baseball, which is to say, the game of baseball is seemingly born inside them. Don Drysdale was one.

His father, Scott, was a Pacific Coast League pitcher whose career dissolved with back trouble in 1935. Drysdale came along a year later, born in Van Nuys, where he was a high school classmate of perhaps the one student who could rival him in looks, Robert Redford.

In Drysdale's childhood, he was the acorn that becomes the hard-throwing oak.

"I wasn't real big then," Drysdale said in his memoir written with Bob Verdi, published in 1990. "Or should I say, I wasn't real tall…I didn't do most of my growing until right after I got out of high school, when I shot up 4½ inches in a hurry. When I was nine, though, I was a little large in other areas, a little chubby, which I guess is why they called me 'Porky.'"

The summer before his senior year, Drysdale was an infielder for his American Legion team—"I had never even given pitching a thought"—when the scheduled hurler was a no-show. Scott put Don on the mound, on a day when Goldie Holt, a scout for Brooklyn, was in the stands. Drysdale threw strikes, and in a sense, his Dodger career was born. (So was Scott's—he became a part-time Dodger scout.)

Two other area scouts, including future Dodger pitching coach Lefty Phillips, added Drysdale to a Brooklyn Dodger Juniors team that also featured George Anderson (later to be known as Sparky) and brothers

Norm and Larry Sherry. The games might not have been anything to write home about, but the connection to a major-league team was. As was the case with Carl Erskine, the interest shown by the local branch of the Boys of Summer meant something.

When, after Drysdale's senior season in 1954, Branch Rickey personally worked him out and then offered $6,000 to sign with the Pirates, compared with the $4,000 proffered by the Dodgers, Drysdale still felt more comfortable signing with the club whose scouts had been nurturing him all along. (Essentially, Pittsburgh had Drysdale and Sandy Koufax in its grasp, and lost both.)

It took Drysdale less than two years to make his big-league debut, and even less time to make an impression. His post–high school growth spurt had injected more fast in his fastball. "Hey, I'm not gettin' in there against that kid!" a smiling Jackie Robinson yelled at spring training in 1955. Roy Campanella told Drysdale that if it weren't for the talent already on the Brooklyn roster, he could pitch in the major leagues then and there. Drysdale was four months shy of his 19th birthday at the time.

He spent the '55 season in Montreal, beginning the year 9–2 before he got angry after being knocked out of a game and broke his hand on a Coke machine. He still finished the season with a 3.33 ERA that was nearly identical to his 27-year-old teammate Tom Lasorda, who had been demoted to make room on the active roster for Koufax. A lanky, youthful 6-foot-5 by this time, Drysdale wouldn't throw another minor-league inning in his career.

"I don't care if he's 15 years old," Alston said. "If Don Drysdale can win some games for us, he'll stay here and pitch."

At 19 years and 269 days, Drysdale made his Brooklyn Dodger debut on Opening Day 1956, pitching a scoreless ninth inning in an 8–6 loss to the Phillies. Within a week came his first start and first complete game, taking a shutout into the eighth inning and finishing with a strikeout in a 6–1 victory at Philadelphia.

"The 6-foot 5-inch youngster pitched with the poise of a seasoned hurler," wrote Roscoe McGowen in *The New York Times*. "He registered nine strikeouts and had the crowd buzzing when he struck out the side in the first inning."

In his next start, Drysdale was roughed up for five runs in 5⅔ innings, and didn't pitch for another 20 days. It wasn't really punitive. The Dodgers had four primary starters in 1956—Don Newcombe, Erskine, Sal Maglie, and Roger Craig—who combined for all but 32 of the team's starts that year. For the remainder, Drysdale emerged as the No. 1 alternative—outpacing 20-year-old sophomore Koufax in the process—making 12 starts along with 13 relief appearances for 99 innings in all, with a 2.64 ERA (152 ERA+). In the borough, he was winning fans fast, in no small part because he went 4–0 with a 1.37 ERA in 26⅓ innings against the Giants.

"Why I was able to beat the Giants so often, I don't know," said Drysdale, who also went 3-for-8 at the plate and hit his first big-league homer against the local rivals. "I only won five games all year."

The opening reviews were all positive, but the Dodgers, with burgeoning confidence in their organizational approach to pitching, wondered if they could take him even further, faster.

"I had established myself as a sidearm pitcher," Drysdale recalled, "a pitcher who dropped his arm down and delivered from there, rather than over the top, because it just felt natural to me. It wasn't conventional, but it was comfortable. Well, on our trip to Japan after the 1956 season, Al Campanis took me over to the side one day and started working with me on an overhand curveball, which was something of a Dodger tradition. That was a pitch Dodgers were taught, and even though it was difficult for me—because I had that unorthodox motion—Campanis tried, which was fine.

"But I was having a heck of a time with it, because I just couldn't get up there. It was too unnatural for me, and watching me struggle on the sidelines one day, Clem Labine and Campanella dropped over and voiced their opinions. Basically, what they told Campanis was, 'Al, he's doing just fine the way he is. Let him throw the way he's used to throwing. Don't change him.' That was the last of my overhand curveball experiment."

The 1957 season was the year Podres led the NL in ERA, ERA+, shutouts, and WHIP. And yet, Drysdale had the better season, throwing 25 more innings with an ERA that was only 0.03 higher at 2.69 (153 ERA+)—and, looking back, leading the NL with 6.1 wins above replacement. Nearly 30 years would pass before a 21-or-younger NL pitcher had a comparable campaign (Dwight Gooden in 1985).

Drysdale was a nice young man. Respectful. Personable. Confident but humble. But an intensity was developing for those moments between the lines, an attitude that for many became his defining characteristic.

Winning mattered above all else. Batters were obstacles to winning, and therefore batters had to be pushed aside, by any means necessary.

"Drysdale sizzled after every defeat," said Duke Snider. "Fantasy camp, training camp, National League season, World Series, All-Star Games—it never made any difference. He could not tolerate losing, and he didn't want anyone on his team to tolerate it either."

Said John Roseboro, who in his rookie season of '57 first caught Drysdale: "He was a good guy, but he could be as mean as Sandy was clean."

Perhaps it was in Drysdale's DNA that he would become the Master of Intimidation, but Sal Maglie, who was 39 years old when he joined the Dodgers in mid-1956—twice Drysdale's age—accelerated its evolution.

"One of the best early lessons I got about pitching was from Maglie on how to move a batter off the plate," Drysdale said. "We talked by the hour about his philosophy of keeping hitters honest, and by the time 1957 rolled around, when I'd had one whole year in the big leagues, I was developing the same ideas as Sal."

Frankly, the approach was more cerebral than hostile, centered on manipulation as opposed to intimidation. Maglie showed Drysdale how he would waste a pitch outside, not necessarily to get a batter to chase but to see how the batter reacted with his feet and what that revealed about his expectations.

> ### Moment in the Sun: Sal Maglie
> - Nicknamed "The Barber," a longtime Dodger antagonist with the Giants who came to Brooklyn in middle of 1956 season
> - In two years with Dodgers, had a 2.89 ERA (140 ERA+) in 292⅓ innings
> - Pitched final no-hitter in Brooklyn Dodger history, smothering Phillies on September 25, 1956
> - Struck out 10 during complete-game, Game 1 victory in the 1956 World Series, but was on losing end of Don Larsen's 2–0 perfect game in Game 5

"The other thing Maglie did," Drysdale said, "was to make sure not to throw just one pitch inside if he was trying to move a batter off the plate. Sal threw two, just for good measure...The batter didn't know what to think, because he had no idea what Maglie was up to next."

So yeah, Drysdale did lead NL hurlers in hit-by-pitches each of the next four seasons, from 1958 to 1961. Every pitcher wants to get a hitter off-balance, yet no pitcher did it more directly than Drysdale. Make of that what you will. But as they say, it wasn't personal. It was business.

"I was called 'intimidating,' and I wasn't about to dispute that," he said. "I never talked about my reputation, but I was very much at peace with having others talk about it...Yet, for all those batters I nailed, I can honestly say that I never tried to hurt any of them, period.

"Also, for all my reputation, I got into only one real fight and that happened because I dinged [Johnny] Logan with a pickoff throw at first base, not a pitch."

Jeff Torborg was as mesmerized as anyone by the Drysdale persona.

"He would come toward the plate to get the ball," Torborg says, "and he wouldn't be looking at me to throw the ball back. He was looking at the hitter, and the hitter would say, 'What's he looking at?' I'd say, 'I think he's looking at you.'"

The baseball world had every reason to believe that the Dodgers had a newly ascendant ace in the indomitable Drysdale. He was young, fierce, and healthy. And on top of it all, he was heading home, moving in 1958 with the Dodgers back to Los Angeles. What could be better?

For one thing, Drysdale (who was in Army Reserves boot camp with Koufax at Fort Dix, New Jersey, when he got the news of the move) had quickly grown emotionally attached to Brooklyn and its fans. If that hurdle was surmountable, a bigger one rose behind it, one that was 40 feet tall, stood 251 feet from home plate, and could intimidate the intimidator.

The left-field fence at the Dodgers' new starter home, the Los Angeles Memorial Coliseum, wreaked havoc on Drysdale like kryptonite on Superman.

It didn't help that in MLB's first West Coast game, Drysdale was knocked out in the fourth inning at the now–San Francisco Giants' new home, Seals Stadium, allowing six runs in an 8–0 loss. He was then hammered in his first two Coliseum games, didn't get his first win until he pitched shutout ball against the Phillies from the 11th through the 14th innings on May 6, and didn't win his first start until May 21.

When the All-Star break arrived, Drysdale's ERA was 5.80. Fortunately for him, he found his equilibrium in the second half with a 2.80 ERA. He also exacted his own revenge on the wall, hitting five homers in 15 at-bats from August 3 to 23, to tie Don Newcombe's season record of seven by a pitcher.

That carried nicely into 1959, when the Dodgers surprised the baseball world by recovering from their seventh-place finish to win the World Series in their second Los Angeles season. Drysdale had a 3.46 ERA (122 ERA+), led the league in strikeouts and shutouts, and won his first career postseason start, Game 3 of the '59 World Series, before an unprecedented

Fall Classic crowd of 92,294, to put the Dodgers ahead of the Chicago White Sox to stay. In that game, Chicago had baserunners in every one of Drysdale's seven innings but went hitless with runners in scoring position.

"On this team, I'm the stopper," Drysdale had said plainly that summer. "When the Dodgers drop a couple of games, I pitch. When we want to get off to a good start in a critical series, I pitch. I'm not supposed to lose."

Drysdale led the NL in whiffs again in 1960, accompanied by a 2.84 ERA (139 ERA+) and a league-leading 1.06 WHIP, before slumping to merely above average in the final Coliseum season of '61 (3.69 ERA, 116 ERA+). In 1962, the Dodgers moved again, and this time the new address suited Drysdale just fine.

Dodger Stadium, with its swaying palm trees, beautiful symmetry, and distant fences, was the ultimate Southern California pad. Walter O'Malley paid for it, but Drysdale called dibs on the penthouse, winning the Cy Young Award by going 25–9 with 19 complete games and a 2.83 ERA (128 ERA+), in the first of four consecutive seasons of at least 300 innings.

"He has reacted to failure in the past by indulging in epic fits of wrath and self-flagellation," wrote Huston Horn in *Sports Illustrated*. "When seized with anger, his pitching declined apace, and it became a maxim around the league that if you couldn't beat Drysdale on your own, get him mad and he'd beat himself.

"But this year, that sort of psychology is not working. Maturity and a fine opportunity to be the man of the hour have apparently hit Drysdale together. There were other reasons for his improvement—a new ballpark, a modified delivery, a strong offensive team—but Drysdale, having learned to swallow his gorge, had reached a kind of middle-aged serenity."

That dominance made the season's disastrous end that much more devastating. Eleven years after '51, the Dodgers had ceded their smaller but still significant four-game lead with seven games to play to the Giants, setting the stage for another three-game playoff. Again, the Dodgers led in the ninth inning of the final game; again, the bullpen couldn't hold on. But in what was likely the most controversial decision of Alston's managerial career, Drysdale's offer to enter the game was ignored.

"Drysdale was raring to go," Roseboro said. "He told Walt he wanted to pitch and would get the last outs. I think he could have. But Alston wanted to save him to open the World Series against the Yankees, which was coming right up. Drysdale said, 'We've got to get there first.' Alston said, 'We'll get there.' He was sure we would. We all were."

In Alston's defense, Drysdale had pitched 5⅓ innings the day before and more than 20 innings in the past week. But the defeat generated enormous anger and recriminations, not to mention furious speculation that the Dodgers would fire Alston, before the manager's contract was renewed for his 10th season on October 18.

Nothing redresses a mess like success, however, and 1963 was all that and a bag of Roger Owens–tossed peanuts. Even as Koufax was winning his first Cy Young, Drysdale lowered his own ERA to 2.63 (though his ERA+ declined to 114), while Los Angeles spent every day after July 1 in first place. The right-hander also pitched the only shutout of the cathartic World Series sweep of the Yankees, a 1–0 victory in which he allowed five baserunners, struck out nine, and withstood a deep fly to right by Joe Pepitone for the final out.

Drysdale's career-best 2.18 ERA (128 ERA+) couldn't forestall a sixth-place Dodger finish in 1964, nor did a jump back to 2.77 (118 ERA+) get in the way of the Dodgers' 1965 championship, their third in seven years. That season, Drysdale pitched the only one-hitter of his career—in which he scored the game's first run after leading off the bottom of the eighth with a single—and finished the regular season by allowing only one unearned run in his final 27 innings.

Knocked out upon being charged with seven runs (three earned) in 2⅔ innings of his Yom Kippur start in place of Koufax in Game 1 of the World Series, Drysdale suffered his first career postseason loss, after he mythically told Alston, "I bet you wish I was Jewish." (In his 1966 memoir, Alston credits Lefty Gomez with the gag.) However, Drysdale rallied with a complete-game, 11-strikeout, 7–2 victory in Game 4 to even the Series, won by the Dodgers four days later.

When Drysdale and Koufax sought better contracts during spring training before the 1966 season, Drysdale later credited his wife, Ginger, for the idea to hold out in tandem. Though the dispute was resolved in time for the season, many Dodger fans weren't eager to forgive any missteps that followed, even for someone owning a treasure chest of achievement like Big D.

"This man who has pitched 173 victories," wrote *Sports Illustrated* scribe Jack Olsen, "won the Cy Young Award, worked harder and oftener and more consistently than any other pitcher in baseball for the last 10 years, this man who should be accepting plaques in Pasadena and attending dinners in his honor in Cucamonga, suddenly hears boos from the fans and reads insulting remarks in the public prints. 'Why should he be subjected to that kind of treatment?' a typical Dodger student says with studied sarcasm. 'Just because he's having a rotten, lousy, miserable year? Is it fair to boo a man who's rotten, lousy and miserable? Is this the American way?' It certainly is."

"I didn't feel strong," Drysdale explained at the time. "I didn't have anything. I didn't have a good fastball. I didn't have a good curveball. You name it, I didn't have it…It all had something to do with this long muscle that runs down from the shoulder along the outside of the arm. That's always the last arm muscle to tone in, and while it was toning in I was trying to find a groove. I'd find a groove and the muscle would tone in a little better and I'd have to find another groove. Normally, all this would've been worked out in spring training."

In what was now his 11th big-league season, Drysdale's 4.25 ERA crept through Dodger Stadium like a rodent of unusual size when he took the mound against the Mets on July 24, the day after his 30th birthday. He struck out 10 in a shutout and just like that, zipped through the rest of the year with an ERA of 2.37 in 121⅓ innings.

With Koufax pitching 27 innings in the final eight days of the season to help preserve the latest NL pennant for the Dodgers, Drysdale got the Game 1 start against the Orioles. But back-to-back first-inning homers by Frank Robinson and Brooks Robinson gave Baltimore a lead it never relinquished, and when Drysdale found himself on the wrong end of a 1–0 shutout in Game 4, thanks to another Frank Robinson blast, the Series—and Drysdale's postseason career—was over.

There was, of course, one last hurrah—one glorious, historical, unforgettable last hurrah.

In 1967—his first big-league season without Koufax as a teammate—Drysdale gave Dodger fans a 2.74 ERA (112 ERA+), albeit in a 91-loss season for Los Angeles. (His 13–16 record was identical to the year before.)

"There was even mention in a couple newspapers that I was trade bait, because I was on the downside of the baseball mountain," Drysdale said. But the 1968 season opened with Drysdale still in Dodger Blue, obliging with a shutout of the Mets in his annual debut.

Then on May 14, the fun began.

First came a 1–0, two-hit shutout of the Cubs, then one by the same score over the Houston Astros at Dodger Stadium four days later. Drysdale took his act out of town, and shutouts at St. Louis and Houston followed.

In the Astrodome, umpire Al Barlick was asked to check Drysdale for doctoring the baseball. The pitcher passed the test, though truth be told, after he retired Drysdale followed in the footsteps of Preacher Roe by admitting that he knew, dating back to his season in the minors with Montreal, more than a little something about throwing a wet one.

"Through the years, I called on my spitter at times to get out of jams," Drysdale said, comparing the pitch to a split-fingered fastball in effect, but one that was less taxing on the arm. "I wasn't the only one, believe me…But my good buddy, Gene Mauch, singled me out. He said I threw the best spitter in the National League because I threw it the hardest."

All Drysdale needed, he explained, was a little saliva. They never found any extra substances on him because he never needed them.

"You'd be amazed at how uncomplicated the process was," he said. "When I wanted to throw a spitter, I would just look at my catcher and call it myself, usually by doing something with my lips, like moistening them in broad daylight. Really cloak-and-dagger stuff, huh? Then I'd stick my fingers in my mouth, dry off my thumb, and let it go.

"Remember, as I said before, if you're going to war, you better bring all your weapons."

Any controversy, real or imagined, over the spitball paled in comparison to the brouhaha punctuating Drysdale's bid for his fifth consecutive shutout May 31.

If you know anything about Drysdale's scoreless streak, you probably know that in the ninth inning against the Giants, he hit San Francisco catcher Dick Dietz with a bases-loaded pitch—but wasn't charged with a run. Umpire Harry Wendelstedt famously ruled that Dietz didn't make an effort to avoid the missile, and called it a strike.

"Dick started to flinch," recalls Torborg, the Dodger catcher that night. "You know, he started to back out with his rear end and then reach right in with his left elbow, and the ball hit his elbow. And I turned around, exaggeratedly yelling that he didn't make an attempt to get out of the way the ball. And the funny part is, I don't know if you've ever done this when you've turned your head too hard and you got that burning sensation in your neck. I got that. It looked like I had some sort of paralysis. I'm hollering, and Harry, immediately he says, 'No, no, no,' and wouldn't allow him to take his base.

"And then of course it was a huge argument with Giant manager Herman Franks, and the coaching staff was yelling. So I'm out on the mound with Don, and he said, 'Go back and find out what happens from here.'"

What happened was that Dietz had to step back in the box, but still with the potential streak-breaking run 90 feet away. On a 3-2 pitch, Drysdale got Dietz to fly to left field, too shallow to score the run. Ty

Cline grounded into a force play at home, and Jack Hiatt popped to first, extending the scorelessness to 45 innings.

"It took a lot of balls on Harry's part to make that call," Drysdale said, "but I felt he was absolutely right. Dietz had made no effort to avoid the pitch, and that was confirmed to me the next day. Juan Marichal, the Giants' great righthander, told me that Dietz had said in the dugout before he came to bat, 'If it's anything but a fastball, I'll take one and that will end [the streak] right there.'"

Records fell in Drysdale's next two starts: Carl Hubbell's NL mark of 46⅓ consecutive scoreless innings tumbled with a June 4 blanking of the Pirates (also the sixth straight Drysdale shutout, a record that still stands), and Walter Johnson's MLB-record 56 was topped in the third inning of Drysdale's June 8 start against the Phillies. The streak reached 58⅔ innings when Philadelphia pinch hitter Howie Bedell delivered the third and final RBI of his major-league career with a fifth-inning sacrifice fly.

"It was an amazing time," Torborg warmly recalls. "It meant so much to all of us with the Dodgers, because Sandy had the no-hitters and the perfect game and Don never had a no-hitter, but he was beloved like Sandy was beloved by his teammates."

Drysdale concluded that "it couldn't go on forever, and it had gone on a whole lot longer than I expected." That night, just a few miles from Dodger Stadium, Robert Kennedy was at the Ambassador Hotel, having officially been crowned the winner of the California Democratic presidential primary, moving him closer to a nomination.

"When Senator Kennedy heard about the ballgame, he announced the score to a ballroom full of supporters," Drysdale said. "He congratulated me and they cheered. Two hours later, he was [shot] by an assassin's bullet. So much for the importance of all those shutout innings."

If the streak itself was unlikely, the idea that Drysdale's career would end 14 months later was nearly incomprehensible. But during spring training in 1969, Drysdale knew the pain he was feeling in his right shoulder was trouble, even before he had learned he had a torn rotator cuff. Surgery was risky, and medication was only making him feel worse about the situation.

"I was so drugged up at times that I couldn't see the scoreboard from the mound," he remembered. "I was a walking drugstore. I had to cover one eye, like a drunk driver does when he wants to see the road. Roberto Clemente hit a line drive through the box that could have killed me. I never saw it…I was that fuzzy, that blurred. But I heard it. Did I ever hear it. And I felt it, too.

"After I'd escaped being hit, I felt a little sensation on the left side of my neck, like I had a mosquito sitting there, waiting to bite it. I brushed the area with my hand and looked down and my hand was dripping with blood. Clemente's line drive had taken the skin right off the edge of my ear. How's that for a gentle reminder that you've about had it?"

Two stints on the disabled list solved nothing, and Drysdale started to feel he was doing more harm than good.

"I knew that I wasn't really helping the ballclub," he said. "We had an outside chance to finish first, and if I hung around, Walt Alston was going to be tempted to pitch me every time my turn came up. Just like he'd always done, just like I'd always done. But I couldn't do it. I can handle pain, but this pain was unbelievable. It was like somebody was sticking an ice pick in my shoulder."

Drysdale's final game came two weeks after his 33rd birthday, on August 5, 1969. He officially retired at a press conference in the Stadium Club, six days later.

"The Dodgers at that time had a lot of pride in their pitching," says Claude Osteen, "and you were well aware of what was expected of you. I remember Drysdale called the group together, I think it was near the time that he was getting ready to retire, and he told all of the young players, 'Just remember one thing. This uniform means a lot. It means a heck of a lot more than the DODGERS that's written across the front of it. There's a lot of history here and a lot of good history.' And I never forgot that."

In his 14-year career, spanning 3,432 innings, Drysdale framed a 2.95 ERA (121 ERA+) and hung it in the gallery with the greatest of Dodger pitchers. Only Dazzy Vance had more wins above replacement than Drysdale's 61.2 in franchise history.

Drysdale hardly faded into oblivion, and we're not just talking about his 1970 guest appearance on *The Brady Bunch*. In 1984, Drysdale was elected to the Hall of Fame. For nearly a quarter century, he was a sportscaster, whose grace interviewing Orel Hershiser about his own scoreless-inning record being broken is remembered by every fan of the era, and whose ecstatic call of Kirk Gibson's 1988 World Series home run remains an exhilarating complement to Vin Scully's.

His 1990 memoir, *Once a Bum, Always a Dodger*, was in part a celebration of his life—by then being spent with his second wife, Ann Meyers Drysdale—and in part a celebration of his teammates, including a lament over the untimely passing of Hodges at age 47.

"Here was a man so strong that you figured he was indestructible, so impressive that you figured he would live forever," Drysdale said, "and he went down just like that."

Three years later, Drysdale himself passed away, so very much too soon, at 56, on a road trip in Montreal, with a despondent Scully revealing the news to Dodger fans midgame. It was an incredibly painful loss, mitigated only by the knowledge of how much joy Big D felt in his thrilling life.

"For all the memories of Brooklyn and Los Angeles and the guys I played with and learned from—Duke, Gil, Pee Wee, Jackie, Sal, Sandy, and the rest—I've never been luckier than I am now," Drysdale had written. "I've never been happier."

PART THREE

THE POST-KOUFAX GENERATION

SANDY KOUFAX AND DON DRYSDALE rode off into the sunset beyond Elysian Park, taking the star power that had blessed the Dodger pitching staff in baseball's promised land at Stadium Way. However real the Dodger pitching tradition, it was vulnerable.

Yet, Dodger pitching thrived in its transition from the 1960s to the 1970s, generating not only another future Hall of Famer in Don Sutton but a fertile supporting cast that was the envy of baseball. Much of this could be attributed to savvy scouting, drafting, and player acquisition led by general managers Buzzie Bavasi, Fresco Thompson (who died five months after succeeding Bavasi), and Al Campanis. (Had the Dodgers signed their 10th-round draft pick from baseball's first amateur draft in 1965, Tom Seaver, it would have been that much more impressive.)

Less celebrated but completely critical was the emerging role of the pitching coach, which in Los Angeles began with two respected men: ex-catcher Joe Becker (1955–64) and former scout Lefty Phillips (1965–68), who had lassoed prospects including Drysdale and Bill Singer.

Then came Red Adams—"the best pitching coach in my lifetime, anywhere around," right-hander Burt Hooton says, and he was far from the only one to say so. Though he pitched but 12 innings in the majors, Adams was a hallowed figure in baseball.

Adams, who passed away in 2017 at age 95, was a Los Angeles baseball hero long before the Dodgers arrived, winning the Pacific Coast League Most Valuable Player Award with a 2.72 ERA (and .349 batting average) in 41 games for the Triple-A Angels in 1946. Like Phillips, he became a Dodger scout immediately after his playing career ended and then ascended to pitching coach before the 1969 season.

"Red Adams was probably as good as it gets for a pitching coach," Singer says. "He would break down everybody's mechanics and find the two or three keys. Everybody's different. And he'd be able to go out to you on the mound and mention the one little thing you weren't doing and turn the game around right then."

Adams could obviously work with pitchers who came up through the system—"a gifted teacher," according to Dodger executive Fred Claire—but he also connected with outsiders whose training might have been alien to the Dodgers. Veteran hurlers might come to Los Angeles with their ideas of how to pitch set in stone. Adams put the chisel in their hands.

"I'm in spring training, and it's my first game," Tommy John says. "I'm coming in second in the fourth inning to pitch my three innings against the Braves at Vero. I always took a big step back off to the side and back, and then I'd come up and have a little pause and then I could go to the plate."

Adams had a good long look, John recalls, then engaged him afterward.

"I really think you would be better off if you would square up and step straight back and take a shorter step back, and then you'd be more in control," Adams said, according to John. "And then when you turn, you could go right to the plate. I just think you'll be better off doing that."

So John worked on that adjustment. Adams monitored his progress. About two weeks later, maybe three, Adams asked to see John throw his old way again. After two pitches, Adams came to his conclusion.

"The next time the old Red Dog tells you to try something, tell me to stick it up my ass," Adams said.

"And right then I knew that he was an outstanding pitching coach," John remembers. "Any time a coach in baseball will admit that he is wrong, it means he is solid in what he does, he's confident—and yet he's got common sense, and Red had all those."

It explains how Adams could go about his business seeming like a godsend but never a threat to his managers, whether Walter Alston or Tommy Lasorda.

Says Claire: "I sat in meetings with Walt where he would say to Red in spring training, 'You take the pitchers, you do what you want to do with them, you pitch them when you want to pitch them, you rest them when you want to rest them, but they'd better be ready for Opening Day.' And in a lighthearted way, Walt had total confidence in Red—total—and never, ever, ever interfered."

With Adams, the role of the Dodger pitching coach was beloved. It continued through the years with Ron Perranoski, Dave Wallace, and Rick Honeycutt (to name a leading trio), but Adams was the godfather. Dodger pitching would never have thrived without the talent, but the nurturing from Adams was the secret ingredient.

"No person ever meant more to my career than Red Adams," Sutton famously said during his 1998 Hall of Fame induction speech. "Without him, I would not be standing in Cooperstown today."

Bill Singer

Sadly but inevitably, the operating table became nearly as much a part of Dodger pitching history as the mound. But before anyone ever heard of Tommy John surgery, there was the little matter of Bill Singer surgery.

Born in 1944, Singer was signed to a $50,000 bonus by the Dodgers out of nearby Pomona in 1962, scouted by his future Dodger pitching coach, Lefty Phillips. After his third minor-league season, the 20-year-old right-hander debuted for the Dodgers, starting before a reclining-room-only crowd of 629 on September 24, 1964, at Wrigley Field. The three-game series drew just fewer than 3,200 fans combined, or as Singer puts it, "not enough to pay the hotel bill."

Despite his initial promise, the 6-foot-4 right-hander spent most of 1965 and 1966 in the minors. Mastering a fastball and a slurve (that is, a curve thrown at slider speed, or a slider with a downward break), he led the Pacific Coast League in strikeouts in '66 and also pitched four shutout relief innings for Los Angeles. Joked John Roseboro: "It's a pity Singer will be around for only 10 or 12 years with that hummer he's got."

But that year, Singer was diagnosed with a largely unknown condition: thoracic outlet syndrome, which disrupted the circulation in his right hand. On November 2, Singer became the first athlete to undergo a pioneering rib-removal surgery to prolong his playing career.

"I was the original," he says. "I was the Tommy John of that. It was experimental—they had never done it before—and so I had to wait about six weeks while they made an instrument that would go in under my armpit and cut out my first rib, without killing me. If they cut out muscle, I couldn't pitch again. If they cut out the collarbone, I couldn't pitch again.

"Now the operation's done arthroscopically, so it's so much different, so much easier. I was 22 years old, I had just had a kid, and rolling the dice to whether I'd live or not. In those days, there was no rehab. So I tried to get a job working at Sears, but I couldn't pass the physical—I couldn't lift any weights."

The Dodgers prepared to have reliever Bob Miller replace the retired Sandy Koufax in the starting rotation—Miller, somewhat bizarrely, started Opening Day 1967 after pitching all 46 of his 1966 games in relief—but by mid-May, Singer had locked down his spot, and in June, he threw his first career shutout, striking out 10 to beat Juan Marichal and the Giants. Singer's first full season, though overshadowed by the disappointment of Koufax's departure and the Dodgers' 91-loss, eighth-place finish, was quite successful: a 2.64 ERA (117 ERA+) in 204⅓ innings, with an MLB-leading 0.2 homers per nine innings, and, for future generations to digest, a league-best 2.22 fielding-independent ERA. A 2.88 ERA followed in 1968, though in the year of the pitcher, that meant he was below average except in strikeout rate, which led the NL.

Singer's 1969 season was his personal triumph: 20 wins, 315⅔ innings, and a legitimately great 2.34 ERA (142 ERA+) in 40 starts. He made one relief appearance that year, and even that was historic. In the first game of the season, on April 7 at Cincinnati, Singer took over for Drysdale with a 3–2 lead to start the seventh, and retired nine of the final 10 batters. According to a new official scoring rule—baseball's first since the RBI was introduced in 1920—Singer's three shutout innings were rewarded with a save, the first to ever appear in an MLB box score.

"We're on the way to the ballpark," Singer recalls, "and Walt Alston says, 'Drysdale's starting—can you finish the game?' And I said, 'Sure.' So he went six and I went three, and that was it, and I never knew anything about [the save] for a long time."

In 1970, a hospitalization for hepatitis rendered Singer's first half something of a lost cause, but by July, he was thriving. In six starts, Singer pitched five complete games and 8⅔ innings in the other. On July 20, "The Singer Throwing Machine" sewed up the first Dodger no-hitter since Koufax's retirement, a 5–0 whitewashing of Philadelphia with no walks, an error, and a hit batter. *Los Angeles Times* sportswriter John Wiebusch noted that because Singer's liver was still recuperating, he couldn't drink any celebratory champagne.

"I had everything going for me," Singer says. "I was what they call 'in the zone,' and everything clicked and it was easy."

Injuries plagued Singer in his final two Dodger seasons, but by the time he was included in the November 1972 trade to the California Angels that yielded Andy Messersmith, Singer had given Los Angeles 1,274⅓ innings with a 3.03 ERA (106 ERA+), along with a prelude of a landmark operation to come.

Claude Osteen

By the 1960s, Dodger pitching development was revving like a Mustang, and it wasn't thanks only to Drysdale and Koufax. To illustrate: of the 1,610 games Los Angeles played during the decade, 83 percent were started by pitchers originally signed by the Dodgers. Of the eight Los Angeles pitchers to start at least 50 games in the '60s, seven were homegrown.

Claude Osteen was the standout, in more ways than one.

Ambling in the shadow of three Hall of Fame teammates and not exactly a household name to 21st century fans, Osteen has to be one of the more underrated pitchers in Dodger history. With 26.3 wins above replacement in nine seasons for Los Angeles, Osteen ranked 15th among the franchise's great arms and eighth in Los Angeles. Osteen's 100 complete games tie him for 12th on the all-time Dodger list, and as for shutouts, only his three Hall of Fame contemporaries plus Nap Rucker had more as a Dodger than Osteen's 34.

"We took a lot of pride in finishing the job," Osteen says. "I took a lot of pride in throwing shutouts—it's probably one of the things I'm most proud of."

Osteen played an enormous role in capturing the Dodgers' final World Series title of the '60s, provided a stabilizing bridge to the pennant-winning Dodger teams of the 1970s and extended the Dodger tradition to a later generation as pitching coach from 1999 to 2000. Though it all began for Osteen elsewhere, he nearly had roots as a Dodger as well.

Don Mohr, his baseball coach at Reading High School in Ohio in 1957, also scouted for the Dodgers and got the franchise interested in the young left-hander. The feeling was mutual. But unlike the Dodgers, whose roster was loaded with stars (as well as their bonus baby, Koufax), the nearby Reds could provide the young prospect a faster path to the majors, so Osteen signed with Cincinnati.

"I could spot my fastball—I wasn't overpowering by any means," the 5-foot-11 Osteen says. "I probably wouldn't have gotten signed today. But I was one of those pitchers in the Tom Glavine, Randy Jones, Tommy John mold. You make good pitches, you put movement on the ball, and you get people out, and that's kind of what my forte was."

Befitting the last four letters of his name, Osteen not only signed with the Reds a month before his 18th birthday, he made his major-league debut the same week. He allowed a run in his first inning of relief and pitched 3⅓ shutout innings across two other games before convention took over, and he spent the better part of the next several seasons in the minors. In September 1961, with a career 3.23 ERA in 627 minor-league innings, Osteen was traded from that year's NL pennant winners to the AL's expansion Washington Senators for 30-year-old veteran righty Dave Sisler.

Still only 21, Osteen began 1962 in the Senators' starting rotation and threw his first shutout in his sixth career start. Pitching for a team that lost at least 100 games each of his three full seasons there, Osteen led Washington with a 3.41 ERA (112 ERA+) in 619⅔ innings. That made him attractive enough to become, in December 1964, the main piece in the Dodgers' biggest move of the decade, coming to Los Angeles with John Kennedy and $100,000 in exchange for five players, most notably

28-year-old outfielder Frank Howard, who had hit 123 homers in 624 games.

"They're gambling," Mark Langill says of the Dodgers' mindset at the time. "They're giving up power in Howard, so you better pick the right pitcher. It did pay off, but it was still nonetheless a big, big gamble, because Osteen hadn't necessarily pitched for a winner before."

Just like that, the star Senator now played third fiddle in a rotation with Sandy and Don.

"I knew I was joining what was going to be a great pitching staff, and I had to find out real quick that I couldn't pitch like them," Osteen says. "I had to do it my way, and I kind of learned how to prepare myself."

From the outset in 1965, he was ready. He pitched a two-hit, 3–1 victory with eight strikeouts at Pittsburgh in his Dodger debut. He had a 1.97 ERA through his first nine starts (though only a 3–3 record to show for it) and threw a one-hitter against San Francisco on June 17, though he downplays the achievement.

"I always thought, unless you were a guy like Koufax, no-hitters were kind of freakish," Osteen says. "The one-hitter I pitched, the Giants probably hit the ball harder off me in that game than the majority of games that I pitched."

Were it not for his better-known teammates, Osteen's performance down the stretch in 1965 would be legendary. As the Dodgers rallied from 4½ games back with 16 to play, Osteen started five times and allowed five earned runs, pitching 37⅓ innings with a 1.21 ERA. By season's end, Osteen had made 40 starts with a 2.79 ERA (117 ERA+).

In the World Series, it was Osteen who carried the Dodgers' entire season on his left arm when he took the mound for Game 3, after the rare, back-to-back losses by Drysdale and Koufax put the Dodgers in a dangerous hole.

"I knew the Minnesota club very well," Osteen says. "I was undefeated against them in my career, and I didn't need any scouting reports. I knew every one of them, having pitched against them for three years with Washington. And so that worked out a little bit in my favor."

At first, that confidence against his opponent also came with the butterflies from making his first World Series start.

"I just had so much pent-up energy that I needed to get it all out in one pitch," Osteen says, "and the first pitch I made to Zoilo Versalles—he was the MVP that year—he hit it into the left-field seats for a ground-rule double."

But with runners at the corners and two out, Earl Battey missed a hit-and-run sign and took a 2-0 pitch. Harmon Killebrew froze between first and second—and then Versalles took off for home. Jim Gilliam tagged out Versalles, ending the threat. Osteen got out of a similar first-and-third, sixth-inning jam in more standard fashion with a double play, and went on to pitch a 4-0, five-hit shutout.

"For a guy to have the biggest game of his career when your team needed it the most, very rarely does that happen," Langill says. "You look back at all the big games in Dodger history, and somehow because of his personality and his low-key nature, Osteen never gets credit for that game. It's always Sandy and Don, Sandy and Don, which is great—but without Osteen in '65, there's no championship."

Even Osteen couldn't quite believe that the Dodgers' first postseason victory in '65 went to neither Koufax nor Drysdale, but to him.

"The first year that I was there, that was like a dream come true," Osteen says. "Things just turned out well for me. In every ballgame, you get breaks or breaks go against you. Sometimes you benefit from it, sometimes you don't. I think the first inning was the key to that game."

Though saddled with a Game 6 loss despite allowing only one earned run in five innings, Osteen was able to take pride in a World Series celebration the following day.

Osteen's second year in Los Angeles neatly resembled his first (2.79 ERA, 116 ERA+, and an MLB-best 0.2 home runs per nine innings). His next two seasons were a bit below average, but he recovered in 1969, the year after Drysdale's retirement, to throw a career-high 321 innings with a 2.66 ERA (124 ERA+). In his first five Dodger seasons, Osteen had a 2.91 ERA (108 ERA+) while averaging 39 starts and 278 innings per year.

"I was kind of expected to be some sort of a leader in the way that I pitched," Osteen says. "I couldn't lead by being an overpowering strikeout guy or anything like that. I just had to lead by example of going nine innings most of the time, and winning the game."

As with other Dodger greats, running played an important role for Osteen.

"I was always in great shape," he says. "I worked hard. I ran—back then, running was the key—and I never varied from my routine. If I was going bad, I ran; if I was going good, I ran. And so I had a lot of stamina, and I had to pitch with my brain, because I couldn't overpower anybody.

"Everybody tried to tell me that I was tired when we went into the World Series, and shoot, I never felt better. I refused to accept that. It's kind of like you hear today: If anybody talks about a four-man rotation, the press goes crazy—'there's no way you can do that'—but we did it for 10 years."

Dodger Stadium was Osteen's happiest of homes, and he credited groundskeeper Chris Duca, who had been tending the team's field since his career began with Brooklyn in the 1940s.

"It was the best place in my opinion to pitch in the league," Osteen says. "Everything was immaculate. The stadium was clean, nice. The mound was the best in the league, and the groundskeeper would fix the mound and tailor it to the person who was pitching that night. I liked to have a certain drop. They didn't have to do too much for me, [but] some guys would throw their two cents in to the groundskeeper and bring up little points, like the area immediately behind the rubber where the pitcher steps back to start his windup."

As late as 1972, Osteen went 20–11 with a career-best 2.64 ERA (127 ERA+), followed by a 3.31 ERA (106 ERA+) season in '73. In his final start in a Dodger uniform, the 34-year-old scattered 12 hits in a nine-inning no-decision.

He was still regarded highly enough to go out as he arrived—in a trade for a slugger, this time Jimmy Wynn, who helped lift the Dodgers to the 1974 NL pennant.

"I could see it coming," Osteen says. "I was starting to lose a little bit of command, and pitchers like Doug Rau and the young set [were] starting to show up. And you knew how the game went; you knew how it was played. You're gonna be replaced sooner or later."

Wrapping up his playing career via short tours with the Astros, Cardinals, and White Sox, Osteen retired after the 1975 season, his 18th in the majors, with a 196–195 won-lost record and 3.09 ERA (106 ERA+) in 2,397 innings. For the first 60 years following his 1957 arrival, only 10 left-handers threw more innings in the majors than Osteen.

"It's been a long time, but I tell you, I loved every minute of it," Osteen says. "We had a great ownership—you couldn't find finer people than the O'Malleys. They treated us great, and they just caused you to have a lot of pride in wearing that uniform."

Don Sutton

With Don Sutton, the conversation rarely telescopes into a single game or even a single season.

His career defines his legacy, and a question defines his career: does Sutton deserve to be in the Hall of Fame?

Much of the evidence favors him, validating his 1998 election to Cooperstown, where he resides with more than 75 pitchers inducted since the announcement of the first Hall class in 1936. In the shorthand of wins above replacement, Sutton's 68.8 ranked 30th in the history of baseball's pitchers, 24th since 1901, and ninth across the three decades in which he pitched, the 1960s, '70s, and '80s.

Some counter that Sutton was less than the sum of his achievements obtained over a 23-year career. Sutton was a lunch-pail man—a dedicated, reliable one—but a VP rather than a president much of the time. His 3.26 career ERA (108 ERA+) flattens in the horizon. His perennial quest for a 20-win season, 11 years in the making and 12 years without being repeated, implicitly portrayed him a wannabe. He had a 3.34 ERA in 10 playoff games for the Dodgers, averaging more than seven innings per start, but never pitched for a World Series champion. Five one-hitters, but never a no-hitter. Sutton himself spoke humbly at times, once saying that "comparing me to Sandy Koufax is like comparing Earl Scheib to Michelangelo."

Sutton had spectacular games, outlandish streaks, and wonderful years, but the longer he pitched, the hazier the memory of them became, until all that seemingly remained was a curly haired vet with, *yawn*, 324 wins, 58 shutouts, 3,574 strikeouts, and (as if it weren't an achievement in itself) 5,282⅓ innings.

Since 1901, Sutton ranked in the top 10 in each of those categories. If he took his time, in the end, Sutton was elite.

"Don Sutton should unquestionably be elected to the Hall of Fame," wrote Bill James in 1994, at the outset of Sutton's eligibility. "Yes, I know Sutton didn't 'seem like' a Hall of Fame pitcher to many of you…The facts are, however, that there is no pitcher with a record remotely comparable to Sutton's who is not in the Hall of Fame, [and] there are many pitchers with much worse records than Sutton who are in the Hall of Fame. So if you don't elect Sutton, then in effect he blocks the door."

The 6-foot-1 right-hander ranked third in big-league history in games started, behind only Cy Young and Nolan Ryan, and seventh in innings pitched. In all his seasons, he averaged seven innings per start, never landing on the disabled list until he was 43 years old.

"I think it's fair to say of baseball history, never missing a start is extraordinary," says Eric Enders. "Even compared to his peer group, which was the most durable group of starters in baseball history, even among those guys Sutton was the most durable, so that's really impressive."

Thomas Boswell of the *Washington Post* wrote that Sutton's delayed election to the Hall was "one of baseball's most ludicrous injustices." In an insightful pop quiz, Murray Chass of *The New York Times* once asked 16 MLB general managers which pitcher they would rather have for his entire career: Koufax or Sutton?

"As intriguing as they all found the exercise, the outcome was just as intriguing because the general managers were clearly divided," Chass wrote. "Eight selected Koufax, six chose Sutton, and two said they could not decide...Those who chose Sutton generally said pitching is so fragile that it would be difficult to turn down the chance to get a pitcher who could last 23 years and win consistently, if not spectacularly."

On the mound, Sutton mixed his offerings like a master bartender. "I don't think too many pitchers have mastered as many pitches as he has," said his first manager, Walter Alston.

"He has such a variety of pitches that he's never dependent on just one," noted Ryan, the Hall of Famer and all-time MLB strikeout leader who was Sutton's teammate in 1981–82 with the Astros. "He has the versatility to adjust. A two-pitch pitcher like me can have problems if one of them—with me, the curve—isn't getting over. Don can just go to something else."

Unlike many hurlers who lead with their heater, Sutton cast his fastball in a beguiling supporting role. Asked to compare himself to Astros flamethrower J.R. Richard, Sutton said, "We all know what he can do with his stuff. He's tremendous. What I'd like to see is what he could do with my stuff."

The star of Sutton's ensemble was his curveball—an "incredible curveball," teammate Charlie Hough emphasizes. "He crimps his index finger atop the ball," wrote Jim Murray, "which makes the ball appear to dive for the ground like a crashing airplane. He can throw this malicious mischief for a strike." But Sutton learned not to lean on it too heavily.

"This goes back to Red Adams," Tommy John says. "Don had a great curveball, outstanding curveball, and Red kept telling him, 'You'll be a better pitcher when you use your fastball more.' And when Don started using his fastball and getting guys out with his fastball, it made his already outstanding curveball even better. And then he came up with a little cutter that he could throw in on lefties. Don was an outstanding pitcher and outstanding competitor."

Yet for all his steadfast ability, Sutton's personality and presence in Los Angeles revealed themselves to be as complicated as his pitching repertoire. Longer than any other Dodger pitcher, he was the centerpiece of serious trade talks. Several times, newspapers reported his departure as imminent. These weren't just wild rumors—often, Dodger executives and Sutton himself openly discussed the possibility of him leaving town. He frequently wondered aloud if the grass were greener elsewhere, either playing for another team or moving onto another profession, namely broadcasting. In practically the same breath, he unabashedly admitted how much he valued his rising place in the Dodger record books. He could be charming and unnerving in the same conversation.

"He's very complex," Adams said.

Sprinkled on top of this restlessness were ceaseless accusations from opponents of doctoring the baseball, nicking it up, sanding it down—allegations Sutton simultaneously resented and encouraged.

"I'll never say what I do or don't do to the ball," he said. "If they think I'm cutting it up, fine. It gives them one more thing to worry about."

Sports Illustrated writer Ron Fimrite related how umpires reached into Sutton's uniform pockets in pursuit of incriminating evidence, recovering notes that read NOT HERE or YOU'RE GETTING WARMER. Accused of moistening the baseball with a "foreign substance," Sutton zippily denied it.

"Not true at all," he said. "Vaseline is manufactured right here in the United States of America."

Amid all his internal and external contradictions, there was no mistaking Sutton's singular desire to succeed.

Born in Clio, Alabama, on April 2, 1945 (the same date as future teammates Mike Kekich and Reggie Smith), Sutton was the son of teenage sharecroppers and fiercely proud of their influence on him. "God gave him the curveball, but Dad gave him the work ethic," Murray wrote.

"He married at 17 and had only a seventh-grade education, but he'd work on the farm all day and then go to night school," Sutton said of his father. "He finally got his high school diploma and things opened up for him. He was an excellent carpenter, and he went to work for a construction company...I think you can see that the work ethic was ingrained in me a long time ago. That's why I feel comfortable working at my profession the year round. I am never not in training."

As opposed to his heroes Koufax and Don Drysdale, the young Sutton didn't stumble into pitching. "Sutton considered himself to be a professional ballplayer by age 11," Fimrite wrote.

"My mother used to worry about my imaginary friends 'cause I would be out in the yard playing ball," Sutton said. "She worried because she didn't know a Mickey, or a Whitey, or a Yogi, or a Moose, or an Elston, but I played with them every day.

"Other kids my age were playing for fun. I was playing to get to the big leagues. It was all just training for me. Everything was a stepping-stone. I don't know that I ever had a childhood."

Sketch an outline of a boy with this level of determination and focus, then color it with the will to seek an education and the precociousness to improvise when necessary.

"I've been fortunate," Sutton said. "Every time I've needed somebody, they've always been there. My sixth-grade teacher, Henry Roper, pitched in the Giants organization. I hounded him until he taught me some things. He got me throwing breaking balls when I was behind the hitter.

All young hitters are looking for the fastball then. It was a break with convention.

"I learned how to throw a curve by raising my index finger and digging the tip into the ball. I have small hands—unlike someone like Koufax, who had long fingers and could wrap them around the ball—so I use a different grip for every one of my pitches."

Sutton signed with the Dodgers in 1964 at age 19 out of Florida's Gulf Coast Community College, choosing Los Angeles over more lucrative offers from the Astros and A's based on the organizational pitch by scouts Monty Basgall, Bert Wells, and John Keenan. His minor-league debut in 1965 screamed potential—a 1.50 ERA in 10 starts (averaging 8.4 innings) for Single-A Santa Barbara, then a 2.78 ERA in 21 starts (averaging 7.9 innings) for Double-A Albuquerque. For the year, he pitched 249 innings with 239 strikeouts, a 1.02 WHIP, and 24 complete games, a prospect for whom innings limits and pitch counts would have meant nothing.

On September 10, almost precisely on the one-year anniversary of signing him, the Dodgers promoted Sutton to the majors, but in the blazing heat of that '65 pennant race he did not pitch, and no one handed him a rotation spot entering the 1966 season. He'd go up against veterans of different ages: 33-year-old Johnny Podres, 28-year-old Phil Regan, and 23-year-old Joe Moeller. For a month, the Drysdale-Koufax holdout opened spots for all, but as the preseason days rolled on, Sutton became the talk of Dodgertown, retaining his rotation candidacy even after the team's twin aces returned.

"The singular attraction about Sutton this spring was that he seemed to throw 20-year-old stuff with a 40-year-old head," *Sports Illustrated* writer Jack Mann reported.

"I may not win the MVP award, but I think I can win in the National League," Sutton said on the eve of his 21st birthday, for which his present would be his first encounter with Willie McCovey and the Giants in an exhibition game. "And I may not be on Mr. Alston's team the whole season, but I am going to be on it at least part of the time, and that's something I've wanted to do ever since I was six years old."

Los Angeles Times beat writer Frank Finch noted that Sutton, who was prone to nervousness on game days, watched the Giants hit several homers during batting practice and then went back into the clubhouse to read George Christian Anderson's book, *Man's Right to Be Human*.

"It deals with psychiatry and religion in man's life," Sutton explained.

Described by Finch as "the likeable Alabaman with the brashness of youth and the pose of an old pro," Sutton fanned four batters across three shutout innings in his unofficial Dodger Stadium debut April 10 in an exhibition against the Indians, clinching his spot in the rotation. "This kid Sutton is going to make the fans like him," Alston said. "He's got the best command of a curveball I ever saw for a youngster."

On April 14, in the Dodgers' third game of the 1966 campaign, Sutton took the mound at Dodger Stadium for real. During his first seven innings, he struck out seven while holding Houston to an unearned run (and went 2-for-3 at the plate), but he walked Sonny Jackson to lead off the eighth and, despite a mound visit by Alston, surrendered a game-tying RBI double to future Dodger Jim Wynn. In relief, Ron Perranoski allowed a two-run homer to Rusty Staub, saddling Sutton with the 4–2 loss.

Four days later in Houston, however, Sutton grabbed his first big-league victory, strolling through eight innings in a 6–3 win. His parents, listening from Florida to a New Orleans station that was part of the Astros radio network, tracked him down by phone in the visitors' clubhouse.

"They've rooted for me ever since I was a Little Leaguer, and they were pretty proud tonight," said a grinning Sutton.

Sutton struck out 10 Atlanta Braves in his first complete game on April 27, pitched his first shutout on May 11 against the Phillies, and two-hit Cincinnati in a 2–0 whitewashing on August 16. At one ballpark after another, future Hall of Famers paid tribute to his confidence and command.

"I like his poise, but I like his stuff even better," Richie Ashburn said. "He acts like he wants to stick around for a long time."

"Hell! He throws that [breaking ball] on 3-and-2 with the bases loaded," Eddie Mathews complained to Murray. "Somebody should explain things to that rook."

Sutton's strangest predicament during his freshman year was that in his first 10 starts, he was hit by batted balls five times. He finished 1966 with a 2.99 ERA (110 ERA+) in 225⅔ innings, striking out 209—the most by an NL rookie since Grover Cleveland Alexander's 227 in 1911. He would have whiffed more if not for a right forearm injury—a rarity in his long career—pulling a muscle September 5 against the Giants. (He was the fourth Dodger starting pitcher in as many days to leave a game early for physical reasons, following Osteen, Koufax, and Drysdale.) Sutton made three more starts in 1966, lasting four innings in each.

Perhaps showing lingering effects of having thrown nearly 500 professional innings in the two years before turning 22, Sutton's 1967 season (at the outset of the Dodgers' post-Koufax doldrums) was his worst in the majors, with a 3.95 ERA (78 ERA+) in 232⅔ innings, though he did have his second two-hit shutout against Cincinnati in as many seasons.

"When he was right, 8 of 10 curveballs broke sharply, but lately, less of them have," Alston said that July. "Maybe, subconsciously, he is afraid to break off a sharp curve because of the muscle injury he suffered last season."

Sutton's topsy-turvy 1968 began with the first of many unfulfilled trade rumors in his career, one that had Sutton going to Baltimore for 34-year-old shortstop Luis Aparicio. Remaining a Dodger, Sutton still commenced the season in the minors, having missed most of spring training while finishing a six-month Army Reserve commitment. Called up in late April to stay, Sutton soon had his first memorable encounter with the baseball patrol. In a June 10 duel against fellow 23-year-old Tom

Seaver and the Mets, scoreless through nine innings, home-plate umpire Sam Sudol investigated Sutton for mischief.

"I did it on my own," Sudol said. "Some of his pitches were doing unusual things. But after a thorough investigation of his cap, uniform, and glove, I was convinced he was using nothing but his hand. As far as I'm concerned, Sutton just has one helluva sinker."

Said Sutton: "Sudol met me as I was crossing the line to start the ninth inning and told me the Mets were protesting that Sutton was using an illegal pitch. I told him to come out anytime. After I threw a strike to Art Shamsky in the ninth, Sudol started for the mound. I met him halfway, handed him my cap and glove. He looked me over pretty good, even felt in both pockets, and then he apologized for doing it.

"I feel I can get by with my natural stuff and don't need anything else."

Later in June, Alston dispatched Sutton to the bullpen for the only time in his career. Combined with two more weeks of Army Reserve duty in July, Sutton went more than a month between starts. He took the sabbatical as a call to action.

"I'm stubborn and I'm ambitious," Sutton said, "and I was angry when I was sent to the bullpen. But it made me want to be a starter more than ever. [Pitching coach Lefty Phillips] started working with me on a new changeup the day I went to the bullpen. It is a modified screwball…it has given me a third good pitch. I've been getting strikeouts on my curve, my fastball, and now my screwball."

Returning to the rotation for good on July 28, Sutton had a 2.06 ERA in his final 109 innings of '68, concluding with a 2.60 ERA (106 ERA+), a 2.08 FIP, and an MLB-leading 0.3 home runs per nine innings (six in 207⅔).

Come 1969, Sutton threw his first career one-hitter May 1 at San Francisco, taking a no-hitter into the eighth inning before Jim Davenport lined a double off the left-field fence. He concluded the one-hit shutout to extend what became a 27-inning scoreless streak. In a tight, three-team race in the newly formed NL West, Sutton's complete-game victory

September 18 over Atlanta tied the Dodgers with the Braves, half a game behind the Giants. But Los Angeles dropped its next eight games, including heartbreaking, back-to-back 2–1, complete-game losses by Sutton—the first despite leading 1–0 with two out, the bases empty, and an 0-2 count in the bottom of the ninth.

Having finished 1969 with a nearly average 3.47 ERA (96 ERA+), Sutton began the 1970s with more sparkling moments in an otherwise disappointing year. He threw a 10-inning shutout July 17 against the Mets with 12 strikeouts. "That's as good a stuff as Don will ever have," said first baseman Wes Parker. "He was absolutely breathtaking." Always on the verge of a breakthrough season, Sutton's latest midseason slump—in this case, a 15.63 ERA in his first four starts of August—set him back.

"He has the same stuff," Alston said. "It's a matter, mostly, of his control. Either he's right down the gun or he's wild high…and when he gets behind the hitters he's forced to come in with fat ones."

Sutton's ERA at the end of 1970 was the worst of his Dodger career: 4.08 (94 ERA+). Ninth in the NL in innings, Sutton was tied for first in earned runs allowed. Through the age of 25, Sutton had already thrown 1,219⅔ innings, but his career ERA of 3.45 (95 ERA+) in that era underwhelmed. Not the first promising Dodger pitcher to struggle well into his twenties—Koufax being the most famous—Sutton confronted some familiar tropes from those trying to explain it.

"Yes, I'm hardheaded," Sutton said during spring training in 1971. "I'm aware that's what some people in the organization say about me, and I admit that it's true. My feeling is that I'd have never made it to the majors if I hadn't been hardheaded. People said I didn't have the ability, I didn't have the right style. I'm hardheaded enough to believe in the way I do things.

"But I'm also not hardheaded to the point that I think I'm smarter than the manager or the pitching coach. I'll accept changes if I think they'll help me."

Having spoken with Alston and Adams, Ross Newhan of the *Los Angeles Times* wrote that "it has been the inconsistency of [Sutton's curveball] compounded by the straightening fastball that has in recent years retarded Sutton's growth." Sutton didn't dispute this.

"I admit that there have been games when I've attempted to grind it out with a bad curve," he said. "It's always been such a good pitch for me that in those games, I just can't believe it won't snap back."

But in '71, the pitcher who became the Hall of Famer emerged. In 265⅓ innings, Sutton finished fifth in the NL with a 2.54 ERA (127 ERA+) and a 1.08 WHIP. Adams, according to Newhan in May, "went back and looked at movies of Sutton's style in 1966 and then made an adjustment that benefited the curve." From May 27 on, Sutton's ERA was 1.91 in 202⅔ frames, despite pitching through elbow pain in June, his worst discomfort since the end of 1966.

Sutton one-hit Houston on June 19, the lone blemish Jim Wynn's slicing liner to center that tipped off the glove of a diving Dick Allen. After finally completing his six-year Army Reserve commitment at the start of August, Sutton had a 1.75 ERA in his final 92⅓ innings. Entering the final day of the regular season, the Dodgers were one game behind the Giants in the NL West. Sutton went the distance for a 2–1 victory, but Juan Marichal's complete game over the Padres pitched San Francisco to the division title.

Then, at age 27 in 1972, came Sutton's masterpiece season, the one that is too often ignored, even by those in the Dodgers' orbit.

In his first 10 starts, Sutton allowed only 11 earned runs while averaging 8⅔ innings per outing, for a 1.14 ERA, including a May 7 Sunday afternoon at Parc Jarry in Montreal when he pitched 10 innings of one-hit, shutout ball. In Sutton's first All-Star Game—"my greatest thrill in sports," he said at the time—his first batter, Reggie Jackson, hit a leadoff single, and the remaining six went down in order: Allen, Carl Yastrzemski, Bobby Grich, Brooks Robinson, Bill Freehan, and Mickey Lolich. Sutton finished September riding 36 consecutive innings without allowing an earned run, including an 11-inning, 1–0 shutout of the Giants for his 100th career victory, then tossed in a complete-game victory October 3 over Atlanta in his final start for good measure.

Sutton's 2.08 ERA, 162 ERA+, and 18 complete games (in 272⅔ innings) were career bests, as were his league-leading nine shutouts, 0.91 WHIP, and 6.1 hits per nine innings. For the first 20 seasons of the post-Koufax era, no Dodger pitcher bettered Sutton's 6.6 wins above replacement. This was the real deal. Unfortunately for Sutton, his greatest season slammed against of the most famous pitching years of all time: that of Steve Carlton, who went 27–10 with a 1.97 ERA (182 ERA+) for a Phillies team that was 59–97 (30–85 when Carlton didn't start). Sutton also lagged in the stat that mattered most in that era, settling for 19 wins.

"People don't acknowledge you as a good pitcher until you win 20, but if I don't, it won't be the end of the world," Sutton said at the time.

In 1973, his second consecutive All-Star season, Sutton affirmed his place among the best in baseball with a 2.42 ERA (144 ERA+) in 256⅓ innings and his fifth 200-strikeout season, hitting the magic number September 25 by striking out Dusty Baker and Davey Johnson to end his 14th complete game of the year. From 1971 to 1973, only Seaver's adjusted ERA bettered Sutton's.

"When Sutton has his control, he ranks up there with Seaver as the best right-hander in the league," said Hank Aaron, who went 0-for-4 on September 25 in his bid for a 713th career homer—then took Sutton on a fishing trip after the season.

In 1974, the final year of his twenties, Sutton threw a career-high 40 starts with a 3.23 ERA (106 ERA+), beginning with an Opening Day shutout of the Padres and including his third career one-hitter, May 9 at San Diego. Oddly, Sutton reached the All-Star break with a 14-start winless streak that dropped his record to 6–8 with a 4.21 ERA. By his own admission, Sutton still struggled not to sabotage himself.

"Sometimes I think my temperament works against me," he said. "After a bad game...I tend to try and double my efforts. Rather than staying and relaxing in a groove, I begin pressing. I guess that might be it.

"The key is in handling the bad times. Henry Aaron has a batting slump but he doesn't change his stance. The great players keep doing the things they've always done. They stay in a groove. They don't fight it."

In the second half, Sutton went 13–1 with a 2.17 ERA, including a 1.79 ERA in seven September starts as the Dodgers fended off a strong challenge from the Reds. Entering play October 1 with 100 wins, the Dodgers had been in first place for 5½ months but led Cincinnati by only two games with two remaining. Sutton took the mound against Houston and won his 19th game of the season with five shutout innings, exiting to a happy reception after news arrived from Atlanta of the Braves' victory over the Reds, eliminating Cincinnati from the race.

Ten seasons into his career, having sat on the sidelines during the 1965 and 1966 World Series, Sutton finally got to pitch for a playoff team. "Now I'm a part of it, and it's a great feeling," he said before shutting out Pittsburgh in Game 1 of the NLCS, 3–0, allowing six baserunners, none of whom would have passed first base except for a Dodger error.

"That was the greatest display of pitching I've seen by anybody all year," Davey Lopes said.

"Sutton's artistry may have come to a surprise to the country at large because he has been living in the shadow of contemporaries like Tom Seaver and Bob Gibson," Murray wrote. "When he broke in, he was in the shadow of teammates Sandy Koufax, Don Drysdale, and even Claude Osteen. He was like the guy who came to shift the scenery or turn the pages at the podium."

On three days' rest, Sutton presided over the 12–1, Game 4 clincher with eight innings of one-run ball before leaving with a blister. "His breaking pitches dipped and hooked and nosedived sharply all afternoon," wrote Jeff Prugh of the *Los Angeles Times*. "They demoralized the Pirate hitters so much that they insisted in their red-faced frustration that Sutton *had* to be illegally doctoring the baseball." Plate umpire John McSherry examined Sutton's glove in the fifth inning, returned it to him, and that was that.

In his World Series debut, Sutton ran his postseason winning streak to three games when his 3–2, Game 2 victory over Oakland evened the World Series at one win apiece. Striking out nine, Sutton took a shutout into the ninth inning, then yielded two baserunners who scored on Mike Marshall's watch before the record-setting relief pitcher closed it out. With the Dodgers facing elimination in Game 5, Sutton left for a pinch hitter as the Dodgers tied the game at 2–2 in the sixth. One inning later, Marshall allowed the final run of the game, and the season. For the 1974 playoffs, Sutton's ERA was 1.50 in 30 innings with 25 strikeouts against 23 baserunners.

Coming back in 1975, Sutton received new guidance from an unexpected source. Juan Marichal, the longtime Dodger nemesis from San Francisco, hooked up with Los Angeles during spring training at age 37. In a brief echo of Sal Maglie mentoring a young Drysdale in the 1950s, Marichal (though he made only two April starts before being released) and Sutton found time to connect. "I used to hate him like everyone else on our club, but since he's been over here he's been a good friend," Sutton said. "We've talked quite a bit about pitching. We're similar. We throw breaking balls for strikes and spot the fastballs."

Others saw the resemblance. "Sutton gets better every time I see him—he's unbelievable," Reds second baseman Joe Morgan said April 15, after Sutton pitched six no-hit innings on his way to his fourth career one-hitter. "The only guy he reminds me of is Marichal, in his prime. Marichal moved the ball around better than anyone I'd ever seen."

After back-to-back complete games August 5 and 10, Sutton was 16–9 with a 2.38 ERA. But he didn't pick up another win that year, not even when he held Montreal to one earned run in 11 innings on August 24. Sutton's season ended September 12 after he sprained his ankle while sliding into second on a double in a 2–1 loss to Atlanta, leaving him with a 2.87 ERA (119 ERA+) and a league-leading 1.04 WHIP in 254⅓ innings. The Dodgers were held to three runs or fewer in 21 of his 35 starts.

For his first 10 seasons, Sutton averaged 15.5 wins per year. Already the team's No. 2 all-time leader in shutouts and fourth in strikeouts, Sutton's inability to reach 20 wins in any season frustrated pretty much everyone, including himself. In the winter, he told Peter O'Malley that he'd happily relocate to the AL, believing that the new designated-hitter rule would allow him to stay in more games and get more wins (and apparently not fretting over having to face an extra hitter in opposing lineups). Before the 1976 season began, talk of a monumental trade involving Sutton and Seaver, winner of the 1975 NL Cy Young Award, broke beyond rumor. Mets general manager Joe McDonald conferred with Sutton's agent, Larue Harcourt, about a contract renegotiation—imagine the shock waves from New York to Los Angeles if this one had gone through. But Seaver stayed put, and Sutton, whose service time gave him veto power over any trade, turned one down shipping him and Dodger infielder Jerry Royster to New York for 26-year-old Jon Matlack.

Thus beginning his 11th year in Los Angeles, Sutton struggled with the longest and toughest opening slump of his career, taking a 4.35 ERA into August—at which point he embarked upon the finest stretch run of his life. Beginning August 10, he won eight straight starts with a 1.17 ERA, boosting his record from 11–9 to 19–9 with three weeks to go, and suddenly, the long-delayed, gleaming "20" was within reach. But it wasn't going to be that easy. In his next start, the first game of a September 17 doubleheader in Atlanta, Sutton pitched 11 shutout innings in a game Hough and the Dodgers lost in the bottom of the 12th on an infield single, sacrifice, wild pitch, and passed ball.

On September 22, Sutton took the mound at Candlestick Park in San Francisco. He fell behind 1–0 in the second inning, but the Dodgers tied the game in the third, took the lead in the seventh, and added an insurance run in top of the ninth. With two out in the bottom of the ninth, Sutton walked Darrell Evans, bringing Jack Clark to the plate as the tying run. Sutton struck him out, and at last, for one year, he had the wins to match the No. 20 on the back of his uniform.

"I'm numb," Sutton said. "This is something I've wanted all my life, something I feel I've pitched well enough to achieve before, and right now I'd say it's the biggest thrill of my career, more exciting even than the first pitch of a World Series. I know that sounds selfish but at this moment I don't really care.

"One of the reasons this is so rewarding is that there are so many people sharing it with me. In fact, of all the people who are relieved and happy right now, I'm probably the least. There are my parents, who made so many sacrifices so that I could pitch. There's my wife and children, who catch hell when I lose because I haven't yet learned to accept the fact that I can't win every time I walk out there. There's Red Adams, who's been like a father to me, and Walter Alston, who stuck with me early this season and parts of the '74 season when I was the ugliest pitcher in baseball."

Finishing the season with two more complete games, Sutton averaged $9\frac{1}{3}$ innings in his final 10 starts of the year, giving him a 3.06 ERA (110 ERA+) in $267\frac{2}{3}$ innings to go with his 21–10 record. For the fifth consecutive year, Sutton finished in the top five in the NL Cy Young balloting without winning.

Then, at the most gratifying moment of his career to date, turbulence returned to Sutton's baseball world.

Alston had managed the Dodgers for 23 seasons, the last 19 of them in Los Angeles, the last 11 with Sutton in his starting rotation. But Alston retired at the end of September, the job officially passing to Tommy Lasorda. The new manager was a hurricane of fresh air for a number of Dodgers, but for those who worshiped the John Wayne–like Alston, it was Tropical Storm Tommy.

The longtime organization man and most recently the Dodgers' third-base coach, Lasorda was obviously no stranger to Sutton. The pair had even traveled together all the way to Fairbanks, Alaska, before spring training in 1967 to conduct baseball clinics in the middle of February. But Sutton's loyalty to Alston and penchant for straight talking put his relationship with his new manager on poor footing.

"The question was posed to me: 'What do you think about Walter Alston retiring?'" Sutton recalled. "And I said, 'I'd rather he didn't.' Next question was, 'Who would you pick to manage the Dodgers?' And I said, 'Jeff Torborg,' because I saw in him a lot of Walt's qualities. And that probably was purely selfish on my part, because I didn't want any change in the atmosphere."

A religious man, Sutton also bristled under Lasorda's evangelistic style.

"I always regarded the Big Dodger in the Sky as somewhat sacrilegious," Sutton said. "For all I know, God may not even like baseball. He may be a football fan. Under any circumstances, I don't think He should be considered a pocket good-luck charm that you can pull out when you need it.

"I know Tommy didn't mean it disrespectfully. He's just a gung-ho, emotional man. He goes sky-high over a win and hits a deep depression over a loss. Walter always said you should never gloat on the peaks and never stay in the valleys. I spent so many of my years with Walter, the transition was very difficult for me. It took me years to understand Tommy. I still don't necessarily agree with him, but at least I think I understand him. For that matter, I doubt whether he agreed with a lot of my hanging curveballs."

If nothing else, the pair learned to coexist.

"I didn't feel we were as close as we should be. But we got along. It never got to the point where we weren't on speaking terms," Lasorda said. "But one thing about Don Sutton—he kept himself in great shape. Great work ethic. Good, clean-living young man. So it was just a feeling that we had, but I think it simmered down and we became closer.

Said Sutton: "One regret I have is that Tommy and I never took a day, just the two of us, and sat down and explained our personalities to each other. But I knew then, and I know now, Tommy will do whatever it takes to give his club an opportunity to win, and I think he knows, and has said publicly, that he could always count on me."

A new contract—a four-year, $1 million deal that was the richest in Dodger history—figured to ease Sutton's mind, along with a wintertime gig as a color commentator for Pepperdine and Long Beach State basketball telecasts, indulging his broadcasting aspirations. Somehow, reports persisted that Sutton remained unsatisfied. In March, the Dodgers proposed trading Sutton to the Red Sox for promising 24-year-old slugger Jim Rice, a deal Sutton would have approved, but Boston backed out.

When Sutton threw his first pitch of the 1977 season and Lasorda's reign, using a baseball intended to be preserved for posterity, San Francisco outfielder Gary Thomasson smacked it into the right-field pavilion—so much for ceremony. But that was the only run to score off Sutton, who won 5–1 to ignite a robust beginning under Lasorda's new regime. Going 10–4 with a 2.58 ERA in the first half of the season, Sutton made his fourth All-Star Game, starting for the first time. Retiring 9 of 11 batters and striking out four in three shutout innings, Sutton was the winning pitcher and MVP in a 7–5 NL victory.

Projecting calm on the field, Sutton's emotions still surfaced in times of stress. After allowing a game-losing ninth-inning grand slam August 12 to Rod Gilbreath of Atlanta, Sutton blew up in the clubhouse. "I put it to five lockers, two tables, two chairs, and the housing for a fire extinguisher," he said. "And I feel a lot better about it. I usually have two blowups a year and I had this one coming. I feel relieved, but then the Dodgers haven't billed me yet."

Ill spirits purged for the time being, Sutton in his next start made his last and best no-hit bid, coming within four outs August 18 before Giants catcher Marc Hill singled to left. In pitching his fifth one-hitter, Sutton tied the NL record (later broken by Carlton), while winning his 187th game, matching Drysdale's L.A. record. Ten days later, with another shutout, Sutton broke the mark.

Sutton finished '77 with a 3.18 ERA (121 ERA+). The Dodgers breezed to the NL West title, outpacing the division by 10 games, and Sutton won Game 2 of the NLCS with a complete-game nine-hitter. In the World Series, Sutton pitched well but with little reward. He held the Yankees to three runs in seven innings of Game 1; the Dodgers lost in the 12th. With the Dodgers facing elimination in Game 5, Sutton dished off six shutout innings while the Dodgers built a 10–0 lead, going the distance in a 108-pitch, 10–4 win, only for Los Angeles to fall under the onslaught of Jackson's three homers in Game 6.

With the years mounting, each new season carried Sutton to one milestone after another. In 1978, Sutton defeated Atlanta in his seventh Opening Day start, tying Drysdale's team record. On June 30, Little D passed Big D to become the Dodgers' all-time strikeout leader. On September 15, Sutton blanked Atlanta to tie another Drysdale record with his 49th shutout as a Dodger.

"I'm definitely thinking about these records, and I don't think that's selfish," Sutton said. "It means a great deal to me to be thought of in the same terms—the statistical terms, at least—as Drysdale and Koufax. I can't think of a better example of ability and durability."

For many other reasons, 1978 was…an eventful year. On July 14, years upon years of accusations came to a head, when umpire Doug Harvey ejected Sutton (seeking his 200th career victory that day) in the seventh inning against the Cardinals for using a defiled ball.

"In the second or third inning, my first-base umpire got the ball back on a third out and said, 'Doug, this ball has been defaced,'" explained Harvey, himself a future Hall of Famer. "I told him to take the ball to home-plate ump Jim Quick. In the sixth inning, there was a fly to [center fielder Bill] North and the ball had an identical-type scuff mark. I went to Lasorda and said, 'Tom, someone's messing with the baseball. If we find another one, we will eject the pitcher.' When we found another, I said, 'We're not finding it at any other time than when Sutton's pitching. He's out of the game.'"

Said Lasorda: "[Harvey] showed me the ball. I didn't see anything wrong with it. I protested because he had no right to throw Sutton out of the ballgame. He's accusing my player of doing something to the ball. I don't think someone can deprive him of a living. He did absolutely nothing to the ball."

That part about depriving Sutton of his livelihood was no idle comment by Lasorda.

"After he had been thrown out of the game," Scott Ostler of the *Los Angeles Times* wrote, "Sutton returned to the discussion near home plate and handed Harvey a piece of paper. Harvey slapped it out of his hands without reading it, but it was apparently a hastily scrawled notice of Sutton's intent to sue."

Subject to a 10-day suspension, Sutton got none. He and his attorney, Ed Hookstratten, met with NL president Chub Feeney for two hours in New York, and came away with a warning from the league office that "additional disciplinary action may be taken in the event repeated violations of this nature are detected." Satisfied, Sutton reveled in his unique style. Wearing a shirt under his uniform that said NOT GUILTY in his next start, closely examining baseballs out in the open—"like a geologist inspecting a series of fascinating rocks," wrote Ostler—as if to make sure he wasn't being framed, Sutton picked up his 200th career victory with a 7–2 complete-game victory July 18 over the Pirates.

For a moment, peace. And then in the next, another war.

Before a Sunday afternoon game on August 20 at Shea Stadium, Steve Garvey confronted Sutton with quotes condensed from a Boswell story in the *New York Post*. "All you hear about on our team is Steve Garvey, the All-American boy," Sutton had said. "Well, the best player on this team for the last two years—and we all know it—is Reggie Smith. Reggie doesn't go out and publicize himself. He doesn't smile at the right people or say the right things…Reggie's not a facade or a Madison Avenue image. He's a real person."

Their tête-à-tête began, serious but quiet. Suddenly, according to UPI reporter Milton Richman, "Sutton leaped at Garvey and flung him against a row of lockers along the opposite wall." They brawled in the visitors' clubhouse in open view of reporters, with teammates needing to separate them. Faces were scratched. Garvey's right eye was bloodied.

Sutton apologized with an emotional public statement that took stock of himself: "For the last few days, I have thought of nothing else and I've tried over and over to figure out why this all had to happen. The only possible reason I can find is that my life isn't being lived according to what I know, as a human being and a Christian, to be right. If it were, then there would not have been an article in which I would offend any of my teammates."

Hugely popular, Garvey had the support of the fan base. Dodger fans booed Sutton, though he pitched better down the stretch than he had in the first half of the season, finishing his year with a 3.55 ERA (99 ERA+). Sutton admitted that the negativity stung.

"Darn right it bothers me," he said. "In 13 years I've experienced a lot of highs and lows. In 13 years I've made some positive contributions and interjected some negatives. I've always tried to be honest, and it seems to me that people are taking a little bit of information and making concrete judgments that have hurt both my family and myself.

"If they're booking on the basis of performance, that's one thing. But I don't think that's the issue here."

Putting the noise behind him and moving into October bearing a 2.13 career playoff ERA, with his path to the summit of the Dodger record book largely carved out, Sutton focused keenly on a title. "A world championship," he said, "is the last of my childhood dreams." But Sutton had his first disappointing postseason, losing once in the NLCS and twice in the World Series, allowing 14 earned runs in 17⅔ innings, including the defeat October 17 in the decisive Game 6.

"An hour after the game," Ostler wrote, "Sutton slumped into the canvas-backed chair in front of his locker and stared blankly at the wall, his back to the busy Dodger clubhouse. His eyes were red and his voice was shaking with emotion."

"It just keeps haunting me that I might never be here again," Sutton said, in what Ostler called a hoarse whisper. "I'm 33 years old, I've played 13 years, I've been here three times before, and I might never be here again.

"Just once I wanna win it all. Just once."

It wasn't going to be in 1979, the Dodgers hitting the All-Star break in last place and scrambling just to finish third. With a 3.82 ERA (95 ERA+), Sutton had his poorest year since 1970, though he did break the Dodgers' all-time win record with his 210th on May 20 against the Reds, the strikeout record with his 2,487th on August 5 against the Giants, and the shutout record with his 50th on August 10 at San Francisco.

Remaining outspoken and occasionally alienated, Sutton vented after Lasorda pinch-hit for him in the sixth inning on June 5 against Pittsburgh. "I have more wins than anyone in this organization," Sutton said. "I don't have to put up with it. I'm not one of his bobos. They can't fire me." When he broke the strikeout record, he talked openly about the possibility of retiring to broadcasting, with his agent Hookstratten eyeing openings in the Angels booth. For the NL playoffs, Sutton joined Joe Garagiola and Tony Kubek to provide color commentary for NBC, shifting back to humility for the national audience.

"Well, Joe, I helped both of these clubs get here—I contributed heavily to their being in the playoffs." Sutton deadpanned in his opening remarks. (It wasn't really true—Sutton's ERA against the two teams was 2.58.)

Sutton returned to the mound in 1980—eventually. When time came for pitchers and catchers to report for spring training, Sutton, in the last year of his contract, wasn't there. Again, speculation about his future in Los Angeles arose. In mid-March, the Associated Press reported that Sutton was on the verge of going to the Yankees, except that the Yankees wouldn't part with 21-year-old pitching prospect Dave Righetti.

"It wouldn't be spring without a Sutton trade rumor," Mike Littwin of the *Los Angeles Times* wrote. "No one really expects him to be traded this time, but no one has rushed forward to quash the rumor, either."

Once more, Sutton was in a Dodger uniform when the season began, but to some surprise, the 35-year-old unveiled quite nearly the best season of his career, leading the NL for the first time with a 2.20 ERA (161 ERA+), along with an MLB-best 0.99 WHIP. He was consistent, with his ERA never rising above 2.50 after May 1, despite pitching with a fractured toe suffered in late August. If there were any individual honor eluding Sutton that year, it was that with the All-Star Game at Dodger Stadium for the first time, six teammates made the NL squad, but Sutton and his 2.27 ERA at the break didn't.

Still, every bit of his performance counted in a taut NL West dogfight with the Astros. Beginning on April 26, no more than 3½ games separated Houston and Los Angeles in the standings for the rest of the season. On October 3, making his final start as a Dodger before impending free agency, on the first night of a three-game season-ending series that the Dodgers needed to sweep, Sutton pitched seven innings of one-run ball before allowing the go-ahead run in the top of the eighth—but the Dodgers rallied to win in the 10th, 3–2.

The teams arrived at the final Sunday, Game 162, one game apart in the standings. Starting pitcher Burt Hooton was removed four batters into the second inning, making it all hands on deck for the pitching staff. In the bottom of the eighth, Ron Cey's two-run home run gave the Dodgers and closer Steve Howe a 4–3 lead. But in the ninth, when singles against Howe put runners at first and third with two out, Sutton emerged from the pen. It took two pitches before Denny Walling grounded to second for the final out.

"I knew I wasn't going to throw the ball by anyone," said Sutton. "But after 15 years, I think I ought to be able to finesse one batter."

With the Dodgers' elimination in the NL West tiebreaker game the next day, Sutton's Dodger career was on the precipice. Conversations continued, but entering his age-36 season, Sutton was looking for a five-year deal at $4 million. Under the free-agency system used at the time, Sutton's tenure as a Dodger came to an official end November 13, when the Dodgers did not join 10 other teams in selecting him for negotiation.

On December 3, Sutton signed with Houston. Though clearly ready for a change, Sutton did ponder what he was leaving behind.

"You don't spend 15 years anywhere except prison without developing an emotional attachment," he said.

The following March, at his first spring training away from Vero Beach, Sutton further reflected.

"Last year was a very exciting year," he said. "That last week, the Houston series, will always be the first thing that comes to my mind when I think back on the Dodgers. Not World Series games or All-Star Games but that week, pitching in the ninth inning of the Sunday game. That's a pretty pleasant memory to leave town on.

"With all things equal or close to equal, I'd like to have spent the rest of my career there, extended the Dodger records. I remember the night they had for Don Drysdale when he retired and they gave him a pickup and a boat. A thought came over me: 'I'd like to have that happen to me.'"

Poetically, his first start as an Astro was at Dodger Stadium, but Sutton was beat, lasting three batters into the fifth inning of a 7–4 loss. His longtime home fans jeered him. But near the end of the year, on September 27, Sutton two-hit the Dodgers (a day after Ryan no-hit them) with nine strikeouts, holding the eventual World Series champions hitless until Ken Landreaux singled to start the seventh. For the strike-shortened 1981 season, Sutton had a 2.61 ERA (126 ERA+) and led the NL for the second consecutive year with a 1.02 WHIP.

However, during a final meeting at Dodger Stadium on October 2, a Jerry Reuss pitch fractured Sutton's right kneecap while he was attempting to bunt, ending his season and any chance of facing the Dodgers in the first National League Division Series or pitching his new team into the World Series.

In 1982, Sutton went from apprentice to full-fledged member of baseball's wandering class. That August, the fading Astros traded him to Milwaukee, where he made his American League debut, won ALCS Game 3 over the Angels, and nearly got his elusive World Series ring. With the Milwaukee Brewers leading the Cardinals 3–2 in the series, the 37-year-old Sutton was knocked out in the fifth inning of a Game 6 loss, and could only watch St. Louis win Game 7.

Milwaukee traded Sutton to Oakland after the 1984 season. Oakland sent him to the Angels in September 1985. In the 1986 ALCS, making his final postseason start, he pitched 6⅓ innings of one-run ball in the Angels' 4–3 Game 4 win. Following a relief appearance in the Red Sox's 7–1 blowout of the Angels in Game 7, Sutton's postseason career passed 100 innings, with a 3.68 ERA.

From 1981 to 1987, seven years of baseball that took Sutton from age 36 to 42, he had a 3.70 ERA (103 ERA+) with 878 strikeouts in 1,466 innings. In the off-season leading into 1988, Dodger general manager Fred Claire, trying to reshape an L.A. team that had endured two straight 73–89 seasons, eyed the free agent who would turn 43 two days before Opening Day.

"I wanted to bring him back so that that some of our young pitchers saw how a championship and indeed Hall of Fame pitcher prepares for a season," Claire says.

Sutton didn't need to keep pitching. He had made money inside the game and invested it well outside of the game. Broadcasting awaited, as did (ironically, given how often Garvey had been said to have such ambitions) a potential political career. But on January 5, he put his name on a contract bringing him back to Los Angeles.

In the first three months of the season, Sutton made 15 starts, never allowing more than four earned runs, before missing the month of July with a sprained right elbow—his first trip, after all those years, to the disabled list. Returning August 9, in the 774th start of his MLB career, Sutton lasted seven innings but allowed five earned runs in a 6–0 loss to the Reds, who whittled the Dodgers' NL West lead to half a game. That night, Claire and Lasorda decided to recall Ramón Martínez—at age 20, less than half Sutton's age.

"Don had been the role model we expected him to be in the spring," Claire wrote in his book, *My 30 Years in Dodger Blue*, "and had given us a veteran presence during much of the season while Martinez gained experience at Triple-A. But now, it was time to make the switch."

Sutton had said publicly after the loss at Cincinnati that he had been inquiring about jobs with other organizations, including the open position of assistant general manager with Houston, but the mini-controversy was quickly defused, and Claire said it bore no impact on the timing of Sutton's departure. Nevertheless, circumstances didn't allow for the fanfare of a ceremonial retirement in front of the home fans for Sutton.

"I guess I would have liked Bob Hope singing 'Thanks for the Memories,'" said Sutton, whose mother tragically died in a car accident on August 12, two days after his release. "It's a business and I understand that. They held a press conference, and I think I said the right things… [but] that was not a good week."

Despite spending seven seasons with other teams, Sutton retired as the Dodgers' all-time pitching leader in wins (233), starts (533), innings (3,816⅓), strikeouts (2,696), and shutouts (52) (and remains atop those leaderboards 30 years later and counting). His place in Los Angeles pitching history was secure. All that remained was Cooperstown.

In 1994, his first year of eligibility, Sutton pulled 57 percent of the vote, the best of anyone new to the ballot. In 1997, he needed 353 votes and tallied 346. The following year, Sutton reached baseball nirvana, with room to spare.

"I just went numb at first," said Sutton, after getting the news while playing golf. "I went through a multitude of emotions, from instant tears to joy to excitement to numbness…There were so many people who are no longer with us who I would have given anything to share this with—my late mother, Walter Alston, the Big D."

Sutton joined Koufax and Drysdale in the Hall to become part of the first trio of Hall of Famers from the same rotation (1966) since Bob Feller, Early Wynn, and Bob Lemon pitched for the Indians in the late 1940s and early '50s.

None other than Lasorda said Sutton was overdue.

"What was special about him is he went to the mound," Lasorda said. "That's what was different about him. He logged a lot of innings. He was a winner. He was a competitor. When you gave him the ball, you knew one thing: your pitcher was going to give you everything he had. You win as many games as he did, to me, that should be automatic Hall of Fame."

PART FOUR

THE MODERN CLASSICISTS

ON MAY 31, 1948, 20 years old and fresh out of military service, Tom Lasorda took the mound for the Class-C Schenectady Blue Jays—and quite nearly never gave it back.

"I wind up pitching against Amsterdam, 15 innings," Lasorda said. "In the bottom of the 15th, I drive in the winning run. I wind up striking out 25. I walked 12. I gave up 14 hits. Bobby Valentine and I [once] sat down and tried to figure out how many pitches I threw. I threw over 350 pitches. Four days later, I got 15 Ks in nine innings, and four days after that I got 13, so I had 53 strikeouts in three games."

This John Henryesque display attracted the attention of the Brooklyn Dodgers, who drafted the 5-foot-10 lefty from Norristown, Pennsylvania, into their organization that November. For virtually all of the next seven decades and across two coasts, that organization is where Lasorda remained, as a player, scout, coach, manager, front-office executive, and life force.

Lasorda's belief in the ability—in the *duty*—of a single pitching arm was practically infinite, and in his most celebrated role, managing the Dodgers from 1977 to 1996, he tacked Dodger pitching toward that boundlessness.

"He was always inclined to go with his starting pitchers, even at the beginning of his career," Bill James wrote. "He adjusted toward using more relievers as the game moved in that direction, but he was always behind the league, always going further with his starters than were most other managers."

Baseball analyst Chris Jaffe corroborated that—except, notably, in 1988—Lasorda used relief pitchers as little as possible. With baseball trending in a more aggressive direction, Lasorda became the last manager of note who never had a pitcher make 70 relief appearances in a season.

"Only once did someone save 30 games in a season for him—Todd Worrell with 32 in Lasorda's final campaign," Jaffe said. "During Lasorda's career, 52 closers broke the 30-save barrier. Only six times did Lasorda's closer get at least 20 saves, including none from 1978 to 1988."

For starting pitchers who liked their jobs, Lasorda gave them all the rope they wanted.

"More than any other manager I played for," Jerry Reuss says. "When I was a starting pitcher, I loved it."

Lasorda's embrace of the iron-man pitcher might seem like a throwback, except it reversed a trend developing under his predecessor, Walter Alston.

Make no mistake: Alston entertained the last of the ultramarathon pitching performances in franchise history. When he found a full well, Alston drank deeply. Sandy Koufax hurled four games of at least 12 innings; no Dodger has done so since or ever will again. Don Drysdale started 165 games from 1962 to 1965—essentially, a full big-league season by himself in the span of four years.

However, Alston helped push the Dodgers to the forefront of baseball's transformation from four-man to five-man starting rotations, making the move temporarily in 1971–72 and permanently in 1976. And relative to his time, beginning with his surprise hiring in 1954, Alston was quicker than most to pull his more mortal pitchers, even with a lead. James noted that Alston's teams often led the league in saves, well before the save statistic held any status in the minds of baseball men.

"He knew how to handle a pitching staff," Bill Singer says. "He'd be willing to lose a battle to win the war. He didn't play every game like it was the seventh game of the World Series. It was the long haul, and so he wouldn't overuse anybody."

It's true that as some pitchers thrived under Alston's style, others chafed. "It was like Walt couldn't wait to get me out of the game," says Tommy John. Conversely, some came to wonder if Lasorda was too slow to catch on to the idea of letting a pitcher, especially a young pitcher, breathe before subjecting him to repeated complete games.

Compared to how they contrasted in style—the stoic Alston versus the bombastic Lasorda—this distinction might feel like splitting hairs on heirs to the Dodger managerial throne, but it teases the role each had in shaping the team's pitching tradition from within. Perhaps more importantly, the franchise never ceased to find pitchers whose abilities transcended any managerial whims. Rolling from Alston's reign into the Lasorda era, the Dodgers enjoyed ongoing success in a new mold of pitchers, modern and classic all at once.

Tommy John

Tommy John pitched 4,710⅓ innings in the major leagues. Since 1901, only 13 players have thrown more.

From the date of John's first MLB game in September 1963 to his last in May 1989, nearly 26 years passed. In the 20th century, only Nolan Ryan played in more seasons.

John was incredible in his consistency and endurance, even without accounting for the operation that made him a household name—in baseball and medical households, anyway.

"I threw the same when I came up to the big leagues as I threw after Tommy John surgery as I threw in the last game I pitched," John says. "I threw two pitches—I threw a sinker and I threw a curveball. I never learned to throw a changeup. Would I have been better had I learned a changeup? Maybe, maybe not—I don't know—but I just threw two pitches. I sank the ball, and I could throw the ball low and away 9 out of 10 times for strikes, or close enough to the plate that they might not be strikes but the umpires would call them strikes. That's the way I pitched—that was my strength."

The one time that anyone insisted on changing his approach paved the way for his becoming a Dodger.

Signed by Cleveland as an 18-year-old in 1961, John had a 2–11 record despite a 3.61 ERA as a part-timer in 1963–64 with the Indians, before the White Sox picked him up in a three-team, eight-player deal in 1965. He spent seven seasons with Chicago, for whom he showcased a 2.95 ERA (117 ERA+), highlighted by a 1.98 ERA (161 ERA+) in a 1968 season cut short by a broken collarbone suffered in a fight.

Before the 1971 season, the White Sox hired Johnny Sain as pitching coach. Sain came highly regarded, but the same regard didn't flow toward John.

"I was trying to pitch like Johnny Sain wanted me to pitch, and he and I were like oil and water," John says. "We just never meshed, and so as a pitcher, you know when your time is up.

"Johnny was big on a short curveball, a slider. And I tried and I tried and I tried. Through six weeks in spring training, through six weeks of the season—so now I'm 12 weeks of throwing the slider—I can't throw a slider, I can't throw my fastball anymore, I can't throw my curveball. So I called my old pitching coach, Ray Berres. And he said, 'God damn, I wondered when you were gonna call.' And I said, 'Why?' And he said, 'Stick that slider up your ass.'"

"Look," Berres continued, "you only have a pitch if it makes your other pitches better. You don't add a pitch if it takes away from any of your other pitches. And the slider's taking away from your sinker and your curveball."

That made sense to John, but John never really found a way to satisfy Sain, and so at the end of the '71 season, the White Sox jumped at the chance to trade him to Los Angeles for 29-year-old outfielder Dick Allen, who posted a .395 on-base percentage and .468 slugging percentage with 23 homers in his only year with the Dodgers. At Chavez Ravine, John found the pitching coach he had been looking for in Red Adams.

John's official Dodger debut was delayed by the 13-day players' strike that April, then came a day early in place of an ailing Claude Osteen, on April 18, 1972. John pitched seven innings of one-run ball that night, and had an ERA of 1.73 after his first six starts. He blanked the Giants on August 3, then struck out a career-high 13 five days later, pitching the first nine innings of a 19-inning, 2–1 Dodger loss at Cincinnati.

John finished '72 with a 2.89 ERA (116 ERA+) before undergoing a relatively minor procedure to remove bone fragments. (In Koufaxian style, a slide on the basepaths forced the issue.) With Allen winning the AL MVP award, many in Los Angeles still bristled at the previous winter's transaction, but that changed in 1973. While a fractured fibula limited Allen to 72 games, John appeared none the worse from his off-season operation, pitching 218 innings with a 3.10 ERA (113 ERA+). No Longer the Villain in Dick Allen Trade, proclaimed a *Los Angeles Times* headline.

Beginning the 1974 season with 18 consecutive scoreless innings, John became the first Dodger pitcher ever to win five games in April, sitting pretty with a 12–2 record and 2.48 ERA on Independence Day.

"I've found that my fastball now keeps its life longer," John said that year. "The other day, in the seventh inning, I threw a fastball past Dave Kingman. It was up and out over the middle of the plate. Two years ago, I couldn't have gotten away with it. The difference is in that fastball and my confidence. I feel I'm at the peak of my career and that barring injuries, I can go on for five or six more years."

About that…

For all his endurance, John was regularly battling a sore elbow, dating to a 1963 injury in Puerto Rico.

"People said, 'What were you doing when John Kennedy was killed?'" John remembers. "Well, I tell you what I was doing. I was getting my first cortisone injection. I was in that doctor's office—I was 20. From that time for 11 years until 1974, I probably had 50 or 60 injections in my elbow. And when I told Dr. [Frank] Jobe that, he went, 'Oh my god, it's a wonder your elbow lasted as long as it did.' But it's what they did back then. That was the protocol.

"Back in that era, you didn't tell somebody that 'my elbow hurt,' because if you did, you wouldn't pitch much. Your job was to pitch. You kept your mouth shut, you took what you had to take, and you zipped it.

"Here's how bad sports medicine was on major-league baseball teams. When I was with the White Sox, 1965, our team physician—you're gonna laugh at this—was an ob-gyn. Sports medicine has come so far, my god, and it's because of Frank Jobe that it's come so far like that."

It was Jobe who came to John's rescue after the day of reckoning: July 17, 1974. Two batters into the third inning against the Montreal Expos, John's left elbow sounded the alarm, as if it had snapped. Walking straight to the dugout, John was soon examined by Jobe and diagnosed with a ruptured medial collateral ligament. Surgery wasn't the immediate recourse, but in September, even as the Dodgers were headed for the NL West title and the playoffs, John conceded that his season was over.

On September 25, Jobe took a tendon from John's right elbow and weaved it into the left elbow while tightening the muscles there. Few at the time of the operation knew its significance. Few today know that John's daughter was born two days later.

"Dr. Jobe was not worried about the surgery working or not working," John says. "You know what he was worried about? My wife was pregnant with our first child. 'Tommy, when this doesn't work'—not 'if this doesn't work,' but 'when this doesn't work'—do you have means to support your family?' And I said, 'Yes.' That tells you the quality of person Frank Jobe was. He wasn't worried about the surgery being a success and making a name for [himself]."

Jobe gave John the green light to begin throwing in February 1975. Decades later, experts prescribed specific measures for Tommy John surgery recovery, but back then, Jobe could offer little in the way of a road map.

"All he ever told me was 'listen to your body,'" John says. "Your body will tell you what it needs. If you need to throw more, throw more. If your body doesn't feel good, if your arm doesn't feel good, throw less."

The surgery had affected nerve endings in John's fingers, threatening his grip of the ball and his ability to throw breaking pitches. "One of the forlorn sights of the 1975 Dodger season was of Tommy John in the clubhouse at home and on the road squeezing balls of putty, bouncing a baseball off a wall, or soaking his shrunken hand in the whirlpool bath," wrote Jim Murray.

"When I first got there, he couldn't hold a baseball yet," says Burt Hooton, whom the Dodgers acquired in 1975. "So I watched him for almost two years go through a regimen which I'm pretty sure 99.9 percent of other people wouldn't go through, and everybody was telling him he would never pitch again. He's the only one who'd believe that he would pitch again. His determination and his patience and his dedication and just how hard he worked was one of the most impressive things I've ever seen."

"I started throwing to my wife, because I knew if I threw to her I couldn't throw hard," John says. "So I would just throw to exercise. I threw every single day but took Sundays off, and my reasoning was if God rested on Sunday, if he worked six and took Sunday off, Tommy John could do the same thing. And then I started finding out that the day I had the worst feel of the ball was Monday, and the next worst was Tuesday, and the best days I had were Friday and Saturday. The more I threw, the better my arm felt, so from that time on until I retired in 1989, I threw a baseball off a mound to a catcher every single day I was out on the baseball field. And the more I threw, the more confidence I got in my arm, the better control I had, the better hop I had on my fastball."

Says Dodger catcher Steve Yeager: "I used to see all kinds of things put on his arm that they would try, because it was the first time they'd ever done that. They didn't know how to rehab it. They didn't know how to get it back. But you could watch him go through his stuff in the training room and on the field, trying this and trying that to get it straight. And when you'd see him try to throw, you'd say good things are happening here. It was a long process for him because it was the very first one. Nobody knew."

One year after the operation, John ventured to the 95-degree temperatures of the Arizona Instructional League to face a squad of minor-leaguers. In his first competitive action in 15 months, he threw three perfect innings. The following spring, John arrived at Vero Beach with the rest of the Dodger staff, breaking the eggs that every pitcher does to make the upcoming season's omelet. His arm gave him little trouble physically, allowing him to focus on his mechanics and feel. He just wanted his stuff back, needed his stuff back—his good sinker, good tail on the fastball, good breaking curveball.

"If I didn't have that, I was dead meat," he says.

On April 16, 21 months after he last walked off the Dodger Stadium mound, John began his official comeback with four shutout innings at Atlanta. The fact that Darrell Evans then hit a three-run homer in the bottom of the fifth fazed not a soul in the organization.

"What Tommy John did tonight qualifies him for the Comeback Player of the Year Award," said Dodger reliever Mike Marshall, who had recently completed his doctorate in kinesiology. "He wins it, flat out. What he has done in coming back from that injury is the greatest accomplishment I've ever seen."

At the end of the season, Marshall's kudos demand came true. John allowed one run in 14 innings for the remainder of April (earning himself a standing ovation after his first appearance at Dodger Stadium), pitching his first post-surgery complete game in June and his first shutout on July 23, almost exactly two years after his injury. He threw 207 innings in 1976—a total that would have led the Dodgers 40 years later—with a 3.09 ERA (109 ERA+) and an NL-best 0.3 homers per nine innings.

"I don't think Tommy was any different before the surgery than after the surgery," Yeager says. "Tommy John was about as good a competitor as you're going to find for a guy that basically had a pitch and a half. He had his sinker—he was able to put it where he wanted. He didn't leave it in the middle of the plate. He had a curveball occasionally, and he just stayed where he wanted to stay and was successful giving up ground balls to short, ground balls to second, every time he went out there. So after the surgery he was the same guy. He didn't change his style at all."

John quickly pushed himself from comeback kid to full-fledged star. In 1977, he finished second in the NL Cy Young Award voting after a 20–7 season in which he threw 220⅓ innings with a 2.78 ERA (138 ERA+) and 11 complete games for the Dodgers, who won the NL West in manager Tommy Lasorda's rookie year.

After being victimized by four unearned runs in Game 1 of the National League Championship Series, John took the mound on a cold and rainy October 8 in Philadelphia, with the Dodgers aiming to clinch the pennant on the road against Cy Young winner Steve Carlton. John did nothing less than go the distance in a 4–1 victory.

"The best game I ever had," John says. "Lasorda, each inning, asked me, 'How do you feel?' 'I'm fine, I'm fine, I'm fine.' And Tommy let me pitch, and I pitched."

With one out in the ninth inning, Bob Boone hit a ball along the turf to third baseman Ron Cey for John's 15th groundout of the game.

"I got the ball back," John says, "and I fingered it and I felt the ball had wet spots on it from where it hit on the turf, and it was right where I gripped the ball. All through that game, that infield was a soggy, AstroTurf mess, but the ball had never felt wet in my hand.

"Bake McBride was the last guy, and I threw strike one, strike two, strike three—and it was over."

John's dream season ended in Game 3 of the World Series with a 5–3 loss to the Yankees, but he took advantage of the Dodgers' return trip to the Fall Classic the following year. In 1978, John's ERA rose to 3.30 (107 ERA+), although his fielding-independent ERA shrunk from 3.05 to 2.91, indicating he was more unlucky than anything else. He made his first All-Star team, and cruised with the Dodgers into the World Series thanks to an NLCS Game 2 shutout of Philadelphia.

He found revenge against the Yankees in a Game 1 victory, allowing three earned runs in 7⅔ innings, then pitched similarly well in Game 4 but settled for a no-decision in the Dodgers' 10-inning loss. Few realized then that the next time the teams met, John would be wearing Yankee pinstripes.

"I didn't want to leave," says John, who became a free agent for the first time that November. "Playing for the Dodgers and the O'Malley family was the greatest part of my life in baseball. But I wanted a three-year contract, and Al Campanis said, 'I can't give you three—I know that third year, you will probably break down.'"

The last thing John was going to do, after all he'd been through, was take this unsolicited medical advice lying down.

"I said, 'Al, how can you sit there and say that?' He said, 'Tommy, you've got to understand. I went to NYU, and I was a P.E. major. And I took all the same science courses that Dr. Jobe took, and I think that third year is an iffy year for you.' And I looked at him, and I said 'Al, my wife went to Indiana State. She was a P.E. major, 40 years after you, when science was better, and she said I'm gonna pitch another 10 years.'"

The last night before John officially became a free agent, Campanis telephoned John's agent, ostensibly to relent.

"Campanis said he will give you the third year," John's agent said, "but you've got to apologize to the Dodger fans."

"What?" John asked.

"He just said you have to apologize to the Dodger fans. What do you want me to tell him?"

John's answer in that moment is best left to one's imagination.

"That was crazy," John reminisces, nearly 40 years later. "That was how I left the Dodgers. I didn't want to leave the Dodgers. Why would anybody want to leave the best team in baseball?"

Among those who have thrown at least 1,000 innings, John's adjusted ERA of 118 ranked ninth in Dodger history, and third among Los Angeles pitchers, behind only Clayton Kershaw and Sandy Koufax. But in that dispute over a third year, his Dodger career was done.

While John went 43–18 with a 3.19 ERA (125 ERA+) in his first two seasons in the Bronx, the Dodgers missed the playoffs. Then, after delivering a 2.63 ERA (136 ERA+) in the strike-shortened regular season of 1981, John threatened to make his former fans and friends in Los Angeles feel even worse, pitching seven shutout innings against the Dodgers in Game 2 of the World Series and two more shutout frames out of the bullpen in Game 4.

To start Game 6, John was on the mound again, with the Yankees needing a win to stay alive. The score was tied 1–1 in the bottom of the fourth, with two on and two out for New York, when John's spot in the batting order arrived. Yankees manager Bob Lemon made the decision to have Bobby Murcer pinch-hit, leaving John sputtering in disbelief on national television at the other end of the dugout. Murcer flied out against Hooton, and the Dodgers began pouring across runs against the Yankee bullpen on their way to a Series-clinching 9–2 victory.

"I don't think we were gonna hit Tommy John," says Hooton, his former roommate. "When Bob Lemon took him out of the game, I couldn't believe it. I still remember watching Tommy John at the end of the Yankee dugout, shaking his head like 'I can't believe it, either.'"

John was 38 at the time. The following year would be his 20th in baseball, and he still had seven more to go after that. He won once more in the postseason, a complete-game win for the Angels to open the 1982 ALCS. He went 13–6 back with the Yankees in 1987, pitched another 176⅓ innings in 1988, and finally, after a May 25, 1989, start, he and his ever-famous left arm went into retirement, three days after his 46th birthday.

Andy Messersmith

Forty years before Zack Greinke graced the Dodgers with three increasingly superb seasons—and then left for a big-money contract—came the pitcher who set that template in Los Angeles.

Andy Messersmith was squarely in the Dodgers' sights as they stared down I-5 toward Anaheim, where the right-hander had debuted at age 22 with the Angels, appropriately enough, as it turned out, on Independence Day 1968. He spent the next four and a half seasons compiling a 2.78 ERA (118 ERA+) in the grasslands below the Matterhorn.

According to Ross Newhan of the *Los Angeles Times*, Al Campanis was in Baltimore for the final games of the 1971 World Series when he asked Tigers manager Billy Martin and Twins manager Bill Rigney who was the best pitcher in the AL—and agreed when each named Messersmith. Looking to improve their offense, the Angels let the Dodgers know that Messersmith would be available, but it took 14 months before the teams found a combination of players each could live with in the biggest trade ever between the two Freeway Series teams: Bill Singer, Billy Grabarkewitz, Frank Robinson, Mike Strahler, and Bobby Valentine to the Big A for Messersmith and Ken McMullen.

"I wanted Messersmith since that night in Baltimore," Campanis said.

The 6-foot-1 righthander began his Dodger career in 1973 impressively with a 2.70 ERA (129 ERA+) in 249⅔ innings—that year, he, Don Sutton, Claude Osteen, Tommy John, and Al Downing started 158 of the Dodgers' 162 games—then topped himself in '74. With a 20–6 record, a 2.59 ERA (second in the NL), and a 1.10 WHIP (best in the league), Messersmith finished second in the NL Cy Young Award balloting, losing to his teammate out of the bullpen, Mike Marshall. Twice in May, Messersmith pitched more than nine innings to get the win.

"Mess was good," John says. "Andy was a hard worker, and he had maybe the best curveball, he and Sutton. He had an outstanding curveball, and he had a good fastball, and he would compete until the cows came home—that was just the way he was."

In the 1974 postseason, Messersmith pitched seven innings of two-run ball to win Game 2 of the NLCS, before taking a hard-luck, 3–2 loss in Game 1 of the World Series when he allowed two earned runs in eight innings, including the first of Reggie Jackson's nine career World Series homers against the Dodgers.

Though Messersmith's remaining World Series game also ended in defeat, his standing among his teammates remained strong.

"I loved Andy—he was my kind of guy," Steve Yeager says. "Great competitor and a great guy who worked well with everybody else.

He helped me, and he helped the other pitchers. He helped the other hitters…Loved to surf, loved the water, and whatever he did, he did it well and did it right. He was laid back—curly hair and a big barrel-chested guy that came out and competed, and that's all you could ask for."

Given his persona, Messersmith might not have seemed one to be on the front lines of baseball's player revolution in 1975. In fact, Messersmith's motive wasn't escape. Having spent most of his life in California—growing up in Orange County and attending UC Berkeley—the pitcher was not only content to stay in Los Angeles at the salary the Dodgers offered, he wanted to come away with a no-trade clause to root him there. But when the parties couldn't agree to terms, the Dodgers followed decades of baseball custom, ostensibly forged by the sport's reserve clause, and renewed Messersmith's contract without his signature.

On the field, all was well. For the fifth consecutive season, Messersmith lowered his ERA, this time to a career-best 2.29 (149 ERA+) while pitching more innings, complete games, and shutouts than anyone in the NL. But with the Dodgers falling 20 games shy of the high-powered Big Red Machine in Cincinnati, the real postseason drama for Dodger fans took place in the office suites. And what a climax: when arbitrator Peter Seitz declared Messersmith a free agent two days before Christmas, baseball insiders weren't shy to declare something of their own—a death sentence to baseball. "Here Lies Baseball, 1975—Victim of a Slave Uprising," Jim Murray provocatively wrote, the former Hollywood writer exaggerating to make his point: just as the entertainment industry reinvented itself after the breakdown of its contract system with actors, so would baseball.

No one knew then exactly how that reinvention would take place, and as people came to realize over the ensuing decades, the process would be reworked again and again. But the end result was that Messersmith, like his left-handed teammate coming back from surgery in 1976, would forever be known more for something that happened off the field than any of his considerable accomplishments on the diamond.

> **Moment in the Sun: Al Downing**
> - Outstanding debut Dodger season in 1971 after spending 10 years in AL, going 20–9 with a 2.68 ERA (121 ERA+) and league-leading five shutouts
> - Most famous for throwing the pitch in Atlanta that Hank Aaron hit for his record-breaking 715th home run on April 8, 1974
> - Finished his Dodger career with a 3.16 ERA (107 ERA+) in 897⅔ innings—similar to overall 3.22 ERA (106 ERA+) in 2,268⅓ career innings

"I'm not a martyr, but I wouldn't change anything," Messersmith told Murray Chass of *The New York Times* that winter. "I've gained a lot of notoriety, but I don't want it. That's not why I did it. It was done for selfish reasons but also for some unselfish reasons. A lot of things had to be changed, and this is the way it has to be done."

After the last appeal was exhausted in March 1976 and Messersmith became a free agent in earnest, a bidding process ensued. Though the Dodgers initially withdrew, they didn't stop having conversations, and the belief remained that Messersmith had no desire to go anywhere else. Initial reports that the Yankees signed him proved to be premature. Ultimately, he went to Atlanta on what his agent ironically (and incorrectly) called a "lifetime contract"—a three-year deal with perpetual renewal clauses that were soon invalidated.

Playing for the last-place Braves in 1976, Messersmith had his last great year, with a 3.04 ERA (125 ERA+). Battling injuries as well as the mental exhaustion of the previous winter, the season represented a slight decline from his Dodger heights, but not one that matched the intense criticism he received from certain pockets of baseball. He made himself a perfect target of schadenfreude in his only start as an opposing pitcher at Dodger Stadium, which didn't come until April 1977 and, perhaps not so ironically, was the worst of his post-Dodger career: six runs in the first inning of a 14–10 loss. His 102⅓-inning season ended in the first inning of a July 3 game, when he suffered the first of two serious injuries on fielding plays that would undermine him across the next nine months, the next coming during spring training in 1978 after he had been sold to the Yankees.

He pitched only 22⅓ innings in '78, then made one last comeback attempt in 1979. It was with the Dodgers.

"As for leaving the Dodgers in '76 as I did, I helped a lot of players' careers," Messersmith said. "In that sense, I felt right about it. But personally, I always regretted leaving the Dodgers. This is the best place in baseball to work. My most enjoyable years in baseball were spent right here. It's a class organization."

Messersmith began his second Dodger career with seven innings of one-run ball in an April 7 win over San Diego, and had a four-start run in May when he averaged 7⅓ innings with a 3.10 ERA, but he left his 11th start of the year with shoulder pain, underwent an operation on his elbow, and never pitched in the big leagues again.

Among 20th century pitchers with at least 600 innings, only Sandy Koufax and reliever Ron Perranoski had a better ERA+ as a Dodger than Messersmith's 129. It's a level of performance not easily ignored, even if his impact was much more profound in baseball's front offices.

On August 28, 1979, the very day of Messersmith's unconditional release from the Dodgers, Mike Littwin of the *Los Angeles Times* spoke to outfielder Dusty Baker about a report that he might be traded in response to a losing season. Baker, it was noted, had a no-trade clause.

"Whatever players make today, they should be sending Andy Christmas cards every year, thanking him," John says. "And the agents should be sending them, too."

Burt Hooton

Preacher was receding into the past and Bulldog had yet to woof, but in the period in between, there might not have been a better nickname for a Dodger pitcher than Happy.

Burt Hooton was Happy, and made Dodger fans happy, even if he might not have looked happy.

"I'm not a real emotional guy," Hooton says. "I mean, I enjoy life—I enjoyed everything about the career I've had and the people I've played with. We had fun. I like having fun just as much as anybody. But I'm not going to be the one who's going to be jumping up and down and going crazy every time something happens."

Tommy John, who became Hooton's roommate, believes it was no mystery why the nickname worked.

"What a great guy," John says. "Laid back, Texas, deadpan humor, funny—God, he was funny. He just had a dry sense of humor. He would say something deadpan and it would be hilarious. He was a great guy, but he just had this sour, dour look on his face all the time."

More than just a chance branding, Hooton's nickname and the way he earned it presaged the biggest turning point of his big-league career.

Born in Greenville, Texas, in 1950, Hooton made his big-league debut with the Cubs nine days after they drafted him No. 2 overall in the secondary phase of the June 1971 draft out of the University of Texas, where his ERA was 1.14 over three seasons. After allowing three runs in 3⅓ innings against the Cardinals, he was dispatched to Triple-A Tacoma, where he had a 1.68 ERA and 135 strikeouts in 102 innings.

When he took the mound a second time for Chicago on September 15, Hooton struck out 15—an MLB record for a player making his second career start—in a three-hit complete-game win over the Mets. In his next appearance, he shut out New York at Wrigley on two hits. Suffice it to say, Hooton never pitched in the minors again, and in his first start the next year, at Wrigley Field on April 16, 1972, though he walked seven, Hooton became the first rookie in 60 years to hurl a no-hitter.

Hooton finished the 1972 season with a 2.80 ERA (135 ERA+) in 218⅓ innings for the Cubs. But his startling debut faded as his next two seasons grew progressively sadder: 3.68 ERA (107 ERA+) in 1973, 4.80 ERA (80 ERA+) in '74.

"We had three managers, four pitching coaches," Hooton says. "I was a young kid. I tried to establish my career pretty much as a four-seam fastball, four-seam curveball, four-seam changeup guy, and all four pitching coaches I had were sinker-slider guys and they wanted me to throw sinkers and sliders.

"Even after all the success I'd had up to that point, at the end of three and a half years I was pretty frustrated, and to make a long story short, I asked them to trade me."

That's when Tommy Lasorda and the Dodgers found their way into the Happy hunting ground. Lasorda, then the Dodgers' third-base coach (and still three years away from becoming manager), recruited Hooton for his winter-league team in Licey.

"He had seen me pitch early in my career right after I was signed," Hooton recalls. "He saw me pitch in the Pacific Coast League when he was managing Spokane, and I was very successful there. And after three years, I was nowhere near the same pitcher. So he invited me to come down and pitch for him in Licey, which was a good experience.

"He nicknamed me 'Happy' when we were in the Dominican Republic on New Year's Eve. I'm not a big New Year's Eve guy, so I was playing solitaire and when the clock struck midnight, he just kind of looked at me and said, 'Well, aren't you happy?' And somehow or another, it stuck."

After the upbeat winter, Hooton began the 1975 season downtrodden in Chicago, allowing 10 earned runs in his first 11 innings, a far cry from the no-hit wonder of three years prior. Enough was enough for the Cubs, and in a rare early-May trade, they sent the 25-year-old Hooton to the Dodgers for left-hander Geoff Zahn and righty Eddie Solomon.

In his first Dodger appearance, Hooton allowed five earned runs, entering against the Padres in relief and surrendering a 6–2 lead. His ERA for the season stood at 9.88. Hooton was eager to make the most of his new opportunity to play for the Dodgers, but now there was no hole he wouldn't have crawled into when Walter Alston approached him after the game.

But Alston, a man of few words, particularly to a newcomer like Hooton, surprised him with these: "I like what I saw, kid." The manager backed up his sentiments by starting Hooton five days later in Pittsburgh, and was rewarded with six innings of one-run ball. On his next turn, Hooton threw a two-hit shutout at St. Louis.

Hooton thanked Alston for the confidence boost and credited Red Adams for enabling the turnaround.

"I was as down as anybody could be," Hooton says. "So that was a big lift, and Red was a big lift. When I first got to the Dodgers, I was throwing in the bullpen and getting really frustrated trying to throw my sinkers and sliders. I knew they weren't very good, but I never could throw one. Red just kind of put a stop to it right in the middle of the bullpen and asked what in the world was going on with me, and I told him. And he said, 'You know, why don't you can the sinker-slider and go back pitching the way you used to?' I mean, the way I did in high school, the way I did in college when I first signed—everything was all good then. So that's what I did. I canned the sinker and slider, and it was kind of like finding an old lost friend.

"I had pitching coaches telling me if I was gonna win on the big-league level, I needed more movement on my fastball and needed a slider. So my mistake was believing them."

Hooton's old friend was the one that had already become famous when he threw his no-hitter as a rookie—the knuckle-curve. It was a pitch that Hooton stumbled upon through a combination of happenstance and ignorance.

"I was 14 years old trying to throw a knuckleball after watching Hoyt Wilhelm pitch on TV one Saturday afternoon," Hooton says, "and I went out to a Pony League practice. And you know, common sense told me if you're gonna throw a knuckleball, you've got to put your knuckles down on it. I've heard people say you push it out, so I pushed it out. I never could really throw a true knuckleball. But when I pushed it out, it always had a rotation on it. And the harder I threw it, the better it got. And I could always control it—that was not a problem. So that ended up being my curveball."

Hooton's ERA was still an unimpressive 4.54 at the All-Star break, but he was improving. In his final start before the break, he threw a strong seven innings of two-run ball at Pittsburgh, but took a hard-luck loss.

He didn't take another the rest of the year. Over his final 15 starts of the season, Hooton went 12–0 with a 1.91 ERA. He won back-to-back NL Player of the Month honors in August and September (in the latter, he averaged $9\frac{1}{3}$ innings per start). The Dodgers went 14–1 with Hooton on the mound, suffering their only loss on a blown save by defending NL Cy Young Award winner Mike Marshall.

"I kind of re-found myself," Hooton says. "For three years, I was treading water, trying to find myself. With all of the information and the people saying I need to do this, I need to do that, it was more confusing than it was helpful."

As a Dodger, Hooton finished his first season 18–7 with a 2.82 ERA (121 ERA+). Even with John recovering from surgery, it was no small feat to hold one's own in a starting rotation that featured Don Sutton and Andy Messersmith, who finished in the top five of Cy Young balloting in '74 and '75.

"That helped kind of solidify myself in my mind as a good major-league pitcher," Hooton says. "Hanging around guys like Don Sutton and Andy Messersmith and Tommy John—the best teacher was just watching how those guys went about their business and how they were successful."

Moment in the Sun: Doug Rau

- Strong mid-'70s run with the Dodgers, ending eight-year Los Angeles stint with a 3.30 ERA (106 ERA+) and 11 shutouts in 1,250⅔ innings
- Highlight season for left-handed Texas native came in 1976, when he finished second in the NL with a 2.57 ERA and 131 ERA+
- On May 11, 1979, pitched a no-hitter for 7⅔ innings against visiting Montreal, before settling for one-hit shutout. It would be the last of his 80 wins as a Dodger, before suffering a torn rotator cuff

In his first seven years in Los Angeles, Hooton ranged from steady to superb. After pitching 226⅓ innings with a 3.26 ERA (104 ERA+) in 1976, Hooton had what he considered his best season in 1977, with a 2.62 ERA (147 ERA+). It was the first of three consecutive years below 3.00 in ERA, a feat he also repeated in the strike-shortened 1981 season, when he finished third in the NL at 2.28 (148 ERA+).

"He threw strikes," John says. "He would challenge you, he wasn't afraid to throw the ball over the plate, and he could throw his breaking ball 0-0, 3-2—it didn't make any difference, because he could throw that for a strike almost every time."

In contrast to his regular-season consistency, Hooton encountered extreme highs and perilous lows in the postseason.

Making his playoff debut—Game 3 of the 1977 NLCS at Veterans Stadium in Philadelphia—Hooton needed only six pitches for a perfect first inning. In the second inning, he gave up a leadoff single to Greg Luzinski, but after a forceout and a strikeout, little seemed to be developing for the Phillies. Then Bob Boone singled, and former Dodger infielder Ted Sizemore walked on four pitches to load the bases. The opposing pitcher, Larry Christensen, worked a 3-2 count.

"I got into a situation where I had to make a big pitch," Hooton says. "I threw what I thought was a called third strike, and I think a lot of other people thought it was, too. The mistake I made was, it was called a ball and I lost my composure, so to speak, and one of the lessons you learn as a pitcher [is] once you lose your composure, it's really hard to get it back.

"And of course, all the fans picked up on it, and it got real loud in there. But I threw a few more pitches that I thought were strikes and didn't get 'em, so I was mentally out of it by that time."

In all, Hooton walked four batters in a row, forcing three runs and his exit from the game (one in which the Dodgers made one of their most dramatic playoff rallies ever, scoring three in the ninth to win, 6–5). John's complete game the next night pushed Los Angeles to the World Series, where in Game 2, Hooton would be back on the hill, on the road, in Yankee Stadium.

Yes, the fans read the papers. They knew in the Bronx that they had a pitcher on the ropes before the game even began, and they savored the opportunity.

"I knew exactly what to expect in the first few innings," Hooton says. "They were all on me. As soon as I walked out of the bullpen to go start my game, they were all over me. I determined the only way I could shut 'em up was to go out there and pitch well, which thankfully, I did."

In the first three innings, Hooton racked up six strikeouts, and the Dodgers took a 5–0 lead on homers by Ron Cey, Yeager, and Reggie Smith before New York had its first baserunner. In a breezy two hours and 27 minutes, Hooton wrapped up a five-hitter with the Dodgers winning 6–1.

"By the fourth inning, they were off of me," Hooton says, calling the night a career highlight. "So that allowed me to pitch my complete game and move on.

"Nobody talks about the New York game. They all talk about the Philadelphia game, [but] that game in New York was enormous for me."

Hooton experienced more downs and ups in October, giving up the first of Reggie Jackson's three home runs in the Series-ending Game 6 loss in '77, then splitting two decisions in the 1978 World Series.

By 1981, Hooton was used to pitching in relative obscurity, being noticed only when something went wrong and rarely commented upon when something went right. The arrival of Fernando Valenzuela that year doubled down on that phenomenon, but quietly, Hooton turned in one of the best postseasons in Dodger history. It began with the first of five do-or-die games the Dodgers played that October, when he took the mound in Game 3 of the best-of-five National League Division Series after the Dodgers scored one run in 20 innings across two losses at Houston.

"Probably one of the hardest competitors to beat is the one who doesn't have anything to lose," Hooton says. "I think when we lost the first two games to Houston, everybody's expecting us to lose—and I'm starting Game 3. So everybody's expecting me to lose. And you know, I really had nothing to lose. So I can relax and go out there and perform, and lo and behold if we didn't win."

Marred only by a harmless solo homer by Art Howe, Hooton pitched seven strong innings, carving the path for the Dodgers to return to the NLCS, where in Game 1 and Game 4 against the Expos, he sauntered through back-to-back, 7⅓-inning starts with no earned runs, setting the stage for the Dodgers' decisive Game 5 triumph.

In Game 2 of the '81 World Series against the Yankees, Hooton extended his streak of playoff innings without an earned run to 24⅔—but still took a loss against his old roommate, John, after New York converted a fifth-inning Davey Lopes error into a run during the Yankees' shutout victory.

Hooton found redemption, for both his Game 2 loss in '81 and his Game 6 loss in '78, on the mound in Yankee Stadium for Game 6, holding New York to one run in his first five innings (while the Dodgers overwhelmed the post-John Yankee bullpen) to become the first winning pitcher in a World Series–clinching victory for Los Angeles since Sandy Koufax.

Overall during the 1981 playoffs, in a feat that too few recall decades later, Hooton pitched 33 innings with an ERA of 0.82.

"Did you take a look at Burt's numbers in the postseason?" asks Jerry Reuss, no stranger to outstanding playoffs himself. "He was phenomenal. Nobody knew how good Hooton was.

"You talk about a pitcher overpowering the opposition? I think Burt underwhelmed the opposition. He just kept throwing strikes, his location was perfect, and when he had to in a key situation, he reached back for something less. And he was successful doing it."

Hooton's importance diminished over his final three seasons in Los Angeles, as his knees started to give out on him.

"I had a basketball injury in high school, and it started to catch up with me in 1982, right after the World Series," he says. "I had it operated on—or maybe probably came back a little too soon—and my left knee started to bother me. Well, before it was said and done, my knees were shot, and back then, we didn't have the abilities to fix things like they do now."

His last hurrah on the Dodger Stadium mound came in 1984, when he pitched mainly out of the bullpen but quite effectively, with a 3.20 ERA in 81⅔ innings as a reliever. He spent one final season in 1985 with the Texas Rangers, but when he retired, he could call himself one of the top Dodger pitchers ever, with 26.1 wins above replacement—16th in franchise history, just ahead of Preacher Roe. In 10 years with the Dodgers, Hooton threw 1,861⅓ innings with a 3.14 ERA (113 ERA+).

His impact extended to future generations as a coach and instructor, counseling pitchers including Pedro Martínez, Pedro Astacio, Ismael Valdez, Darren Dreifort, and Chan Ho Park.

"You take the whole 10 years and the 9 years I coached in the organization," Hooton says, "I got to spend 19 years with, in my mind, the best organization to work for."

Bob Welch

Bob Welch is the greatest starting pitcher in Dodger history who is remembered for basically nothing he did as a Dodger starting pitcher. Because he did so much more.

Reggie Jackson is, of course, his touchstone. The electric showdown between the baby-faced Welch and the charismatic Yankee slugger in Game 2 of the 1978 World Series was only the most memorable Fall Classic moment for the Dodgers between Sandy Koufax and Kirk Gibson.

For an encore, on a dreary October afternoon in Montreal, it was Welch who preserved an NL pennant for the Dodgers, relieving Fernando Valenzuela with two on and two out in the bottom of the ninth and retiring Jerry White to save the 2–1, all-or-nothing Game 5 of the 1981 NLCS.

Welch went on to win a Cy Young Award, but that came in 1990, three years after the Dodgers traded him to the Oakland A's. And after Welch's 27–6 season, even in an era when won-lost records still mattered to most people, some wrote off his success to the 5.2 runs per game provided by Oakland's "Bash Brothers" offense.

For 99 percent of the baseball world, Welch's career is tied to those three bullet points and one other defining legacy. He was one of the first athletes, and perhaps the youngest, to admit that he had a drinking problem. His memoir, *Five O'Clock Comes Early: A Young Man's Battle with Alcoholism*, written with George Vecsey and published when Welch was still only 25 years old, stunned in its honesty and power, and reverberates decades later.

"The first book I read [in rehab] was called *Five O'Clock Comes Early*," Yankees pitcher CC Sabathia said in 2016, "and it hit so incredibly close to home…Bob was a source of inspiration for me."

If Welch had done nothing more than strike out Jackson and ride off into the sunset, he'd still be cherished by Dodger fans. That's what makes it so striking that in the end, he has been underappreciated for what he did in the rotation. Since the Dodgers moved to Los Angeles, only six pitchers accumulated more wins above replacement for the team than Welch: Don Drysdale, Clayton Kershaw, Koufax, Don Sutton, Orel Hershiser, and Valenzuela. Add in Dazzy Vance, Nap Rucker, and Jeff Pfeffer from Brooklyn if you like, and Welch remains one of the 10 most statistically valuable pitchers in franchise history.

"What an arm, what a competitor," knuckleballer Charlie Hough says. "He was the real thing. He'd throw a little bit of a curveball, but he was basically a hard thrower. He just went after 'em."

It doesn't help Welch's reputation that in his three postseason starts as a Dodger, he lasted a combined four innings, beginning with a 1981 World Series Game 4 outing in which he was pulled immediately after the first four batters reached base.

Nevertheless, Welch had a 3.14 ERA (114 ERA+) in 292 regular-season games for the Dodgers, all but 25 of them coming as a starting pitcher. He was a fixture in the Dodger starting rotation for eight seasons (1980–87), and except for the first two months of 1985, was always available to take his turn.

Those who saw Welch firsthand, from the moment the Dodgers called him up in the middle of the 1978 season, speak of him in awe.

"I loved him, I loved him," says Tommy Lasorda. "I didn't like it when they traded him, to be perfectly honest with you. He was such a great guy, and I loved him real good."

The 6-foot-3 right-hander was the Dodgers' first-round draft pick in 1977 out of Eastern Michigan University, where he had a 1.63 ERA and 205 strikeouts in 166⅓ innings. As early as 1976, renowned baseball writer Roger Angell wrote about Welch in *The New Yorker*, saying "he threw with a kind of explosive elegance." Al Campanis said Welch wouldn't have lasted long enough for the Dodgers to get him with their 20th overall pick if not for a strained flexor tendon in his junior year in college that scared off some teams, while a clean report from Dr. Frank Jobe eased any anxiety in Los Angeles.

Tommy John remembers running laps in the outfield with pitcher Rick Rhoden as the Dodgers began to tinker with their new toy.

"Al Campanis was down there," John says, "and Al was showing him how to throw the Johnny Podres changeup, and he was showing him how to throw the Sandy Koufax curveball. Now here is a guy that they just drafted in the first round, and you got a guy down there that never pitched in his life showing him how to throw the Podres pull-the-window-shade-down changeup and the Koufax 12-to-6 curveball, and Rhoden and I, as we're running, we're laughing, and we said, 'We wonder if Welch is going to be the same after his session.'"

Welch himself said that Sutton told him, "Listen, I don't care what anybody says. You know what got you here. You've got to be your own pitcher."

Welch made his major-league debut on June 20, 1978, with two shutout innings against the Astros, striking out the first batter he faced, Mike Fischlin. The next night, Welch entered the game against Houston in the top of the 10th inning and struck out the side, pitched a shutout 11th inning, and came away with his first win. After two more relief appearances and a six-inning spot start, Welch had 12⅓ scoreless innings with 13 strikeouts and no walks to begin his MLB career.

In August, he entered the Dodger starting rotation, kicking off the month against the Giants at Candlestick Park, no less. The Dodgers had lost six straight games, falling out of a tie for first place in the NL West to 4½ games behind the Giants. Two of the losses had been walkoffs, a fresh memory when Welch and the Dodgers led 2–0 but San Francisco put the tying runs on base with one out in the bottom of the ninth.

More than 50,000 fans at Candlestick Park were in a frenzy. Millions more in a national *Saturday Game of the Week* audience watched. The batter was Jack Clark. It was, though people didn't realize it at the time, the dress rehearsal for Jackson. Lasorda went to the mound to tell Welch he was going to the bullpen.

"No you're not," Welch said.

"Do you want this guy?" asked Lasorda. "How bad do you want to pitch against him?"

"I want to pitch against this guy real bad. You can't take me out."

Years later, Lasorda still remembers the exchange vividly. "That's what I wanted to get out of him. I said, 'Okay, you got him.' Threw the fastball belt high, strike one. Raised it a couple inches, strike two. Raised it a couple more inches, strike three."

Clark sat down, Hector Cruz then flied to left, and the game was over.

Welch pitched two more shutouts in September, finishing his rookie season with a 2.02 ERA (174 ERA+) in 111⅓ innings. But with the Dodgers' stacked starting rotation, led by Hooton, John, and Sutton, Welch slid easily back into the bullpen for the playoffs. In his first career postseason appearance, he pitched the final 4⅓ innings of NLCS Game 1, allowing one Phillies run and earning the win. In his second career postseason appearance came Jackson.

Actually, before Jackson, there was Thurman Munson. Clinging to a 4–3 lead entering the ninth, the Dodgers tried to get a third inning out of Terry Forster, but a Bucky Dent single and a Paul Blair walk with one out put the tying and winning runs on. With Munson up and Jackson on deck, Welch entered the game.

"I think he was a take-charge guy," says Dodger announcer Ross Porter. "He liked to be in those situations, and he was very confident in his abilities—'Give me the ball and let me do my job.' I never saw him shaken or put in a position where he wasn't very cool about it. I thought he was very composed and obviously had a good arm."

On Welch's second pitch, Munson lined to a perfectly positioned Reggie Smith in right, before the epic nine-pitch at-bat with Jackson began.

"What was I thinking at the time?" Welch asked. "I would have to say I wasn't thinking much at all. Just following my instincts. If I start fooling around, I lose my concentration. Concentration is not the same as thinking. It's almost the opposite."

"For a young kid in that situation, he had the ice water running through his veins," says his catcher that night, Steve Yeager. "He didn't care who it was. He was thinking he just had a job to do, and he went and did it. He wasn't afraid of nobody.

"It was fastball after fastball. We were going right after him. We just needed to go a little higher, a little higher, a little higher. Finally, we got up where he wasn't going to swing and hit it. He'd swing and foul one off, but the way that Bobby went out for him and the way Reggie went after him, it was a contest, it was a battle. And Welchy won."

It was, unfortunately for the Dodgers, the last game they won in 1978, including their controversial Game 4 loss in which Jackson got revenge on the Dodgers, first with his hip knocking a Bill Russell throw into right field to enable a sixth-inning run to score, then with a 10th-inning single off Welch (in his third inning of work) that set up Lou Piniella's game-winning RBI.

Still, during spring training at Vero Beach before the 1979 season, no less than Koufax himself commented on the potential of Welch. "He's got the stuff," Koufax said. "All he needs is to come up with that curveball. Then, who knows? He might go on to be one of the greatest."

During a first half of the season that left the defending league champions in last place in the NL West, Welch was a rare bright spot. Used both as a starter and a closer, Welch had a 2.76 ERA at the end of May. But all the work during the past year plagued him with a tired arm, and he only pitched $35\frac{2}{3}$ innings the rest of '79.

Something else was fraying as well.

No one really seemed to know what went on inside Welch's head. He was eccentric, and he drank, but those were not unprecedented characteristics in a big-league clubhouse. That Welch harbored what was essentially a life-threatening condition wasn't obvious to anyone at first.

"I found out, I guess, when everybody else on the team found out," says Reuss, who joined the Dodgers in 1979. "There were some guys who were more aware of it, but I was surprised—I said I had no idea. Because I had been on teams where guys did drink a lot. They weren't called alcoholics, but by today's standards or standards that were established back in the '80s, oh yeah they were…It was kind of hidden from sight, but when it wasn't, you just figured the guy had a little too much and about the most you would say to him was, 'Come on, we can't do this every night,' and that was that."

In his book, Welch said that he was a drinker in high school and that as early as a college All-Star trip to Japan, USC coach Rod Dedeaux told him that he was acting just like an alcoholic. Welch said he was "stone sober" when he struck out Jackson, but for the most part, the issue wasn't that he was under the influence of liquor 24/7. It's that it was his frequent escape.

"The booze helped soften the losing and helped heighten the winning, but the main thing was, I couldn't face reality," Welch said. "The reality was too intense, so I would use a chemical to give me the mood I wanted."

At the same time, it hadn't registered with Welch that he was really an alcoholic. Don Newcombe, at this time the Dodgers' director of community relations, gave talks about the perils of drinking, explaining how he lost his career and nearly his life, and Welch didn't think that applied to him, no matter what happened over his first two years in the majors—showing up 10 minutes before game time after a night of binging, or taking his Bronco for a late-night drive on the beach and rolling it over. After striking out Clark during his rookie-year shutout, Welch had eight beers and missed the team bus from Candlestick.

In spring training of '79, Lasorda suggested to Welch that he needed to take better care of himself.

"He told me not to stay out so late," Welch said. "He said there was nothing wrong in having a beer, but I didn't have to stay out till the wee hours of the morning and get drunk. But the truth is, there *was* something wrong with my having a beer. I couldn't stop at one or two. I don't think anybody realized it at the time.

"What should people have done when I was acting like this in spring training? Probably, the Dodgers and my family should have confronted me with my behavior. Just pull me in a room and say, 'This is what you have been doing.' To confront alcoholics, you have to love them enough to hurt them, to cut through their defenses, their denial. I was putting up a wall, trying to frighten people away."

Midway through the '79 season, Welch admitted, he started drinking during games. Newcombe got wind of Welch's habits. So did Dale McReynolds, the Dodger scout who signed him. Campanis attempted an intervention with Lasorda, but neither knew how to conduct one—and Welch blew up at them.

One night in San Francisco that September, Welch drank all night and into the next day, barely making it to the ballpark for the finale of the road trip. He was openly out of control of his faculties during batting practice, nearly stumbling unsolicited into a pregame brawl with Terry Whitfield of the Giants, almost a complete stranger, and any notion that Welch didn't have a serious problem was out the window. All that remained was Welch's denial.

That off-season, Welch was given a 20-question quiz about his condition. Answering yes to at least three of the questions meant you were an alcoholic. Welch said yes to eight. Led by Newcombe, the Dodgers' program for addressing alcoholism was coming together. They encouraged Welch to check into a rehab center, The Meadows.

"The truth is, I was tired of having problems with my drinking," Welch said, "and I wanted to help myself. I didn't want to ruin my life. But on the other hand, I wasn't ready to admit that I was an alcoholic, and the idea of not drinking at all seemed very distant. I just wanted to 'control' my drinking, whatever that meant."

Nearly 100 pages of Welch's book is devoted to the 36 days he spent at The Meadows. He emerged a different person, and he made amends to the Dodger organization at spring training in 1980.

"I could see some guys were shocked, but the reaction was kind of positive," Davey Lopes said. "There are very few people in the world able to accept something negative about themselves. I don't think I would have…He knows he's going to take a lot of hell from some ignorant people, but he's ready for it. He can handle it now."

"Everything seemed easier in 1980," Welch said. "I was no longer going around mad at people, suspecting they were checking up on my drinking. I was running to get myself in better shape, not to burn the alcohol out of my system. I had better control of myself in every way."

The Dodgers put Welch in the rotation to stay that year. He made every start, highlighted by a one-hit shutout of Atlanta in which he faced the minimum 27 batters. He finished the year with a 3.29 ERA (108 ERA+) in 213⅔ innings.

"To me, it was more than symbolic that I could finally throw a change of pace," Welch said. "Before, I never could relax enough to let up on my fastball, to permit the ball to float toward the plate, to throw the hitter off stride. In 1980, sober for the first time since I was a young teenager, I started learning the changeup."

Welch pitched three one-hitters in his career, and also homered for the only run in a 1–0 shutout of the Reds in 1983. From 1980 until the end of 1987, when he was included in the three-team deal that brought Alfredo Griffin, Jay Howell, and Jesse Orosco to Los Angeles, he was—as unlikely as it might have seemed at one point—as stable as they come.

The trade meant Welch was on the wrong side of the '88 World Series, but he got his second ring the following year with the A's. He retired after the 1994 season with a 3.47 ERA (106 ERA+) for his career in 3,092 innings.

Shockingly, Welch died on June 9, 2014, at age 57, after an accidental fall in his home. He left behind great memories and a greater impact.

"I have heard from dozens of people," Vecsey wrote after Welch's passing, "who were sober, day by day, because Bob Welch, star pitcher, had gone public about his addiction to that dangerous drug called alcohol, and how he took treatment for it."

Jerry Reuss

You could joke—and Jerry Reuss was no one if not someone who liked a good joke—that the left-hander's first playoff experience quite endeared him to Dodger fans, with the small detail that he was wearing a Pirates uniform at the time.

Reuss was the losing pitcher in the first and last games of the 1974 NLCS that sent Los Angeles to the World Series against Oakland. He took a hard-luck defeat in Game 1, allowing one run in seven innings while Don Sutton was pitching his shutout, before earning a quick hook (three runs in 2⅔ innings) in the Dodgers' pennant-clinching 12–1 Game 4 victory.

That might have been Southern California's lasting memory of Reuss, who largely (at 6-foot-5, that is) pitched out of mind and sight of Elysian Park. Reuss debuted in the majors with seven shutout innings for St. Louis at age 20 in 1969, then apprenticed two years there before a trade to Houston on the day the 1972 baseball season began. After leading the NL in starts in 1973, he was forwarded to Pittsburgh, spending five years there, summed up by a 3.52 ERA (103 ERA+) and highlighted by an All-Star selection in 1975, when he finished with an ERA of 2.54 (139 ERA+).

Then, almost out of nowhere, Reuss reentered the Dodgers' world, exchanged straight up for Rick Rhoden three days after the 1979 season began. The trade might seem strange: Rhoden had a 3.40 ERA (105 ERA+) in 670⅓ career innings—not to mention four homers swinging the bat—and was about to turn 26, while the soon-to-be 30 Reuss was coming off his most disappointing season in the majors, with a 4.90 ERA (76 ERA+) in 82⅔ innings.

The Dodgers already had five starting pitchers in Sutton, Burt Hooton, Doug Rau, Bob Welch, and the reacquired Andy Messersmith, and there wasn't room for Rhoden, who had suffered through a sore shoulder the year before. There wasn't room for Reuss either, but on a staff that leaned heavily to the right side, Reuss' southpaw arm could be more of an asset, whether starting or relieving.

On April 9, in his first game for Los Angeles, Reuss pitched four innings of shutout relief to preserve a 2–1 Dodger victory. The first time an opening came up in the starting rotation, it went not to Reuss but to Rick Sutcliffe, who became NL Rookie of the Year. For the first two months of the season, Reuss pitched strictly out of Tommy Lasorda's bullpen.

As it happened, Reuss' first start in a Dodger uniform came against his recent Pittsburgh teammates in June 1979, with him allowing one earned run in seven innings. But for a Dodger team that had to rally in the second half of the season just to finish in third place in the NL West, Reuss remained a mystery piece, fluttering in and out of the pen. A sizzling September (six starts, 43⅓ innings, and a 1.25 ERA) should have guaranteed him a full-time spot in the rotation, but there was still a waiting game to be played.

Reuss' first spring training with the Dodgers came in 1980, when he really saw the depth of the Dodger pitching tradition, meeting Carl Erskine, Preacher Roe, Johnny Podres, Sandy Koufax, and Don Drysdale.

"There were always pitchers of note," Reuss says, "monuments of Dodger pitching history. And because of that, you believed that there was continuity and there was something special with the Dodgers, simply because of that personal connection. And that made a huge difference. Those were living, breathing historical figures that you'd only read about, and they knew your first name. So there was a connection with the team that came from Brooklyn, and the team that transitioned into Los Angeles and developed, and all of the guys in between—which included Sutton, who was still an integral part of the ballclub when I joined it."

Sutton, in fact, was already laying down guidelines for Reuss.

"Sutton came to me when I first joined the club," Reuss recalls, "and said, 'It's my job to tell you this—you take it how you want. You've been around a long time, so I'll tell you different than I'd tell a kid. But we have a workout program here, and because this workout program has been successful, we're allowed to monitor our own program. So you get your program, and let Red [Adams] know what you want to do, then you go out and do it—it's your responsibility. Lasorda's on board with this, with a reservation, and that reservation is if he finds that a pitcher is not doing his work, then all the pitchers will revert back to the traditional running program that the Dodgers had at one time and other teams were employing at that time.'"

Sutton then circled back to his point.

"'I'm telling you this because I don't want you to be the guy to screw things up for everybody else.'"

Nothing to worry about. Reuss fine-tuned his workout program upon arriving with the Dodgers, and stuck to it.

"How much did it help? Well, I believed in it," Reuss says. "I liked it. And by virtue of that, if nothing else, that worked for me. You can get into a workout program, and if you don't believe in it, if you don't commit to it, you're not going to get results. You see, there were a lot of guys who never even touched a weight because they said, 'I don't need this.' I had one teammate with the Dodgers who said, 'Babe Ruth was one of the all-time greats, and he never lifted a weight.' And my comeback to that was, 'Well, guess how good he could have been had he done weights and not alcohol and carousing.' That kind of shut that up."

On top of everything else, Reuss' time in the bullpen had produced an unexpected benefit: a cut fastball that ignited the best phase of his pitching career.

"I think it was accidental," Reuss says. "Warming up in the bullpen pitching in relief, I had to get ready in a hurry. And somehow the normal release that I have with the ball on my fingertips—particularly with the middle finger, which was the last finger to leave the ball when it left my hand—went from the outer tip to the inner tip. And that was the difference in the movement of the pitch. [Bullpen catcher] Mark Cresse said, 'Nobody has a pitch like that, and you're throwing it at a pretty good velocity and you're right on mark with it every time.'"

Perhaps the most famous cutter for the Dodgers belongs to Kenley Jansen, but Reuss' approach was different.

"He pitches up a lot, and I was exactly the opposite," Reuss says. "I worked down a lot. Everything that I threw in those four years that I'm talking about was in the lower region of the strike zone. And because I was so consistent there, there were times that I believe I got a pitch called my way, even though it was an inch, maybe two inches off the plate. And that forced batters, knowing that the umpire was going to call it a strike, to go after a pitch that was out of the strike zone."

If left-handed batters made contact with Reuss' cutter, they usually cued it off the end of their bat. Righties might pull the ball hard, but foul.

"I can't tell you the number of rockets I saw go down the third-base line that ended up in the stands," Reuss says. "Boy, I would have brought a garbage can lid to Dodger Stadium when I was pitching if I had seats down that third-base line, particularly over that auxiliary scoreboard."

Though he didn't make his first 1980 start until mid-May (thanks in part to the Dodgers' off-season free-agent signing of Dave Goltz), what followed for Reuss was one of the best four-year runs in Dodger history and the best four years of the 22 he spent in the majors. From 1980 to 1983, Reuss' 2.76 ERA and 127 ERA+ were second only to Steve Carlton among NL starting pitchers. The cutter was the missing piece of the puzzle.

"I could put that ball where I wanted on the inside corner to a right-handed batter," Reuss says, "and because I could do that, it made my other pitches better, because I could go to the opposite side of the plate with the sinker, and I could also change speeds with that sinker, thereby making two different kinds of fastballs, one with a change of speed to it, somewhere in between a fastball and a changeup. Plus, I had a couple of different curveballs. It was the first time in my career that I had an extended run of running on all cylinders."

In 1980, Reuss was spectacular at times, not the least of them being the June 27 no-hitter he threw at San Francisco that was a Bill Russell error shy of a perfect game. His ERA dropped to 1.87 that night, firming up his position for the 1980 All-Star Game, where before a Dodger Stadium crowd of 56,088, he struck out all three hitters he faced and emerged as the night's winning pitcher. He also pitched a complete-game, 2–1 victory over Houston on the season's final weekend, part of the Dodgers' three-game sweep to force a one-game playoff for the NL West title against Houston.

"Here came a big guy that had a lot of ease and a lot of elbows flying at you," Steve Yeager says. "He'd throw tremendously hard from the left side. He had a little bit of a breaking ball. Great competitor and a goofy individual. And that's the kind of guy you like."

Outside of being scratched from his Opening Day start in 1981 because of sore calves (the Dodgers got some rookie named Fernando Valenzuela to take his place) and the interruption of the strike at midseason, Reuss found himself sailing like '81 Grammy-winner Christopher Cross, concluding the regular season with a career-best 2.30 ERA (146 ERA+) and an NL-leading six shutouts. In 18 NLDS innings against the Astros that October, Reuss allowed 15 baserunners and no runs, leaping into the air from the mound to celebrate the final out in the winner-take-all Game 5.

If it appeared Reuss was running out of gas following a losing effort in Game 3 of the '81 NLCS and a third-inning exit in Game 1 of the World Series, his heroics in Game 5 of the Fall Classic forever etched him into the Dodger pitching pantheon he had first encountered as an outsider.

The Yankees scored a second-inning run on a double, an error, and an infield single, but Reuss pitched out of a first-and-third jam in the third inning and survived New York loading the bases with one out in the fourth, buying time for the Dodgers to rally off the Yankees' Ron Guidry with home runs by Pedro Guerrero and Yeager. With two out and one on in the ninth, Reuss fanned Aurelio Rodriguez to finish the 2–1 victory.

At this point, it was impossible for Reuss not to be a fan favorite. On top of all his success, Reuss was forming a lasting reputation as a merry prankster of the clubhouse.

"I always loved a good laugh," Reuss says. "In the major leagues, there are certain things you just don't do. There are unwritten rules. There are codes. My sense of humor developed over time once I learned what could be done and what guys laughed at."

Among the many stories Reuss tells in his book, *Bring in the Right-Hander*, is of the time the Dodger plane had to make a refueling stop in Chicago on its way home from Montreal. Challenging Lasorda's vaunted celebrity, Reuss bet him $50 that he couldn't have a dozen pizzas waiting on the tarmac when they landed in the Windy City. Lasorda took the challenge, and sure enough, as soon as the doors of the plane opened, a kid came up the steps with the pizzas. Lasorda met him, then grabbed the plane's intercom.

"I bet Reuss $50 that I could have a dozen pizzas delivered when we landed here. I want him to pay up in front of all of you!" he announced boldly.

Reuss gave him a crisp $50 bill, then grabbed the mic.

"Where else could you get 12 pizzas for $50?" he called out. "The food's on me, everybody. Enjoy!"

As Reuss began passing out the pizzas to his grateful, laughing teammates, Lasorda realized he'd been had.

No pizza gag in the world would have gotten laughs if Reuss hadn't continued to deliver on the mound. He had a 3.11 ERA (113 ERA+) in 1982, highlighted by another near-perfect game in which he gave up a leadoff double to the Reds' Eddie Milner on June 11 and retired the next 27 batters in a row, as well as the day in Chicago on August 11 in which he initially pitched innings 18 through 21 in the resumption of a game that had been suspended because of darkness, and then the first five innings of the regularly scheduled game, winning both. That was followed by a 2.94 ERA (123 ERA+) in '83 and two more postseason starts, albeit less rewarding ones. A Mike Schmidt home run in the first inning of Game 1 of the 1983 NLCS, for the only run of the game, preceded a duller Game 4 loss.

After a 1984 season in which he was slowed by elbow and heel injuries, Reuss' last strong season came in 1985, when his 2.92 ERA (119 ERA+) helped lift Los Angeles back into the playoffs, where they met the Cardinals in the NLCS. Pitching in Game 4, Reuss and the Dodgers unraveled in a nine-run second inning by St. Louis. In Game 6, he was in the bullpen, a candidate to face Andy Van Slyke in the top of the ninth, if the Dodgers could get past the bat of Jack Clark with the lead. But they didn't.

The Dodgers hung on to Reuss one game into the 1987 season, when they released him—the third team, across a period of 15 years, to part ways with him in April. His Dodger career ended with a 3.11 ERA (113 ERA+) in 1,407⅔ innings, not to mention the best ratio of home runs per nine innings—0.48—of any pitcher in Los Angeles Dodger history with at least 1,000 innings.

Like Sutton and Tommy John, Reuss pitched into his forties, becoming a four-decade player in 1990 back with the Pirates. He wound up throwing 3,669⅔ innings in 22 seasons, with a 3.64 ERA (100 ERA+).

While contemplating his legacy and that of his fellow Dodger pitchers, Reuss emphasized that any success they had did not come without help.

Two gifted men behind the plate shepherded the Dodger staff for most of the 1970s and '80s, and however much credit Yeager and Mike Scioscia have been given, it's not enough.

"Yeager was an outstanding defensive catcher," Reuss says. "I didn't see a whole lot of guys in the American League, so you have to qualify my opinion here, but Yeager was the best defensive catcher I've seen outside of Johnny Bench. He would do things defensively, that it was like having a fifth infielder. That's why I'm surprised when they talk about the [Ron Cey–Bill Russell–Davey Lopes–Steve Garvey] infield, they don't include Yeager. Yeager was so good, he could field bunts that should have been an infielder's play or a pitcher's play—he was so quick out of the box and his footwork was so good and the accuracy and the strength of his throws were so good."

Yeager played 14 of his 15 big-league seasons with the Dodgers, from 1972 to 1985, and was in his eighth year when the Dodgers acquired Reuss. By that time, his preparation for the game to come was more instinctual than anything else.

Says Reuss: "Yeager would take a drag off his cigarette, tap the ashes, and look at me and say, 'Here's what I'm gonna do. I'm gonna use my index finger and my little finger for a fastball. You throw either fastball you want, I'm gonna catch it. Now as far as your curveball, we'll use it, we'll mix it in. Your changeup is nonexistent—so don't even think about that. Now, let's go get 'em. You have any questions?' And that was a pregame meeting with Yeager."

In the bygone era of lawless plays at the plate, Yeager and Scioscia were brick walls, risking life and limb in shattering collisions to stop freight trains like Dave Parker from scoring. But Scioscia, who was promoted to the majors as a 21-year-old during Reuss' second Dodger season in 1980, was more studious in his game preparation, according to Reuss, breaking down the opposing lineup batter by batter, planning not only for that day's start but starts to come.

"He would say, 'What I want to do is show him a pitch first or second time through the order and see what kind of reaction we get, because that I think is the kind of pitch we can use later on in the ballgame to get an out with runners on base,'" Reuss notes. "And he would remember this, and he said, 'If we don't use that, we'll use it the next time you pitch, because you're scheduled to pitch to him when we go to their place. We'll just keep that as a card in our pocket.'"

Robert Schweppe, a longtime executive with the Dodgers, kept an ongoing notebook on the Dodger pitching philosophy, replete with his own observations and tidbits from conversations up and down the organization. In his view, Dodger receivers deserved awards as best supporting actors in the team's pitching tradition.

"There was an emphasis on complete involvement of the catchers in the organization for pitching development," Schweppe said. "The line of Dodger catchers for 40 years ran through Roy Campanella, John Roseboro, Steve Yeager, Mike Scioscia, and Mike Piazza. Campanella was a regular visitor to spring training for minor-league catchers and always available for the catchers on the major-league team when he would attend games at Dodger Stadium. Roseboro, Scioscia, and Yeager would also become catching instructors for the team after their playing careers with the organization."

Before their playing careers ended, Yeager and Scioscia each caught more than 1,000 games for Los Angeles. While Yeager coxswained the boat for many of the Modern Classicists, Scioscia emerged in the 1980s to shepherd the two biggest pitching luminaries since Koufax and Drysdale—one left-handed, one right-handed, both legendary.

PART FIVE

EL TORO AND THE BULLDOG

The left-hander arrived in a soft rumble over a few weeks as late summer glided into the fall of 1980, a low-level gathering storm, before tearing across the baseball sky in an awe-inspiring flash during the spring of 1981.

The right-hander materialized even more quietly, downright unobtrusively, in the waning days of 1983. Even in the summer of 1984, when the light first shone on him, it's not clear that Dodger fans could understand what they were seeing, could process the first colors of what became a full-blown aurora borealis by the fall of 1988.

The glow of Fernando Valenzuela and Orel Hershiser might never land in Cooperstown. Neither had the sublime five years of the supernova Sandy Koufax, nor the durably dominant longevity of a baseball Jupiter such as Don Sutton. At the same time, Valenzuela and Hershiser were two comets, each shattering illusions of impossibility, delivering poetry on the field and inspiring the same off the field. Their legacies resonate decades later, as if descended from the stars.

Fernando Valenzuela

He rocked back into his windup, his head dropping back slightly, his eyes tilting upward, as if having a secret, personal communication with the heavens.

The eyes had it.

"He turned the game into a religion," broadcaster Jaime Jarrín once said. More than a pitcher, Fernando Valenzuela was, of course, a mania. His dusty cinematic background, his cuddly youth, and his quietly wry air of mystery fused with his preternatural talent, creating in Los Angeles an immediate sensation and an enduring love affair.

It was nothing that could have been foreseen before the 1980s, least of all by Valenzuela, born the youngest of seven boys and five girls in his family in the Mexican town of Etchohuaquila, near the eastern shore of the Gulf of California, on the first day of November in 1960. Like Sandy Koufax, like Don Drysdale, he didn't begin pitching until his teens.

"I started playing ball when I was maybe 13," Valenzuela says. "From that time I liked the game, but I think what I remember more is I had a chance to play with my brothers. We had a large family and I've got a lot of brothers, so everyone was playing on the same team. I think that helped me a lot, and they gave me some good advice."

Valenzuela had older relatives at second base, short, third, the outfield, and, yes, on the mound, for which he had to wait for his own opportunity.

"We had a winter league that played only Sundays, once a week," he says. "It was open—no age limit. They told me, 'You're gonna play but you're not gonna pitch, because you're too young—your arm is not ready to throw the ball.' And I think that helped me a lot, because I wanted to pitch—that was my favorite position, but they told me, 'You're not ready—your arm is not ready.'

"Probably I was almost 15 years old when I started pitching. That's when they let me pitch one inning. Little by little—they didn't let me go all the way and let my arm get tired and throw many pitches. But I had a chance to pitch every week, because it was once every Sunday, so that wasn't a problem."

As his talent became apparent, Valenzuela aimed to play professionally —first in Mexico, then in the U.S.—a goal that became more and more realistic once scouts began circling. One of those bird dogs was the Dodgers' Mike Brito, though partly by happenstance—Brito was scoping a shortstop when he first came upon the precocious southpaw.

The Dodgers officially purchased the 18-year-old Valenzuela's contract from his Mexican League team in July 1979 for a reported $120,000, of which $20,000 went to the teenager, who passed it on to his family.

"We made one offer," Dodger general manager Al Campanis later said, "and the Yankees made one. Then we came back and closed the deal before the Yankees had a chance to make another bid."

Fourteen months later, Valenzuela would be in Dodger Stadium.

His American journey began with three starts before the end of the 1979 minor-league season for Single-A Lodi, allowing three earned runs in 24 innings for a 1.12 ERA—though he walked 13. In the fall of '79, he went to the instructional league, where Brito broke the news that the Dodgers wanted him to learn another pitch.

Dodger reliever Bobby Castillo (another Brito signee) obliged by showing Valenzuela a pitch that was mostly a relic, whose most famous practitioner, Carl Hubbell, had retired in 1943.

Many remember Valenzuela mastering the screwball almost immediately. Castillo, who died of cancer in 2014, once said that Valenzuela had the proper rotation on the first screwball he threw, and that within a week, the pitch had stopped flattening out. But Valenzuela, who took the pitch with him to Double-A San Antonio in 1980, says it took months to command it (not that "months" is so bad for a prospect still in his teens).

"That was hard in the beginning," Valenzuela says, "but I kept practicing and practicing, because the Dodgers gave me confidence: 'Don't worry, don't look at the numbers. Whatever score or whatever record you have does not count. We want you to learn that pitch.' I wanted to stop throwing it—I was a good control pitcher, but I was giving out a lot of walks. But the Dodgers told me not to worry—'Just keep practicing, keep throwing.' So I said, 'Well, if that's going to put me up there, I'm going to keep working on it.'"

Valenzuela recalls a game against Amarillo in the second half of the season that marked the first time he felt he was controlling the screwball, instead of the screwball controlling him.

"That's when I started to say, 'Okay, I think it's ready,' because every time I wanted to throw inside, outside, the ball was there," Valenzuela says. "Finally, I started to get more and more command, I threw more over the plate, and the hitters started chasing bad pitches. Normally, the hitters let it go because they knew it was a ball, but when the hitters started seeing I got more control with that pitch, then I could throw it off the plate and they'd chase it, because they were saying, 'Now he can throw it for a strike—now where's it going to be?'"

At the same time, Ron Perranoski, then the Dodgers' minor-league pitching coordinator, had taught Valenzuela to start busting his fastball inside to counter right-handed batters leaning out after the right-to-left movement of the screwball. The results were devastating. Valenzuela completed seven of his final eight starts in 1980 with four shutouts and didn't allow a run in his final 35 innings with San Antonio, enabling him to reach 174 innings for the Missions with a 3.10 ERA and 162 strikeouts.

The Dodgers, in the midst of spending a week in September tied with Houston for first place in the NL West, matching the Astros win for win and loss for loss, called up the kid to help out their bullpen. It was all circumstance, no pomp—and Valenzuela's mixed feelings initially nixed the gig in exchange for a Texas League title.

"I didn't want to come up, because we were in the playoffs," Valenzuela says. "My manager in Double-A, Ducky LeJohn, said, 'You're going to the big leagues.' And I said, 'No, I want to finish here. I want to be a champion here.'"

LeJohn wasn't sure Valenzuela understood.

"No, they need you there, so you have to go," Le John said. "If not, we're going to send another one."

"Okay, send another one," Valenzuela replied, calling his bluff.

LeJohn folded his hand—and then put his foot down, directing Valenzuela to nearby Houston to meet up with his new major-league teammates. The youngster didn't get into a game there, nor on the next stop of the Dodgers' road trip, in Cincinnati. On September 15, 1980, Valenzuela entered his first major-league contest in the sixth inning of what would be a 9–0 loss to Atlanta. He was 19 years and 319 days old.

"If I say I wasn't nervous, I'm not from this planet," jokes Valenzuela, who decades later still remembered his first batter, Bruce Benedict, popping out to center field. "Everybody gets nervous. But not, 'I don't want to do it.' I wasn't nervous because I didn't know if I was going to fail. I was just excited—I wanted to just get in the game and just see what would happen, because I didn't expect anything. I wanted to do my best, and whatever happened was fine."

After a perfect sixth, Valenzuela fanned Jerry Royster for his first career strikeout to start the seventh, though thanks to errors later in the inning by third baseman Ron Cey and shortstop Derrel Thomas, Valenzuela allowed two unearned runs. He didn't give up multiple runs in a big-league inning for another eight months.

"When I joined the team, everybody gave me a nice welcome," Valenzuela says. "The veteran players, they had been playing for many years, so I think that helped me a lot—for that part, I felt more comfortable. I got some friends, and they helped me."

It was like seeing Christmas thank the children for being so cheerful. In his debut month in the majors, Valenzuela was the unexpected present under the tree, throwing 17⅔ innings with that 0.00 ERA, striking out 16 and walking five. He quickly became invaluable. On September 27, he bailed out NL Rookie of the Year Steve Howe and 1979 World Series veteran Don Stanhouse by pitching the final 1⅓ innings against the Padres for the first of his two professional saves, then was the winning pitcher in back-to-back two-inning shutout outings. Those two wins more or less equaled the number of English words people believed Valenzuela knew at the time.

"They'd say, 'How do you communicate with Fernando?'" recalls Steve Yeager. "I said, 'With my fingers. That's all I need.'"

In the final-weekend sweep of the Astros that forced a 163rd game, Valenzuela came out of the bullpen twice, including two innings in Game 162, helping extend the season but eliminating any chance of him starting the Monday afternoon tiebreaker, as much as alternate history would have happily used him instead of Dave Goltz. Tommy Lasorda later expressed regret that he wasn't bold enough to start the kid with the division on the line.

"I had no idea what he was like until you catch him for a couple of times," Yeager says, "and you realize that as young as this young man is, he's pitching as though he's five years older."

"All I'm worried about," Red Adams said, "is that someone will make him lose 25 pounds, and he'll be the most physically fit pitcher in Lodi."

Heading into the 1981 season, it was clear that the Dodgers didn't plan on keeping Valenzuela from starting much longer—illustrated by their willingness to let Don Sutton go as a free agent. Valenzuela's maturity continued to stun everyone who came in contact with him, leading to questions about whether he was really as young as he was reported to be. Campanis told reporters he had a copy of Valenzuela's birth certificate on his desk. "Anyone who doubts it can come up and see it," Campanis said.

Valenzuela threw well in the spring, with a peak outing of six innings, to punch his ticket for the starting rotation, but it hadn't crossed anyone's mind he would take the mound on Opening Day. No rookie ever had for Los Angeles. But then his fellow pitchers started dropping like pawns in an Agatha Christie mystery. Bob Welch developed a bone spur in his right elbow. Goltz had a virus. Burt Hooton was vexed by an ingrown toenail. When Jerry Reuss strained a muscle in his left calf while running the day before the season opened, the Dodgers turned to Valenzuela.

"I was throwing on the side a little bullpen, a little warmup, working out," Valenzuela remembers. "And when I finished, they told me, 'We don't have a pitcher for tomorrow.' I said, 'Yes.' I didn't wait—I didn't wait to answer that question."

Says Lasorda: "I had no concern about it, because I saw him all spring."

In front of the festive red-white-and-blue bunting and 50,511 fans with no idea what to expect, Valenzuela took the mound on April 9, 1981. He began the game more wily than dominant, pitching around baserunners in each of the first three innings, including a couple of early walks, setting the tone for his bodacious big-league journey.

"From the first game through the 400 to 500 starts I had in my career," Valenzuela says, "early in the game, I always tried to be too fine, working in the corners, and that's when I'd maybe fall behind the hitters. And that made me get in trouble, because pitching like that to big-league hitters is not recommended. My style is not coming up right over the middle of the plate—I had to work in the corners."

Facing Joe Niekro, the winner of Game 163 the previous October, the Dodgers went ahead in the bottom of the fourth on Steve Garvey's triple and Cey's sacrifice fly. Valenzuela battled to hold the lead. With runners on second and third and one out in the top of the sixth, he broke Dodger nemesis Jose Cruz's bat on a soft liner to short, before inducing an Art Howe comebacker that Valenzuela—soon to be revealed as an expert fielder—flagged on one hop.

In the bottom of the seventh, 24-year-old Pedro Guerrero's RBI double provided a luxurious 2–0 lead for Valenzuela, who responded by pitching a perfect top of the eighth and retiring Cesar Cedeno and Cruz to start the exuberant ninth. Howe singled with two out, but on Valenzuela's 106th pitch, Dave Roberts (same name, different DNA from the future Dodger manager) whiffed. On a screwball.

In Dodger Stadium—and soon, throughout Los Angeles—the delight was indescribable. The baseball world didn't know what to think. The next day, a photograph in the *Los Angeles Times* showed Valenzuela in his windup, arms high above head, eyes looking up.

Mike Scioscia, himself only 22 and with 54 big-league games to his name, was also making his first Opening Day start and caught Valenzuela's shutout, as well as all but two of his starts in 1981.

"Even though he was 20 years old, he was pitching baseball like a veteran," Scioscia says. "Just the whole experience of when you would catch Fernando, just the way he was in command and control and never got flustered out there, all the things that are important in a championship-caliber pitcher, that was him."

Valenzuela's second start came April 14 in frigid Candlestick Park. In the eighth inning of that game, he finally allowed his first MLB earned run, on a two-out double by Larry Herndon and RBI single by Enos Cabell, in what was otherwise a masterful 10-strikeout, 7–1 victory over the Giants. Adding in his San Antonio scoreless streak, it was the first earned run he had allowed in 69⅓ innings.

"Fernando's way of doing things was working around the screwball," Reuss says. "Fernando's pitches, if you grade 'em out just on velocity or movement, they may be average, maybe a little bit better. But where his numbers really jumped were in his mixing of pitches and his ability to be just as deceptive as he was. That's what Fernando was all about. It wasn't about his stuff. It was about deception."

Lasorda took quick advantage of his amazing new talent. Valenzuela made each of his next two starts on three days' rest and threw back-to-back shutouts, first 2–0 at San Diego, then 1–0 at Houston, where he drove in the game's only run with an RBI single off Sutton.

"When he had to make pitches, he made them," Sutton said after the game. "With men in scoring position, he never gave one of our hitters a good pitch to hit."

In the first two weeks of the 1981 season, Valenzuela had thrown 36 innings and struck out 36, while allowing only the one run. By this time, the media frenzy had begun, with pregame sessions becoming press conferences. "This is where we get set to say good-bye to Valenzuela's childhood," wrote Mark Heisler of the *Los Angeles Times*. A day later, on April 27, the headline on Scott Ostler's column was one word, appearing in print for the first time: FERNANDOMANIA.

"I was excited," Valenzuela recalls. "It was fine—hard, at the same time. On the field, I was fine. Off the field, after the games—sometimes people or the media didn't understand—they wanted the interview right away, and I had to work, I had to be with the team. In that time, that was the hard part, but when I went on the field, that was exciting, because I knew what I had to do. I had a lot of confidence in my stuff."

"The Mexican people in Los Angeles were clamoring for an idol," Jarrín says. "When he started pitching in 1981, not only Mexicans, not only Latinos, but the Anglos also took notice of this kid, a little bit chubby, long hair, who couldn't speak any English. The American people fell in love with him. Everybody."

Rather than deploy a teammate or coach like Manny Mota to translate, vice president of public relations Fred Claire asked Jarrín to do so. On road trips, Jarrín and Valenzuela began flying to the next city a day ahead of the team in preparation for the next media onslaught, and when Valenzuela pitched, Jarrín left the broadcast booth in the eighth inning to be ready for the postgame Q&A from dumbstruck reporters.

"He was always very reserved," said Jarrín, who at the outset of his third decade with the Dodgers became a mini-national celebrity in the process. "In 1980, the writers didn't pay much attention to him because he was just a member of the bullpen. Then '81 started, and everything became a madhouse there. But he was always a very reserved person, very private person. Many people wondered if he knew exactly where he was and what was happening around him—and he knew exactly. Extremely sharp guy, very intelligent."

With his teammates, Valenzuela was generally quiet, but his sense of humor snuck up and delighted them.

"Fernando liked to play around," Reuss says. "Liked to play jokes too. Did anybody tell you about his lasso? He made a lasso out of clothesline, maybe he had a couple of different ones. And when somebody wasn't looking—they'd put their foot up or cross their legs and sit comfortably on the bench, in a conversation or watching the game—he'd get his lasso out and just like a cowboy, he'd spin it over his head and catch somebody's foot and then yank it off their knee."

The night the FERNANDOMANIA headline appeared, Valenzuela pitched his fourth shutout of the month, 5–0 over San Francisco—while going 3-for-4 to raise his batting average to .438. His career ERA at that moment was 0.14.

"We had no idea that he would rise as fast as he did," Hooton says, "but it was fun to watch. He handled it amazingly well. Here's a kid that was 20 years old, and he's got to do press conferences before every game he pitches. He's got a whole half a world watching everything he does. And for a 20-year-old kid to handle things the way he handled, it was pretty remarkable—and then still go out and pitch the way he pitched."

"It was a little bit like when you throw a rock into water and you see it splash," says Reuss. "Fernando was the splash. I was one of the ripples on the wave. I was one of the ones close up, so I saw it happen right there in front of me."

In his sixth start of the season and first start of May, Valenzuela gave up his second run and his first lead of the season when Montreal's Chris Speier tied the game at 1–1 in the bottom of the eighth with an RBI single. Valenzuela finished the ninth inning, then came away a winner when Los Angeles scored five times in the top of the 10th. In his next start, Valenzuela returned to his familiar ways, making a 1–0 lead stand up in New York for his fifth shutout, with 11 strikeouts. He then improved to 8–0 on the season when, after Speier and Andre Dawson hit the first home runs ever off him, sending the game into the bottom of the ninth tied 2–2, Guerrero hit a walkoff blast to win it.

It's tempting to believe that Valenzuela had arrived in the big leagues fully formed, but he continued to be a student.

"Fernando was very coachable," Scioscia says. "And I think that he was trying to absorb knowledge and have an understanding of just the path he needed to be as good as he could be. Ron Perranoski had a positive influence on him. But everything from game plans to how to work in between starts, Fernando absorbed information like a sponge."

The scope of Valenzuela's impact could be seen not only at Dodger Stadium but throughout the community—on May 17, thousands attended a Dodger clinic with Valenzuela in East Los Angeles—and indeed, across the country.

"I'm half Mexican American," says the historian Eric Enders, an El Paso native, "and the community I grew up in is 80 percent Mexican American, and everybody in town was so excited about Fernando. The first memories I have of him was that everybody wanted to talk about him, not only Dodger fans, not only baseball fans even. I remember at all our family gatherings, my *tío* [uncle] Manuel, who didn't care about baseball one bit, he would always ask me, 'How's Fernando doing? How's Fernando doing?' And we'd talk about that. It just seemed to really galvanize this community, even a community that has nothing to do with Los Angeles, that's 900 miles away. People were just really proud of him."

Valenzuela's grip on those hearts held firm even after his stranglehold on baseball loosened. On May 18, in his ninth start, there was another shutout, but this time, it was Los Angeles on the scoreless end, with Valenzuela giving up four runs (on three hits and two walks) in seven innings for a loss—an actual loss. Despite throwing an 11-strikeout complete game on June 1, Valenzuela had become mortal. In his final six starts before players went on strike in mid-June, Valenzuela had a 6.16 ERA in 38 innings. He started and pitched a shutout inning for the NL in the All-Star Game after the labor dispute ended, but struggled more in his first two starts for the Dodgers in August.

A few years earlier, baseball had been visited by a charismatic phenom in Tigers rookie Mark Fidrych, who threw 24 complete games and led the AL in ERA in 1976—talking to baseballs all the while—only to be out of the majors within five years. There were those who thought Valenzuela was about to vaporize even more abruptly. But Valenzuela rebounded—and in the process, helped seal his NL Cy Young and Rookie of the Year honors—by finishing his season with a 1.85 ERA in his final nine starts, leaving him with a 2.48 ERA (135 ERA+) and league-best 11 complete games, eight shutouts, and 180 strikeouts. In the closest NL Cy Young vote ever at that point, Valenzuela edged Tom Seaver (2.54 ERA, 140 ERA+), with Steve Carlton (2.42 ERA, 151 ERA+) third. Nolan Ryan, who led all pitchers with a 1.69 ERA and 195 ERA+ but pitched the fewest innings of the top quartet, finished fourth.

"In hindsight, you get some room in your rearview mirror and you kind of get some perspective," Scioscia says. "And looking back, it was unbelievable how all the stars aligned, that this young superstar pitcher from Mexico is pitching in L.A. And the immense amount of pressure that possibly could have built on his success as he pitched shutout after shutout—he was just marvelous that year—diffused because he was just a kid playing baseball. That's what he felt."

Valenzuela hardly stopped there. With his veteran teammates on a mission to finally win their first World Series for Los Angeles, Valenzuela had a superb postseason, beginning by allowing two runs in 17 innings in the NLDS against the Astros, including a 2–1, complete-game four-hitter in Game 4. In the NLCS against the Expos, Valenzuela dropped Game 2, 3–0, but got a second chance in the decisive Game 5.

Montreal jumped ahead against him in the first inning, when Tim Raines doubled, Rodney Scott reached on a fielder's choice, and Raines scored from third on a double-play grounder by Dawson. Valenzuela himself tied the game with an RBI grounder in the fifth, and allowed only three other baserunners until the ninth inning, retiring 18 of 19 at point, before Rick Monday hit his unforgettable two-out home run to give the Dodgers a 2–1 lead and ultimately the pennant.

Valenzuela allowed six baserunners in 8⅔ innings. In his first four postseason starts, he had a 1.71 ERA. His fifth start was nothing like the first four—and yet, it was incredible.

The Dodgers lost the first two games of the 1981 World Series, giving them six straight losses to the Yankees in postseason play dating back to the '78 Fall Classic. Minutes after Valenzuela took the Dodger Stadium mound in Game 3, Cey's first-inning homer gave the Dodgers a 3–0 lead, but a rocky Valenzuela, who had walked two in a scoreless first inning, wobbled more.

Bob Watson hit the second pitch of the second inning over the wall in center. So concerned were the Dodgers with Valenzuela that when Rick Cerone followed with a double, Goltz began warming up in the bullpen. Valenzuela had faced six batters to this point. One out later, Larry Milbourne singled home the Yankees' second run, and in the next inning, Cerone hit a two-run shot to left-center off a screwball to give the Yankees the lead.

"This might be the worst game I've ever seen Valenzuela pitch," Vin Scully said on the national radio broadcast.

Through three innings, Valenzuela had already thrown 71 pitches, New York bombarding him with 10 baserunners to go with the four runs. But keen to preserve their lead, the Yankees made a fast pitching change, pulling Dave Righetti for George Frazier when Garvey and Cey reached base to begin the bottom of the third. Lasorda wasn't beyond making a quick move himself, sending Scioscia up with two out to bat for Yeager.

Scioscia grounded out to end the inning, leaving Valenzuela in the on-deck circle, holding perhaps one more chance to right his ship. With two out, he issued his fourth walk, to Dave Winfield, before surviving a Lou Piniella liner to left. Valenzuela batted for himself in the bottom of the fourth, only to give up a leadoff double to Watson in the top of the fifth that sent Tom Niedenfuer to get warmed up.

"He was struggling pretty bad," Lasorda says. "But I said, 'No, I'm not taking this guy out. I'm leaving him in.' I'm depending on this guy. I believe in him, and I told him, with as much Spanish as I could speak, 'I'm leaving you in here because you can work your way out of here and pitch this game.'"

For the second time in five innings, Valenzuela walked Milbourne intentionally to get to the pitcher's spot and escape the inning. In the bottom of the fifth, the Dodgers tied the game on Guerrero's RBI double, then took the lead on a run-scoring double-play grounder by Scioscia. When Valenzuela batted for himself with a runner on third, having thrown 95 pitches in five innings, the crowd, still fully behind him, roared with approval.

Valenzuela grounded out. He then walked Randolph to start the sixth inning, but after another visit to the mound by Lasorda, with Niedenfuer and Steve Howe warming up in the bullpen, Scioscia threw out Randolph trying to steal, helping Valenzuela finish his third consecutive shutout inning.

"Sometimes, you're not gonna have the best stuff," Valenzuela says. "I kept fighting and fighting, but my control was the problem. Like I mentioned before, sometimes early in the game, that's when I had a problem, because I'd try to be too fine. So if I didn't have command on any pitch, that's when I'd get in trouble, and that happened in that game, that third game of the World Series.

"But I started not using a lot of screwballs. I started using fastballs inside on the hands of right-handers"—remembering what Perranoski taught him—"and they started hitting but in front, pulling foul balls, and that's the only way they could do it: hit it hard, but foul balls. And after that, I came up with the screwball. And that's when it started working."

The remainder of the game doubled down on suspense. In the seventh, Baker flagged down a Watson drive to the left-field wall. In the eighth, after Aurelio Rodriguez and Milbourne singled—the 15th and 16th baserunners allowed by Valenzuela—Cey spectacularly dived to catch a Bobby Murcer bunt in foul territory and then doubled Milbourne off first, then made a difficult play on a Randolph grounder and tagged Rodriguez running from second to third.

One inning remained.

"The whole year was amazing," Jarrín says. "The whole year was fantastic, and the beginning was unbelievable. But then everybody believes, as I do, the best game he ever pitched was in the World Series against the Yankees. He didn't have his best stuff, and he was in trouble during the whole game, and Lasorda went to the mound several times, but Fernando, he wanted to finish. That was one of his trademarks—he wanted always to finish what he started. He didn't care if he had thrown 130, 135 pitches. He wanted to close. And that game against the Yankees, he didn't have his best stuff but he was so valiant. He came through unbelievably."

In the ninth inning, Jerry Mumphrey grounded out. Winfield flied to right center. Piniella took two balls before a called strike and a foul evened the count. On pitch No. 147 from Valenzuela, Piniella swung and missed.

"I don't know how many pitches he threw," Scioscia says. "But he was just as fresh at the end of the game as he was at the beginning."

"This was not the best Fernando game," Scully famously said at the end of his broadcast. "It was his finest."

The victory was the first of four straight by the Dodgers, depriving Valenzuela of what would have been a Game 7 start at Yankee Stadium but more than compensating him with a World Series celebration.

"That was an exciting game," Valenzuela says. "The two best moments in my career—I think the first game I started against Houston on Opening Day, and that game, the World Series—I think those were my best moments."

Amazingly, Valenzuela's big-league life was only 13 months old. It had been less than two and a half years since he first came to the United States. He turned 21 eight days after the World Series ended. The rest of his career lay before him.

"I put in my head, 'That's only one season,'" he says. "It's easy to reach the big leagues, but to stay in the big leagues and do it successfully, that's the hard part. So I had to keep going, had to keep working. The season was in the past, the World Series was in the past, and so I had to be looking forward."

Barely taking time off, Valenzuela pitched for Navojoa in the Mexican Winter League, hurling a no-hitter in January 1982, before beginning the first year of the rest of his big-league life.

While lacking the pyrotechnics of his rookie year, Valenzuela went 19–13 with a 2.87 ERA (122 ERA+) in a sophomore season that was arguably more impressive, if perhaps naive, in its endurance. Still only 21, Valenzuela pitched nearly 100 more innings, shooting up to a career-high 285, including 18 complete games.

"He came to the mound like a general going to battle," Jarrín says. "He was unbelievable."

Lasorda wasn't quick with a hook, and when it did come near him, Valenzuela ducked away.

"In the '80s, that's the way we played," Valenzuela says. "I had a lot of confrontation with Tommy, because he'd tell me 'You're up over 100 pitches already.' I'd say, 'No, I'm fine, I want to stay in the game, I want to finish the game.' So I don't know if I would change anything, because that's the way I liked to play. But it's hard to compare now and the old days. I'd have to play now to see how my head would change."

This was also the year that Valenzuela hit the first of his 10 big-league home runs, on August 25 at St. Louis. In his MLB career, Valenzuela batted .200, and his 158 hits while pitching for the Dodgers (not including his 5-for-15 pinch-hitting record, a stat he knows by heart) trailed only Newcombe, Drysdale, and Hershiser.

Ask Valenzuela to talk about his pitching accomplishments, and he's a minimalist. Ask him about his hitting, and a steady flow of words floods his shyness.

"For shutouts, you need defense," he says. "Sometimes good defense will save you a run. On a home run, nobody helps you out. Really for me as a pitcher, a lot of good things happened when I was on the mound. But at the plate, things didn't happen like that every day. So hitting a home run, that was more exciting for me. When you hit in the sweet spot in the right spot of the bat, you're not gonna feel anything on your hands. You're gonna make contact and the ball's gonna fly. That's the best feeling, as a hitter, not only when you hit homers but when you hit it solid."

By this time, Valenzuela had a strong reputation in all aspects of the game. Despite his teddy-bear physique, he was obviously an athlete, and a fundamentally sound one at that. No one was a better decision maker on the field than Valenzuela.

"You have to anticipate before the batter hits the ball," he says. "So that helped me out a lot—just to be ready and thinking in that situation. If the ball is coming up to me and I have first and second, where do I go? I go third or go first or go where? No, I go for the double play, second to first."

When the Dodgers ran out of position players in their 21-inning, two-day win at Wrigley Field during the summer of 1982 and Valenzuela had to play outfield, it was just an extension of his normal routine between starts. "I liked to go to the outfield and practice catching fly balls—you never know," he says. "You've got to be ready for anything. But that was exciting."

The rumbliest of Valenzuela's first seven seasons as a starting pitcher came in 1983, though as such seasons go, it wasn't bad: 257 innings, a 3.75 ERA (96 ERA+), plus the Dodgers' only victory in the NLCS, when he threw eight innings of one-run ball against Philadelphia. He recalibrated to a 3.03 ERA (116 ERA+) in 1984, with the most memorable start coming May 23 at Philadelphia, when he took the mound following a pregame thunderstorm and struck out a career-high 15—the most in a game by a Dodger since Koufax—outdueling Steve Carlton in a 1–0 shutout in which he drove in the only run.

"I learned a lot from Fernando, just the way he went about from day to day," says Rick Honeycutt, who pitched for the Dodgers from 1983 to 1987 (3.58 ERA, 100 ERA+) before becoming their longtime pitching coach in 2006. "His personality and persona just never changed. You wouldn't know if he had thrown a no-hitter or if he had given up five or six runs in his start. He was just upbeat and happy every day, and always interacted with the players and the other pitchers with a smile on his face. I learned that you just give everything you have and then let that game roll off your back and go be ready for the next game. It was an eye-opener for me, how you should take every day and just enjoy it and work hard and just have fun here."

Fernandomania II: Electric Boogaloo returned to Los Angeles in 1985, when Valenzuela started the season with 41 consecutive innings without allowing an earned run, before Tony Gwynn hit a solo homer in the ninth inning of a 1–0 Padres victory at Dodger Stadium on April 28. Crazily, that left Valenzuela with a 0.21 ERA but a 2–3 record in a month in which he pitched two shutouts but twice lost 2–1 games on unearned runs.

No game that season, however, drew more attention than the one the night of September 6, when he faced off against baseball's newest 20-year-old sensation, Dwight Gooden. The Mets right-hander dazzled Dodger Stadium, striking out 10 in nine shutout innings. Valenzuela two-upped him, pitching a career-high 11 shutout frames, in a game the Dodgers lost in the 13th. A season-high Chavez Ravine crowd of 51,868 gave Valenzuela two standing ovations.

He finished the regular season with a career-best 2.45 ERA and 141 ERA+ in 272⅓ innings. That October, Valenzuela made the final two postseason starts of his career. Facing St. Louis in the NLCS, he was a Game 1 winner with 6⅓ innings in a 4–1 victory, pitching with the veteran maturity that made it easy to forget he was, unbelievably, still not yet 25 years old.

"We had a meeting before the game to talk about how to pitch their guys, where to throw, what to throw, all that," said Enos Cabell, the Dodger first baseman that day. "Fernando went out there and threw 'em exactly like we talked about. Exactly! I couldn't believe it."

In Game 5, Valenzuela allowed two runs and lasted eight innings and 132 pitches despite walking an NLCS-record eight, leaving with the score tied before Ozzie Smith's walkoff homer off Niedenfuer floored Los Angeles.

Though Valenzuela's ERA declined in 1986 to 3.14 (110 ERA+), he remembers the year most fondly, because he broke the 20-win barrier, going 21–11, along with a career-high 20 complete games. He finished second in the NL Cy Young voting and won his first Gold Glove Award. His 20th victory was a two-hitter at the Astrodome, the *let-them-play* pen where he first put on a Dodger uniform and where, two months earlier, he stole the All-Star Game by striking out the first five batters he faced— Don Mattingly, Cal Ripken Jr., Jesse Barfield, Lou Whitaker, and Teddy Higuera—to begin three shutout innings.

"A lot of good things have happened to me in that stadium," Valenzuela says. "I've got good memories. For the hitters, it's batting .300. For pitchers, the magic number is 20. To win 20, I think that's the greatest."

Valenzuela's 1987 season began well, but a lack of dominance and command began to catch up to him, and he finished with a 3.98 ERA (101 ERA+), allowing 382 baserunners—the most by a Dodger in 46 years—in 251 innings. The same pattern of a solid start and midseason struggle returned in 1988 (the year he began wearing glasses on the mound) but worsened. On May 22, he was knocked out of a game in the second inning for the first time ever. On June 25, he gave up three first-inning homers to the Reds and left before he got the third out.

Finally, on July 30, he called the trainer to the mound during the fifth inning of a start against the Astros. After taking 255 consecutive turns in the Dodger starting rotation, Valenzuela went on the disabled list on the last day of July with a stretched left anterior capsule, which contained the ligaments that stabilized his left shoulder. The 26-year-old Valenzuela's fastball had lost between five and 10 mph, and his screwball was ineffective.

"When he would bring the arm up to throw, he would feel pain," Dr. Frank Jobe said at the time. "Then, he would drop the shoulder down to protect it. It stiffens the muscles in the shoulder. When you drop your arm, you lose your fastball, and then he'd try to throw too hard to compensate."

Valenzuela came back September 26 to test his ability to pitch in the playoffs, and actually started the game in which the Dodgers clinched the 1988 NL West title, allowing a two-run homer in three innings while on a 60-pitch limit. A four-inning relief outing with no earned runs October 1, in which he earned his second career save, was encouraging on the surface, but even Valenzuela, whose career playoff ERA for Los Angeles was exactly 2.00, said he didn't trust himself enough to pitch in critical games, and his season ended with his absence from the postseason roster.

"It was extremely hard for him not to be able to help the ballclub," says Jarrín, who recalls asking Valenzuela why he never wore his 1988 World Series ring.

"Because I didn't do anything," Valenzuela told him. "I don't deserve that ring."

"Come on, Fernando," Jarrín replied. "Come on."

"No, no," Valenzuela said. "I never wear that, because I was not helping the ballclub."

Before his 28th birthday, Valenzuela had thrown more than 2,000 innings as a Dodger. The wear and tear was enormous, reflected not only in the innings but the number of pitches he threw within them. Returning for his 10th season in the majors in 1989, Valenzuela knew he had to reinvent himself, according to Scioscia.

"He understood what he needed to do to be successful, and he found ways to do it," Scioscia says. "So he came up with a little cut fastball to help him get inside on right-handers more, which would keep the outside corner still open for a screwball or his fastball. He understood about changing speed—he always changed speeds great, but he didn't have the 91-mph fastball anymore, so he had to try and adapt, and actually had some pretty good seasons after he hurt his arm."

After a second-inning May 4 knockout that left his ERA at 4.91, Valenzuela had a 3.17 ERA the rest of the '89 season, finishing with a 3.43 ERA (100 ERA+) in 196⅔ innings. On June 3, he returned to position play, taking over first base while Eddie Murray moved to third in the Dodgers' 22-inning game against the Astros, another memorable day for Valenzuela in Houston. Third baseman Jeff Hamilton was on the mound, throwing upward of 94 mph in his bid to keep the Dodgers alive. Valenzuela caught a pop fly in foul ground for Hamilton's first out in a perfect 21st inning, then was on the receiving end of a toss from Hamilton for the first out in the 22nd. But with runners on first and second and two out, Astros shortstop Rafael Ramirez lined one the opposite way.

"I jumped," Valenzuela says, "and it tipped my glove and went into right field. So close. And it scored the run. And [Hamilton] was so mad. He was pissed. And I went to see him and I said, 'You know what, that's the way we feel when we lose games too—so don't worry.'"

In 1990 came the capstone of his Dodger career. It had been an uneven year. His ERA was as low as 2.68 in mid-May, then rose to 4.09 two weeks later. To start June, he fanned 22 in 27⅔ innings with a 2.28 ERA, before taking a 10-hit, eight-run beating June 24 at Cincinnati. He was inconsistent and unpredictable from game to game.

The day of his next start, June 29, former teammate Dave Stewart was throwing a no-hitter for Oakland.

"They told me had a no-hitter for six innings," Valenzuela says, "and I said, 'That's good, that's great.' So I went to do my routine, my preparation, for the game. I kept going and going, and then when I was walking to the bullpen, walking right next to the video room, they told me, 'Dave Stewart just got a no-hitter.' I said, 'It's good for him. You guys were watching?' They said, 'Yeah.' 'So you guys were watching one on TV, now you're going to watch one live.' They said, 'You're crazy,' and all that."

Left fielder Stan Javier's first-inning error enabled the only baserunner against Valenzuela until one out in the seventh, when former teammate Guerrero and future Dodger Todd Zeile drew consecutive walks, but Valenzuela retired the next two batters to escape the jam. As the night's drama mounted, Lasorda pierced the tension and drew laughs by yelling for Mickey Hatcher to pinch-hit for Valenzuela in the bottom of the eighth, but there was no way El Toro wasn't going out for the final battle.

After fanning Vince Coleman on a called third strike to start the inning, Willie McGee walked on four pitches, bringing Guerrero up to the plate.

"We were teammates for a long time, for eight seasons," Valenzuela says. "I thought that he wasn't going to be that aggressive, because I was throwing cutters right on the hands, but he was swinging hard. So I said, 'He's serious.' So I kept the ball right there on the hands, and that's when he got that ground ball right back there to the middle. I'm not sure if that hit tipped my glove or not, if it took a little bit of velocity off that ground ball. It surprised me."

Less surprised was second baseman Juan Samuel, who had shaded toward second base before the pitch and saw the ball come almost exactly to him. Samuel stepped on second and threw to first, doubling up Guerrero, on his 34th birthday, for the final out.

"If you have a sombrero," exclaimed Scully, in what might have been his most famous post-1988 call, "throw it to the sky."

Unfortunately for Valenzuela, the sky was no longer the limit. If the no-hitter capping a strong June seemed to show that Valenzuela was back, an 8.40 September ERA spoke otherwise, leaving him with a 4.59 ERA (80 ERA+) in 1990. That November, he became a free agent, but other teams were wary of giving up draft-pick compensation to sign him, and he returned to the Dodgers on a one-year deal but without a guaranteed spot in the 1991 starting rotation—nor a contract locked at its full value unless he was on the Opening Day roster.

Throughout spring training, Valenzuela's future was a huge question. Before 27,000 in a mid-March exhibition in Monterrey, Mexico, he pitched five shutout innings and hit an RBI single, a vintage and emotional day for everyone in attendance. But in other games, opponents pounded him. On March 28, 12 days shy of the 10th anniversary of his first Dodger start, the Dodgers parted ways with the author of Fernandomania.

"I think that's part of the game, part of the business and all that," Valenzuela says. "I understand that. The only hard part for me was they told me about a week before the season started. By that time, all the teams, they're already ready to go. I think that's the only thing that hurt me a little bit, because I didn't have any other team, any other options. If they had said, 'Okay, we don't have a plan for you, we'll let you go to find another team, early in spring training,' that's [a better] choice for me."

In his Dodger career, Valenzuela threw 2,348⅔ innings (seventh in team history) with a 3.31 ERA (107 ERA+), 1,759 strikeouts (sixth in Dodger history), 915 walks (second, behind Don Sutton), 107 complete games (11th), and 29 shutouts (tied with Dazzy Vance for sixth).

Valenzuela was 30 years old, the same age as Koufax when he threw his last pitch. But Valenzuela continued for six more years. His initial comeback attempt, with the nearby Angels in 1991, generated much attention but lasted only two big-league starts, and he didn't pitch in the majors at all in 1992. However, coming back yet again in 1993, this time with Baltimore, he threw 178⅔ innings in 31 starts. He remained inconsistent, as a 4.91 ERA (91 ERA+) signaled, but had several strong performances, including a six-hit shutout three years and a day after his Dodger no-hitter. For San Diego in 1996, he threw 171⅔ innings with a 3.62 ERA (110 ERA+).

His major-league career ended July 14, 1997, with St. Louis, though as late as 2006, at age 46, he made 11 starts for Mexicali in the Mexican Winter League. Moving on to become a Dodger broadcaster, Valenzuela professes to like all sports, but his love for baseball never wavered.

"It's almost—I don't want to say perfect—it's almost a perfect game," Valenzuela says.

Heavenly, even.

Orel Hershiser

While Fernando Valenzuela graced the world with his skyward eyes, the definitive image of Orel Hershiser might be the sight of him walking off the mound, almost in a trance, before looking up in exhilaration and gratitude upon completing the 1988 season as a World Series champion and baseball's most dominant pitcher, equal parts thoughtful and fearsome.

The tale of how Hershiser became that pitcher is hardly less improbable than that of Valenzuela, and features one of the Dodgers' top-flight origin stories, including what might be the greatest nickname-to-name ratio in baseball history.

Orel Leonard Hershiser IV was born in 1958 in Buffalo, New York, and went to high school in Cherry Hill, New Jersey, where it would have been quite a stretch to say he was a phenom.

"I was a suspect, not a prospect," he says.

In 1979, the Dodgers drafted Hershiser out of Bowling Green University in the 17th round, several rounds after lefty pitcher Steve Howe, first baseman Greg Brock, and even future MLB umpire Kerwin Danley.

"I had a fastball coming out of college and I had a curveball, and that's pretty much all I had," Hershiser says. "My fastball probably had what would be considered life, but I don't think it had sink. And then my curveball was more of a curveball that kind of popped out of my hand, more of a high school curveball where it was a big breaker and you could spin it. But as far as for a big-leaguer or a minor-leaguer, it was very much a breaking ball that was telegraphed coming out of my hand."

With his relatively limited arsenal and pedigree, Hershiser pitched primarily out of the bullpen during his five seasons in the minors, even at the highest levels, dropping scattered hints of the starting pitcher he was to become.

Signing with the Dodgers the week he was drafted, Hershiser appeared in 15 games for Single-A Clinton in '79, starting four, with a 2.09 ERA. The following year—as a teammate of Valenzuela in Double-A San Antonio—Hershiser relieved in 46 of 49 appearances, with a 3.55 ERA and 14 saves. In 1981, while Fernandomania was igniting in Los Angeles, Hershiser returned to San Antonio to make 38 relief appearances in 42 games, his ERA ballooning to 4.68, though he also had 15 saves to go with three complete games in his four starts.

Less important than the numbers were the lessons Hershiser absorbed—about location, about changing speeds, about making your breaking ball tighter. Sandy Koufax made a powerful impression, while Ron Perranoski, who had become the Dodgers' minor-league pitching coordinator, made the steadiest impact. In a sense, Hershiser got a big *So You Think You Can Pitch* kind of awakening, developing the kind of precision that was necessary to elevate his work from athlete to craftsman. "Low" isn't just between the thigh and the knees, but between the top and the bottom of the knee. An ordinary breaking ball lands in the strike zone—a worthy breaking ball needs to finish at the knee or below.

"To make the ball be that precise, you have to be more precise with your body and be more precise with your mind," Hershiser says. "So you start to refine your mechanics, to be able to have a higher level of what you're trying to repeat. When you step back in your delivery, the step back needs to be more precise. It can't be three inches one time and eight inches another, and you can't rock your head back off your back foot one time and keep your head over your back foot the next time. You have to start to be more precise with your body movements.

"And it feels really restrictive at first. It feels like, 'I have no freedom and I can't be an athlete.' You feel like somebody's almost put a straitjacket on you. But you come to find out that as you do restrict yourself and get more precise with exactly whatever movement you want or what the coach is asking you to do, you find the right thing that lets you execute things more consistently. All of a sudden, it moves from restriction to foundation. That becomes the foundation of your delivery."

It was a sensible process, but for Hershiser, a painstaking one. After spending 1980–81 in San Antonio, Hershiser clocked in two more years at Triple-A Albuquerque, with a 3.71 in 47 games (seven starts) in '82 and a 4.09 ERA in 49 games (10 starts) with 16 saves in '83. By this time, Valenzuela was a three-year MLB veteran. Righty reliever Tom Niedenfuer, another former minor-league colleague, came up in 1981 and was a regular member of the Dodger bullpen in 1982.

Still, Hershiser didn't worry about playing leapfrog with his teammates.

"I didn't perceive beating them out as much as I thought about getting to be as good as them," he says. "I never felt like I was competing with Fernando. I thought, *Wow, what a talented guy with this great ability to locate the ball inside and out, with his ability to throw the screwball that Bobby Castillo taught him, with his ability to throw a breaking ball.* Tremendous poise, tremendous location, tremendous movement. But I never felt like I could beat Fernando, because he's left-handed and he's got a screwball.

"What I started to really realize was that there's just so many different ways to skin a cat. Some guys are going to have high velocity. Some guys are going to have great movement. Some guys are going to have borderline control, and some guys are going to have precise control. Some guys can change speeds, and some guys can go up the ladder with their velocity from 92 all the way up to 97 [mph]. And you've just got to figure out, with all those different formulas or all those different ways to get people out, which one are you? Which one can you do at a high level?"

As a result, Hershiser didn't model himself after any particular pitcher. Even in his most inexperienced days, he was simply trying to be the best Orel Hershiser he could be, asking himself, "What do I need to do today to get better?" Koufax & Co. were never models to conform to. They were purely teachers.

"It was these guys at the very beginning saying, 'That's the pitch I want. That's the fastball movement I'm looking for,'" Hershiser says. "And maybe you can execute it two out of 10 times. But when they said, 'That's it,' you remember the feel. You remember what the ball did. You remember the location they liked, and you start working on how to do that again consistently: 'That's the breaking ball we're looking for. That's the spin I'm looking for. That's the arm angle that's going to work.'

"After you learn that, I actually then became a guy who knew how to do it, from moving my feet to moving my hands to making my turn to throwing the ball—and go, 'That's it.' And I wouldn't even need to watch the ball. I could tell from what I did that the ball was going to do the right thing. So almost like Michael Jordan could close his eyes and tell you he was going to make a free throw...I will tell you when the ball left my hand, I knew it was a perfect pitch."

The reward for these years of study and toil came in 1983. Hershiser received his big-league call-up once rosters expanded, making his Dodger debut September 1 by retiring Gary Carter, Al Oliver, and Tim Wallach—6,529 career hits between them—in a perfect seventh inning, then allowing his first earned run in the eighth. Before the season ended, Hershiser dipped in eight innings that September with a 3.38 ERA.

That led to Hershiser beginning the 1984 season in the Dodger bullpen, where he pitched erratically for the first two months. By now, there was a prevailing belief that this skinny, almost gawky suspect was now a prospect, but at the same time, frustration that he hadn't marshaled his potential into a more reliable weapon. Hershiser needed another transformation, and Tommy Lasorda pushed him through it.

"Well, I saw a lot of weaknesses in him, which I didn't like," Lasorda says. "He didn't have the confidence you want a pitcher to have. I called him in and told him he was the most negative pitcher I'd ever seen. I didn't like his attitude, I didn't like his willingness to challenge hitters, and I said, 'You're just out there pitching so defensively that you're gonna have problems. But for me, you've got good stuff, and you've got to pitch and you've got to believe in yourself. And from now on, I'm gonna call you "Bulldog," because a bulldog has drive, a bulldog has determination, a bulldog walks around just looking for other dogs he can whip.'"

Hershiser seconded the story, though he said he "heard through the rumor mill" that bullpen catcher Mark Cresse was the one who gave Lasorda the idea for the nickname. In any case, it was Lasorda who made the nickname count.

"What I walked out of that meeting kind of processing was, he really believes in me, and he believes I'm a big-league pitcher," Hershiser remembers. "He just doesn't believe I'm tough enough. He doesn't believe I am brave enough. He thinks I'm too timid. He thinks I respect the big-league hitter too much. He thinks I'm going to back down from situations, big situations. But ultimately what he does believe is he believes that I am good enough. And so I need to take on a persona and be strong enough and brave enough to just say, 'I can compete at this level.' And the way that that manifests itself is in attacking a strike zone."

Elaborating on that point, Mike Scioscia notes that Hershiser had a "really good curveball, and he thought he had to throw it every pitch." With the confidence Lasorda gave Hershiser, the righty adapted to using the curveball to complement his heavy sinker.

"You know Tommy—one thing he would do, because he did communicate with guys, was that he had an uncanny ability to reach people," Jerry Reuss says. "A lot of managers wouldn't have tried, but Tommy did. Tommy saw something and was going to do his best to get whatever he saw out of Orel and make him a success. Of course, that kind of attention didn't always work, but Tommy was creative enough to deal with people and try to reach a level where he could communicate.

"Orel's very intelligent, and he thought his way: 'If I do this, I could develop that, add to this, add to that.' And it worked."

By itself, the nickname wasn't a magic bullet. But it was a way to harness all that labor, all that training throughout his professional career, to make his pinpoint location more than a party trick. The "Bulldog" mentality didn't mean pure firepower, but rather fearlessness in executing his plan.

"As a youth and as a young professional, it's all about, 'If I try harder, then I must be doing my best,'" Hershiser says. "'More' is not better if your priorities are out of line. More velocity with less movement is not better. More velocity and more effort with less location is not better."

If this were an after-school special, we could say that Hershiser established himself as an elite pitcher then and there, but Hershiser still needed to prove he could succeed—not only to the Dodgers, but to himself. When he came to work May 26 at Shea Stadium and found a lone baseball sitting on the stool in front of his locker, he didn't know what to think.

"I was thinking I was getting called in to be sent down to the minors," Hershiser says. "But Rick Honeycutt and Jerry Reuss both got hurt in about the same week, and they needed a starter. And Tommy, knowing my personality, didn't want to tell me that I was going to start against the Mets the next night on a road trip. So my first start, I didn't know. I didn't know that I was pitching until I got to the ballpark on the team bus and there was a baseball sitting on my chair. And I'm thinking, *Who wants my autograph?* Because I've got like a 5.00 ERA.

"And I pick up the ball. Tommy's waiting for me to walk in, and he's in the doorway of his office, and he said, 'You got the ball today, kid.' And that's how I found out I had my first big-league start."

That afternoon, Hershiser took a 1–0 lead into the seventh inning before Hubie Brooks hit a game-tying home run that left him with a no-decision. Even then, mixed results continued for the better part of June, including an unsuccessful start in Atlanta. But in five relief outings from June 13 to 23, Hershiser allowed two runs in 12 innings, capped by three sparklingly perfect shutout innings at Atlanta.

It was the prelude to greatness.

On June 29 against the Cubs, he went the distance in a 7–1 victory, striking out eight. On Independence Day, he shut out the Pirates with 11 strikeouts. After a relief appearance just before the All-Star Game, Hershiser returned from the break with back-to-back two-hit, nine-strikeout shutouts at Chicago and St. Louis. Then after 8⅓ innings in a 4–2 loss to Atlanta came his *third* two-hit shutout of the month, 1–0 over the Reds.

From his last two innings June 29 through his first three innings July 24, Hershiser pitched 33⅔ consecutive scoreless innings. Had it happened in April, the headlines might have read ORELMANIA. As it was, after allowing 28 baserunners in 46 innings that July with a 0.78 ERA and 48 strikeouts, Hershiser was named NL Pitcher of the Month for his first full month as a starter.

He finished his rookie season with a 2.66 ERA. Hershiser was 26 years old—two years older than Valenzuela, but fast on his way to becoming the Dodgers' preeminent pitcher.

"He showed all of us at a very young age that he had the ability to go out and perform and produce and win, and that's just what you want," says Steve Yeager, who at age 35, in his second-to-last season with the Dodgers, caught two of Hershiser's four July shutouts.

The 1985 season confirmed this, a year some argue was superior to his legendary campaign three years later. Hershiser went 19–3, with a 2.03 ERA (171 ERA+) and a 1.03 WHIP in 239⅔ innings, finishing third in the NL Cy Young vote behind Dwight Gooden and John Tudor.

Hershiser allowed three earned runs or fewer in 31 of his 34 starts and pitched two one-hitters.

He carried that momentum into 1986, with a 1.95 ERA after his first 10 starts, then fell out of his groove, finishing the season with a 3.85 ERA (90 ERA+) in 231⅓ innings. Though the Dodgers lost 89 games for the second consecutive season in 1987, Hershiser rallied to go 16–16 with a 3.06 ERA (131 ERA+) while leading the league in innings for the first of three consecutive years—and volunteering for extra relief duty to boot.

"I remember he came to me in St. Louis," says Fred Claire, who had just become the Dodgers' new general manager that year, "and I told him, 'Your chances of going to the bullpen are as good as my chances of going to the moon, because that's not going to happen.'"

Then came 1988.

The year did not begin auspiciously. Playing golf a week before spring training, Hershiser hit an 8 iron onto the 18th green, then dropped to his knees in pain. Thinking he had the flu, he drove himself home.

"I threw up in my car the whole way," Hershiser says, "and got myself home and got up to the bathroom, and my wife found me wrapped around the toilet, passed out. She got me in the car and got me to the hospital, and I had an emergency appendectomy."

Hershiser had no intention of letting the removal of a silly body part slow down his schedule. Hours after the operation, he was taking his IV pole with him up and down the hospital stairs to get in his cardio.

"And the doctor said, 'What are you doing?…Will you get back in bed?'" Hershiser remembers. "And I go, 'No, I'm not going back to bed, I've got a few more things to do, and then I'll come back and rest.'"

Hershiser reported to spring training on time, determined to be ready to go at the first bell. The Dodgers planned to hold him back, but after watching him go through workouts on day one, they let him throw on day two.

"The last thing I wanted to have our team think is that one of our pitchers is not going to be ready," Hershiser recalls. "That's not the vibe

I'm sending. I'm sending a vibe of 'We're going to be tough' and 'We're going to fight.' And I was excited about our team. I was like, 'Holy smoke—we've got a chance, and I don't want to be the reason we don't have a chance.'"

One thing energizing Hershiser was the Dodgers landing Kirk Gibson late in the off-season, as one of a group of free agents set loose following a ruling that MLB owners had colluded to keep salaries down. That meant Hershiser was present for the famous moment when another new arrival, Jesse Orosco, soiled Gibson's cap with eyeblack in a practical joke so enraging the outfielder that he threatened to storm out of the clubhouse and possibly America. In full uniform, Hershiser followed Gibson into the showers to talk him back, but in the process found a validating message.

"Gibson," Hershiser says, "made it cool to care."

Hershiser's '88 season began, appropriately enough, with a shutout of the Giants, but when the All-Star break arrived, his 2.62 ERA was nearly half a run off John Tudor's MLB lead and outside the top 10. After a brutal August 14 in San Francisco, when he allowed eight runs (five earned) before leaving for a pinch hitter in the bottom of the second, Hershiser's ERA was a respectable but not exactly exceptional 3.06. Tim Leary, his less celebrated teammate, stood at a much more stylish 2.37.

However, the next time Hershiser was removed from a baseball game, he would be baseball's all-time leader in consecutive scoreless innings.

Hershiser finished August with three straight complete games. In the third, August 30 at Montreal, the Expos scored two runs in the bottom of the fifth inning. Beginning with the remaining four innings of that contest, no one scored on Hershiser for the rest of the regular season. The zeroes rolled on as the opponents rolled over: Atlanta. Cincinnati. Atlanta again. Houston. Taking the mound September 23 at Candlestick Park, his scoreless streak was at 40 innings.

For Hershiser, it was all a matter of probability. What's the best pitch to throw in a given location and situation? Execute that pitch, and if the odds play out in your favor, runners stay put. Keep working the odds, runners continue to stay put—with a little help, anyway.

"I think I only averaged about seven strikeouts during the streak," he says. "So it wasn't like I was striking so many people out that there were no odds of the ball possibly being a hit. I think John Shelby made a couple really good running catches in center field. There were some great plays in the infield. It's very much not an individual record. It's a team record.

"If I was striking out 14 guys a game and the other outs were mostly pop-ups and a few toppers on the mound because I just had unbelievably dominant stuff, then I would say it's a little bit more of an individual record. When you're giving up ground balls and fly balls and striking out six or seven, I think it's more of a team and a strategy and an execution record."

But if it were that easy, anyone could do it, points out Claire.

"I know it was a combination of talent and intelligence," Claire says. "I mean, I can remember Orel being on a computer, it seemed like, before anybody. And it was just Orel's makeup, the way that he thought about things and dealt with information.

"And he was a gifted athlete. You wouldn't necessarily think that he was the type of athlete that he really was. Hand-eye coordination—it's like a scratch golfer. It's not surprising that actually a lot of the great pitchers, most of them are the better golfers than the hitters, the Madduxes and the Glavines and the Orels and the others, because they know how to use their body and keep it in a rhythm and in sync. And that's what Orel had. There was this whole flow to Orel. Nothing was forced. Everything was in sync."

At Candlestick that night, there was no probability to account for what happened when the Giants had runners at the corners with one out in the third inning. Ernest Riles grounded to second. Future teammate Brett Butler, running from first, broke up the double play, apparently allowing Jose Uribe to score the streak-breaking run from third, but umpire Bob Engel barked interference on Butler—recalling the Harry Wendelstedt call against the Giants 20 years earlier that saved Don Drysdale's streak—and awarded an inning-ending double play. The Dodgers then broke a 0–0 tie with Mickey Hatcher's only regular-season homer of 1988, and Hershiser finished the game with his scoreless innings streak intact at 49.

"I remember running off the field yelling, 'Dick Dietz revisited! Dick Dietz revisited!'" Hershiser said. "I think Tommy Lasorda was the only one in the dugout who knew what I meant."

With one start remaining, there was no reason to think that Hershiser could break Drysdale's record before the season was over. At best, he might tie it—and that was even with the record, originally set at 58⅔ innings, subsequently being reduced to 58 when MLB decided fractional innings were déclassé. But sharing a spot atop the record book with Drysdale was just fine with Hershiser. And in any case, he had to get there first.

"[Pitching coach] Ron Perranoski and I are standing on the first-base line down in the bullpen warming up," Hershiser says. "And during the national anthem, I say to Ron, 'I'm kind of nervous.' And he goes, 'Me too.' And I'm like, 'Really good advice from a pitching coach.'"

Foreshadowed by the San Francisco game, the Dodgers had as much trouble scoring runs for Hershiser at San Diego on September 28 as opponents did scoring against him. The first pitcher to complete 10 shutout innings that night was not Hershiser but the Padres' Andy Hawkins, who allowed six baserunners but no one past second base. The question then was whether Hershiser would come out for the bottom of the 10th.

"I didn't want to," Hershiser says. "Everybody shook my hand, and they were going, 'Are you gonna to keep going or not?' And I said, 'This is so selfish, I'm not going to keep going back out there. We clinched it, we're going to the playoffs. We don't need this game as a win. I've tied Don. We have two Dodgers at the top. Let's just leave it alone.' But [Lasorda] said, 'Bulldog, I'm sending you back out there.'

"Well, if he's going to send me back out, I'm going to try and throw a zero. And that's when I saluted Don. I'd completed my warmups in the 10th and I looked up into the booth in the press box to find him. And he wasn't there. But I saluted the press box anyway. None of that's on camera because we didn't have TV [for the game], so nobody knew what I was doing. But the reason I couldn't find him is he was in the dugout already getting ready to do the interview with me."

Dodger announcer Ross Porter verifies that Drysdale was completely on board with Hershiser breaking his record. "Don handled that perfectly," Porter says. "Don had said to him, 'No, no, no, no, no. It's not gonna hurt my feelings. You go on and break it.'"

Drama struck fast when Marvell Wynne struck out but reached first base on a wild pitch—not exactly what you want when you're in your 10th inning of work. Benito Santiago sacrificed him to second base, and on a Randy Ready groundout, Wynne moved 90 feet from home—the first runner for either team to reach third base. Hershiser intentionally walked Garry Templeton, who moved to second base on defensive indifference.

On a 1-2 pitch, pinch hitter Keith Moreland hit a delicate fly ball to right field. Jose Gonzalez gloved it, and history—all 59 innings of it—was Hershiser's.

"What he did in 1988, I don't recall ever watching something like that before, even with Sandy Koufax," Jaime Jarrín says. "When he broke the record, I couldn't believe it. And he's such a nice guy, such a professional guy. He loves what he does, and he studies the game very, very much."

"I picked up the paper in Arizona the next day, and I didn't quite know how to feel," said Koufax. "I cared so much about both of them, having worked with Orel and having played with Don for so long. I was proud of Orel, but a little sad for Don. It's an amazing record, when you think about it. I can believe most anything that happens in a single game, but such sustained excellence over such a long period, with no margin for error, is unbelievable."

Hershiser marched from the 1988 regular season into the playoffs with a league-leading 267 innings, 15 complete games, and eight shutouts. His 2.26 ERA was third, his 149 ERA+ was fourth. Though he won the NL Cy Young Award unanimously, he probably needed every bit of the scoreless streak to fend off Danny Jackson, who had an identical 23–8 record, and David Cone, whose .870 winning percentage and 2.22 ERA bested Hershiser.

As the NLCS against the Mets began, there were two levels of intrigue: whether the Dodgers would win and whether Hershiser would keep putting up zeros, even if they didn't count toward his official record. Hopes were shockingly dashed on both fronts in Game 1. Hershiser took a 2–0 lead into the ninth inning, but an RBI double by Darryl Strawberry shattered the shutout, forcing Hershiser's exit from a game that the Dodgers lost 3–2, when on an 0-2, two-out Jay Howell pitch, Gary Carter lunged and hit a dying liner that center fielder John Shelby charged but couldn't glove.

"The press tried to make a big thing out of my getting pulled at that point," Hershiser wrote that off-season for his 1989 book, *Out of the Blue*. "The fact is, it was the right move. I said and I meant I had no problem with it. It made sense. I had thrown 99 pitches. I was not tired. I had not choked. But I *had* been hit hard three times and had made mistakes with the last two pitches. Baseball sense tells you it's time to shut the door with a hard-throwing reliever."

Four nights later, in Game 3, the Dodgers lost a second time with Hershiser on the mound. Though he allowed only one earned run in seven innings, New York saddled Los Angeles with an 8–4 defeat to take a 2–1 NLCS lead. The Mets positioned themselves to go to the World Series without having to face Hershiser again. Or so they thought.

The following night in Game 4, New York was one inning away from a commanding 3–1 series lead when Scioscia's two-run homer off Gooden in the ninth inning tied the game. Then, with two out in the top of the 12th, Gibson homered to give the Dodgers the lead. However, in the bottom of the 12th, Leary gave up two singles to put the winning run on base. Gregg Jefferies flied to right, but Orosco walked Keith Hernandez to load the bases.

Around this time, ABC's broadcast of the game showed Hershiser warming up beyond the outfield fences.

"I went down to the bullpen when we didn't have any more pitchers left," Hershiser explains, "and Tommy didn't know it. I had already told him when Jay Howell was suspended [for having pine tar on his glove in Game 3] that 'I'll be your Jay Howell.' And he goes, 'Bulldog, get out of my face! You already pitched seven innings the night before.' And I'm like, 'Yeah, okay, whatever.'

"And then Sosh hits the home run and then Gibson hits a home run, and I'm like, 'Oh my gosh, we're out of pitchers and we might need help. Jesse's the only one left.' So I ran into the locker room and got my stuff on, and I went down there and told Cresse to warm me up and that he didn't have time to ask Tommy if I was allowed to do it. And then I said, in the middle the inning, 'Tell him I'm ready.'"

Orosco stayed in the game to strike out fellow lefty Strawberry, but right-handed Kevin McReynolds awaited.

"And Tommy goes back out," Scioscia says, "and I didn't even see if anybody was warming up down in the bullpen. So, all of a sudden you see Orel trotting out from the bullpen, and we're all going, 'You've got to be kidding me.'"

"Fun," says Hershiser. "Unbelievable pressure. But I volunteered to do it."

On a 1-1 pitch, McReynolds hit a shallow ball to nearly the same spot Carter's game-winning hit landed in Game 1. But it had a little more elevation, and Shelby snagged it. One night after throwing seven innings, Hershiser saved the game.

As if he hadn't pitched in enough pressure already, three nights later came Game 7. But the Dodgers broke the game open early, with Hershiser scoring one of the Dodgers' five second-inning runs before catching Howard Johnson looking at a third and last strike to send the Dodgers to their final World Series of the 20th century.

Even from the NLCS into the World Series, Hershiser evolved his approach, looking for ways to catch his opponents off guard. Against the A's, for example, Hershiser says he threw a sidearm pitch to Jose Canseco "when I hadn't probably thrown a sidearm pitch all year."

"There are tactics," he says. "There are surprises. There are things you can do in playoff baseball that can give you an edge. That scouting report is coming into the playoffs with you, and [the postseason] is time to change."

Moment in the Sun: Tim Belcher

- Right-hander went 3–0 with a 4.88 ERA in 1988 playoffs for the Dodgers, winning two against the Mets and one against the A's (plus a no-decision in 1988 World Series Game 1)
- Pitching 806 innings for Dodgers from 1987 to 1991, his 118 ERA+ (2.99 ERA) ranked 11th in Los Angeles history
- Opening Day starter in 1989 led MLB in shutouts with eight that year

Taking the mound the night after Gibson's improbable, impossible homer to win Game 1, Hershiser pitched his second consecutive 6–0 shutout of the playoffs, matching the Oakland's hit total with three of his own, including two doubles. "Gibson went 1-for-1 [in Game 1] and I went 3-for-3, and I'm really still mad to this day that I got more hits than him and he gets all the popularity," Hershiser jokes. The Dodgers then needed only to split their next two games to set up Hershiser to pitch the potential clincher in Game 5, and that's exactly what happened.

By this time, Hershiser was more than a streaking hot pitcher. He fascinated the baseball world, embodying what might be called a cerebral physicality, coaxing himself on the mound, singing quietly to himself on the bench, his parents' support from the stands serving as the wind at his back. His mental and physical toughness were at a supreme state, even as he began to feel the fatigue of the struggle.

"I was running out of gas, but I wanted that Whitney Houston thing, you know, my one moment in time," Hershiser told Steve Wulf of *Sports Illustrated,* which named the pitcher Sportsman of the Year. "Now, I don't want Tommy to know I'm tired, so I have to act confident. But if I act too confident, he's going to know I'm faking it, so I have to strike the right balance there."

Leading 5–2 in the bottom of the ninth, at the end of a season that began with an emergency appendectomy, Hershiser stood straight on the mound. He brought his hands up with the ball in his glove, then dropped them and straightened his cap. His spikes clawed at the dirt. His shoulders rolled as he stared home. His gaze held through two perceptible breaths as he went into his windup, calmly but sharply lifting his left knee above his waist, then rapidly uncoiling with his right arm and whipping the ball toward home, the fulfillment of all the precisely tuned mechanics honed during those long minor-league seasons. Like a high-speed train, the ball sliced the air. From his crouch at home plate, Tony Phillips took a late, lamentable swing that came not at all close to making contact to the ball as it popped into catcher Rick Dempsey's glove.

Hershiser finished his follow-through and turned to his left, taking three mesmerized steps before leaning his shoulders and head back in a galactic catharsis. Dempsey tossed off his helmet and mask and emerged beaming, arms outstretched, glove raised in his left hand, ball held out in his right. Barely a moment before Dempsey came to him, Hershiser came to, as if returning from another dimension. Dempsey hugged Hershiser before the ace had a chance to get his arms out. Only after being hoisted into the air did Hershiser make a fist, cock his elbow, smile, and reveal his triumph.

"Does everyone really appreciate what Orel has done?" Gibson asked. "I don't know if we will ever again see the likes of what he's done through all of this. It may be that no pitcher in history stayed in that kind of groove so long or so well."

What only the most dedicated fans realize is that although he allowed a run in the first inning of his first start the following season (ending his regular-season scoreless streak) and his won-lost record declined to 15–15 for a Dodger team that slipped to 77–85, Hershiser had every bit as a good a year as he had before, with a 2.31 ERA and matching 149 ERA+. That season also ended with a dominant extra-inning performance, though with a more questionable legacy. With nothing on the line on the season's final day, before a crowd of 4,840 and after a 143-minute rain delay, Hershiser endured 169 pitches in 11 innings of a 3–1 Dodger win at Atlanta. Hershiser himself doesn't second-guess the manager who left him in.

"That's who Tommy was," Hershiser says, with full support.

The moment was quickly forgotten. But in the seventh inning of his fourth start of the 1990 season, April 25 against St. Louis, Hershiser walked off the mound in distress. He had thrown his final pitch of the year.

"I had no idea any trouble was coming, because I didn't throw with my arm, I threw with my legs," he says. "The arm for me was more about the end of a whip, and the reason the whip moves so fast, the reason the whip is accurate, is because of what you did with the handle. So when you supposedly got tired or when you supposedly aren't able to throw the ball well at the end of the game, I was not using my arm. I was using my legs and my body, and my arm was just going along for the ride."

But over time, the ligaments and labrum that formed the structure of Hershiser's arm began stretching and wearing out. Dr. Frank Jobe said that the front of Hershiser's shoulder looked like pounded veal. And so, to a Dodger tradition that had featured Tommy John surgery (and before that, the less prominent Bill Singer surgery), you could now add Orel Hershiser surgery. Jobe had previously done labrum cleanup operations on pitchers—Alejandro Peña, for one—but hadn't implemented a way to actually repair the labrum. That changed with Hershiser, with whom he experimented by inserting bone anchors with sutures in a method so ingenious, that with the help of physical therapist Pat Screnar, it essentially enabled Hershiser's scar to be molded into a new anterior labrum.

It took two years for the scar tissue to harden and for nerve endings to die down, relieving Hershiser of the pain. But with an ability to suffer stoically, Hershiser returned to the mound much sooner, on May 29, 1991. It was a rough go, with four runs and 12 baserunners in four innings, but in his next game, he pitched 6⅓ shutout innings and was on his way to a successful comeback season with a 3.46 ERA (104 ERA+).

"When I had pain, I was actually improving," Hershiser said. "I was getting better. I was molding the scar tissue. I made it back in 13 months…So when I came back I was pitching in pain for a good 11 months. I'd walk around the mound and rub the ball up and wait for the pain to subside to get ready to throw the next pitch."

Though his 3.67 ERA (95 ERA+) in 1992 and 3.59 ERA (106 ERA+) in 1993 betrayed that he was not as effective as in years past, Hershiser still broke the 200-inning barrier in both years. And Hershiser's aura of all-around skill further blossomed, thanks to rather astonishing developments in his hitting. A career .214 hitter as a Dodger (.250 in the postseason), Hershiser went 26-for-73 with two walks and four doubles in 1993 for a .356 batting average, the highest by a Dodger pitcher since Ben Chapman went 11-for-29 (.379) in 1944.

As with pitching, Hershiser's hitting success was a matter of improving his odds and exploiting probabilities. He never tried to hit a home run—and never succeeded, either. But he did spend his time in batting practice working to make contact, perfecting the bunt (successful sacrifices didn't count against your batting average), and practicing the bastard play (faking a bunt and then slashing the ball past the oncoming infielder). How else, trying it every fifth day during a game, could he succeed at the hardest job in sports?

"When you watch me hit, it's really ugly," Hershiser says, "but it had nothing to do with trying to be pretty and had nothing to do with trying to hit the ball far. It had only to do with making contact, and that year the ball fell in and I got all my bunts down and I was really good at the bastard play. I remember the hitting more than I do the pitching—and when I stole bases." Hershiser in fact holds the Dodger franchise record for a pitcher with six steals. "That was the fun part."

In 1994, his 12th year as a Dodger, Hershiser stood to become a free agent at season's end. Now 35, he was driving toward a similar performance as 1993 (3.46 ERA, 112 ERA+), when he took the mound August 7 for the last time before he and his fellow MLB players had threatened to go on strike. At Mile High Stadium in Colorado, he carried a no-hitter into the sixth inning of a 6–2 victory, then talked to teammates and reporters afterward about how it could be his last outing as a Dodger.

In fact, both the Dodgers and Hershiser were interested in extending his stay, though there was an understanding that another tradition dating back to Branch Rickey—that it was better to get rid of a player a year too early than a year too late—was in play. But the real game changer was the secret, impending arrival of a unique free agent from Japan named Hideo Nomo. That prevented the Dodgers from guaranteeing Hershiser a spot in the 1995 starting rotation and forced them into requesting a hometown discount on salary that Hershiser, still being pursued by Cleveland and San Francisco, among others, had no need to grant. Cleveland won the tug of war.

"There was no animosity at all, no ugliness," Hershiser says. "We completely talked it out, and then it was just go on and see who else wanted me."

Hershiser spent three years with Cleveland. The first was a bit of a renaissance, with a 3.87 ERA (121 ERA+, his best since 1989) in the regular season, followed by a 1.53 ERA in 35⅓ postseason innings over five starts for the AL champions. With a 1.64 ERA in 13 playoff games dating back to 1985, Hershiser established one of the greatest October reputations in baseball history.

At age 39, he moved on to pitch for the rival Giants in 1998, which put him on the mound against Los Angeles three times, winning the first two. Asked if he treated the Dodgers as any old opponent or if it mattered to be pitching against his longtime team, Hershiser responded in a way that revealed his true competitive fire.

"It always matters," he says. "You're always looking for a buzz before the game starts. You're always looking for a reason to try. You're always looking for a reason to get angry. You're always looking for a reason to get the adrenaline going. So when somebody says, 'It doesn't mean anything, they're just another opponent,' I think they're lying. It definitely means something. It's somebody who said, 'We don't want you anymore.' It's somebody who said, 'Hey, good luck somewhere else.' It's somebody who said, 'We've got somebody better for the job.' So there's always a little extra edge, and you're always looking for that as an athlete—at least, I was. I was always looking for a reason—somebody yell at me and swear at me and say 'Your mother' to me. Okay, thank you. You just helped me. You have no idea. You think you're hurting me. You just helped me."

Hershiser's fire could also be found in the way he went after pitching until every last spark had been extinguished. After spending his age-40 season with the Mets, Hershiser made one last trip back to Los Angeles in 2000. Good vibes in the spring fed into six innings of one-run ball in his second start of the season. In his third, however, he allowed seven runs in 1⅓ innings, tying a franchise record by hitting four batters with pitches.

"I was terrible," Hershiser states. "My body was shutting down. When I would work out, my body would need to miss it. The workouts were not making me stronger. They were actually tearing me down, and it becomes a balance between 'I need to work out to get stronger to be ready for my next outing, but if I work out too hard, then I don't recover in time and now I'm not ready.' So slowly, slowly you actually start to deteriorate. There is just not enough rest to recover to get ready to go perform. If somebody said I could have pitched in a rotation that was once every 10 days, I could have done it. You haven't lost the ability completely, you've lost the ability to do it in the time frame necessary for the big-league schedule.

"And then slowly, the ability goes away completely. The wiring of your eye-hand coordination and the strength go away."

On June 26, Hershiser started against San Diego, the team he faced for his 59th consecutive scoreless inning 12 years earlier. Of the 14 batters he faced this day, 10 reached base and eight scored. When manager Davey Johnson pulled him from the game and Hershiser took a seat in the dugout, the Dodger Stadium fans had a feeling. They rose to their feet. They didn't know that Hershiser would later return as a Dodger broadcaster, or how often he would be around to share his wisdom with young players.

"I had my head back on the cement," he says. "And I could feel the coldness of the cement of Dodger Stadium, knowing this was it. It was over. But it was great, because the fans gave me a standing ovation. They knew how bad I pitched, but they respected me. They knew it was over, too. It's pretty good when thousands of people understand that you were really bad, but respect you enough to do a standing ovation."

As the years passed after the 1988 World Series title, Hershiser's feats loomed larger and larger in Dodger history, for all except the man who made them happen.

"I don't ever think about it," he says. "I never think about any of this stuff. I don't even watch the film. I'm such a present-tense person, 'What have we got for tomorrow? What have we got for today?' The only time I think about '88 is when somebody else brings it up or a fan asks to look at the championship ring, but [otherwise] I never, ever, ever think about it. I'm thinking about my golf swing that I need to have in a couple of days."

PART SIX

The International Rotation

IN THE TWO DECADES FOLLOWING the championship season of 1988, not a single Dodger pitcher won a postseason game except for the lovably beguiling Jose Lima, whose Game 3 shutout in the 2004 NLDS against St. Louis glorified a slim, one-season tenure in Los Angeles.

No future Hall of Famer emerged, save for the lost treasure that was Pedro Martínez, traded away after his second season in 1993 with the best of intentions but the worst of outcomes.

Not until a forty-something Greg Maddux came to Los Angeles in the twilight of his career in 2006 did a future Hall of Famer again wear a Dodger uniform.

Even so, the 1990s enhanced the Dodger pitching mystique in a specific but meaningful way. Rooted in a far-sighted mentality established decades earlier by Dodger ownership—first Walter O'Malley, then his son, Peter—the Dodgers, and particularly their pitching staff, expanded baseball's global evolution. The ultimate flags-of-our-nations festival came in 1996, when the Dodger starting rotation featured pitchers from an unprecedented five different countries, with Ramón Martínez (Dominican Republic), Ismael Valdez (Mexico), Chan Ho Park (South Korea), and

Hideo Nomo (Japan) joining the lone American, knuckleballer Tom Candiotti.

A number of factors were at play, not the least being the longstanding O'Malley interest in promoting baseball internationally, particularly in the Far East, where the Dodgers' 1956 monthlong postseason goodwill tour of Japan inaugurated a series of cultural exchanges. The Dodgers made a commitment to use baseball as a means of improving players' lives, whether they would succeed as major-leaguers or not.

Nowhere was this more evident than the Dominican Republic. Drawing from the talent pool of Spanish-speaking nations in the Americas wasn't revolutionary, but paying attention to their development and well-being was. That's what made the creation of the Dodgers' complex in the Dominican Republic so important. Dodger special assignment scout Ralph Avila explored several possible locations before settling on what became Campo Las Palmas in Santo Domingo, which opened in 1987.

"Before we built that camp, I went down there a year or two earlier and looked at the facilities," Peter O'Malley says. "At that time, Toronto had the best, but it was in my opinion not good enough. And the other boarding houses where the teams, the major-league clubs, had their players, it was really embarrassing. I said at that time to Ralph, who was with me, 'Ralph, we've got to do something. If *60 Minutes* ever came down here to look at the facilities the major-league clubs have—literally boarding houses with chickens jumping in and out the windows—it was terrible."

Avila, a Cuba native and baseball lifer who began working for the Dodgers as a Latin American scout in 1970, took the baton, making it a personal mission to mold Campo Las Palmas into something more than utilitarian, more than a place to play and sleep. There, players would learn English, develop healthy eating habits, grow as people.

"He and [his wife] Gloria lived there," O'Malley said. "There's a little house across the street that we also bought, fixed it up. He walked across the street to the camp. He oversaw not only baseball but the kitchen. He had a farm there, he grew vegetables that he was very proud of, he raised pigs that were used for food. It was a farm in addition to a baseball camp, and he oversaw the whole thing."

Simply stated, the Dodgers' philosophy toward a global game changed baseball, and one needed look no further than the international rotation to see the proof. Martínez, Valdez, Park, and Nomo won't set foot in the Hall of Fame except as visitors, but each had historic moments and several seasons of sustained excellence. That success, underscored by their unique journeys to Dodger Stadium, makes them a worthy bridge connecting 21st century Dodger pitchers back through time to Hershiser, Valenzuela, Sutton, Koufax, Drysdale, and Newcombe.

Ramón Martínez

Thanks to unforgettable hitters like Manny Mota and Pedro Guerrero, it's easy to imagine a steady pipeline of talent to Dodger Stadium from the Dominican Republic. But the Caribbean nation, joined with Haiti on an island tucked off the Florida coast between Cuba and Puerto Rico, didn't produce a homegrown pitcher for the Dodgers until the World Series year of 1981, when Alejandro Peña broke in. Next came Balvino Galvez, who drank a 10-game cup of coffee in 1986. Ramón Martínez was only the third.

Decades later, Martínez looms largest—not only as the most valuable Dodger pitcher between Orel Hershiser and Clayton Kershaw, but as the ultimate big brother to those who followed him to Los Angeles (including his actual little brother, Pedro).

"Ramón Martínez was a great pitcher," says his manager, Tommy Lasorda. "I thought he was so much better than his brother at that time, and Ramón was one of the nicest human beings that you ever want a player to be like. He was a leader of the people from the Dominican that were on the team—he'd invite them to the suite on the road and feed them and talk to them and have fun with them—and he did such a good job both on the field and off the field. One of the nicest human beings that God ever put on the earth."

Praising Martínez's intelligence, Jaime Jarrín says he was special because he not only "tried to be the torch among the Latino players that were with the Dodgers," but the others as well.

"He was a good leader, a good person," says Martínez's teammate from South Korea, Chan Ho Park. "I liked him a lot, and how he treated teammates very well. We used to enjoy following his routine, his training—we all followed him. We all looked up to him. Even though it was a different culture for everybody, the team worked very well."

Lanky as an L, Martínez was 6-foot-2 and 132 pounds when the Dodgers signed him as a 16-year-old in 1984 from Mota's hometown of Santo Domingo, weeks after he was the youngest player in the Olympic baseball competition at Dodger Stadium. After pitching 170⅓ innings with a 2.17 ERA and only three home runs allowed for Single-A Vero Beach at age 19 in 1987, Martínez was untouchable in general manager Fred Claire's off-season dealings, so much so that the Dodgers, though gunning for a title in 1988, were more willing to trade stalwart veteran Bob Welch in the three-team deal with the A's and Mets than their teenage righty.

Through the minors, the Dodgers' sizeable concern with Martínez, who grew up (to 6-foot-4) but not out, remained his lack of size. "Martínez looks like something Pedro Guerrero might swing in the on-deck circle," Sam McManis wrote in his feature introducing Martínez to *Los Angeles Times* readers. Officially listed at 165 pounds, Martínez struggled in the minors to adapt to American culture in general and cuisine in particular, sometimes shrinking to about 150 pounds. But with that golden arm and winning poise, he was the needle in the prospect haystack.

"Everybody in the organization said, 'Wow, this is a special young man,'" recalls Peter O'Malley. "The quality of the person impressed everybody in the camp when he came to Vero Beach, and later when he came to L.A."

In '88, Martínez carved up Double-A San Antonio, pitching 95 innings with a 2.46 ERA and 89 strikeouts, earning a promotion to Triple-A Albuquerque in June. Not even two months later, with a 2.76 ERA in 58⅔ innings for the Dukes, Martínez answered the call to the show when the Dodgers released Don Sutton, who at 43 was more than twice Martínez's age.

The youngest pitcher to debut for the Dodgers since Fernando Valenzuela—and even more highly anticipated, given the fervent desire to find the next El Toro (*Los Angeles Times* columnist Mike Downey quickly tested out the phrase "Ramónomania")—Martínez's August 13 inauguration surprisingly became an afterthought in one of the most memorable games of the '88 season, when pitcher Tim Leary's pinch-hit single in the bottom of the 11th gave the Dodgers a 2–1 victory over San Francisco. Martínez retired the first five Giants in a strong 7⅔ innings (throwing 123 pitches, a little-noticed figure then that would be worthy of full-scale alarm in the 21st century), allowing one run on four hits and four walks while striking out five.

Moment in the Sun: Mike Morgan

- Pitched exactly 600 innings in three seasons for Dodgers with a 3.06 ERA (117 ERA+), 18th-best adjusted ERA in Dodger history
- On July 28, 1991, matched Montreal's Dennis Martínez by retiring first 15 batters, before losing to Martínez's perfect game thanks to unearned runs
- Made MLB debut at age 18 with Oakland and retired 24 years and 12 big-league teams later with 2,772⅓ career innings, winning first World Series at age 42 with Arizona

"However anxious he might have felt inside, he certainly looked relaxed and thoroughly big-league on the outside," Downey wrote.

Martínez followed that start with seven more innings and 130 pitches of one-run ball against the Phillies, once again another no-decision that later became a 2–1 Dodger win. Eleven days later, the Dodgers played a third 2–1 game, but this time the baseball gods granted Martínez the W, following seven efficient innings with 92 pitches and no earned runs, when Alfredo Griffin hit his only home run of the season in the top of the eighth.

A Paul O'Neill shot up the middle off Martínez's right index finger short-circuited his first outing of September, and as the end of an exhausting season neared, Martínez made only one start the rest of the way and didn't pitch more than three innings in a game. His 1.73 ERA at the end of August rose to 3.79 (90 ERA+) by year's end, and he was left off the postseason roster.

That zig preceded some zags as 1989 unfolded. He pitched inconsistently in spring training, particularly with his curveball, and returned to Albuquerque while the Dodgers retained Tim Belcher, Hershiser, Leary, Valenzuela, and Mike Morgan in their rotation. Disappointed but not daunted, Martínez dominated the high-scoring Pacific Coast League, with 88 strikeouts and a 2.61 ERA in his first 76 innings, when the Dodgers called up him up for a June 5 doubleheader at Atlanta.

Pitching like a man with a statement to make, Martínez smothered the Braves like the summer humidity, weathering a 105-minute rain delay and throwing his first career shutout, a 125-pitch six-hitter with nine strikeouts, one walk, and a whole lot of "Here I am, folks." No Brave reached third base until the ninth inning. Martínez was the youngest Dodger righty to throw a shutout since Sutton in 1966.

"I feel more confidence because I've got better stuff, better control, and a better curveball," Martínez said after the game. The catcher, Mike Scioscia, said the curveball still wasn't where it needed to be, "but he had command of his fastball in and out, and his changeup was just tremendous."

Despite all that, Martínez was still an extra man in the rotation, and he was dispatched right back to Albuquerque for another six weeks. The Dodgers were 26–28, but pitching was not their problem—Morgan, the No. 5 starter when the season began, had a league-leading 1.36 ERA. Nevertheless, try explaining a demotion to a pitcher who just threw a shutout. "It's hard for me to understand," Martínez said. "My feeling was, I would never go back to Albuquerque. It's a bigger surprise now than in the spring."

When the Dodgers recalled Martínez in mid-July, however, it was a one-way ticket. He had plenty to learn, but at times, Martínez schooled the NL, especially last-place Atlanta. In his second start against Atlanta, he struck out nine in eight innings of one-run ball, and on September 15, he blanked the Braves again, no-hitting them for 4⅔ innings, fanning a career-high 12, and finally displaying a curveball to Lasorda's satisfaction.

"I was very disappointed that a young man who throws the ball as hard as he can does not have a good curveball," Lasorda said of Martínez, who finished his 1989 Dodger campaign with a 3.19 ERA (108 ERA+) in 98⅔ innings. "When this happens, either the guy has a stiff wrist and can't throw a curve, or he just doesn't know how to throw a curve. In Ramón's case, he just didn't know how."

Now he knew. In 1990, he showed just how much.

At age 22, Martínez dined on the NL's dime, pitching 234⅓ innings, including an MLB-leading 12 complete games, with a 2.92 ERA (126 ERA+), 223 strikeouts, and a 1.10 WHIP, throwing a shutout inning (despite two walks) in the All-Star Game and winning the silver medal in the NL Cy Young Award voting behind Pittsburgh's Doug Drabek.

The most memorable game of that 20–6 season, if not his career, arrived June 4, against his familiar playthings from Atlanta. Martínez's first six outs came by strikeout. Through four innings, he had 10 whiffs. When Jeff Blauser went down on three straight pitches to make the second out of the eighth inning, Martínez tied Sandy Koufax's franchise record with 18 strikeouts, with four potential outs remaining.

Despite going to two strikes on three more occasions, Martínez couldn't corral the record-breaking K, settling for a place in history alongside Koufax, along with a 6–0 shutout.

"I was throwing as hard as I was in the beginning," Martínez said. "I was doing everything I could do…I still got the complete game and the shutout, and we won. And I am with a superstar like Sandy Koufax. I feel honored."

"Ramón always had that ability to go out there and put up big numbers and strike guys out," Scioscia says. "Everything seemed like it flowed that game. He just had that fastball with great life, was getting it in good zones, and used the changeup. It was just one of those nights that everything came together."

Because of Hershiser's shoulder surgery in 1990 and Valenzuela's release the following spring training, the 23-year-old Martínez was the only homegrown member of the starting rotation when the 1991 season began, with Morgan, Belcher, Bob Ojeda, and Kevin Gross. Throwing 220⅓ innings, Martínez's ERA diminished slightly to 3.27 (110 ERA+), but his strikeout rate dropped significantly, from 8.6 per nine innings in 1990 to 6.1 in '91, the neighborhood where it remained for the next four years.

Correlation is not causation, but in 87 big-league starts before his 24th birthday, Martínez threw at least 120 pitches 31 times on Lasorda's watch, including games of 145, 147, and 148 pitches in 1990.

"When you put Ramón on the mound, you're gonna get at least six innings out of him and probably more than that, and a real good fastball, and he had the command—just an outstanding pitcher," Ross Porter says. "Now, I think there are those who would say Tommy overused him, and again, you have to look at his innings."

Martínez's ERA was as low as 2.25 at the end of July, but in his final 68⅔ innings of the season, he allowed 42 earned runs with 31 walks.

"Ramón was quiet but talented, and Ramón had a great pitcher's body," Claire says. "But when you're as tall as Ramón and your arm is as long as Ramón's, it's like hitting a driver compared to a 7 iron. It's easy to get off track."

Martínez's struggles became more pronounced in 1992, admittedly a year when practically nothing went right for the 99-loss Dodgers. Starting on Opening Day, he left after 11 of the 19 batters he faced reached base, throwing 87 pitches in 2⅔ innings. Plagued by a bothersome left hip, he strung together three quality starts only once in the first half of the season. A five-start stretch from July 24 to August 15 with a 2.86 ERA offered hope, but he allowed seven runs in his next start with declining velocity, and on August 25, completed only two innings, his ERA for the year rising to 4.00 (87 ERA+). Diagnosed at this point with tennis elbow, Martínez didn't pitch again in '92.

On September 24, the day that the Dodgers confirmed that the 24-year-old Martínez wouldn't return to action, a 20-year-old Martínez debuted for the Dodgers with two shutout innings of relief. This was Ramón's *hermano más joven* by the name of Pedro, five inches shorter but brimming with talent, and someone Ramón long insisted was the best pitcher in the family. (A third brother, 18-year-old Jesus, had also entered the Dodger farm system.)

"The Martínez children grew up poor, but they were well dressed for school and they took their education seriously," Norm King wrote in a SABR essay. "They also took baseball seriously…very seriously.

"In the grand tradition of annoying little brothers everywhere, 13-year-old Pedro tagged along when Ramón went to the academy. [Ralph] Avila eventually noticed him tossing a ball around and decided to put the radar gun to his fastball—it clocked in at 80 miles per hour. Wisely, Avila told Pedro to keep on pitching. Pedro did just that, and in 1988, Avila signed Pedro, now 16, to get him into the Dodger fold before he could turn professional."

Despite missing a month of the Triple-A season himself with a sore shoulder, Pedro had healed enough for a late-season trial in '92. Six days later, Pedro started and struck out seven with no walks in six innings, allowing two runs on four hits.

"What I know of baseball, and life off the field, I owe to Ramón," Pedro said. "Everything I am I learned from Ramón."

Ramón and Pedro spent the 1993 season as teammates—a comeback season in the rotation for big brother (211⅔ innings, 3.44 ERA, 111 ERA+), a breakout season in the bullpen for little brother (107 innings, 2.61 ERA, 146 ERA+, 119 strikeouts). The only discordant note was the ongoing deterioration of Ramón's control—he led the NL with 104 walks, 35 above his previous career high. Still, 25 of his 32 starts lasted at least six innings.

With Ramón still only 25, it was easy to envision the Martínez brothers buttressing the Dodger staff for years to come, but infamously, the Dodgers saw Pedro primarily as a reliever—and a fragile one at that. On November 19, the Dodgers acquired second baseman Delino DeShields from Montreal, and Pedro Martínez was the price they paid.

"His shoulder had come out once," Dr. Frank Jobe said, "and once an injury of that type occurs, you can't say it won't reoccur. He had kind of a delicate stature to start with, and there were already questions about his stamina. It's a judgment call, but you had to kind of wonder, 'Golly, is this kid going to break down?'"

Without his brother on the team, Ramón made the rest of the Dodgers' international rotation into his family and his protégés. For Ismael Valdez, among others, Martínez was a role model.

"His work ethic, his attitude about being the best," Valdez says. "He worked really hard before and during the season. He was very disciplined; he had extreme order in his life. Very good command of his personal life."

Martínez averaged more than seven innings per start in 1994, pitching 170 innings with a 3.97 ERA (99 ERA+), his improved control negated by an increased homer rate. On the afternoon of August 11 in Cincinnati, he threw his league-leading third shutout of the season, his final pitch the last any Dodger threw that year, before the season-ending players' strike.

In 1995, Martínez allowed a career-high eight earned runs in a July 2 start against the Colorado Rockies—in Los Angeles, not Denver—sending his ERA sprawling to 4.97 amid boos at Dodger Stadium. He recovered with six innings of two-run ball against the Reds in his final start before the All-Star break, but in the shadow of Hideo Nomo's launch in Los Angeles, Martínez's star seemed to be dimming.

Then, almost out of nowhere, came July 14. While the Dodgers built a 7–0 lead over the first six innings, Martínez efficiently set down every Florida Marlins hitter he faced—the first 23, in fact—his fastball, which had been a question for some time now, hitting 95 mph.

With Todd Hollandsworth, in his first career start, making a running catch deep in right center of a Terry Pendleton drive to start the eighth, the perfect game continued until Tommy Gregg walked on a full-count pitch with two out.

"That was the only time I felt nervous," Martínez said. "I felt myself shaking a little bit."

Recovering, Martínez struck out Kurt Abbott looking to end the top of the eighth, then Charles Johnson to launch the top of the ninth. Jerry Browne grounded to second on the next pitch. The final batter, leadoff hitter and fellow Santo Domingo native Quilvio Veras, fouled off a pair of 2-2 pitches.

"We don't talk about no-hitters during the game or in the dugout," Valdez says. "We don't get even close. And one of the things he taught me: 'Rocket, throw it down the middle…When it's meant for you, you're gonna have it.'"

Veras hit a fly ball to left field, to the waiting glove of Roberto Kelly.

His last start had brought all the catcalls, but now Martínez felt nothing but celebration and adulation. O'Malley came down from the owners' box to the clubhouse to congratulate him. Among the phone messages awaiting him at home was one from Pedro, who had thrown nine perfect innings in an extra-inning game a month earlier.

For Ramón, it was a most gratifying moment.

"I have pride," the 27-year-old said, "and I wanted to let people know that I can still pitch. You know something, I think people had forgotten about me."

The no-hitter kicked off a second-half resurgence for Martínez, who stuffed 111⅔ innings into his final 15 starts with a 2.66 ERA, to finish '95 with a 3.66 ERA (103 ERA+), punctuated by back-to-back eight-inning wins. In his final start of the regular season, Martínez's 4–3 victory over Colorado pulled the Dodgers a half-game ahead of the Rockies with five to play, in a division race Los Angeles won by a single game.

Seven years after missing out on the 1988 playoffs, Martínez made his postseason debut in Game 1 of the NLDS against the Reds, though it didn't go well. Cincinnati ambushed Martínez with a two-run double by Hal Morris and a two-run homer by Benito Santiago in the first inning of a 7–2 loss, in which Martínez was knocked out with one out in the fifth.

In his second start of 1996, Martínez tore his right groin muscle when he slipped on his way to first base in sub-40-degree temperatures at Wrigley Field. Six weeks later he returned to complete his season with a 3.42 ERA (114 ERA+), his best adjusted ERA since his breakout 1990 season. He even emerged victorious in an emotional duel with Pedro in Montreal on August 29.

"I only wish I'd gotten along with either Martínez half as well as they got along with each other," Mike Piazza said. "They really did have a special relationship. Pedro was known to sit in the dugout and pray for Ramón when his brother pitched against his team—or slip back to the Montreal clubhouse, where he could cheer more openly. On the night they opposed each other, Pedro was asked what he was thinking after Ramón walked three straight batters in the bottom of the third to let in the first run of the game. He said, 'I was hoping he'd make some adjustments.' Ramón did, and we won, 2–1, on back-to-back homers by me and Eric [Karros] in the fourth."

Returning to start Game 1 of the NLDS, this time against the Braves, Martínez pitched more than well enough to win, going toe-to-toe with Greg Maddux and allowing only a sacrifice fly in eight innings of a game the Dodgers lost in 10, 2–1.

After throwing 168⅔ innings in '96, a small rotator cuff tear diagnosed in mid-June 1997 limited Martínez to 133⅔ innings, his lowest total since he was a rookie in 1989, with a 3.64 ERA (197 ERA+). Avoiding surgery, Martínez made seven more starts before the end of the year—and then 15 starts in 1998 with an ERA of 2.83 (143 ERA+). But on June 14, in his 102nd inning of the year, facing fellow Dominican and former Dodger protégé Pedro Astacio, Martínez departed with shoulder stiffness.

"I was trying to throw hard and get my good fastball, but I was uncomfortable," said Martínez. "This [pain] is in the front of the shoulder, not the back like last year."

Martínez had an increased rotator cuff tear as well as a cartilage tear, and consulted three different doctors (Jobe, Lewis Yocum, and James Andrews) before assenting to surgery, ending his season—and his Dodger career. In October, the Dodgers declined Martínez's contract option for 1999, and that January, Martínez signed to join Pedro in Boston.

For two years, Ramón pitched sparingly for Boston while enjoying a front-row seat as Pedro had two of the finest seasons in baseball history: a 243 ERA+ (2.07 ERA) in '99 and an MLB-record 291 ERA+ (1.74 ERA) in 2000. Ramón attempted a second term with the Dodgers in 2001 but didn't make it out of spring training (Eric Gagné won his spot in the rotation), and after a short stint with the Pirates in 2001, the godfather of Dodger pitchers from the Dominican retired.

"Ramón is the greatest guy," Gagné said. "He talked to me the whole spring, always encouraged me the whole time. It could have gone the other way."

If injuries prevented Martínez from sustaining the level of excellence that he sometimes achieved, they didn't stop him from installing his name across the Dodger leaderboards. With a 3.45 ERA (109 ERA+) in 1,731⅔ innings, Martínez ranked 16th in franchise history in innings and in wins above replacement (26.1). Moreover, he placed in the top tier of pitchers leading by example.

CHAN HO PARK

At his first game at Dodger Stadium, the 16-year-old sat at the top of the ballpark, the language on the scoreboards inscrutable, the players nearly too small to see, the pitcher's mound a speck of dust in the faraway universe below.

At his second game at Dodger Stadium, the language remained foreign but the players were life-size, because at age 20, the mound in that universe was his.

For all the international men of history amassed by the Dodgers in building their pitching staffs, no one was more of a pioneer than Chan Ho Park when he became MLB's first South Korean player in April 1994.

He could have been a novelty, but instead proved worthy of the uniform, amassing 18.2 wins above replacement—the bulk of them between 1996 and 2001—to rank 24th in Dodger history and 14th since the team moved to Los Angeles, ahead of his more celebrated Asian counterpart, Hideo Nomo.

Park's presence in the United States owes itself to his talent. His presence in Los Angeles owes itself to the Dodgers' globally minded front office, as well as the seductive power of Blue Heaven on Earth.

Born in 1973 in the modestly populated city of Gongju, 150 miles south of Seoul, Park made his first trip to the United States—and, unbeknownst to him, his first appearance in front of Dodger scout Bobby Darwin and scouting director Terry Reynolds—in 1990, when he played for a youth all-star team in an international tournament against players from Japan and the U.S. Before heading home, he joined his teammates in a pilgrimage to baseball's holy land in Chavez Ravine.

"We sat in the very top deck, right in the middle area, red seats, and so very far away," Park says. "So I can see the stadium, the whole thing, but I can't see the players barely at all…I didn't even know the players' names anyway. I just saw the baseball field and how they played the game.

I didn't even know how good major-league players are. For me, the huge stadium and big crowd—and the 'ba-da ba-da, ba-da—charge!'—that made it for me a special moment.

"I can't see the pitches, but I can see the fans reacting, and how great it would be to be playing there. Imagine being a baseball player playing the game in front of this crowd."

When the game ended and the stands emptied, Park continued to gaze at that mound as he and his group stuck around. Then before leaving, he went to the Top of the Park gift shop to buy gifts for his hometown friends who had helped raise money for him to go on the trip to the United States. He looked at Dodger keychains, Dodger pencils. Then he saw a shiny blue Dodger jacket hanging on the wall.

"The seller said, 'That's the same jacket the players wear,'" Park recalls. "I saw the players wear the same blue jacket in the dugout. So I'd like to buy that, so I checked the price."

The cost of the jacket nearly staggered him, but he had a solution. He bought the jacket, and then when he got back to Korea, he passed it around so that everyone could wear it. It was a direct connection to a memory of Dodger Stadium that profoundly affected him.

"I never imagined I could pitch there, or I'm gonna pitch there," Park says. "I'd just think about *if* I were there. Nervous, big crowd, big stadium, and palm trees in the outfield—that's so beautiful. This I had in my memory, and this jacket every day would bring it up."

Park took his baseball dreams to Hanyang University in Seoul. He had gotten a copy of Nolan Ryan's guide to pitching—all in English, but with pictures of exercises and mechanics that Park paged through so relentlessly, the book nearly disintegrated. (His distinctive high leg kick was inspired by Ryan.)

As all this transpired, the Dodgers hadn't forgotten about Park. They tracked him, both in Korea and as he pitched internationally in 1993 for the Korean national team in the Asian Games in Australia and the World University Games in Buffalo, New York. Quietly, Dodger owner Peter

O'Malley made multiple trips to Seoul to meet with Park, his family, and his college president, bringing Dr. Frank Jobe along for one.

> ## Moment in the Sun: Tom Candiotti
> - Durable knuckleballer pitched 1,048 innings for the Dodgers from 1992 to 1997, with a 3.57 ERA (106 ERA+)
> - His 14.8 wins above replacement ranked 24th in Los Angeles history
> - Perhaps Los Angeles' unluckiest pitcher ever: no one with an above-average ERA had a lower winning percentage than Candiotti's .448 (52-64)

"Dr. Jobe, he didn't show up [at school] because they didn't want to let anyone know Dr. Jobe was here," Park says. "I had to tell to the coach at the school—'I had to go out to see my uncle.'"

While Park was passing his examination for Jobe at a nearby hospital, O'Malley was giving reassurances that the Dodgers would look out for him.

"Getting permission from his college was a challenge, as well as from Chan Ho's parents," O'Malley says. "They had to understand where he's going, who's gonna take care of him. And I think we convinced the university and his parents that we were going to take good care of him. I remember telling his father in the lobby of the hotel, 'I'm gonna take care of your son just as I would take care of my own son.' I remember saying that. And it's been a pleasure, because he and I are good friends and have been forever."

O'Malley, who had been active in the international baseball community for so long, said there was no concern about pursuing a ballplayer from a country that had yet to produce a single major-leaguer.

"The scouting reports spoke for themselves," O'Malley says. "We did our homework, talked to people in Korea at that time…I asked those friends in Korea what they knew about him, and they all said, 'This guy's for real, not just as a ballplayer but as a person.' Well-educated, good family guy, just a darn good man."

Park flew to Los Angeles to seal the deal, which included a signing bonus of $1.2 million—as well as a requirement releasing him to return to Korea for college if he did not make it as an MLB player within three years. On New Year's Day 1994, he arrived at Dodger Stadium. By this time, his old Dodger jacket had been stolen, so he sported a different one he had purchased in Korea.

"I didn't know it was a Yankee jacket—I didn't know what it said," Park remembers with a laugh. "Before Peter saw it, the people there realized. They changed it right away to a Dodger jacket."

On January 11, the Dodgers announced Park's signing to media from two continents, as well as his enrollment at an English-language school that enabled him to postpone his two-year commitment to the South Korean military. He arrived at spring training that year with a fastball in the high 90s, a slider, a curveball, and an occasional forkball.

"You can tell he didn't grow up pitching in the United States of America," Dodger teammate Delino DeShields said. "The way he changes his delivery, he has different looks, and that is confidence. I'm not an expert, but I think the Dodgers have something here."

A healthy four-pitch mix is a nice icebreaker, but Park's efforts to learn English and connect with everyone regardless of any language barrier endeared himself to his new employers, including manager Tommy Lasorda.

"Chan Ho would eat early with the players, and Tommy would eat late," O'Malley says. "While Tommy's having his late dinner, Chan Ho looks at the dining room, and Tommy waves him over, and Chan Ho would eat a second dinner with Tommy and whoever's at Tommy's table. Tommy deserves a lot of credit for the support he gave Chan Ho. Everybody in the organization knew it was an important project, an important signing."

"On his wall in his room is a poster with a runner crossing the finish line and it says, BECAUSE GOD SEES ME AS A WINNER, I AM," Lasorda said. "So Chan Ho says to me, 'Because Tommy sees me as a winner, I am.' You have to love this guy."

When final roster cuts for Opening Day were made, not only did Park become the first South Korean player in the major leagues, he also became only the 18th ballplayer since the MLB draft began in 1965 to skip the minor leagues before making his debut. (One day earlier, Darren Dreifort had become the 17th—together, they were the first Dodgers to play their first professional game in the majors since Sandy Koufax.)

On April 8, 1994, Park warmed up for his first official action, against the Braves in the top of the ninth inning at Dodger Stadium. Because translators weren't allowed on the field at that time, Park recalls, bullpen coach Mark Cresse had preprinted cards with English-Korean translations: ARE YOU READY? ARE YOU OK? Park simply nodded. Kent Mercker happened to be three outs away from completing a no-hitter against the Dodgers, but that didn't relieve Park of any of his delirium.

"When they opened the gate, I ran hard to the mound," Park says. "You know why, right? I remember how my legs felt, because I felt like I was flying." Park was so nervous, he was seeing double and triple. "As soon as I'm on the mound, Mike Piazza, he'd keep moving, moving like this, moving like that. I didn't understand why he kept moving."

Bowing to the umpire before commencing, Park walked Fred McGriff and David Justice on a combined 10 pitches. Terry Pendleton then lined his 11th to left for a double. It cost him two runs, but it cleared Park's senses—Piazza was no longer multiplying before his eyes—and Park struck out two of the next three batters in completing his first big-league inning.

Walking back to the dugout, he still felt embarrassed about the two runs. But as he approached the steps, everybody stood up, fans cheering, teammates offering handshakes and hugs.

"I didn't understand," Park says. "I gave up two runs, we're losing, but they're still happy for me. It makes me feel something special, right? Then I'm sitting in the dugout, and then I think about two years ago [in the top deck]. Look at Brett Butler there, Tim Wallach there, Eric Karros there. That's really a big moment for me."

Nevertheless, midway into April, the Dodgers decided that it would help Park's long-term development and confidence to log some time in the minor leagues, and sent him to Double-A San Antonio.

"Some guys are sent down because they are not doing the job," Lasorda told reporters. "This wasn't the case with him. We're sending him down for his betterment…This guy has an outstanding arm and, believe me, he's going to be an outstanding pitcher."

The Korean community in San Antonio was a bit smaller than the one in Los Angeles, to say the least, but Park did find comfort in Missions pitching coach Burt Hooton, the former Dodger pitching great. "He was like my uncle, and I respected him," Park says. "He was the only person I felt like I could lean on, because we talked a lot in the bullpen about pitching."

"I ended up picking him up at the airport," Hooton says. "You know, he's a 20-year-old kid halfway around the world trying to make a living in professional baseball. Basically he's over here by himself. And English and Korean, you couldn't get two languages more directly opposed to one another. And I remember him being very lonely. Good kid, good sense of humor, just good personality. He had the whole country of South Korea watching everything he did—even in Double-A they would broadcast his games back to Korea, and he wasn't doing real well then. He was getting a real quick education on the field and off the field.

"You stop and think the situation he put himself in. Really, I'm not so sure that me or a lot of other guys like myself could have gone to Korea at 20 years old trying to make a living. The culture is different, the diet's different, everything over here is different. And for him to do what he did and make a success out of himself is a pretty remarkable story…He just needed time to grow up."

Park remained in the minors until the end of the 1995 season, when he appeared in two games, including his first big-league start, in which he allowed a run in three innings at San Diego while striking out five. He began the 1996 season in the Dodger bullpen, winning his first MLB game with four innings of shutout relief April 6 at Wrigley Field—Park called Hooton to tell him the news before calling his own parents—then notching a W as a starter April 11 with five shutout innings against the Marlins.

In his first 55 innings that season, Park had a 1.96 ERA but walked 39 batters, signaling obvious problems of control issues and less obvious issues of fear. In the summer, he found almost nowhere to hide, allowing 27 earned runs in 35 innings that ballooned his ERA. Confidence meant survival.

"I learned how to use the fastball more," he says. "I got more confidence with it. American hitters, I gave them [too much] credit, so I was always trying to go away, being careful. When I had to throw the 2-0 pitch, sometimes I'd throw the breaking ball, because I'd think they were looking for the fastball. At the time, I learned, I could still throw the fastball. I could throw it inside or throw it a little bit lower. When I learned that, I was ready to pitch in the major leagues."

For the entire 1996 campaign, the 23-year-old Park struck out 119 batters in 108⅔ innings across 48 games, 10 of them starts, with a 3.64 ERA (107 ERA+). Two decades later, Park's 9.9 strikeouts per nine innings might seem commonplace, but for Dodgers with at least 100 innings in a season during the 20th century, it was topped by only Nomo, Koufax, and Pedro Martínez.

The next year, Park stepped into the starting rotation in a big way, throwing 192 innings with a 3.38 ERA (115 ERA+). In the first half of

1998, he suffered a setback, practically taking the fetal position at his clubhouse stall after getting knocked out in the third inning of a May 24 game at Arizona, with his ERA swelling to 5.36 after the Rockies tagged him with 10 runs in 5⅓ innings June 21 at Denver. But in his remaining 131⅔ innings that season, Park's ERA was a nifty 2.60—including 1.05 over six July starts to become NL Player of the Month—leaving him at 3.71 (109 ERA+) in 220⅔ innings that year.

Perhaps the 6-foot-2 right-hander's most memorable start—and certainly his most infamous—came on April 23, 1999. With the bases loaded and none out in the third inning against the Cardinals, Fernando Tatis pounced on a Park pitch and sent it into the Dodger bullpen for a grand slam. Nine batters but only two outs later, Tatis did it again, a sacks-stacked second slam to the bleachers in left-center, setting an unfathomable MLB record and capping an 11-run explosion. Park became the first pitcher since the Pirates' Bill Phillips in 1890 to give up two slams in one inning.

"That happened," Park says. "It was bad luck for me, but I had to take it. It made me stronger. I'm glad people ask me about that. I'm not embarrassed anymore. At the time, I was embarrassed. If that was the last game of my career, it was going to be very embarrassing."

It wasn't his last game, but it also wasn't the only low point of his season. In June, with his parents and 91-year-old grandfather in attendance, Tim Belcher made a hard tag on Park on a sacrifice bunt and said some words. Park retaliated, thrusting his forearm at Belcher's face and kicking him. Park was suspended for seven games, but the worst came in the public reaction.

"I got a lot of threatening letters at the time," Park says. "I thought I might get killed by somebody. Every day I felt like that. That's why I was always nervous going to the stadium. Hard to focus."

With his ERA at 6.07 entering August, Park salvaged his year's final lap, finishing with four consecutive quality starts to alight at 5.23 (82 ERA+).

"It was the best year for me, because I learned the most," he reflects. "Now I can say that. At the time it was tough—I didn't know what was going on."

Park set career bests in 2000 with a 3.27 ERA (132 ERA+), leading the NL with 6.9 hits allowed per nine innings and finishing second in strikeouts with 217. Five times he fanned double-digits, including a career-high 14 on August 29 against the Brewers.

"He just dominated us," said no less an authority than Hall of Famer Rod Carew, Milwaukee's batting coach.

Over the final two months of the season, Park's ERA was 1.79 with 10.8 strikeouts per nine innings. In his final two starts, he pitched 17 shutout innings with 26 strikeouts. In his final at-bat, he even homered—one of three he hit in his career.

That set the stage for a 2001 season in which Park was named to the All-Star team, taking a 2.91 ERA into July and finishing at 3.50 (114 ERA+) in a career-high 234 innings. He did allow a home run to Cal Ripken Jr. in the shortstop's final All-Star Game, as well as the record-breaking 71st (and then 72nd) homers of the year by Barry Bonds in October. Park was unapologetic, citing his determination not to be afraid of any hitter, the way he might sometimes have been earlier in his career.

The homers by Bonds didn't reduce any of the attraction Park held for teams looking for pitching when he became a free agent for the first time at age 28. But Park wasn't putting any moving vans on hold.

"I really liked the Dodgers," he says. "The Dodgers were my home. To leave the Dodgers, it would be the same feeling like I left Korea."

But the Dodgers, who had signed Dreifort to a five-year contract after the 2000 season, barely spoke to agent Scott Boras during the negotiation period, while the Rangers, who weren't even a consideration for Park when the off-season began, made Park the proverbial unrefusable offer, signing him to a five-year contract.

Dogged by injuries and inconsistency, Park never acclimated to Texas, pitching only 380⅓ innings for the Rangers and struggling to a 5.79 ERA

(83 ERA+) from 2002 until the July 2005 trading deadline, when they dispatched him to San Diego. He did little better for the Padres (5.08 ERA, 79 ERA+, 182⅓ innings), who nonetheless left him with special memories in 2006. When Park was battling intestinal problems in the summer, eventually needing surgery, teammate Jake Peavy's wife was among those who donated blood to match Park's rare type. That October, at the end of his 13th MLB season, Park was able to pitch in his first playoff game, throwing two shutout innings against St. Louis.

After being limited to four big-league innings in 2007 (with the Mets), Park, in a manner of speaking, phoned home.

"I asked the Dodgers, 'Can you invite me to spring training?'" Park says, "because I wanted to wear the Dodger uniform one more time before I retired. They said 'yes.' When I went to spring training, I felt great."

Even if I retire here, even if this is the last opportunity of my career, I'm so happy to wear a Dodgers uniform, he recalls thinking.

"But I pitched so well, I'm dreaming again of Dodger Stadium."

In fact, Park became a surprisingly effective swingman, pitching 95⅓ innings with a 3.40 ERA (123 ERA+). That put a bow on his Dodger career with 1,279 innings, 1,177 strikeouts, and a 3.77 ERA (108 ERA+).

Park fulfilled remaining dreams by pitching for a World Series champion as a Phillie in 2009, and even put on a team-issued Yankee jacket in 2010, in his 17th and final season in the big leagues. Moving on to Pittsburgh, Park became the winningest Asian pitcher in MLB history, passing Nomo, when in his final big-league game, on October 1, 2010, he struck out six in three perfect innings of relief.

He was done pitching in the U.S., but he wasn't done pitching. In 2011, he took the mound in the Japan League, and in 2012, at age 39, more than 20 years after O'Malley came to bring him to the Dodgers, Park came full circle, making 23 starts for the Hanwha Eagles in Korea.

"If you feel like you really want it, it's going to come true," Park says of his baseball experience. "I'm lucky. Being a pioneer is so lonely and hard, but it's special."

Today, Park and O'Malley work together, partnering with Nomo to run Historic Dodgertown, the Dodgers' former spring training home in Vero Beach. In many ways, Park is focused on making the next generation of ballplayers' dreams come true.

"He's a very deep guy," O'Malley said. "I saw that early. He's an intelligent young man who understands life, what's it all about."

Ismael Valdez

Despite the boundless, practically epic legacy of Fernando Valenzuela, only nine men born in Mexico pitched for the Dodgers before Julio Urías made his big-league debut in 2016, and even with his career sidetracked by shoulder surgery in 2017, Urías had already moved into the No. 3 spot in career starts among his countrymen.

In fact, for all the attention to Valenzuela's heritage, not one Mexico native pitched in a Dodger game for the entire decade following the launch of Fernandomania.

Growing up in Ciudad Victoria, Tamaulipas, about 200 miles south of the Texas border, Ismael Valdez had zero idea he would be the Dodgers' next Mexican prodigy after Valenzuela—much less that he would become, it might surprise people to realize, one of the 25 best Dodger starting pitchers ever.

With 19.1 wins above replacement, Valdez ranked 22nd in franchise history and 12th in the first 60 seasons of baseball in Los Angeles. With an adjusted ERA of 115, Valdez was 13th among Dodgers with a minimum of 1,000 innings and sixth among Los Angeles pitchers, trailing only Clayton Kershaw, Sandy Koufax, Tommy John, Don Drysdale, and Orel Hershiser.

The story of Valdez (who originally spelled his last name "Valdes" before learning at age 26 that his birth certificate had a "z") not only illustrates the lengths the Dodgers would go to make a pitcher, but the lengths a pitcher would go to make it with the Dodgers.

Resembling Hershiser more than Valenzuela, the skinny, right-handed Valdez had little in common with his famous baseball countryman, except for nationality and the fact that neither began pitching on a regular basis until well into their teens. Before then, Valdez might have spent as much time trying to imitate slugger Pedro Guerrero as either of the Dodgers' star pitchers, and couldn't have been a starting pitcher if he tried.

"At age 14, I couldn't throw the ball 10 feet away from me," says Valdez, who experimented with other sports including basketball, tennis, and even football. "It was because I was growing up. My tendons, my nerve, I didn't know why—it was not mechanical. It just felt uncomfortable in my elbow."

When his baseball team went to a national tournament, Valdez was its first baseman. But during one game when the team's starting pitcher was getting hammered and needed emergency relief, Valdez suddenly raised his hand. It had been more than half a year since he had tried pitching.

"It was a blessed day for me," he says.

Within two years, Mike Brito signed Valdez the pitcher to the Dodgers. ("I knew who he was," Valdez says, "because he was the one who signed Fernando.") But Valdez's journey from there to a Dodger uniform was an adventure, not the least because it had a ticking clock. To get permission to sign his deal, his mother asked him to promise that if he didn't succeed within three years, he would go back to school.

"I said, 'Okay, Mom, that's fine,'" Valdez says, not knowing how close to the deadline he would come.

In 1991, Valdez made his first trip to spring training. By coincidence, it was the final trip to Vero Beach for Valenzuela. But Valdez was with the lowest of the minor-leaguers. Valenzuela was so close yet so distant.

"I was from far away seeing Fernando Valenzuela—my idol, man," Valdez says. "Far away. Extended-camp guys, they couldn't get close to the big-league ballclub. No chance—no way."

Valdez had a satisfying first year—he excelled in extended camp, went back to Mexico, then the Arizona Fall League. The second year was another story. At first, farm director Charlie Blaney wanted to send him back to extended camp, but Valdez requested an alternative, so off he went to the Mexican League, where he was held hostage by a manager who had no use for him.

"Two months passed, and I just threw 2⅓ innings, so my mind was getting crazy," Valdez says. "I would have no confidence in myself. They didn't give me any chance or opportunity."

Hoping to escape, he again called Blaney, who arranged for him to pitch in Venezuela. This was 1992, a year in which Hugo Chávez led an attempted coup d'état.

"I was 18 years old, arriving in Caracas, with war tanks in the streets," Valdez says. "I mean, it was amazing. I just wanted the opportunity… That's when I started taking a shower in the rain, sleeping with the heat."

Valdez had been there only two weeks when Blaney called to say that all the major-league teams were removing their foreign players from the country.

"So remember how this year's travels started," he says. "From United States to Mexico, Mexico to Venezuela. From Venezuela, they sent me to the Dominican Republic, all in the same year. This is my second year as a professional, and remember, I only have three years. So in the Dominican Republic, I was low in trust in myself. None of the confidence. I was a little skinny guy who just wanted an opportunity."

At this critical moment, the Dodgers' pitching coach in the Dominican, Eliodoro Arias, provided a lifeline. "He worked with my mind, he strengthened my mind," Valdez says. "He was one of the guys to give me confidence, because I had none when I got there."

Valdez's odyssey continued into 1993, but that summer he reached Double-A San Antonio, where he forged another pivotal relationship, this time with Missions pitching coach Burt Hooton. Valdez's progress bought him a one-year extension of his agreement with his mother, and that's all he needed.

Moment in the Sun: Pedro Astacio

- Statistically made the best pitching debut in Los Angeles history, striking out 10 in a July 3, 1992, shutout of the Phillies
- In 10 starts as a rookie, had a 1.98 ERA (177 ERA+)
- Pitched for Dodgers through 1997: 886⅔ innings with a 3.68 ERA (104 ERA+)
- Ranked 18th in Los Angeles history with 15.8 wins above replacement

In 1994, Valdez shuttled back and forth between San Antonio and Triple-A Albuquerque to start the season. Pitching in one of the toughest environments in baseball, Valdez had a 3.40 ERA in nine starts for Albuquerque, but he had already been demoted once that year and was not eager to have it happen a second time.

"[Onetime Dodger infielder] Rafael Bournigal was my roommate," Valdez recalls. "And I had really good discipline to not drink any alcohol, of not doing anything like that during the season. But I went out that night, with my roommate, and we went back to the hotel to about 2:00 in the morning, something like that. Curfew was probably at 1:00. At 7:00 in the morning, Rick Dempsey, my manager in Triple-A, gives me a call and says, 'See me in the office.' I say, 'All right.' I went to his office, and he says, 'You know what—sorry, man, I can't have you here anymore. This is a plane ticket.'

"I say, 'Rick, what happened? I'm 3–0, I'm averaging seven-plus innings per game.' I was kind of getting crazy. 'What's the big deal? I'm just enjoying the night with my roommate. You know my work ethic. What's happening, Rick?'"

"Well, there's nothing I can do," Dempsey said. "I fought for you. I wanted to keep you here longer. But you know what? The big club is waiting for you in Chicago."

The relief and elation that filled Valdez can be heard in the "Whoooooa!" he exclaims in telling the story. Ten weeks shy of his 21st birthday, only a year older than Valenzuela was when he got his promotion, Valdez was in the big leagues.

Valdez didn't pitch for the Dodgers at Wrigley Field, making his major-league debut June 15 at Dodger Stadium against the Reds with two perfect innings. Outside of a spot start in New York a month later, the 6-foot-3 right-hander pitched 20 times in relief over the next eight weeks, including a stretch of four shutout appearances in five days in July.

Then came the players' strike, cutting off the MLB season at the knees—as the youngest player in MLB that year, Valdez finished with a 3.18 ERA (125 ERA+) and 28 strikeouts in 28⅓ innings—but not stopping him from finishing his year back with Albuquerque, where he walked away with something the NL West–leading Dodgers didn't: a championship ring (from the Pacific Coast League).

That winter, Valdez put the lessons that Ramón Martínez had given him to good use.

"He taught me how to work, how to work really hard," Valdez says. "I committed myself to that work ethic. I took it to wintertime, so I prepared myself and rested my mind and worked my body and strengthened my body to go into 1995. So when I went to spring training in March, I was ready."

In '95, harnessing his four-pitch mix of fastball, curve, slider, and changeup, Valdez took a regular rotation spot in mid-May. In his first eight starts, he had a 1.74 ERA in 62 innings (7.8 innings per start) with three complete games and a June 18 shutout at Wrigley Field. Still only 22 when the season ended, Valdez finished with a 3.05 ERA (124 ERA+) in 197⅔ innings. Though it was overshadowed by Nomo's tornado of a debut, Valdez had one of the 10 best seasons by a rookie pitcher in Dodger history, his adjusted ERA topped in Los Angeles only by the freshman years of Nomo, Valenzuela, and Hershiser.

"I had that great command, because I had a two-foot slider in the big leagues," says Valdez, who also counts Dave Wallace (minor-league pitching coordinator from 1987 to 1994, big-league pitching coach from 1995 to 1998) and Mexican pitching star Chito Rios among his top mentors. "I was throwing to Sammy Sosa all the way to his back, and it was breaking to the outside corner. And then I doubled up my slider [with] my curveball. So I had a 12-to-6 breaking ball, 3-to-9 slider, and then I added a changeup."

Valenzuela, who by this time was pitching for San Diego, also finally blessed Valdez with his long-awaited meeting.

"He called me," Valdez recalls fondly. "'*Paisano*'—that's countryman—'Why don't we go for lunch?' Fernando called me—man, I'm in shock. He was awesome. To this very day, we have a great relationship. I admire him."

Making the playoffs for the first time since 1988, the Dodgers tapped Valdez to start Game 2 of the 1995 NLDS against the Reds. In seven innings, he allowed only four baserunners and no earned runs, but left for a pinch hitter with the score tied 2–2, thanks to a two-out, fourth-inning throwing error by Chad Fonville and an ensuing homer by Reggie Sanders. The Dodgers ended up losing 5–4 on their way to getting swept by Cincinnati.

Valdez returned in 1996 to pitch a career-high 225 innings with a 3.32 ERA (117 ERA+), again starting Game 2 of the NLDS, this time against the Braves, again with the Dodgers losing by a single run. In 6⅓ innings, Valdez walked none and gave up five hits, but three of them were home runs—two in the seventh inning by Fred McGriff and Jermaine Dye to give Atlanta a 3–2 victory.

That lack of run support reached an apex in 1997, when despite a 10–11 record, Valdez had a 2.65 ERA—his 146 ERA+ was the best of any Dodger in the 1990s except for Nomo in his rookie season. From 1995 to 1997, Valdez walked 2.2 batters per nine innings.

"He had great control," says Charlie Hough, who became the Dodgers' pitching coach in mid-1998. "Fastball, slider, curve, change—a four-pitch mix, but he had great command. When he was on, it was pretty solid stuff."

While still effective, Valdez declined from his peak in 1998 and 1999, with a 3.98 ERA in both seasons, a product of inconsistency. Twice in June 1998, he nearly threw no-hitters, starting on June 10 at Oakland, when a seventh-inning single by Matt Stairs ended his bid for history. Valdez still had to finish the game with only a 1–0 lead.

"Roger Cedeno was playing left field," Valdez says. "In the ninth inning, I got a fly ball from the first hitter, and he dropped it—and suddenly I have a man on second. I'm about to lose or tie the game. So the very next hitter hit a line drive, and Roger Cedeno got that ball."

Valdez finished the two-hit shutout with a strikeout of Stairs, then went into the eighth inning June 27 against Pittsburgh with a perfect game until Kevin Young singled. Valdez retired the final six batters to finish with the 28-batter one-hitter.

Unfortunately, Valdez's inability to build upon the success of his previous seasons put him under increasing scrutiny as someone who lost focus at times and pitched scared during others. In April 1997, Bob Nightengale of the *Los Angeles Times* reported a clubhouse fight between Valdez and Eric Karros after Karros "openly ridiculed" the pitcher for a poor performance. (The Dodger offense failed to score during Valdez's next 16⅓ innings on the mound after the incident.) On multiple occasions in 1998, *Times* beat writer Jason Reid reported that teammates and club officials were "angered" by Valdez's reluctance to challenge batters. The pitcher's reputation took a beating.

"Ismael was a very talented pitcher, but to do it, he really had to overcome letting things that would happen in a game be a distraction for him," says Fred Claire, the general manager for most of Valdez's Dodger career. "You know, the pitcher has to be mentally tough—and not that Ismael wasn't. He was a talented player. But I think that's something that he kind of had to get through, to have the confidence in his teammates and for teammates to have the confidence in Ismael."

For most of 1999, Valdez locked in. He had 20 quality starts, and his ERA on September 1 was down to 3.27—best on the Dodger staff except for Kevin Brown—before allowing 20 runs over his next 10 innings.

"We were out of playoff contention," Valdez says. "I don't think I got tired, but I think emotionally, my mind was tired."

Dating back more than a year, Valdez's name had popped up in trade rumors, including one sending him to the Seattle Mariners with Darren Dreifort in a package for Randy Johnson, before Seattle nixed it. Following the '99 season, Valdez's Dodger career veered into an off-ramp, when only a couple weeks after his November 27 wedding, Los Angeles traded him to the Cubs with infielder Eric Young in a December deal that brought back Terry Adams, in what was widely reported as a salary dump. At the time, Valdez still ranked 10th among all active pitchers in ERA.

"I was hurt in my heart," Valdez says. "I never thought I would leave the Dodgers."

Having fallen behind on his winter workouts because of the wedding, then needing to adjust to a new team, then unable to make an official appearance until May because of shoulder tendinitis, then ending his first start after the All-Star break with a 5.70 ERA, Valdez's chapter as a Cub could hardly have gone more poorly.

Trying to stay afloat in an NL West race in which they were 2½ games behind co-leaders San Francisco and Arizona, the Dodgers gambled that Valdez needed an un-change of scenery, reacquiring him for struggling right-hander Jaime Arnold and minor-leaguer Jorge Piedra. But the old magic wasn't there, and the clearest memory of his second stay with the Dodgers was a bizarre rematch August 27 against the Cubs. Though Kerry Wood was leading in the game, the fireballing prodigy had given up two homers to a nondescript Dodger outfielder named Bruce Aven. Immediately after the second, Wood threw a pitch behind Dodger shortstop Alex Cora's head.

Valdez took the mound in the bottom of the fifth, facing his recent teammate, Mark Grace. His fifth pitch hit Grace in the right shoulder.

"You didn't need to tell me that I had to knock him down," says Valdez, who received a six-game suspension (compared to three games for Wood). "I missed the first one. There were warnings for both teams. And I drilled him, obviously below the head. He walked to first base. I got tossed out of the game. Mark Grace looked at me and said hello with his helmet."

Valdez had one final strong outing for the Dodgers on September 1, allowing an unearned run to the Phillies in seven innings, but he became a free agent, never to return except as a visitor—most notably the following June while wearing an Anaheim Angels uniform, with another former Dodger as his manager, Mike Scioscia.

"It was not my turn to pitch in that series," Valdez says. "I said, 'Mike, I want to pitch. I want to pitch against my team. I want to beat 'em, to let 'em know what they let go."

Backed by a Garret Anderson homer, Valdez not only went 6⅔ shutout innings in a 1–0 victory, he singled and stole the fourth and final base of his career.

He made the rounds for the final five seasons of his MLB career, going from Anaheim to Seattle, Texas, San Diego, and Florida, with a 4.89 ERA (91 ERA+) to show for it. "Either I'm good or bad, but never in between," Valdez says. "I was not enjoying the game like I was supposed to. I didn't have butterflies in my stomach before a start."

Valdez also says he was having trouble compartmentalizing his personal life while he was on the mound.

"I was thinking personal on the mound facing Chipper Jones, when I was supposed to be concentrating 100 percent on Chipper Jones instead of leaving my personal stuff outside," Valdez says. "I was having personal issues, some family matters that were affecting me.

"I said, 'You know what, I'm gonna have a year off and then come back. I'm tired of it. I don't want to be traveling, I need to give some time to my family.' Because it was 12 years preparing and traveling, and I have my newborn. I wanted to give it one year and then come back and settle down. But that was the main reason…When I don't feel that in my gut in my stomach, it's time for me to leave."

Valdez's big-league career ended in 2005, at age 32. Among Mexican pitchers, only Valenzuela (2,930 innings) and Esteban Loaiza (2,099) hurled more innings than Valdez's 1,827. And even though his Dodger career ended at age 27, his statline is an impressive one: a 3.48 ERA (115 ERA+) in 1,065 innings. If he didn't reach his maximum potential, he achieved more than he is often credited for.

"Every single game for me, they were so special," Valdez says. "Facing an opportunity to be at the big-league level, with 55,000 souls rooting for you, that was special. My very first day that I pitched in the big leagues, I was in the bullpen, and they called me in. My very first batters were Kevin Mitchell, Tony Fernández. Feeling that adrenaline before the game, and then you throw the first pitch—here we go. This is what I prepared for. And that is unique."

Hideo Nomo

In 1988, the Olympic Games came to Seoul. And baseball, still trying to gain a toehold in the world's biggest athletic extravaganza, came with it. A teenager from a nearby Korean city went up with his friends to check it out, seeing among other players a right-hander from Japan who himself had just turned 20.

From that moment on, Chan Ho Park followed the career of Hideo Nomo, and would have happily offered a scouting report to anyone who was interested. Growing up, he and his friends didn't see American baseball on TV. But they saw plenty of Japanese ball, and most of all, they saw Nomo.

"He was the best pitcher in Japan," Park says. "He was so popular in Korea. In high school, Hideo was my hero. He had a good forkball and fastball. I liked him because he threw the hardest pitch in Japan at the time."

Many of those who were thrilled by Nomo becoming a sensation with the Dodgers beginning in 1995 couldn't appreciate that he had already been the Next Big Thing once before. In Japan, he was a phenom.

Born in Osaka in 1968, Nomo was predisposed to three things—a quiet demeanor, a love of baseball, and a precocious sense of innovation. The combination led to his signature pitching style and success. Originally looking to impress his father, Nomo developed a pitching motion in which, with his pitching hand in his glove, the right-hander stretched his arms high and even behind his head, brought them down to his waist and then up again to shoulder level as he lifted his left knee up, all while pivoting clockwise hard on his right leg—leaning almost impossibly backward, his body nearly in the shape of a 7—before dropping his pitching arm to knee level as he uncoiled and windmilled home.

They'd call him "The Tornado," and soon he laid waste to opposing batters.

Because he still struggled with control, Nomo joined a semipro team in the late 1980s, where he developed the forkball that so impressed Park.

"To develop his grip," Japanese baseball expert Robert Whiting wrote, "he slept each night with a tennis ball wedged in between his first two fingers, stabilized with masking tape. His mastery of the forkball, combined with improved control on his blazing fastball, elevated him to the next level as a pitcher. Now the pro scouts were paying serious attention.

Drafted and signed by the Kintetsu Buffaloes, the 6-foot-2 Nomo immediately sparkled, leading the Japan Pacific League in every major category including ERA and strikeouts, not only winning Rookie of the Year honors but also the Sawamura Award (equivalent to the Cy Young) and the MVP. For the next three seasons, Nomo "was as consistently good as any pitcher in all of Japanese baseball," Whiting wrote.

High pitch counts, particularly under a new manager in 1994—including a 191-pitch, 16-walk complete game—led to arm trouble that limited Nomo to 114 innings that year. By that time, Nomo was already hoping to find a new challenge, in the United States.

Not since Masanori Murakami pitched for the Giants in 1965 had a Japanese player found his way to Major League Baseball, in part because of a rule that Japanese players couldn't become free agents until after their 10th season, in part because of American skepticism over how their skills would translate, in part because of the vilification a player stood to receive upon leaving his country behind.

"Feelings were very strong then," Japanese home run king Sadaharu Oh once said about the temptation to go to the States. "The fans never would have forgiven me."

Undeterred, Don Nomura, a Japanese-born, Los Angeles–based agent, worked with U.S. agent Arn Tellem to set Nomo free. They confirmed a loophole in Nomo's contract, a clause that stated a player who "voluntarily" retired was free to play for another team—as long as it wasn't in Japan.

"My parents were against the idea from the start," Nomo said. "They told me, 'You've got everything in Japan: wealth, status.... Why are you going to throw it all away?'"

Nomo wasn't lacking for interest stateside. Globally minded and always looking to replenish their pitching depth, the Dodgers gravitated to a player like the 26-year-old Nomo.

"It was tough in those days," Dodger owner Peter O'Malley says. "If you were in contention, as you well know, you'd get a first-round pick down the ladder, and we had to find talent someplace. And that's part of what motivated me to look around the world, because you weren't dependent on getting a good pick—you'd sign a player."

The more O'Malley and Dodger general manager Fred Claire learned about Nomo, the more they wanted him.

"The international baseball representatives in Japan," O'Malley says, "from top to bottom, they also gave him good reviews. They said, 'This guy, he's got a nasty forkball. He's a professional, he's committed, he wants to do well, he's focused.'"

A year after the Dodgers successfully courted and signed Park, Nomo and Nomura came to Dodger Stadium for a tour late in 1994.

"We met in the office, and he's got Atlanta and New York to go to [for meetings with Braves owner Ted Turner and Yankees owner George Steinbrenner], and he's going to leave the next day," O'Malley notes. "I say, 'Why don't we talk again tomorrow?' And as I recall, we delayed his trip by a day. He came by the office again the next day, and he had heard good things about us—I can't deny that, because I was fairly well known in Japan and in baseball. And I had heard very good things about his professionalism, and we got along great. And he never went to Atlanta or New York. He canceled the rest of trip and said, 'I'm gonna stay here.'"

Claire worked to finalize the deal.

"We actually signed him to a National Association contract, not a major-league contract," Claire says. "I can remember being in my office, and they were wanting a major-league contract. And at that time I said to them, 'There has never been a player who has come to the Dodgers'—and of course Hideo had pitched professionally, but I was referring to players that we had signed out of college or high school—'who's ever received a major league contract. Major-league contracts are earned and not given.' And Nomura interpreted that to Hideo."

"The only thing he asks that he will be given an opportunity to make the club," Nomura said.

"I can give you my word that he will have an opportunity to make the club in spring training," Claire told him.

It was no hollow promise.

"No. 1, I knew he deserved that," Claire says. "And No. 2, I now knew after I signed him I had no more budget to sign anybody else. So I was very sure that he was going to get the opportunity—because I didn't have any more money."

Nomo's signing was announced February 13, 1995, at a press conference filled with Japanese reporters and camera crews. Before his first pitch, the new mania had begun, and spring training in Vero Beach didn't temper the excitement. Tommy Lasorda, for one, thought Nomo was a hot ticket the moment he saw him.

"I thought he had a great arm, great ability," Lasorda says. "He just came out of nowhere and the people just loved him, and everybody wanted to see him pitch, just like they did with Fernando."

"His windup is so slow," outfielder Reggie Williams said after an intrasquad game, "when the ball finally comes out of there, it looks like 100 mph."

Said Yankee left fielder Luis Polonia, "I don't want to see that guy again in my life. He got me all confused. I only saw him one time, and I don't like him. Thank God he's in the National League so I don't have to worry about it."

If the Dodgers had any major worries, it was that MLB umpires might tame The Tornado.

"The one thing that we were concerned about that I can remember was having Bruce Froemming watch him in spring training warming up with that delivery, that there was going to be any issues in terms of balk calls or anything else," Claire says.

Nomo also had a contentious relationship with the Japanese press, which was invasive in its presence and, in many ways, skeptical in its reporting. Many remained offended by Nomo's escape from Japan and looked for him to fail. Nomo did little to court media approval, focusing instead on his mission.

"He knew we wanted to succeed," O'Malley says. "He had confidence that he would be successful, and that he would not let those long telephoto-lens cameras from around a tree or interview requests or anything else disrupt him. He would not get distracted at all. He just hung right in there and knew he had a job to do."

Nomo essentially made the Dodger starting rotation out of spring training, but it was an odd spring, disrupted by the late settlement of the previous year's strike—plus Nomo hadn't signed until right before pitchers and catchers reported. So Nomo's first recorded U.S. appearance came April 27 for Single-A Bakersfield (5⅓ innings, two runs, six strikeouts), before it was off to San Francisco for his major-league christening.

Moment in the Sun: Jose Lima

- Charismatic creator of "Lima Time" surprised Dodger fans with joyful 13-5, 4.07 ERA (101 ERA+) season in 2004
- Won the Dodgers' first playoff game and pitched their first playoff shutout after the 1988 season, 4-0 over St. Louis on October 9, 2004
- Passed away suddenly at age 37 in 2010

The importance of his debut, on May 2, transcended the traditional Dodgers-Giants team rivalry. The game was televised beginning at 4:30 AM on Constitution Day in Japan, and numerous Giants fans suddenly found themselves rooting for the man in the Dodger uniform.

"They rose as one from their seats, and with tears streaming down their faces, unfurled the Japanese flag in Section 12 at Candlestick Park, waving it proudly," wrote Bob Nightengale in the *Los Angeles Times*. "They erupted with cheers the moment Japanese pitcher Hideo Nomo emerged from the Dodger dugout, and as Nomo slowly walked to the mound, Section 12 truly realized the significance of every step."

"This is a very, very special day for our country," a fan, Mitsuko Iwama, told Nightengale. "I wanted my son to see this because young people see him as a symbol of excellence…I'm a Giant fan, and always will be a Giant fan, but like a lot of people here today, I'm a Nomo fan."

Nomo's first inning was nothing if not eventful. In his 33-pitch first inning, he struck out his first batter looking, walked three in a row with two outs, then whiffed Royce Clayton with the bases loaded. He pitched five frames in all, walking four but only allowing one hit while striking out seven. (The game itself lasted more than five hours, the Dodgers scoring three runs in the top of the 15th before allowing four in the bottom.)

After getting his Coors Field baptism in a seven-run, seven-strikeout, 4⅔-inning outing, Nomo made his Dodger Stadium debut a memorable display of extremes, allowing no hits but walking seven in four innings and giving up three runs, one earned. The Dodgers granted 150 media credentials for the game.

"When he would wind up, there were these flashes all throughout the stadium," O'Malley says. "I don't think that happened with Fernando. Fernandomania was big, I don't deny that—but the flash of the cameras [was new]."

And the media coverage was simply more intense. Valenzuela, for all the attention showered upon him, didn't inspire the level of international press that Nomo did.

"With all the fanfare going on here before the ballgame, he just didn't have the time to relax and prepare himself for the game," Lasorda told reporters. "He wasn't wild, he was just missing. There were so many pitches that he just missed."

Nomo's next start May 17 thrust him from curiosity to star. Facing the Pirates, Nomo struck out nine of the first 12 batters he faced and 14 in all—the most by a Dodger since Ramón Martínez's 18 in 1990—in seven innings of shutout ball. That outing launched Nomo into a run of 15 starts in which he allowed only 21 earned runs, with a 1.63 ERA and 135 strikeouts in 115⅔ innings.

Taking on the Pirates a second time on June 14, Nomo struck out 16, breaking Karl Spooner's 40-year-old Dodger rookie record. In back-to-back shutouts (the first of his MLB career) June 24 and 29 against the Giants and Rockies, Nomo fanned 13 apiece, followed by consecutive games of 10 whiffs.

Fandom begat fanaticism. Nomomania (or more succinctly, Nomonia) shook up Los Angeles.

"They began chanting his name Thursday night before the national anthem," wrote Nightengale. "They unfurled Japanese flags. The playing field and Dodger clubhouse were crammed full of reporters. There were sights and sounds of Hideo Nomo everywhere. Four teenage girls were wearing Nomo T-shirts. Three middle-aged men walked out of the Dodger gift shop with nearly $600 in Nomo memorabilia."

Nomo transcended the sports pages, drawing coverage from national outlets including the *CBS Evening News*, *Good Morning America*, *People*, and *The Wall Street Journal*.

"Sometimes, I wish I was just another player," Nomo said. "My privacy is very limited. At least here, I can go out. They know my name, but they don't know my face yet. In Japan, they know everything about me. I feel so restricted."

The massive attention didn't deny Nomo the gratification of having succeeded so resoundingly in his quest for American success. Nomo not only made the NL All-Star team, he became the starting pitcher (the first Dodger rookie to do so since Valenzuela). "This is a dream for me, one I thought was unreachable," Nomo said. "Now, to go to the All-Star Game, I can't even imagine the feeling. I can't even express it in words. It'll be the biggest game of my life. I will cherish it forever." Under the glare of the worldwide press, including the Japanese contingent that now embraced him in print as a hero, Nomo fanned Kenny Lofton, Edgar Martínez, and Albert Belle in two scoreless innings.

On August 5, Nomo not only struck out 11 Giants, he outhit them, collecting two singles while coming within Clayton's seventh-inning, safe-by-a-half-step infield single of a no-hitter. A couple of subpar mid-August starts took Nomo's ERA out of the sub-2.00 range for good, but he finished the year at 2.54 (149 ERA+), the best by a Dodger pitcher in the 1990s, with a league-leading 236 strikeouts, 11.1 strikeouts per nine innings, and 5.8 hits per nine innings. Nomo edged Atlanta's Chipper Jones to win a Rookie of the Year Award for the second time in his career—a rare feat to be sure—and finished fourth in the NL Cy Young balloting.

As a sophomore, Nomo had a 3.19 ERA (122 ERA+) in a career-high 228⅓ innings, striking out 234, including 17 on April 13 against the Marlins, one shy of the team record and a total no Dodger surpassed for more than two decades. But even by the standards of Nomonia, nothing prepared the baseball world for what happened September 17 at Coors Field in Denver.

The 1996 Rockies had more hits in their home games than any major-league team ever. In their mile-high environment, they were the least likely team in MLB history to be held without a hit in a game. And Nomo, for all his magic at the outset of his big-league career, hadn't come close to figuring out Denver in two previous starts, allowing 12 earned runs on 18 hits in 9⅔ total innings.

For better or worse, Nomo was deprived of his usual pregame routine. Rain delayed the start of the game by two hours, and when Nomo finally set foot upon the slippery mound, the temperature was 46 degrees. By the second inning, he began pitching out of the stretch even with the bases empty.

In his favor, the air was thick. Two hard-hit first-inning fly balls settled harmlessly into the glove of right fielder Raul Mondesi, who later made a seventh-inning diving catch. Greg Gagne, the shortstop, dove to snag a grounder that, thanks to Ellis Burks having walked, allowed him to make a short throw to second base for a force.

Nomo walked four batters, but reaching the ninth inning with a 9–0 lead, he had thrown 101 pitches without any being converted into a hit. Eric Young and Quinton McCracken grounded to Delino DeShields on consecutive pitches, leaving Nomo to face Burks, a .348 hitter, who worked the count to 2-2. Nomo threw his forkball, and Burks' looping swing went right through it.

"Got him!" exclaimed Vin Scully.

Nomo pumped his fist modestly, then ambled off the mound as if he were going to pick up the morning newspaper, with only a smile betraying his excitement before Mike Piazza and his frenetic teammates mobbed him.

"Hideo Nomo has done what they said could not be done," Scully continued. "Not in the Mile High City. Not at Coors Field in Denver. He has not only shut out the Rockies, he has pitched a no-hitter, and thank goodness they saw it in Japan."

Through all his adventures in Los Angeles, Nomo's personality remained a constant. Park, whose place in the Dodger starting rotation was effectively delayed until '96 by Nomo's presence, had reason to resent his former idol. Instead, they bonded.

"He was always very serious, but he's very friendly to his close friends," Park says. "My locker was right next to Hideo's, so I always felt honored, because he was my hero in high school. I thought about pitching at Dodger Stadium, but I never thought he'd be one of my teammates."

Another member of the international rotation, Ismael Valdez, said he has "awesome memories" of Nomo.

"He couldn't speak English and obviously not Spanish, and we had a great, awesome chemistry," Valdez said. "Because it went beyond language. It was a comprehension, it was understandable. It was just friendship. He was very special to me. Hideo got along with everybody."

Inevitably, Nomo couldn't match the heights of his first two seasons, but the first major decline struck more abruptly than people were prepared for. For the second consecutive NLDS, Nomo was the losing pitcher of the Dodgers' final game, allowing five runs in 3⅔ innings at Atlanta. Similar disappointments continued throughout 1997, when Nomo's ERA rose to 4.25 (91 ERA+). Theories abounded, from the specific (uncertain aftereffects of taking a Scott Rolen line drive off his pitching arm in July) to the general (declining velocity, disrupted mechanics). Days after the season ended, surgery removed loose bodies in Nomo's right elbow.

Nomo truly began struggling in 1998, his ERA hovering just shy of 5.00 in the first two months of the season. It was a bad time to underperform—on May 14, less than two months after the O'Malley sale of the Dodgers to Rupert Murdoch's Fox Group became official, the trade of Piazza and Todd Zeile shattered the earth. Nothing on this ship was nailed down—and moreover, Claire had entered his keen pursuit of Randy Johnson from the Mariners. When Valdez wasn't the right-hander in the rumors, Nomo was, though Claire reportedly turned down a deal that included Nomo, and Nomo essentially pitched himself out of Seattle's interest. On May 30, Cincinnati knocked him out in the fourth inning with back-to-back three-run innings. "He's not throwing as hard as he did last year," Reds catcher Eddie Taubensee said. "You lay off his forkball and just wait for his fastball."

On June 1, the Dodgers designated Nomo for assignment, barely three years into his Los Angeles career, 20½ months after his no-hitter. Four days later, he was packaged with reliever Brad Clontz in a trade to the Mets for pitchers Dave Mlicki and Greg McMichael.

Nomo left Los Angeles with a 5.05 ERA (80 ERA+) and finished the season with New York in similar straits (4.82 ERA, 87 ERA+). To start 1999, both the Mets and the Cubs released Nomo without him throwing a big-league pitch, but he signed with Milwaukee at the end of April and began to resurrect his career. His ERA remained above 4.50 that year and in 2000 with Detroit, but baseball's offensive environment was so overheated that Nomo was a league-average pitcher. This wasn't his last gasp—this was Nomo putting the brakes on his slide.

He landed with Boston in 2001, and in his first start of the season, on April 4 at Baltimore, Nomo threw his second MLB no-hitter, stunning the Orioles with 11 strikeouts in a 3–0 victory. The following month, he threw arguably the best game of his career outside of Coors Field, striking out 14 Toronto Blue Jays and walking none while allowing only one hit in a 4–0 shutout. Though his ERA+ was exactly 100 for the second time in three years, he led the AL in strikeouts.

That winter, as Park walked out the door to Texas, Nomo returned to Los Angeles, signing a two-year deal. Dave Wallace, who was Nomo's original pitching coach with the Dodgers, had joined the front office as a senior vice president of baseball operations in 2000 and recommended the signing to new general manager Dan Evans.

Nomo's second term in Los Angeles went from good to great—a 3.39 ERA (112 ERA+) in 2002, leading into a 3.09 ERA (131 ERA+) in a 2003 season that began on Opening Day with an 8–0 shutout of Arizona and Johnson, the long-sought-after lefty who had won four consecutive Cy Young Awards as well as a World Series with the Arizona Diamondbacks.

For a second time, things fell apart. He allowed seven runs in five innings in his first start of 2004, went on the disabled list (inflammation in his right rotator cuff) at the end of June with his ERA at 8.06, and finished the year with an 8.25 ERA (50 ERA+) in 84 innings, the worst in franchise history by a pitcher with at least 10 starts. The Dodgers did not attempt to re-sign him. His last full season was with the Tampa Bay Devil

Rays in 2005 (100⅔ innings, 7.24 ERA, 60 ERA+), and he threw his final big-league pitch for Kansas City on April 18, 2008, at age 39.

Nomo's two-term, Grover Cleveland–esque Dodger career (interestingly, he, Valdez, and Park all had split tenures in Los Angeles, and Martínez nearly so) added up to 1,217⅓ innings with 1,200 strikeouts and a 3.74 ERA (104 ERA+). Among those who threw at least 1,000 innings in Dodger history, Nomo's 8.87 strikeouts per nine innings ranked behind only Clayton Kershaw and Sandy Koufax. In his entire MLB career, Nomo fanned 1,918 in 1,976⅓ innings.

At times, he was the best pitcher in baseball and, he could claim more than anyone else, the world. He was his own phenomenon, yet remained the eye of the hurricane—or rather, the tornado.

"There's no baloney in Hideo," O'Malley says. "It's straight. What you see is what you get. He doesn't care about grandstanding or [his] picture in the paper or endorsements. It's not important to him."

In 2014, Japan's Baseball Hall of Fame made Nomo its youngest-ever electee and only the third to achieve enshrinement in his first year of eligibility. One year later, MLB honored Nomo and Park as the first recipients of the Baseball Pioneer Award, celebrating their role in paving the way for Asian players to get to the big leagues. It was a worthy salute to members of a pitching tradition gone global.

PART SEVEN

THE HIRED HANDS

RIGHT UP UNTIL THE FINAL DECADE of the 20th century, the Dodgers signed or scouted, domestically or internationally, every significant starting pitcher they ever had as an amateur—or parlayed that homegrown talent into a trade for one. While the best things in life aren't always free, the Dodgers rarely risked big dollars on pitchers from rival area codes. You could say it was pride. Or a conservative streak. Or feeling scorched by the relatively fruitless expenditures on the Dave Goltzes of the world.

In the 1990s, Los Angeles turned a bit more aggressively toward free agency, signing such pitchers as Kevin Gross, who threw a 1992 no-hitter, and Tom Candiotti, who knuckled through six seasons at Chavez Ravine. Hideo Nomo was as close as they came to an ace-for-hire, though his previous experience was limited to the other side of the Pacific.

Two times in particular, however, the Dodgers broke their unwritten rule—and the bank—in a big way, with big results. Bold ideas weren't new to the Dodger pitching tradition, but bold gambits like these were, and they radicalized the lineage of Dodger pitching in unforgettable ways.

Kevin Brown

Few odes have been written to the Kevin Brown era in Los Angeles, a time of great disturbance in the Force, with fans adjusting uncomfortably to Fox's 1998 takeover of the Dodgers during the franchise's longest playoff drought (seven seasons, from 1997 to 2003) since Sandy Koufax retired.

Two Kevins—Brown and the general manager who signed him, Kevin Malone—personified that alienation, a level of disaffection unseen since the Dodgers arrived from Brooklyn.

Malone, the Dodgers' third general manager of 1998, succeeded two men (Fred Claire and interim GM Tommy Lasorda) with three-quarters of a century of service to the organization between them, tearing a new page in team history by declaring himself the "new sheriff in town." Three months after his hiring that September came his marquee acquisition, the 33-year-old Brown, who swept into town as the shiny new showpiece—the highest-paid player in baseball history with a seven-year, $105 million deal, a mammoth contract that demanded real results.

Aside from his inability to sprinkle pixie dust on his supporting cast, that's what Brown did for you. The Dodgers' most valuable arm between Ramón Martínez and Clayton Kershaw, this chemical engineering major from Georgia Tech also became the best pitcher ever in Los Angeles to put on a Dodger uniform in the regular season but never in the playoffs, a contradiction that, combined with mixed reviews on his clubhouse persona and behavior, makes him something of a black sheep in the Dodger pitching line—but a noteworthy sheep nonetheless.

The 6-foot-4 right-hander featured a murderous sinking fastball and hard slider among his multi-pitch mix. "His sinker explodes in on the hands, the same as a tailer," longtime MLB catcher and broadcaster Tim McCarver said. "The bottom falls out, and it resembles a splitter. It's very tough to hit the bottom part of the ball against him and get any lift on it."

With his wingspan, Brown could "scratch his knees without bending over," his first big-league pitching coach, Tom House, riffed to *Sports Illustrated* writer Tom Verducci.

"Though Brown's windup is unorthodox—he has an exaggerated hip turn, leading with his butt, and can throw any pitch from any arm angle—he maintains flawless balance, and his amazing extension maximizes the effect of his long arm," Verducci wrote.

Brown came to Los Angeles fresh off two consecutive World Series with two different teams: the 1997 Marlins (the upstarts who won it all) and the 1998 Padres (the upstarts who didn't). Throw in the 1996 season with Florida, when he led the majors with a 1.89 ERA (215 ERA+) and a 0.94 WHIP, and Brown stood behind only Roger Clemens—and ahead of such luminaries as Greg Maddux, Pedro Martínez, and Tom Glavine—as the best pitcher of that time, at least as measured by wins above replacement.

He nearly lived up to his résumé in his first Dodger season, finishing fourth in the NL with a 3.00 ERA (143 ERA+) and third in WAR. But the limits of his impact could be found in the Dodgers' 77–85 record, with the team falling 10 games out of first place by Independence Day, 23 out by season's end. Los Angeles went 22–13 (.629) in games Brown started, 55–72 (.433) in the rest.

"I think everyone is out there playing hard and doing the best they can, but I also think everyone is kind of looking to the finish line," Brown said that September. "I think everyone is looking to the off-season and wanting to put this year behind us."

First baseman Eric Karros was among several Dodgers who publicly praised Brown for his efforts in the clubhouse, but added that "you can only talk so much. When guys are out there, they're on their own."

Neither the franchise's struggles nor his 35th birthday prevented Brown from coming back with an exceptional season in 2000, leading the NL with a 2.58 ERA (his 167 ERA+ was third), a 0.99 WHIP, and a 4.6 strikeout-walk ratio. It was an improved Dodger team as well, and as late as August 4, Brown's 7⅔ innings of one-run ball against Milwaukee helped keep Los Angeles within 2½ games of first place in the NL West. But the Dodgers lost 11 of their next 15, sliding out of the race and leaving Brown's All-Star efforts for naught.

For five consecutive seasons, from 1996 to 2000, Brown had thrown at least 230 innings. In 2001, the workload demanded payback, sending him to the disabled list three times, the last for season-ending surgery to repair a torn flexor muscle. When he did pitch, he was still among the very best: averaging seven innings in his first seven starts, his ERA was 1.09, and opponents reached base at a .212 clip. In his final 17⅓ innings, he allowed two earned runs. For the year, in 115⅔ innings, his ERA settled in at 2.65 (151 ERA+). But for the first time as a Dodger, he couldn't bear a full load.

It's possible the timing of Brown's health woes cost the Dodgers a division title in 2001, when they finished six games out with him limited to 19 starts. In 2002, there was nothing else to wonder but what might have been. Fielding their best team in more than a decade, the Dodgers pulled together a 92–70 record—but it was only good enough for third place, six games shy of first. Brown's battle with arm woes extended into a second season, compounded by a herniated disc that required surgery June 11, leaving him with 63⅔ largely ineffective innings (4.81 ERA, 79 ERA+).

"He's gone through so much pain and stuff for the last couple of years," pitching coach Jim Colburn said. "It's just unfair to any human being to go through that."

A sense of dread entered any contemplation of Brown. In 2003, he would be 38, with two incomplete seasons in his recent past and three high-salaried years remaining on his contract.

"When you have a Kevin Brown, you know what you can expect, but you can't expect that if he's not himself physically," manager Jim Tracy said.

Defying the doomsayers, Brown opened his '03 season with six shutout innings at Arizona, and after an unnerving three-start setback later in the month, went on an outstanding roll, allowing 10 runs in 10 starts (1.27 ERA), with Los Angeles winning all 10.

"He can be hard to catch," said Dodger catcher Paul Lo Duca. "I told him sometimes I just go back there trying to knock it down. His fastball moves so much, and he can throw it 95, 96 mph, just right by you. When he needs to reach back, he can. The previous two years, he couldn't."

Earning a spot in his sixth All-Star Game, Brown wrapped up his season with a 2.39 ERA in 211 innings and his best adjusted ERA (169) since '96.

"I don't think as long as I'm playing, I'll ever be satisfied," Brown said. "I don't think I'll ever sit back and say, 'Hey, I'm where I want to be; I'm comfortable.' I think there will always be a drive to find a way to get a little bit better, because of that attitude and that mentality. You learn how to harness it through experience."

Asked what Brown was like as a teammate during this time, relief pitcher Paul Quantrill answered in Rorschach.

"The sky's a different color in his world on the days he pitches, that's for sure," Quantrill said. "'That's his drive, his direction. Kevin puts on a game face and he doesn't talk much. He just gets in his little world and will not come out of it, even once he comes off the field. Good outing, bad outing, it makes no difference. He's just locked."

Rather than rehabilitating his status in Los Angeles, Brown's 2003 season paved the way for his departure. Despite being owed $30 million for his age-39 and age-40 seasons, Brown suddenly had trade value again, and the Dodgers were wary of assuming that he would remain healthy—particularly amid front-office concerns, later revealed in the 2007 Mitchell Report on performance-enhancing drugs in baseball, that Brown was among the users.

"Kevin Brown—getting to the age of nagging injuries," said notes from the October 2003 meetings of the Dodgers' baseball operations department, according to the Mitchell Report. "Question what kind of medication he takes."

When Brown himself encouraged the Dodgers to shop him to an East Coast team that played closer to his Georgia home, Dodger general manager Dan Evans (who had arrived at the end of 2001 after the unceremonious firing of Malone) began poking around, finding an interested party in the Yankees. Exactly five years after they signed him, the Dodgers sent Brown to New York in exchange for starting pitcher Jeff Weaver, two minor-leaguers, and $3 million.

In cutting ties with Brown, they ensured the remaining good returns of their initial investment in his contract. It was Weaver, not Brown, in the starting rotation for the Dodgers' long-awaited playoff return in 2004, after pitching 220 innings that year with a 4.01 ERA (102 ERA+), followed by a similar performance in 2005. The Dodgers even got a contribution from one of the prospects in the deal, the affably named Yhency Brazoban (aka "Ghame Over"), who had a 2.48 ERA in 32⅔ innings as a late-season rookie in 2004 and 21 saves as a substitute for the injured Eric Gagné the next year. Together, Weaver and Brazoban outpitched Brown, who lasted 205⅓ innings with the Yankees in the final two years of his career, with a 4.95 ERA (89 ERA+).

For what turned out to be their seven-year investment in Brown, Weaver, and Brazoban, the Dodgers received 24.2 wins above replacement, an average of 3.5 per year. That's the equivalent of Hideo Nomo's 2003 season (218⅓ innings, 131 ERA+), seven times over.

As a Dodger, Brown pitched 872⅔ innings with a 2.83 ERA. Through 2017, his 20.6 WAR ranked 20th all-time for the Dodgers, 11th in Los Angeles, and third since 1988. At the moment he boarded his jet for the Bronx, no starting pitcher in Dodger history had a better adjusted ERA (147 ERA+) than Brown. With a 127 ERA+ in 3,256⅓ lifetime innings, Brown even has a stealth case for Cooperstown.

"Brown won 211 games, authored a career ERA of 3.28, enjoyed a peak from 1996 to 2000 that was among the best of his era, and pitched in three different postseasons," baseball analyst Dayn Perry wrote in 2010. "If you knew nothing else, you would call Brown a borderline Hall of Famer. But when you consider his WAR, his ERA in context, and his excellent WPA (win probability added), he becomes something more than 'merely' a strong candidate for Cooperstown. Brown's dossier certainly isn't of 'inner circle' quality, but it's not unreasonable to argue that he's one of the 50 greatest pitchers of all time. In fact, such an estimation might even be a bit conservative."

Not too many people look back at Brown's time in Los Angeles with much fondness, or argue that he deserves much of a place, spiritually at least, in the Dodger pitching tradition. This was not a particularly serene marriage. Yet it has to be acknowledged, even in passing, that in terms of pure quality and pure performance, he was one of the top Dodger pitchers ever.

ZACK GREINKE

You look at how Zack Greinke pitched for the Dodgers in 2015, and it would have been easy enough to think he was simply an output of a computer program, what with all those alternating zeros and ones.

From Opening Day through the final out of the playoffs, Greinke took the mound for 239 different innings, and he allowed no more than a run in 231 of them. The number of ones and (mostly) zeroes was staggering—almost robotic—and went ever so far toward outputting the 1.66 ERA that was the lowest by a major-league pitcher in two decades.

And yet, there has hardly been a pitcher less automated and more human than Greinke, who possessed the unique combination of being one of MLB's most natural athletes, cerebral thinkers, and fascinating characters.

Did they break the mold when they made Greinke? There could never have been a mold like this to begin with.

The journey was in some ways predictable, in some ways remarkable. Precocious from the get-go, Greinke was a Kansas City Royals first-round pick in 2002, made his big-league debut at age 20 in 2004, and had 328 career innings before turning 22.

That birthday came in October 2005, and it was quite nearly the last birthday he celebrated as a major-leaguer. Suffering from what later came to be diagnosed as social anxiety disorder, Greinke left the Royals during spring training in 2006 and missed most of the season while seeking treatment and understanding.

"In life, you have to do things you don't want to do, but I was raised to do what you enjoy doing, whether you are making several hundreds of thousands of dollars per year or $30,000 per year," Greinke said later. "That was my thought: *Why am I putting myself through torture when I didn't really want to do it?* I mean, I enjoyed playing, but everything else that went with it [the media, the downtime between starts] I didn't."

Throughout the baseball world, a swath of people doubted that he would ever return to a mound, doubted once he got to the mound that he would ever return to the majors, doubted once he got to the majors that he would ever again be an effective starter.

"When he really struggled with his social anxiety and really thought about quitting the game, I think that was very real," says columnist Joe Posnanski, who began covering Greinke as a minor-leaguer. "He didn't really see a way at the time to get through all the difficult emotions and feelings he was going through."

But once his off-field concerns were addressed, the path to on-field success emerged anew. By 2008, when he was still only 24, Greinke was back in business, throwing 202⅓ innings with a 3.47 ERA (125 ERA+).

A year later, he became a superstar. In 2009, Greinke led the majors with a 2.16 ERA, a 205 ERA+, and a 1.073 WHIP. He won the AL Cy Young Award in a landslide, tallying 25 of 28 first-place votes.

"There was a tremendous misunderstanding about what he went through as a young player," Posnanski says. "People thought, *He doesn't like attention. He doesn't like the crowds.* It was none of those things. I remember him and people close to him telling me the one time he was comfortable was on the field. It was everything else [that was difficult]. He's a guy that very badly wants to win."

From 2010 to 2012, Greinke navigated a period of transitions, moving in trades from the Royals to the Brewers and then the Los Angeles Angels with a 3.83 ERA (106 ERA+). After the 2012 season, he was the most coveted free-agent pitcher on the market. The Dodgers, who had missed the playoffs for three straight seasons but had emerged from their Frank McCourt–era gloom into their first year of Guggenheim ownership, eyed a crafty complement to the phenomenal Clayton Kershaw.

Little did they know the free-thinking potential front-office advisor soon walking through their door. When Greinke came to visit Dodger Stadium shortly after Thanksgiving, he came alone, without any representation or entourage. "Instead of getting to know the agent or the dynamics around the player, we got to know the kid," Dodger general manager Ned Colletti said. "He was stunning. It was probably the best free-agent meeting I've ever had in decades of doing this."

On December 10, the Dodgers signed Greinke to the new record-holder for richest contract for a pitcher in baseball history: six years, $147 million. At his introductory press conference, true to form, Greinke didn't deny how important the money was, but he also noted that he was partly attracted to the Dodgers thanks to their first-round draft pick that year, a big 18-year-old shortstop named Corey Seager.

"He's so in tune with the business of baseball, the future of baseball," Dodgers catcher A.J. Ellis said. "It makes me gravitate toward him anytime there's free time to have a conversation, because I'm going to learn something new and I'm gonna get some outside-the-box thinking."

Some of that thinking was quite pointed. Midway through the 2013 season, when Ellis asked Greinke how he would improve the Dodgers,

Greinke mulled, then told Ellis, "The first thing I'm doing is trading you and signing Brian McCann," Greinke said.

"A lot of conversations with Zack are almost like a test to see if you're worthy," Kershaw said. "Whether it's from the front office to fantasy football to all sorts of different things, it's almost like he's trying to get a gauge on your ability to think along with him on certain decisions. I enjoy listening to him talk about baseball and the way he looks at certain players, because sometimes it's different from the way I do."

None of this would have been more than a distraction had Greinke not done so well from the get-go. In his first season with the Dodgers, Greinke threw 177⅔ innings with a 2.63 ERA (135 ERA+), while also rolling a .409 on-base percentage to win the Silver Slugger Award for pitchers. His most singular game came July 13, when he threw a two-hit shutout with one walk against the Rockies in which no outfielders were required to record a single out: nine strikeouts, 14 groundouts, two popouts, a soft liner to third, and a caught stealing. His steady season extended to the playoffs, where in three starts Greinke averaged seven innings with a 2.57 ERA, though two of the starts ended in hard-luck Dodger losses after Greinke left the game.

The following year, Greinke increased his innings count to 202⅓, accompanied by a 2.71 ERA (129 ERA+), with the pièce de résistance September 13 in San Francisco. That night, the Giants were looking for a win to create a tie with the Dodgers atop the NL West. Instead, Greinke pitched six scoreless innings, doubled and hit his first homer for Los Angeles in the 17–0 victory, the biggest shutout ever in the Dodgers-Giants rivalry. He then pitched seven run-free innings against the Cardinals in his only playoff start of 2014.

As impressive as this was, the world wasn't prepared for his otherworldly 2015. Not since Greg Maddux in 1995 did anyone have a lower ERA than Greinke's. Not since Roger Clemens in 2005 did anyone have an ERA+ better than Greinke's 222.

"A big part of Greinke's excellence that year could be attributed to his changeup," says FanGraphs analyst Eno Sarris. "It was harder than it had ever been. Most people espouse a big velocity gap between the fastball and the change, but Greinke's was the second-smallest in baseball. Research by Harry Pavlidis at Baseball Prospectus, though, suggested that movement is more important than velocity. And Greinke's somehow had the most drop of his career, even though it's going so fast."

On June 18, Greinke began a scoreless streak that lasted 45⅔ innings, the sixth-longest in MLB history and longest since Orel Hershiser's record 59 innings in 1988. At the All-Star break, his ERA was an unreal 1.39, the tiniest by any pitcher since 1968, before the pitcher's mound was lowered.

"Greinke's command of all his pitches improved over time, and I think that's important," Sarris says. "He found ways to get batters to reach for pitches they shouldn't reach for, and make weak contact, and it's not always about being in the zone.

"He also tinkered with his pitches. He had a cutter for a couple years, in order to have another velocity range to complement his fastball. But then he found that the slider and the cutter interacted poorly and made both worse. So he stopped throwing the cutter, and he got more whiffs on the slider after doing that. The new changeup was getting the most whiffs of his career."

"I've probably changed more than anyone else in baseball over the past 10 years," Greinke himself said before the All-Star Game. "There have been a lot of changes—going from control pitcher to power pitcher to power pitcher that wasn't very good to control pitcher that was okay. I'm kind of a mix right now."

"He has so many weapons," Kershaw noted. "If, going into a game, he thinks one pitch is going to work and it doesn't work, he can go to one of his other four or five. And he's a big thinker, but it's one thing to think and another thing to execute. When he thinks about the way he pitches, it's so that he can execute a game plan."

On top of everything else, Greinke's athletic abilities—the ones that earned him a Silver Slugger in 2013 and Gold Gloves in 2014 and 2015—hinted that he was some kind of closet decathlete.

"The stuff that comes easy to him is pretty obvious," Posnanski says. "He's got a very loose and easy motion. He's a shortstop playing pitcher. That's the thing I always thought of him when he was young. That kid on your Little League team who's your best shortstop, and when you put him on the mound, he's your best pitcher. He's never lost that."

Greinke's feats of baseball alone would make him an object of fascination, but the added allure of his personality traits and quirks transformed him into a cult hero.

"He sniffed his bat one night," says Molly Knight, author of *The Best Team Money Can Buy*, the 2015 bestseller on the Dodgers. "I don't remember a hitter sniffing his bat that deliberately—it was like he was smelling chocolate chip cookies or something. I love it when he yells 'Good take!' at a hitter when a hitter takes a particularly tough pitch.

"I think he really came into his own. I think that he is more outgoing than he thought he was, growing the hair out and walking up [to bat] to 'Careless Whisper'—that's not something that I think a wallflower would necessarily do. Friends say once he knows you, you can't get him to shut up. It just shows me he became very comfortable in his surroundings, and that's a beautiful thing for someone who felt so uncomfortable when he was younger."

His celebrated honesty when being interviewed, which hit some people sideways earlier in his career, now came off as simply charming, a core aspect of his appeal. (True to form, Greinke said he pitched better in 2009 than 2015, when he was "kind of getting some breaks.") Even the notion that he never smiled was put to rest, as he was frequently captured on camera with a grin on his face.

"You talk to him now, there's still some of that quirky Greinke stuff," Posnanski says. "He'll still look at the ceiling when he's talking to you, as if there are answers written up there. You ask him a question that gives him an opening to make a smart-aleck remark, he'll still do that in a fun way. But he's a pro now. There's a different vibe about him than when he was young."

In 26 of his 32 starts in 2015, Greinke allowed two runs or fewer. In four other starts, he allowed three runs. Twice all year did he allow more. Once was, not surprisingly, at Coors Field in Colorado. In the other, Philadelphia stunned him with a five-run first inning. But Greinke, who batted .224 that year, came back with two singles and a home run of his own and ended up winning the game anyway.

That Greinke didn't become the sixth player to win the Cy Young Award in both leagues was nearly impossible to believe. It wasn't for lack of a strong finish: his post–All-Star ERA was 1.99. In his final four starts, he threw 30 innings with a 1.50 ERA. However, Jake Arrieta of the Cubs came charging down the stretch, allowing only four earned runs in his final 88⅓ innings, including an August 30 no-hitter at Dodger Stadium. Arrieta's season-ending 1.77 ERA (215 ERA+) and 8.7 wins above replacement didn't better Greinke's, but the voters' what-have-you-done-for-me-lately focus enabled him to edge out Greinke for the honor.

In the 2015 NLDS against the Mets, Greinke pitched seven innings of two-run ball for a Game 2 victory, then was on the mound in Game 5 for one of the more bizarre plays in recent Dodger playoff history, when the Mets' Daniel Murphy took advantage of a fourth-inning Dodger defensive brain cramp and went from first to third on a walk. Murphy scored the game's tying run on a sacrifice fly in foul territory, then homered off Greinke in the sixth for the decisive run in the winner-take-all contest. Across six playoff starts with the Dodgers from 2013 to 2015, Greinke had 41 strikeouts in 41⅔ innings with a 2.38 ERA and a 0.79 WHIP, yet the Dodgers split the six games.

Entering the post–2015 off-season, there was a strong belief that at age 32, Greinke still had room to develop, that he would morph into his generation's Greg Maddux—and that the likelihood was that he would continue to do so in Los Angeles, even though he had opted out of his contract to become a free agent. Few could afford his price tag, and the biggest fear among Dodger fans was that the rival Giants would make the top bid.

Then on the morning of December 4, Arizona Diamondbacks owner Ken Kendrick, previously too conservative to enter the high-stakes bidding, woke up and threw together an offer that would give Greinke the highest average annual salary in MLB history. Minutes away from signing a new Dodger contract, Greinke turned toward the desert, without even having spoken to any of the Arizona executives, inking a new six-year deal for $206.5 million.

Thus ended a run for Greinke in Los Angeles that was as stunning in its success as it was in its brevity: a 2.30 ERA in 602⅔ innings with 555 strikeouts. Greinke had an adjusted ERA of at least 128 in each of his three seasons, an achievement only five pitchers in Dodger history can top: Kershaw, Hershiser, Sandy Koufax, Don Drysdale, and Dazzy Vance. Among pitchers with at least 600 innings in a Dodger uniform, only Kershaw had a better ERA+ than Greinke's 160.

Above all, that supreme 2015 season won't soon be forgotten. Producing 9.3 wins above replacement, it is the greatest season by a right-hander in Los Angeles Dodger history, topped among franchise pitchers by Vance (1924, 1928) and Koufax (1963, 1966). Sometimes, some of the best things in life are brief.

PART EIGHT

THE BULLPEN ACES

FOR NEARLY THE ENTIRE HISTORY of the Dodgers before the end of World War II, when their pitching tradition was incubating, almost every pitcher they used in relief was a moonlighting starter. Only three players in Brooklyn history totaled more than 200 innings in relief before 1940, and two of those were swingmen—Watty Clark and Sherry Smith, who started more games than they relieved. The lone exception, Rube Ehrhardt, did mainly pitch out of the pen from 1926 to 1928, with modest effectiveness.

Starting with Hugh Casey in the 1940s, the game changed, and the Dodgers began transforming pitchers who weren't cut out to be full-time starters into pitchers who were primarily relievers, and later purely relievers. In the history of Dodger pitching, they play a supporting but key role, occasionally grabbing headlines—some heartbreaking, some thrilling.

One Dodger reliever was a World Series MVP, two others won the NL Cy Young Award (out of five bullpen winners in the history of the league). And while the bar for relief pitchers to reach the Hall of Fame is exceedingly high, one modern-day Dodger pitcher laid the foundation to build a viable case.

In this brief sabbatical from the starters comes a series of snapshots, highlighting the most significant relief pitchers in Dodger history.

Note: saves prior to the institution of the official rule in 1969 have been calculated retroactively by Baseball-Reference.com.

Hugh Casey

In 1939, his first season in Brooklyn, Hugh Casey made 25 starts in 40 appearances, finishing with a 2.93 ERA (139 ERA+). Showing that much promise at age 25, Casey offered little reason to think he would become the godfather of Dodger relievers.

Over the next two seasons, however, the Dodgers took advantage of his versatility. On July 5, 1940, he pitched 9⅓ innings out of the bullpen, facing 39 batters while holding the Boston Bees scoreless from the 10th inning into the 19th. As time passed, the scales tilted decisively toward Casey becoming a reliever. After the All-Star break in 1941, 22 of Casey's 25 games came out of the pen, the Dodgers won the NL pennant, and manager Leo Durocher didn't see a coincidence. "We couldn't have won without Hugh Casey's great relief pitching," Durocher said. As a starter in 1941, Casey had a 4.81 ERA and a 1.44 WHIP. As a reliever, it was 2.14 and 1.07.

The 6-foot-1 right-hander relieved in three of the Dodgers' first four World Series games, and it was the last of those that proved fateful, when what should have been a game-ending strikeout pitch to even the Series at two games apiece got past catcher Mickey Owen, allowing Tommy Henrich to reach first base. That triggered a four-run Yankee rally that enabled New York to win its third game of the Fall Classic, and the Series ended the next day.

Come 1942, there was fascination over a brawl between Casey and Ernest Hemingway in Havana, while the Dodgers were at spring training.

But there was no confusion about Casey's role. He relieved in 48 out of 50 games, finishing 29, with 13 saves (the most in baseball) and a 2.25 ERA (146 ERA+). Then, despite missing three seasons for military service, Casey came home even more proficient in 1946 with a 1.99 ERA (171 ERA+).

Casey led the majors in saves again with 18 in 1947 (3.99 ERA, 103 ERA+), then set a new record by pitching in six World Series games, allowing one run in 10⅓ innings. He also gained revenge on Henrich and the Yankees by inducing a double play to end the top of the ninth in Game 4, before Cookie Lavagetto's double in the bottom wrecked Bill Bevens' no-hitter and won the game.

Relieving in 237 of his 293 career games with Brooklyn, Casey had a 3.34 ERA (115 ERA+) in 867⅔ innings. Life took a bitter turn thereafter. Suffering from personal problems, Casey's Dodger career ended in 1948, and his big-league career a year later. On July 3, 1951, Casey committed suicide in an Atlanta hotel room at age 37.

Clem Labine

The reliever most directly linked with the Boys of Summer, Clem Labine pitched for the Dodgers' final eight years in Brooklyn and first two in Los Angeles, coming out of the bullpen in 388 of his 425 appearances, which makes it all the more interesting that his most memorable moment came as a starter.

For Game 6 of the 1956 World Series, the day after Don Larsen's perfect game put the Dodgers one defeat from elimination, Walter Alston turned to the righty from Rhode Island—in a precursor to Eric Gagné, a descendant of French Canadian parents. Labine had relieved in 59 of 62 games in '56, topping the majors with 19 saves, but on the final Saturday of the regular season, the 6-footer struck out 10 in a complete game that put the Dodgers a game ahead of Milwaukee in the pennant race. Somehow, Labine topped that feat by pitching 10 shutout innings against the Yankees, holding them off long enough for Jackie Robinson to hit his game-winning RBI double.

Nevertheless, Labine retained the spirit of a reliever. "I always thought Clem would've had a great career as a starting pitcher," Carl Erskine once said. "But he told me, 'I didn't want to start. I liked the pressure of coming into the game with everything on the line.'"

Labine's best overall season might have been in 1953, with a 2.77 ERA (155 ERA+) in 110⅓ innings, though it's hard to argue he had a more meaningful year than 1955, the breakthrough for the Bums, when he led MLB with 60 games and pitched a career-high 144⅓ innings with a 3.24 ERA (126 ERA+). He was the winning pitcher with 4⅓ innings of relief in Game 4 of the '55 World Series, then came back the next day to be credited with a save in Game 5 thanks to three more innings. In 1956, Labine became the first Dodger reliever to be invited to the All-Star Game, repeating in 1957.

"Clem Labine was one of the best relief pitchers for several years because he had a wicked curve and a terrific sinker," Cardinals legend Stan Musial said. "He had powerful forearms...I found it difficult to pick up his curveball, and I tried to pull his sinker without success."

Scoring his second World Series ring in 1959 with Los Angeles, Labine concluded his Dodger career the following year with a 3.63 ERA (113 ERA+) in 933⅓ career innings, along with 56 relief wins—a Dodger bullpen record. Until 1967, no other Dodger pitched more innings in relief. Having retired to Vero Beach, Labine passed away at age 80 in 2007.

Joe Black

Three years after Don Newcombe became the first African American pitcher in MLB history, 28-year-old Joe Black debuted as a Dodger in 1952 with his own flourish. Black became the first reliever to win the Rookie of the Year Award and the first African American pitcher to win a World Series game.

After his military service ended in mid-1945, Black pitched the rest of the decade in the Negro Leagues before being acquired by the Dodgers from the Baltimore Elite Giants (along with Jim Gilliam) in 1950. Barely 18 months later, he was in the majors. It was almost unprecedented in baseball to launch a pitcher as a late-inning reliever in his first season, but so it went for the Dodgers with Black, who rewarded them with a team-best 15–4 record, a 2.15 ERA (171 ERA+), a 1.01 WHIP, and 15 saves in 142⅓ innings during the '52 season, relieving in the first 54 of his 56 regular-season appearances and becoming the first NL rookie ever to finish at least 40 games in relief. Racism and death threats were still a horrific par for the course in major-league parks, but the 6-foot-2 right-hander pitched 15⅓ innings in his first nine games before he allowed a run, and marathoned eight innings of relief August 5 against the Giants. So respected was Black that he finished third in the NL MVP vote.

A week before the end of the regular season, the Dodgers drafted Black into starting for the first time, and he responded by throwing a complete-game, 8–2 victory with no earned runs. That emboldened manager Chuck Dressen to have Black start three times in the World Series against the Yankees, beginning with a 4–2 victory in Game 1. He took a heartbreaking Game 4 loss despite holding New York to one run in seven innings, then allowed Mickey Mantle's tiebreaking sixth-inning homer in the Dodgers' Game 7 defeat.

Black's success was fleeting, his ERA swelling to 5.33 (81 ERA+) in 1953, and by June 1955, he was traded to the Reds for Bob Borkowski. His Brooklyn career ended with a 3.45 ERA (113 ERA+), and his playing career two years later.

"Irony ringed Joe Black's life in baseball," Roger Kahn wrote. "He appeared without acclaim, determined and fearless, and quickly became the strongest pitcher on the team. Then, with success, came dread. These afternoons as hero might vanish as suddenly as they had come. He had longed to succeed. Now nightmares warned of a sudden end. All of Joe Black's dreams came true, the good ones and the bad."

Even so, Black became a successful vice president with the Greyhound bus company and remained active in the game in various ways, including community relations, until his passing in 2002.

Larry Sherry

Born with club feet that required a series of operations to correct and special shoes to manage during his childhood, Larry Sherry unexpectedly became one of the first local heroes for the Los Angeles Dodgers. He actually signed with Brooklyn out of Fairfax High School in 1953, then spent five nondescript seasons in the minors and a bitter 1958 cup of coffee in the majors (4⅓ innings, 18 baserunners) before his older brother Norm, himself a Dodger catching prospect who later played that pivotal role in Sandy Koufax's career, helped Larry learn a slider.

On Independence Day 1959, the Dodgers again promoted Larry, who started his first five games before shifting mainly to the bullpen in August, setting the stage for his timeless heroics. In the first game of the Dodgers' best-of-three tiebreaker series for the NL title against Milwaukee, Sherry relieved Danny McDevitt in the second inning and threw 7⅓ shutout innings while the Dodgers rallied to victory. In the World Series, the 6-foot-2 right-hander pitched in all four Dodger victories, saving the first two and winning the last two, including 5⅔ innings of scoreless relief to seal Los Angeles' first championship. He became the first reliever ever to be named World Series MVP.

"Sure, this has to be the greatest thrill of my life," Sherry said after the game, leaning against his locker. "No, I didn't get tired today, but I'm glad there's no game tomorrow."

Sherry never surpassed that glory, nor his 2.19 ERA (193 ERA+) in '59, but his 97 strikeouts out of the pen in 1960 were a Dodger relief record until Mike Marshall came around, and he remained an effective component of the Dodger bullpen through 1963. For Los Angeles, he had a 3.47 ERA (112 ERA+) in 505⅓ innings. His final contribution to the Dodgers was his trade to Detroit that brought in return Lou Johnson, the surprise hero of the 1965 championship season. Cancer took Sherry's life in 2006, at age 71.

Ron Perranoski

Beginning in his rookie season in 1961 and continuing through 1967, Ron Perranoski took Dodger relief pitching to a new level. The 6-foot left-hander from New Jersey grabbed the Dodgers' all-time lead in relief innings with 762⅔, including 198 relief appearances of at least two innings.

Basically, whenever you needed a shutdown reliever, for however long you needed that shutdown reliever, Perranoski was your man.

"Perranoski is the first guy who caused the Dodgers to just say, 'This is our relief ace, he's only going to be our relief ace, we're only going to use him that way,'" historian Eric Enders says.

In his first two years, Perranoski pitched a combined 199 innings with a 2.76 ERA (143 ERA+), prelude to a glorious 1963 season, when he threw 129 innings in 69 games with a 1.67 ERA (179 ERA+), not to mention a 16–3 record and 21 saves. Perranoski finished the final 16 days of the regular season with 19 consecutive scoreless innings, six of them in the famous 13-inning victory over St. Louis that featured rookie Dick Nen's game-tying homer. He capped the year by saving Game 2 of the Dodgers' four-game World Series sweep of the Yankees—the only relief Los Angeles needed that October.

"He is so relaxed he would stop to brush his teeth and comb his hair if his room caught on fire," *Los Angeles Times* columnist Jim Murray wrote.

Perranoski never had a bad season with the Dodgers, who miscalculated with the November 1967 trade that sent him to Minnesota (along with John Roseboro and Bob Miller) for Mudcat Grant and Zoilo Versalles. Neither Grant nor Versalles remained with the Dodgers beyond 1968, while Perranoski's career rolled on steadily until 1972, when the Dodgers reacquired him following a brief downturn in Detroit and pulled out another effective 16⅔ innings. That left Perranoski with a 2.56 ERA in his Dodger career, as well as a 132 ERA+ that ranked fourth all-time among Dodgers with at least 500 innings (pending Kenley Jansen's arrival on that list).

"Perranoski threw a curveball that broke in enormous proportions, both horizontally and vertically," Steve Jacobson wrote in the 1975 book, *The Pitching Staff*. "He also threw from a 'drag-arm' delivery. His arm came around a count after he took his stride, an instant later than the batter expected it."

The fifth big-leaguer ever to exceed 700 games in relief, Perranoski retired from pitching in 1973. He soon became a minor-league pitching coordinator for the Dodgers, and succeeded Red Adams as pitching coach in 1981—the year of Fernandomania and a World Series title—until 1994. No relief pitcher in Dodger history has had a greater impact on the organization than Ron Perranoski.

Jim Brewer

Ron Perranoski pitched 456 games in relief for the Dodgers. Jim Brewer pitched…456 games in relief for the Dodgers. Together, they sat atop the franchise's all-time leaderboard until Kenley Jansen passed them in 2017. Even so, Brewer could share bragging rights with Clem Labine for the longest tenure among Dodger relievers: 12 seasons.

Shortly after his 26th birthday, in what seemed an uneventful trade at the time, Brewer came to the Dodgers from the Cubs with catching prospect Cuno Barragan (who retired the following spring) in exchange for pitcher Dick Scott. At the time, Brewer had a 5.66 career ERA (70 ERA+) with Chicago in 163⅔ innings, marred by a 1960 fight will Billy Martin that left Brewer with a broken cheekbone and a fractured eye socket. But beginning with a 3.00 ERA (108 ERA+) in 93 innings in his debut Dodger season, the 6-foot-1 lefty parlayed his sly screwball into longstanding success.

In 1965, a sore elbow—exacerbated by a five-inning shutout relief appearance August 28 that was followed by 3⅓ more scoreless innings in an emergency start September 4 at Houston—limited Brewer to 49⅓ innings, but his 1.82 ERA (180 ERA+) rightfully earned him his first World Series ring. By 1967, he had recovered sufficiently to throw a career-high 100⅔ innings with a 2.68 ERA (115 ERA+) and clocked in at least 70 innings for seven consecutive years, highlighted by nearly untouchable seasons in 1971 (1.88 ERA, 173 ERA+, 0.97 WHIP) and 1972 (1.26 ERA, 267 ERA+, 0.84 WHIP). His '72 ERA and WHIP each set Los Angeles Dodger records for relievers that lasted more than three decades.

When Brewer, suffering from recurring back trouble, was traded to the Angels in July 1975 for Dave Sells, he had become the Dodger bullpen's all-time leader in strikeouts (a record eclipsed by Jansen in 2016) and, despite pitching in an era when complete games still roamed wild and free, held the club save record of 126 for more than 20 years. As a Dodger, he threw 822 innings with a 2.62 ERA and a 1.12 WHIP, and his 127 ERA+ ranks close behind Perranoski's.

A native of Merced, California, Brewer finished his career with the Angels before retiring in 1976, but he met a premature death in an automobile accident in 1987, two days after his 50th birthday.

Phil Regan

He spent little more than two years with the Dodgers, but Phil Regan made a fast impression in Los Angeles, thanks largely to a 1966 season that bequeathed him the nickname "The Vulture."

Breaking in with Detroit in 1960, the 6-foot-3 Regan started more than half his games for the Tigers, never really faring much better than average (4.50 ERA, 86 ERA+) in 746⅔ innings. In December 1965, the Dodgers traded Dick Tracewski for Regan, with the potential of slotting him into the starting rotation behind Sandy Koufax, Don Drysdale, and Claude Osteen. When Koufax and Drysdale held out during spring training in 1966, the path briefly widened for Regan to become a starter. But the holdout ended, Don Sutton emerged to take the No. 4 spot in the rotation, and Regan didn't open a game for the Dodgers all year.

Instead, bringing his starter's four-pitch mix to the bullpen, he became a fierce right-handed complement to Ron Perranoski. The 6-foot-3 Regan pitched 116⅔ innings in 65 games—all in relief—with a 1.62 ERA (203 ERA+) for the NL champions. "He has better stuff than I had been led to believe at the time of the trade," Walter Alston said. "Phil isn't overpowering, but when he gets you looking for the breaking stuff he can blow the fastball by you."

The first Los Angeles All-Star reliever and the 1966 NL Comeback Player of the Year and Reliever of the Year, Regan was credited with an NL-leading 21 saves, but his calling card was a 14–1 win-loss record. After Regan won his 10th game on August 1, Frank Finch of the *Los Angeles Times* first reported that "Phil's pals playfully call him 'The Vulture,' a bird which feeds on the remains." Still, despite any negative connotations the nickname might have, Regan didn't steal victories thanks to his own ineptitude. Twelve of his 14 wins came after he entered the game with the Dodgers tied or losing, and in only one of those games did he allow an earned run.

Regan came back in 1967 with a solid enough season: 96⅓ innings and a 2.99 ERA (103 ERA+), though his record slipped to 6–9. Two weeks into the '68 campaign, the rebuilding Dodgers traded Regan and Jim Hickman to the Cubs for Jim Ellis and Ted Savage. Regan closed his Dodger career with a 2.28 ERA (140 ERA+) in 220⅔ innings—the best years of his career. He retired as a player in 1972 with a 3.84 ERA (98 ERA+), but among other later activities, he was the pitching coach under manager Tommy Lasorda of the gold-medal-winning 2000 United States Olympic Team.

Charlie Hough

When the Dodgers drafted Charlie Hough in 1966, they didn't know if they had a pitcher, a first baseman, or a third baseman. "A couple of minor problems," Hough says. "I couldn't play third, I couldn't play first, and I didn't hit very good."

For a while there, the Dodgers weren't sure Hough could pitch either, or that he'd stay healthy enough. In 1968 and 1969, the 6-foot-2 righty kept taking the mound despite a sore arm. But in the fall instructional league, roving minor-league pitching coach Goldie Holt—the scout who discovered a teenage Don Drysdale—showed Hough how to grip a knuckleball. In 1970, with Triple-A Spokane under manager Tommy Lasorda, Hough shifted to the bullpen, throwing nothing but the knuckler. That year, he began drinking big-league cups of coffee, finally getting the whole pot in 1973.

"My way of making the team was being that kind of utility pitcher who could pitch in any situation, who would throw every day if I had to," Hough says. "I pitched a lot. When I was coming through the minor leagues, baseball was managed differently, so you put in whoever was throwing good and you just kept using him until they didn't throw good, and I never gave it a thought. You're a pitcher: okay, you show up at the park and you might pitch tonight."

Hough did anything but knuckle under, proving himself a durable and reliable reliever, highlighted by a 1976 season in which he pitched 142⅔ innings in 77 games with a 2.21 ERA (153 ERA+). For his Dodger career, he pitched 799⅔ innings in 401 games with a 3.50 ERA (102 ERA+). No one might ever approach his franchise record of 204 relief appearances of at least two innings.

To say the least, the knuckler added years to his career. Two years after the Dodgers traded Hough to Texas in July 1980, he entered the Rangers' starting rotation at age 34. He started 417 games from that point, extending his big-league life until his final game for the Marlins in 1994—at age 46.

Putting it in perspective, Hough's big-league teammates spanned 50 years in birth dates, from Hoyt Wilhelm (born in 1922) to Kurt Miller (born in 1972). Upon retiring, Hough had pitched 3,801⅓ innings in 858 MLB games, with a 3.75 ERA (106 ERA+).

"I got tired—I had a bad shoulder for 25 years," said Hough, who later served as Dodgers pitching coach in 1998 and 1999 and as a player development advisor for years. "But, I didn't get tired of competing, let's put it that way."

Mike Marshall

At age 29 with the Expos in 1972, Mike Marshall had a great season out of the bullpen with a 1.78 ERA (198 ERA+). He pitched 116 innings, not an insubstantial amount.

He was just getting started.

The next year, Marshall set MLB records with 92 games and 179 innings out of the pen. He had a 2.66 ERA (142 ERA+), finishing second in the NL Cy Young voting and fifth in the MVP voting.

He was just getting started.

When the Dodgers traded their all-time hits leader in Los Angeles, 33-year-old Willie Davis, for Marshall in December 1973, they knew they were getting someone who wanted the ball like none other. "I have to work a lot," said Marshall, a modest 5-foot-10. "It's not only a matter of control, but feeling a part of the game."

Marshall had a master's degree in education from Michigan State and was working on his doctorate in kinesiology at the time of the trade. An unconventional pitcher for an unconventional time, he consistently maintained he was an educator first and an athlete second, and said after the trade that an attractive teaching position could take him away from the Dodgers. But the righty showed up at spring training in 1974, and then had a season like none before.

Obliterating his own records, Marshall pitched 208⅓ innings in 106 games, finishing with a 2.42 ERA (141 ERA+). His durability was astounding. From June 18 to July 13, he set another MLB mark by pitching in 13 consecutive games, with a 1.69 ERA in 26⅔ innings.

Marshall's achievements were so stunning that he beat out teammate Andy Messersmith, who pitched 292⅓ innings with nearly the same ERA, for the NL Cy Young Award.

"I don't talk nonsense," Marshall said. "I said last winter I could pitch in 100 games and work 200 innings, and that's what I did."

Marshall appeared considerably less in 1975, missing most of May and all of September because of rib cartilage injuries, though many would have gladly settled for his output: 109⅓ innings in 58 games with a 3.29 ERA (104 ERA+). Pitching more inconsistently in 1976, however, Marshall became expendable, and he was traded to Atlanta on June 23 for Elias Sosa and Lee Lacy.

Despite spending fewer than two and a half years with the Dodgers, Marshall ranked eighth in franchise history in relief innings upon his departure. He played in the majors until 1981, by which time he had completed his PhD and was known as Dr. Mike Marshall.

Steve Howe

It has to be said that Steve Howe was an extraordinarily talented pitcher. It doesn't make what happened to him more or less tragic.

Picked by the Dodgers in the first round of the 1979 draft, Howe made his MLB debut the following April at age 22 and won the NL Rookie of the Year Award, throwing 84⅔ innings with a 2.66 ERA. Then, capping a strong sophomore year (2.50 ERA, 135 ERA+), the 6-foot-1 lefty was on the mound for the final out of the 1981 World Series, pitching 3⅔ shutout innings to close out the Yankees.

The 1982 season was Howe's best yet: 99⅓ innings, a 2.08 ERA (169 ERA+), and his first All-Star Game selection. But it was also the year Howe's addiction to drugs and alcohol surfaced, when the Dodgers announced in November that he spent five weeks at the Meadows, the same treatment center Bob Welch had checked into two years before. During spring training in 1983, Howe admitted that he had snorted cocaine during games.

Perhaps it was naiveté or simply optimism that made people think Howe was cured in 1983, or just the stat book: through May 17, he pitched 22⅓ innings without allowing an earned run. Dodger fans couldn't have asked for a more reliable fireman. But he suffered a relapse that took him out of action for more than a month for more treatment. Howe returned in late June to finish the '83 season with a 1.44 ERA (251 ERA+) in 68⅔ innings, but the Dodgers suspended him more than once for team violations, and in December, MLB commissioner Bowie Kuhn shelved Howe for the entire 1984 season, citing multiple positive drug tests.

When Howe returned to action in 1985, he struggled both on and off the field. On July 3, the Dodgers and Howe agreed to part ways, with the team granting his unconditional release. "Steve does not feel that he can any longer handle the pressures of playing in Los Angeles, and he is currently unable to perform," the team said.

Howe's final pitching line for the Dodgers is objectively superb: 328⅔ innings, a 2.35 ERA, and a 1.16 WHIP. His 150 ERA+ is the best by a lefty reliever in franchise history. His major-league career endured in scattershot fashion—seven suspensions in all, all the way to 1996. Even at age 39 in 1997, he was still showing off his talent, with a 1.98 ERA for an independent-league team in Sioux Falls.

Howe died in 2006 when his pickup truck overturned and he was thrown from the vehicle. He was 48 years old. "It makes you numb when you hear about a situation like this," Mike Scioscia said, hearing the news. "He had a roller-coaster ride."

Tom Niedenfuer

It is the sad reality for relief pitchers that, given the repeated cliffhangers of their profession, they might be most remembered for a mistake, no matter how much good they do.

Such is the case for Terry Forster, who had a 3.04 ERA (116 ERA+) with the Dodgers but gave up the Joe Morgan home run that cost Los Angeles a division title in 1982, and such is also the case for Tom Niedenfuer.

A 36th-round pick by the Dodgers in 1977, Niedenfuer went on to play at Washington State, then signed with Los Angeles as an amateur free agent on August 14, 1980. One year and one day later, the 6-foot-5 right-hander was in the majors, pitching a shutout inning against Atlanta, and showed enough to make the postseason roster. You'll rarely hear it mentioned that he pitched five innings in the 1981 World Series without allowing an earned run.

In 1982, his first full season, Niedenfuer pitched 69⅔ innings with a 2.71 ERA (130 ERA+), though his year ended sourly—it was his two baserunners who scored ahead of Morgan on the home run. Niedenfuer returned in 1983 as the Dodgers' most reliable reliever amid the Steve Howe trauma, providing a 1.90 ERA (190 ERA+) and a 0.89 WHIP, while stranding 37 of 47 runners. In the NLCS, he pitched two more shutout innings, extending his career playoff run to 7⅔ with a 0.00 ERA.

Niedenfuer's success strolled into 1984 (2.47 ERA, 144 ERA+) and 1985, his busiest season: 106⅓ innings with a 2.71 ERA (128 ERA+). In Game 1 of the 1985 NLCS against St. Louis, he pitched 2⅔ shutout innings for a save that would have been considered utterly heroic in the 21st century. In the first 10⅓ playoff innings of his career, his ERA remained 0.00.

But baseball, man. In consecutive games, the final two of the Dodgers' 1985 season, came the twin disasters—in Game 5, the walkoff homer by Ozzie Smith, and in Game 6, one out away from a three-inning save to keep the Dodgers alive, the three-run, top-of-the-ninth shot by Jack Clark. The Dodgers' season was over, and Niedenfuer's name became a curse word.

"Looking back on it," Niedenfuer said, "it's a very proud feeling that your manager had enough confidence in you to be the guy he put in that situation. I wouldn't trade that for anything in the world because I loved being out there. But when it happened, all I can remember is…you let the team down."

Niedenfuer pitched another year and change for the Dodgers before his May 1987 trade to Baltimore for center fielder John Shelby and pitcher Brad Havens. His Dodger career stands proudly in the abstract: 2.76 ERA (128 ERA+) in 440⅓ innings. But under the scrutiny of history, two pitches remain villainous.

Alejandro Peña

What is a former ERA champion doing on a list of the Dodgers' most important relievers? While it's true Alejandro Peña was the right-handed ace of the 1994 Dodgers, thanks to his NL-best 2.48 ERA (142 ERA+) and four shutouts in 199⅓ innings, he most often came out of the bullpen in a career that included four World Series appearances, two with Los Angeles.

Peña broke in with the Dodgers in August 1981 (two days before Tom Niedenfuer) with a 2.84 ERA (120 ERA+) in 25⅓ regular-season innings and 2⅓ scoreless frames in the NLCS. An unimpressive 1982 followed, but after excelling in two spot starts early in the 1983 season, the 6-foot-1 Peña moved into the rotation in June and completed that year with a 2.75 ERA (131 ERA+) in 177 innings. That led straight into the ERA title of 1984, the only year of Peña's career without a relief appearance.

That triumph came with a price. Peña threw 195 of his innings before September, and made only one start thereafter. His shoulder was nagging at him, and at first, the Dodgers couldn't figure out what the problem was. But in February 1985, Peña underwent surgery, and though he attempted to return to the rotation over the next two years, by mid-1987, he was a full-time reliever.

That worked out just fine for Los Angeles. Once he committed to relief in '87, his ERA was 2.40. In 1988, he became a prime set-up man, pitching 60 games and 94⅓ innings with a 1.91 ERA (176 ERA+) and a 1.08 WHIP. He also happened to be the winning pitcher with three shutout innings the night of Kirk Gibson's 12th-inning homer in Game 4 of the NLCS, and again with two scoreless frames the night of Gibson's unreal smash in Game 1 of the World Series.

Peña spent one more season with the Dodgers (2.13 ERA, 162 ERA+ in 76 innings), then took his talents elsewhere, pitching until he was 37. In 23 career MLB playoff games, his ERA was 2.03. As a Dodger, he ended up with a 2.92 ERA (122 ERA+) in 769⅓ innings. It was not a conventional career, but it was a quietly effective one.

Jay Howell

At age 31 in 1987, Jay Howell had fallen on not-so-prime times for the A's. He had a 4.86 ERA at the All-Star break but somehow made the AL team, nearly drowned in boos by the Oakland crowd during pregame introductions, coughed up a two-run triple to Tim Raines in the 13th inning to lose the game, allowed 11 runs in his next 11 regular-season innings, then went on the disabled list for surgery to remove bone chips in his right elbow.

Somehow, Dodger general manager Fred Claire considered Howell to be a missing piece of the Dodger bullpen puzzle. Despite one noteworthy blip, 1988 proved Claire right.

A rejuvenated Howell shot out of the gate for the Dodgers with a scoreless April, finished the regular season with 18 consecutive scoreless innings (nicely complementing Orel Hershiser) and no inherited runners scoring, and became the first Dodger in a decade to save more than 20 games. For the year, the 6-foot-3 right-hander had a 2.08 ERA (162 ERA+) and a 1.00 WHIP in 65 innings.

Now the playoffs, they didn't start so well. In the NLCS opener, Howell gave up the heartbreaking sinking liner that cost Hershiser and the Dodgers the win. Four days later, Howell had thrown five pitches to Kevin McReynolds with a 4–3 lead in Game 3 when Mets manager Davey Johnson asked umpires to examine Howell's glove. Pine tar was found, and though the Dodgers swore (Tommy Lasorda literally so) by the unwritten rule that pitchers commonly used it to improve their grip in cold weather, Howell was ejected from the game and suspended for two days. The next time he pitched, in Game 3 of the World Series, former teammate Mark McGwire took him for a walkoff homer in Oakland's only Fall Classic victory.

None of these events cost the Dodgers a title—and in fact, Howell came back to save Game 4 with 2⅓ scoreless innings, so he avoided the gloomy denunciations shouldered by others struck with misfortune. What's more, he returned in 1989 with an even better regular season, taking a 0.75 ERA into September before allowing eight runs in a five-inning stretch, long after the Dodgers had been eliminated from contention. Still, the 1.58 ERA (218 ERA+) in '89 was nothing to dismiss, and three more quality years followed. By the time Howell was done in Los Angeles, he could claim a 2.07 ERA (170 ERA+)—the best by a Dodger reliever with at least 200 innings in the 20th century—and top billing in the bullpen of a championship team.

Todd Worrell

On September 14, 1997, Todd Worrell pitched a shutout inning at Houston for his 127th career—and final—save as a Dodger, breaking Jim Brewer's club record. It's a moment that is simultaneously a legitimate achievement and an illustration of that stat's limitations in commemorating Dodger relievers.

Signed as a free agent following the Dodgers' 99-loss 1992 season, the 33-year-old Worrell brought bona fide credentials from St. Louis as one of the top relievers of his generation, with a 2.56 ERA (145 ERA+) in 425⅔ innings, a 1986 NL Rookie of the Year Award, and a 1988 All-Star selection. As it happened, Worrell had just set a new Cardinal career save record with 129.

But the 6-foot-5 righty also missed the 1990 and 1991 seasons because of arm trouble, making him a risky investment, and his first year as a Dodger was challenged and then some. Beset by more health issues, Worrell was limited to 38⅔ innings with a 6.05 ERA (64 ERA+).

The right-hander did begin to rebound in the strike-shortened 1994 season, with a 1.88 ERA and a 0.96 WHIP entering July, though he faltered in the final six weeks, allowing 15 runs in his final 16 innings. Finally in 1995, Worrell had a strong full season: a 2.02 ERA (188 ERA+), a 1.11 WHIP, and a club-record 32 saves. That mark lasted for less than a year—in 1996, Worrell came back with 44 saves to complement a 3.03 ERA (129 ERA+). His 0.32 ERA at the All-Star break was also a Dodger reliever record, netting him his second consecutive selection to the Midsummer Classic.

Needing 35 saves in 1997 to surpass Brewer, Worrell tallied exactly that, though it came with more of the inconsistency (5.28 ERA, 74 ERA+) that had plagued him as a Dodger. That December, at age 37, Worrell retired.

With a 3.93 ERA (99 ERA+) and a 1.28 WHIP in 268 innings as a Dodger, Worrell was statistically less valuable than such lower-profile teammates as Tim Crews (tragically killed in a 1993 boating accident months after he pitched his final game for the Dodgers), Jim Gott, and Antonio Osuna. Even so, it's hard to imagine telling the story of Dodger relief pitching in the 1990s without spending some time on the worth of Worrell.

Jeff Shaw

As with Todd Worrell, Jeff Shaw's reputation as a proven closer preceded him to Los Angeles—only his acquisition was more shocking, and his Dodger success more immediate.

In 1998, Shaw was in the midst of his third consecutive sharp season with Cincinnati, for whom he had a 2.31 ERA (185 ERA+) and a 1.09 WHIP in 249 innings. That July, he was named to his first NL All-Star team. But before he suited up for the NL, Tommy Lasorda—who had become the Dodgers' interim general manager amid the tumultuous changes under the new Fox ownership—made a daredevil maneuver, trading rookies Paul Konerko and Dennys Reyes to the Reds for Shaw. Among other things, it meant that Shaw put on his Dodger uniform for the first time at the All-Star Game.

Many immediately questioned the deal, even assuming—correctly, as it turned out, that Shaw would pitch well for the Dodgers, and even without knowing that Konerko would hit 439 homers in his career. With the team trailing distantly in the division and wild-card races, was this the best time to be giving up prospects for a closer?

In any case, the 6-foot-2 right-hander pitched as the Dodgers hoped in 1998 (2.55 ERA, 160 ERA+, 1.19 WHIP) and 1999 (2.78 ERA, 155 ERA+, 1.16 WHIP). Vin Scully's "Shaw 'nough, here's Jeff," whenever the right-hander came in for a save, became a familiar and pleasing addition to the broadcaster's repertoire.

Shaw's 2000 season carves neatly into two parts—a stomach-churning 8.00 ERA with seven blown saves through June, and then, after a short stay on the disabled list to combat tendinitis in his elbow, a 0.89 ERA from mid-July on, converting all 15 of his save opportunities. In 2001, Shaw reached a Dodger high in saves with 43, one shy of Worrell's record, and his best WHIP (1.09) with a 3.62 ERA (110 ERA+).

That winter, Shaw became a free agent, and although he had talks with several teams, he ended up retiring. He left the Dodgers with a 3.37 ERA (124 ERA+). On the 2001 season's final weekend, he picked up his 128th and 129th saves for Los Angeles, edging past Worrell for the team record.

Within five years, that mark would be blown away.

Eric Gagné

Welcome back to the Jungle.

Eric Gagné was a relief pitcher the way Axl Rose was a vocal stylist. The 6-foot-2 right-hander came as close to a Fernando- or Nomo-like mania as anyone out of the Dodger bullpen ever (the French Canadian even brought his own international flavor), and the best part was, you didn't have to wait for his turn in the rotation. At any given game, that door in the left-field fence could open, the signature Guns N' Roses song would blast through the speakers, and electricity would shoot through every seat in the park.

The phenomenon was days in the making. After Jeff Shaw became a free agent the previous winter, the Dodgers entered spring training in 2002 without a closer. The 26-year-old Gagné, who had a 4.61 career

ERA (90 ERA+) in 283 innings, mostly as a starter, figured at best to land the last spot on the pitching staff. Even at the end of a flawless exhibition season, the idea that Gagné *might* even become the Dodgers' ninth-inning specialist caught nearly everyone by surprise. In three seasons, Gagné hadn't thrown a single pitch in the ninth inning of a major-league game.

"If Eric's role is anything other than a starting pitcher, that's certainly not something that was communicated to Eric and myself," said his agent, Scott Boras.

And yet, after three scoreless appearances in non-save situations, manager Jim Tracy handed the begoggled Gagné his first save opportunity April 7 against Colorado, and he locked it down. And the next. And the next. Before they knew it, the Dodgers not only had a closer, they had *the* closer. The smoke of his fastball, the filth of his changeup, and the relentlessness of his dominance put a bear hug on baseball.

"Oh, yes!" a besotted Vin Scully exclaimed at Gagné's final strike to close a game against the Yankees in June 2004. "Oh my gosh, what a pitch! That's amazing! That's not fair. After a 97-mile-per-hour fastball, you can't tell, but that pitch was in the 60s…a rainbow curve."

From 2002 to 2004, quirkily pitching exactly 82⅓ innings each year, Gagné had a 1.79 ERA (223 ERA+), a 0.82 WHIP, and 13.3 strikeouts per nine innings. In an unbelievable 2013 season, Gagné won the NL Cy Young Award with a 1.20 ERA (337 ERA+), 15.0 K/9, and 55 saves in 55 opportunities, the meat of an MLB-record streak of 84 consecutive saves.

"Gagné thrives on the dizzying oscillation between his changeup and his fastball," Daniel G. Habib wrote in *Sports Illustrated*. "They have the same release point and the same arm speed. The fastball is straight gas… but the changeup is a devious thing, a bowling ball rolled off a picnic table."

Game Over splashed on the scoreboard when he entered games, and the slogan seemed essentially jinx-proof. But the game was over all too soon for Gagné. Trying to come back quickly from a knee sprain, he hurt his arm and underwent Tommy John surgery, missing all but a month of the 2005 season and all but two innings of the 2006 season, when he saved his club-record 161st and final game as a Dodger. Gagné later said that this was the period when he first took human grown hormone in order to speed his recovery, though the revelation opened the door for suspicion about the sanctity of his highest achievements.

Fans may still debate the merits of Gagné's accomplishments. The memories of the experience remain utterly unforgettable. In their entire history, the Dodgers have never seen anything like the Jungle.

Takashi Saito

The accidental closer worked so well for the Dodgers with Eric Gagné, why not stumble into another?

Takashi Saito arrived at spring training in 2006 with a minor-league contract and considerably less fanfare than Hideo Nomo. Though Saito had a successful career pitching for the Yokohama Bay Stars, it ended rather unceremoniously with his release at age 35. Few gave thought to an aging righty whose ERA in his final three Japanese seasons was 4.65.

Nevertheless, the 6-foot-2 Saito made the Dodgers out of spring training as a set-up man, moved into the closer role in place of Gagné, and smoothly dazzled. In his first season, Saito had a 2.07 ERA (218 ERA+) and a 0.91 WHIP in 78⅓ innings, besting all big-league relievers with 107 strikeouts. In 2007, he was an All-Star, with a 1.40 ERA (319 ERA+) and a 0.72 WHIP, the third-lowest in NL history by a reliever, along with a strikeout-walk ratio of 6.0, wielding a mid-90s fastball that bore in on righties and a slider that moved the opposite way.

"If you can hit both pitches, he's got a curveball for you," Dodger catcher Russell Martin said. "And if you can hit that, too—which most guys don't—he has a splitter he uses once in a while. Normally he doesn't even need to use that."

Saito was on his way to another fine season in 2008 when, with a 2.08 ERA, a 1.11 WHIP, and 11.5 K/9, he went on the disabled list with a sprained elbow ligament. He didn't return until September, when he pitched ineffectively for six games. Looking less like the bargain he had been and about to turn 39, Saito wasn't retained by the Dodgers. He finished his stay in Los Angeles with a 1.95 ERA (227 ERA+), a 0.91 WHIP, and 11.6 K/9 in 189⅔ innings. Only Gagné and Kenley Jansen had lower WHIPs or higher K/9s as Dodger relievers than Saito.

Proving the doubters wrong yet again, Saito went on to have three more effective seasons—one each for Boston, Atlanta, and Milwaukee—before calling it a career after 12 innings in Arizona in 2012 at age 42. For a pitcher who arrived in MLB at baseball middle age, Saito's cumulative numbers are exceptional: his adjusted ERA+ of 185 ranks fifth in big-league history among pitchers with at least 300 innings.

Jonathan Broxton

We won't ignore the elephants in the room with Jonathan Broxton, even if Broxton was the one Dodger big enough to block the elephants from view.

In Game 4 of the 2008 NLCS, the 6-foot-4, 285-pound right-hander gave up the game-winning home run to Matt Stairs in the top of the eighth inning that cost the Dodgers their chance to even the series against the Phillies.

In Game 4 of the 2009 NLCS, Broxton walked Stairs, hit Carlos Ruiz with a pitch, and then, with two out in the bottom of the ninth, surrendered the game-winning double to Jimmy Rollins that cost the Dodgers their chance to even the series against the Phillies.

Two traumas, directly derailing the Dodgers' two best chances of advancing to the World Series after a two-decade absence. As with Tom Niedenfuer, for many, those two pitches are all that matter with Broxton.

Still, he deserves credit for all he did to put the Dodgers so close to postseason glory in the first place.

After debuting as a 21-year-old in 2005, Broxton spent two impressive seasons as Takashi Saito's set-up man, then rumbled right into the role of closer in mid-2008 without missing much of a beat.

Neither playoff mishap affected Broxton the following year. In 2009, he had a 2.61 ERA (154 ERA+), a 0.96 WHIP, and 13.5 strikeouts per nine innings. To begin the 2010 season, he was purely dominant, with a 0.83 ERA, a 0.95 WHIP, and 13.2 K/9…until June 27.

That night, the Dodgers stranded a heavily worked Broxton on the mound to throw 48 pitches against the Yankees. Thereafter, he tumbled to a 7.58 ERA and a 2.06 WHIP for the remainder of 2010. The following year, Broxton lasted 12⅔ innings before he landed on the disabled list, and he never pitched for the Dodgers again.

Broxton's final numbers as a Dodger befit his brawn: 3.19 ERA (132 ERA+), 1.23 WHIP, 11.5 K/9. His 503 strikeouts as a reliever rank third all-time among the Dodgers, behind Kenley Jansen and Jim Brewer, and when his MLB career ended in 2017, just before his 33rd birthday, he led all active NL relievers in strikeouts, with 758.

Pitching for the Reds in the 2012 playoffs, Broxton said that he didn't lose sleep over his playoff setbacks, but acknowledged, as Dylan Hernandez wrote in the *Los Angeles Times*, that "he didn't always channel postseason adrenaline the right way."

"Compared to when I first was in the playoffs, I've calmed down a lot," he said. "And if you control yourself, you make better pitches."

Kenley Jansen

Who is the greatest relief pitcher in Dodger history? Before 2016, you could make a case for a few players. Jim Brewer was effective for the better part of 12 seasons, Clem Labine for 11, Ron Perranoski even more so for eight. Maybe for one guy to get you one inning, there's no one you'd take before Eric Gagné.

Then, to the forefront of that conversation, to the tune of "California Love," strode Kenley Jansen.

A minor-league catcher from Curacao who was Clayton Kershaw's batterymate when they were 18-year-old Gulf Coast League rookie-leaguers in 2006, Jansen showed such fire in his throwing while sporting his catching gear that when his hitting went nowhere, it made sense to give him a shot on the mound.

"He was a different kid," says Charlie Hough, who tutored Jansen in his transition. "In the first half of the year he was catching, and he was very kind of backward with people, you know what I mean? Which I thought was maybe language and stuff, but it wasn't. I think he just felt like he couldn't hit, like he couldn't play, and he wasn't having fun playing. And then when we put him on the mound, he only pitched a few innings before he had a little success—and he became this other kid. He just had new life, and he knew he could play."

Jansen rose rapidly through the minors, needing only 60 innings before getting called up to make his MLB debut on July 24, 2010. He struck out two Mets in a perfect inning, and his strikeout rate didn't drop all that much in the years to follow. With 13.9 strikeouts per game for his career midway through the 2017 season, Jansen was the best ever in that category for the Dodgers and fourth in MLB history.

He achieved that success using a cut fastball that came in hard and tailed with devastating effect. Every batter knows he's going to throw it, but through 2016, they were only hitting .170 with a .238 on-base percentage and .279 slugging percentage in 1,590 plate appearances against him.

"It's just a regular four-seam fastball, and it just has a natural cut," Jansen said. "I think it's just more of a blessing, that's how I look at it. I'm not trying to manipulate it. I'm not trying to cut it. Long hand, long fingers—it just cuts. I know now, if I throw it a certain way, it's not gonna end up straight. It's gonna move."

"I remember one time somebody talking about trying to get him to straighten it out," pitching coach Rick Honeycutt adds with a laugh. "I was like, 'Why are you messing with that?' He's got a natural throw that just does something that people can't square up. He's always had pretty good command, and there was really no reason to make any changes with him."

Whether pitching as a set-up man, as he did in 2010 and 2011 and parts of 2012 and 2013, or as a closer for the other games of 2012 and full-time beginning in June 2013, the 6-foot-5, 275-pound Jansen was a heavy blanket smothering a fire. He never had an ERA above 2.85 or an ERA+ below 127.

So what happened in 2016? Like the Wonkavator blasting through the glass ceiling, Jansen elevated his game to a level you never realized was possible. It wasn't only that he had his best ERA (1.83 ERA/217 ERA+) or his best success with inherited runners, stranding 13 of 14, or that he blew past Gagné to become the Dodgers' all-time saves leader. In the 2016 postseason, the Dodgers realized they could ask more of Jansen—and he was ready to answer. Look no further than 2⅓ innings he threw protecting the Dodgers' one-run lead over the Washington Nationals in the final game of the NLDS, or even the three perfect innings he dished in vain in the Dodgers' season-ending NLCS Game 6 defeat.

"Kenley's always been an unselfish man," Honeycutt says. "I wasn't surprised by Kenley doing it. I think Kenley just cared about winning, and he was willing to do whatever he could do…that 'I'll give you everything that I have, I'll go out there and do the best I can for as long as I can' attitude, and didn't play the 'I'm just a closer,' one-inning, role guy. I thought it was extremely powerful."

The throwback mentality carried into 2017, with Jansen displaying even more mastery of the mound. Making several closing appearances before the ninth inning, Jansen not only had a 1.32 ERA (318 ERA+) in 68⅓ innings with a 0.67 WHIP (second-best in NL history), he didn't walk a single batter until June 25, setting a big-league record for most strikeouts (51) before his first walk.

"I'm more focused now on that one hitter," he said that June. "That one pitch. Like, what is the meaning behind this pitch?"

At the age of 30, Jansen had the best career strikeout-walk ratio (5.88) and best WHIP (0.87) for relief pitchers in NL history.

In the long-awaited run to their first World Series in 29 years, the Dodgers put their considerable weight on the more considerable Jansen, who pitched in 13 of their 18 postseason games, striking out 20 in 16⅔ innings while allowing 13 baserunners. He saved five games, including two in the World Series, though he faltered in two other critical opportunities. He gave up a tying ninth-inning home run in Game 2 on a hanging 0-2 cutter to Houston outfielder Marwin Gonzalez, and threw the 417th and final pitch of the wildest, most exhausting Fall Classic game in Dodger history, their 13–12, 10-inning, 317-minute Game 5 loss.

Jansen self-corrected with a two-inning save in Game 6 and a shutout inning in Game 7, giving him a 2.19 ERA, a 0.86 WHIP, and an MLB-record 13.4 K/9 in his playoff career through the end of 2017. He might need to maintain his brilliance for several more years—and a winning World Series showcase wouldn't hurt—for it to happen, but based on the first eight seasons of his career, Kenley Jansen is not only the greatest relief pitcher the Dodgers ever had, it's legitimate to wonder if he'll be their first Hall of Famer out of the bullpen.

PART NINE

THE MAGNIFICENT

SANDY KOUFAX RETIRED one year before I was born. I was raised in Los Angeles, and being raised in Los Angeles, I was raised on stories of Koufax, told by my dad, told by Vin Scully, told by anyone alive at that time. Koufax was mythic, a Zeus throwing thunderbolts from the sky. He was legend. He was everything except a flesh-and-blood pitcher that I could actually lay eyes upon.

As time passed, I captured glimpses, facsimiles, of men providing brief examples of the god. Fernando Valenzuela was a great cosmic joy ride, rolling zeroes on the scoreboard with the panache of Santa Claus hopping in and out of chimneys. Orel Hershiser rewrote history with his steely, down-the-stretch dominance. And I can't let this entire book pass without noting that, to this day, no pitcher impressed me from his mere presence at Dodger Stadium as much as James Rodney Richard of the Astros in the late 1970s. When he took the mound, the Dodgers swung at vapor trails, and although J.R. was never part of the Dodger pitching tradition, I certainly nominate him as an ambassador in the Dodger Stadium pitching parade.

But Koufax remained the standard, the impossible dream. For five years, he ruled the world. But those five years were the last five years before I got to this world, and I had to assume I would never see anyone like him. Many a Dodger pitching prospect had come in four decades following his retirement. None could even be mentioned in the same sentence as Koufax.

And then, on a blissfully normal March day in 2006, the heavens opened one more time...

Clayton Kershaw

"So this young left-hander was pitching," Vin Scully recalls one winter, describing the moment when a broadcasting legend discovered a pitching legend. "And Boston had this big first baseman—they used to call him 'The Mayor'—Sean Casey, a big likeable guy who talked to everybody on the field. Casey was a very good hitter, and a contact hitter. But with two strikes on Casey, this young left-hander, whom I had never seen before, threw the most hellacious curveball and struck Casey out looking.

"I mean, it was an awesome pitch. It's not as if you remember pitches very often, but I've never forgotten that pitch. And probably, in the recesses of my mind, I thought perhaps, *Wow, that was a Koufax curve.* So I always remember that."

Clayton Kershaw didn't come from nowhere. He was the seventh overall pick in the 2006 MLB draft, the highest draft choice in 23 years by the Dodgers—a consolation prize for losing 91 games in 2005. In his senior year at Highland Park High School in Dallas, Kershaw had gone 13–0 with a 0.77 ERA and 139 strikeouts in 64 innings, including one mercy-rule game in which he struck out all 15 batters he faced. Gatorade and *USA Today* named Kershaw their national prep player of the year.

Still, Kershaw wasn't an automatic superstar. When he began playing sports in high school, he was a big, cuddly offensive lineman with baby fat. Six MLB teams with the chance to draft him passed. The last first-round pick by the Dodgers to so much as make a single All-Star team was Steve Howe, selected 27 years earlier.

Kershaw came to the Dodgers with high expectations but no guarantees. By all rights, he should succeed. By all realities, he quite easily wouldn't.

But on that Sunday morning, March 9, 2008, when Kershaw eased out of the stretch and threw that 1-2 looper to Casey, Scully's voice rang like church bells.

"Oh, what a curveball!" Scully exclaimed with genuine shock and glee, "Holy mackerel! He just broke off Public Enemy No. 1."

That pitch showed that it wasn't crazy to believe that Kershaw could be for real. What it failed to show, perhaps, is that Kershaw would be so unreal.

In his first 10 seasons with the Dodgers, Kershaw did nothing less than roll out a Hall of Fame career on the blue carpet. At the end of the 2017 season, the final year of his twenties—one year younger than Koufax was when he retired—Kershaw had a lifetime ERA (2.36) nearly half a run lower than Koufax (2.76) despite pitching in a tougher offensive environment. Kershaw's 1.00 WHIP was the best of any starting pitcher in the past 100 years, and his 160 ERA+ the best of any starting pitcher in baseball history.

Matching Koufax in the honors circuit as well, Kershaw won three NL Cy Young Awards (receiving first-place votes in four other years) and the 2014 NL MVP Award. With 57.4 wins above replacement, he had surpassed Koufax to rank third in Dodger history, with Dazzy Vance (61.8) and Don Drysdale (61.3) in his sights.

In the throes of his career, none of that résumé mattered to him.

"I think all the individual stuff is something you can look back at when you're done," Kershaw says, "if you want to do that, and say, 'I had some success in the game.' But when you're in the game and you're on a team, it's just so much more important to be focused on winning the game."

With Kershaw on their roster, the Dodgers made the playoffs in 7 of his first 10 years, reaching the NLCS four times and winning their first pennant in 29 years in 2017. A World Series title still stood tantalizingly beyond Kershaw's reach entering 2018, and he deserves some responsibility for that—though not nearly as much as his October detractors would assign. Never, however, has there been anything close to a pitcher like Kershaw for the Dodgers—a pitcher of this level of excellence for this length of time.

The curveball that Scully spotted in the Vero Beach sun in 2008 played a major part, as Tom Verducci wrote in *Sports Illustrated*.

"The wizardry of Kershaw's curve is in how much it resembles a fastball out of his hand," Verducci stated. "Kershaw throws each pitch from an identical release point, depriving hitters of an early 'tell.'

"Kershaw also disables hitters' second level of decoding: the reading of spin...Kershaw spins his curveball at a similar rate to his fastball. Though they spin in opposite directions, because he throws both with a true overhand delivery, creating pole-to-pole rotation, the pitches first look exactly alike to a hitter: a gray circle. The four-seamer holds its plane, while the Kershaw curve can drop nine inches."

Moment in the Sun: Brad Penny

- Two-time All-Star for the Dodgers struck out the side in first inning of the 2006 game, pitched perfect inning on seven pitches in 2007
- With a 3.03 ERA (147 ERA+) in 2007, 6-foot-4 righty finished third in NL Cy Young vote
- Hurled 678⅔ innings for Dodgers through 2008, with a 4.07 ERA (106 ERA+)
- Listed at 270 pounds, the heaviest starting pitcher in Dodger history

Though Kershaw's artistry on the mound evolved every year of his career, he jumped to the major leagues based on those two pitches, fastball and curve, and he was quick rising. Kershaw zipped through rookie ball and Single-A Great Lakes to reach Double-A Jacksonville at age 19 in August 2007, 14 months after the Dodgers signed him. He returned to Jacksonville to begin the 2008 season but was called up to make his MLB debut against St. Louis on May 25, two months and one week after his 20th birthday.

On a sun-dappled Sunday at Dodger Stadium, wearing his rookie uniform number of 54, Kershaw threw his first big-league pitch, a 94-mph fastball, high and inside for ball one. Next came two fastballs of the same speed, one swung at and missed, the other fouled back. Kershaw then tried his first curveball, grounded foul. Another fastball at 95 and a curveball at 74, and Skip Schumaker, a 28-year-old outfielder batting .299, fouled them both off—four fouls in a row off the just-unwrapped pitcher. On the seventh pitch of the at-bat, Kershaw fired the ball 95 mph, shoulder-high—and Schumaker whipped his bat right through it.

"Fastball, that just exploded around the letters!" Scully called.

The broadcast cut quickly to Kershaw's mother, Marianne, applauding wildly, as the strikeout baseball went into the dugout for posterity. Kershaw even smiled, a counterpoint to the all-business countenance on the mound that later helped define him.

And then Brian Barton, a 26-year-old rookie playing in his 40th big-league game, walked on four pitches.

"I think I was so nervous on that first guy that I probably just exhaled," Kershaw says.

That brought up the third batter, a 28-year-old nobody named Albert Pujols, who…let's check the notes…hmm, it says here he would win his second NL MVP that season. "Mr. Kershaw, Mr. Pujols. Mr. Pujols, Mr. Kershaw," Scully said by way of introduction.

This at-bat went to eight pitches, with Pujols fouling off two 96-mph fastballs.

"I remember Albert," Kershaw says. "I think I might have thrown a 3-2 curveball—he hit a double down the left-field line and the run scored."

Three batters into his first game, Kershaw was already losing, 1–0.

With off-the-charts adrenaline, Kershaw settled in to strike out Ryan Ludwick and Troy Glaus, one on a fastball, the other on a curve. Kershaw went on to complete six innings of two-run ball, allowing six baserunners and striking out seven in 102 pitches.

"You don't like losing, but that was fun to watch," St. Louis hitting coach Hal McRae said, after the Cardinals fell to the Dodgers in 10 innings. "He obviously has a lot of ability. He's got a future."

Do tell.

In the short term, there were hiccups. Kershaw's debut turned out to be the best start of his initial stint with the Dodgers. With 24 walks in his first 38⅔ innings and a 4.42 ERA, Kershaw returned to Jacksonville for a tune-up.

"When the book gets out on you, that's when things happen," Kershaw says. "The first couple of games, you can get away with stuff, just because they haven't seen you, they don't know what you have, they don't know how you're going to try to attack hitters. It gets around the league that 'this guy has two pitches, and he doesn't throw them for strikes very much, so just wait for a fastball in'—and from there, it makes it really difficult."

Kershaw made three more starts for Jacksonville, finishing on a 16-inning scoreless streak with two walks, then returned to the Dodgers. After taking a 10-hit, three-inning beating in Colorado, Kershaw pitched six shutout innings in each of his next two starts. For his rookie season, he registered a 4.26 ERA (98 ERA+), 100 strikeouts in 107⅔ innings, as well as a spot on the postseason roster (the youngest Dodger to pitch in a playoff game since Drysdale, he relieved in two games, allowing one run) and his first sense of what he needed to excel in the show, with manager Joe Torre and pitching coach Rick Honeycutt guiding his way.

"That first year was tough," Kershaw says. "I kind of felt out of place, and the guys did a great job and Joe and Honey did a great job of helping me out, but I just didn't really know what I was doing. I think I was probably a little bit out of my element that first year, and the performance showed."

In 2009, on a Jackie Robinson Day start April 15 against the Giants, the world first glimpsed a truly dominant Kershaw. In seven innings, he allowed a second-inning Bengie Molina home run, a fifth-inning Rich

Aurilia walk, and nothing else, all while striking out 13, making him the youngest to do so since Koufax was a rookie in 1955.

Nevertheless, Kershaw was cuffed around in his next two starts, allowing 15 runs in nine innings. He needed more consistency. Kershaw was still a two-pitch pitcher, and when he couldn't throw his curveball for strikes, he was his own worst enemy.

"What had gotten me to that point wasn't going to be enough," Kershaw says of his 21-year-old self. "I really needed to figure out a third pitch, figure out how to throw more strikes. That's when I went from being a little stubborn to being more open-minded, trying different things to make sure I could stick in the big leagues.

"I don't think age has so much to do with it. I was failing. I wasn't pitching well. Sometimes it takes failure to understand how you need to change. You need to figure out something to get better, and that was definitely the case with me. I was tired of getting beat up, tired of walking so many guys."

Talking at length with Honeycutt and Dodger bullpen catcher Mike Borzello, Kershaw finally made the leap of faith into experimenting with a slider on flat ground. Like Fernando Valenzuela with the screwball, Kershaw took to his new pitch like Monet to the brush.

A.J. Ellis, seven years older than Kershaw but a teammate of his in Jacksonville, first saw the lefty's third dimension at a bullpen session while the Dodgers were on the road at Wrigley Field during the last weekend in May 2009.

"He gives me the slider sign," said Ellis, who had been called up as a third catcher at the time. "And I play dumb. I get on the inside of the plate. He throws the first one and it's like, the perfect slider, the perfect shape, the perfect speed, right underneath where a right-handed hitter's hands would be, back-foot slider.

"Borzi is right there next to me, about three feet away, just off the side of the bullpen mound on the first-base line. Him and I just kind of look at each other, this big wide-eyed look. Our mouths were open. He throws a couple more, then Kersh finishes his bullpen, walks down, says, 'That slider, what do you got? Is it any good?'"

Oh, yes. Kershaw dipped into the shallow end of the pool, offering the slider maybe once every 15 or 20 pitches at first, but bit by bit, he was transcending into something almost ethereal.

"Slowly from there, things just started to click," Honeycutt says. "When he just started perfecting that slider, his career really took off."

Moment in the Sun: Derek Lowe

- From 2005 to 2008, pitched 850⅓ innings for Dodgers with a 3.59 ERA
- Ranks 10th in Los Angeles Dodger history (minimum 500 innings) with 120 ERA+
- With strong sinkerball, 6-foot-6 right-hander tops in franchise history with 63.9 percent ground-ball rate

Kershaw entered June 2009 with a 4.34 ERA. Over his remaining 115 innings that season, his ERA was 2.03 with 130 strikeouts. For the year, his ERA was 2.79 (143 ERA+) in 171 innings, with the fewest hits per nine innings of any NL starting pitcher. He still walked too many (4.8 per nine innings) and exited too quickly (5⅔ innings per start), but the development was breathtaking.

His first career playoff start came in Game 2 of the 2009 NLDS, and as natural as can be, Kershaw threw 6⅔ innings of two-run ball in a 3–2 Dodger win over the Cardinals. Torre tapped him to open the NLCS against the Phillies: 21 years old, starting Game 1. Kershaw began with four shutout innings, lowering his postseason ERA at that point to 2.13, before a fifth-inning unraveling with three walks, an NLCS-record three wild pitches, and two big extra-base hits—a three-run homer by Carlos Ruiz and a two-run double by Ryan Howard.

T.J. Simers, the mordant *Los Angeles Times* columnist, was no one to share a sympathetic word on behalf of victims of a car crash like this one, but he praised Kershaw for his maturity in facing the "mob of reporters and cameras" after the game.

"I lost the strike zone," Kershaw said. "You do that, and they make you pay for the mistakes…We didn't win the game. I didn't get the job done."

But who could complain about Kershaw's first full year in the majors? Respect for his process flowed from every corner of the Dodger clubhouse.

"A lot of young guys with bullpen [sessions], they're just going to throw and throw, throw and throw and throw their pitches until it feels right," future Tigers manager Brad Ausmus said in the spring of 2010, ahead of his second season as a Dodger backup catcher. "The pitching coach usually has to drag them off the rubber. Clayton sticks to his routine regardless of how he feels and he sticks to that routine every single bullpen. When he's done, he steps off the mound. The only guy I've ever seen do that is [Roger] Clemens."

That year, Kershaw reached the 200-inning and 200-strikeout plateaus for the first time, with a 2.91 ERA (133 ERA+). Perhaps most importantly, his walk rate also declined for the first time, to 3.8 per nine innings.

"By 2010, the slider supplanted his curve as the go-to breaking pitch," wrote baseball columnist Jonah Keri. "Per PITCHf/x data, Kershaw's slider was the second-best in the game in 2010, and the best in 2011. If Kershaw's supernatural talent wasn't blatantly obvious before, it certainly was now. A pitch he'd never thrown in his life just two years earlier was now his best offering."

When Kershaw threw his first career shutout—a 1–0, 111-pitch whitewashing of the Giants on September 14, he walked no one.

"I don't feel any different," Kershaw said after the game, "but I guess the results speak for themselves. I expect to put some zeros up there. Fortunately, I got nine of them tonight."

If Kershaw still lacked anything when he took the mound to begin the 2011 season, it was the relentless consistency that would become part of his trademark. On March 31, starting on Opening Day for the first time, Kershaw began his season with seven shutout innings, one walk, and nine strikeouts, but in two of his final three starts in April, he allowed a total of nine runs in a combined 10 innings. Following a three-baserunner, 10-strikeout shutout of the Marlins on May 29, Kershaw gave up six runs in consecutive starts. He finished June with back-to-back 11-strikeout complete games, then allowed six earned runs again to the Angels beginning July.

But Kershaw's work through June—a 2.93 ERA, with an NL-leading 128 strikeouts against 121 baseunners in 116⅔ innings—sealed an invite to his first All-Star Game, in which he threw a perfect inning, retiring David Ortiz, Robinson Cano, and Alex Avila on eight pitches. After that, there was no more waiting at Cape Canaveral. Kershaw, you're cleared for launch. Averaging 7⅓ innings across his remaining 14 starts that season, the 23-year-old allowed 15 runs for a 1.31 ERA, a blazing stretch run that led to a league-leading 21–5 record, a 2.28 ERA (161 ERA+), a 0.98 WHIP…and his first NL Cy Young Award, with 27 of 32 first-place votes.

Moment in the Sun: Chad Billingsley

- Debuted at age 21 for Dodgers in 2006
- At 24, the 6-foot-4, 240-pound righty led 2008 division champs in ERA (3.14/133 ERA+)
- Pitched 1,212⅓ innings (all but 37 with Dodgers) with a 3.72 ERA (108 ERA+) before arm trouble ended career at age 30
- Eighth among starting pitchers in Dodger history with 7.9 strikeouts per nine innings

Kershaw was the eighth Dodger to win the award, after Don Newcombe, Don Drysdale, Koufax, Mike Marshall, Fernando Valenzuela, Orel Hershiser, and Eric Gagné. (For dessert, Kershaw also won the Gold Glove Award, making him the fifth Dodger pitcher named the league's best fielder at his position.)

"Just thankful to be a part of it—undeserving when you see some of the other names up there," Kershaw said of his first Cy Young. "I've got a long way to go to have the career those guys did."

In 2012, Kershaw led the big leagues with a 2.53 ERA (150 ERA+) and a 1.02 WHIP, but couldn't overcome the media's fascination with 37-year-old Mets knuckleballer R.J. Dickey and finished second in the NL Cy Young vote. In one sense, though, Kershaw came away with a more meaningful prize, becoming the youngest person ever to win baseball's Roberto Clemente Award, recognizing the player who best represents the game off the field as well as on, through sportsmanship and community involvement.

The average age of Clemente honorees had been 35. Kershaw was 24. But in the winter of 2010–11, when he married his high-school sweetheart Ellen Melson, Kershaw went on a missionary trip to Zambia with the Arise Africa organization, and became enchanted by the children he met there and determined to channel his off-field energies toward them.

"It just touched him in a way he probably never could have expected," Ellen Kershaw says. "He just realized there was so much he could be doing, and the platform we have is so strong. He just immediately fell in love with those kids and how joyful they were when they have nothing."

With his personal life in place, gnawing at Kershaw was the fact that the Dodgers were now three seasons removed from their last playoff appearance, amplified by the rival Giants winning the World Series in two of those three years. On Opening Day in 2013, Kershaw began his on-field mission to rectify matters.

On a day when Koufax threw the ceremonial first pitch, kicking off the 50th anniversary of his first Cy Young Award season, Kershaw faced two-time NL Cy Young Award winner Tim Lincecum in the day's marquee pitching matchup, the game scoreless heading into the bottom of the eighth inning. Having thrown only 85 pitches to that point, Kershaw batted for himself against Giants reliever George Kontos.

"I figured I'd better swing at the first pitch," Kershaw says. "I had struck out twice and didn't want to strike out again."

The ball exploded from Kershaw's bat toward deep center field, carrying over the wall. Kershaw's first career homer gave the Dodgers the lead and opened the gates for a four-run inning. Minutes later, Kershaw finished his 94-pitch shutout, the most efficient game of his career, and one that made him the first pitcher to hit a homer during an Opening Day shutout since Cleveland's Bob Lemon in 1953.

After the game, Kershaw respectfully objected to questions linking him to Koufax. But you had to excuse the reporters for posing them, given what was right in front of their eyes, not to mention that the two managers Kershaw had in his career up to that time, Joe Torre and Don Mattingly, joined in.

"I know Joe made comparisons early on between Clayton and Sandy," Mattingly says. "I'd be lying if I said it didn't flash through my mind in the sixth inning, as he's rolling."

Even Kershaw's best friend on the team couldn't shy away.

"It made the day complete, [Koufax] throwing the first pitch and Clayton the last pitch," says Ellis, who had become the Dodgers' starting catcher. "Like a passing of the torch."

If Kershaw wanted to kill the juxtaposition, he did himself no favors by continuing to pitch like Koufax. After throwing a season-low five innings in a 7–2 victory over the Mets on April 23, Kershaw's ERA for the season sat at 2.14. It went no higher for the rest of the year, ending at 1.83 (194 ERA+)—best in the majors for the third straight season, along with his 0.92 WHIP and NL-leading 232 strikeouts. Netting 29 of 30 first-place votes, he reclaimed the Cy Young Award, presented to him at the Baseball

Writers Association of America awards dinner that winter, where none other than Koufax introduced him.

"Clayton Kershaw is not my protégé," Koufax said. "Clayton Kershaw is his own person, his own man, and he's done it all himself. It takes a very special pitcher and some great years to win your second Cy Young Award by the age of 25. Clayton Kershaw is a very special pitcher. He's a very special teammate. He's a very special person."

The Dodgers surged into the 2013 playoffs despite a 30–42 start that put them 9½ games out of first place on the first official day of summer. With Kershaw contributing a microscopic 1.40 ERA and 0.65 WHIP, Los Angeles went on a 42–8 run, the top 50-game stretch by a major-league team since 1942, and won the NL West by 11 games.

Riding baseball's best pitcher into October, the playoffs began exactly as any Dodger fan would have hoped. In Game 1 of the NLDS against Atlanta, Kershaw struck out 12, the most by a Dodger postseason pitcher in 50 years and a day, dating back to Koufax's 15 in Game 1 of the '63 World Series. Despite throwing 124 pitches in seven innings of the 6–1 victory, Kershaw came back on three days' rest for the first time in his career for Game 4 and allowed no earned runs. (Errors enabling two unearned runs to score left the lefty with a six-inning no decision in the series-clinching victory won by Juan Uribe's eighth-inning homer.)

Traveling to St. Louis for the NLCS against the Cardinals, Kershaw pitched six more innings without an earned run, but once again left deprived of a win, the Dodgers suffering a 1–0 defeat. To this point, Kershaw's playoff ERA was 2.88 for his career and 0.47 through 19 innings in 2013. Let's be clear: the idea that Kershaw would come to wear the postseason like any kind of albatross was just shy of preposterous.

However, with the Dodgers facing elimination in Game 6, the bottom dropped out. In a scoreless tie with one out in the third inning, Matt Carpenter fouled off an excruciating 8 of Kershaw's 11 pitches before ripping a double to right field, and Carlos Beltran singled to right for the game's first run. Kershaw rebounded to tally five consecutive strikes, putting him within one pitch of escaping the inning without further damage. Instead, Yadier Molina singled, and the next three Cardinals reached base, capped by Shane Robinson's two-run single to make the score 4–0.

Three more runs were charged to Kershaw in a fifth inning in which he didn't retire a batter before exiting, and the Dodgers lost, 9–0. The game ended the Dodgers' season. Moreover, in the zeitgeist, it obliterated the memory of Kershaw's strong October résumé in 2013, tossing his postseason reputation into misery for years to come.

On a personal level, Kershaw resolved to tune out the naysayers and look to the future.

"I just try to keep it simple," Kershaw says. "Completely forget about last year—good or bad—and then this year come in and not really set any goals. I'm going to win every time I pitch—that's my only goal, my only mindset. And you can just erase the past, regardless, and then focus on the next start. I feel that's the only way I can go about it, and it helps."

Moment in the Sun: Hiroki Kuroda

- The fifth Japanese native to pitch for the Dodgers, beginning his MLB career at age 33 in 2008
- In four seasons, pitched 699 innings with a 3.45 ERA (113 ERA+), topped by a 3.07 ERA (120 ERA+) in 2011
- Retired first 21 batters in 91-pitch one-hitter against Braves on July 7, 2008
- Won both starts in 2008 playoffs, allowing two runs in 12⅓ innings

In 2014, the recovery began oddly, with the Dodgers and Kershaw starting over down under in Australia against the Arizona Diamondbacks. Kershaw delivered a typically authoritative performance in the March 22

Sydney start—6⅔ innings, one run—but immediately after landed on the disabled list for the first time in his career, with a strain of the teres major muscle in his upper left shoulder. He didn't make his second start of the season until May 6, throwing seven shutout innings, and all was well…until 11 days later, when in a bizarre second inning at Arizona, the Diamondbacks hit three triples and knocked Kershaw out with seven runs charged to his account. Kershaw's ERA ballooned to 4.43, and the media crackled with "What's wrong with Kershaw?" tweets and commentary.

As it turned out, nothing. In his remaining 23 starts that season, Kershaw allowed only 28 earned runs. He went on a magnificent, mesmerizing 41-inning scoreless streak from June 13 to July 10 that put Hershiser's record in realistic jeopardy. During the run, only three opponents even reached third base, and two of those were thanks to errors.

"I'm neither his teammate nor his coach, but I've walked in his shoes and tried to do what he's done—not to the level he's done it, surely—but I know how much work and commitment it takes to get better and stay disciplined and continue to reach for more," Hershiser says. "Too many big-leaguers toss their lives away and never reach their potential. Not so with Clayton."

Within that shutout skein came Kershaw's triumphant individual moment, against Colorado. On a lovely cusp-of-summer evening, the 18th night of June, Kershaw retired the first 18 Rockies he faced. The 19th, Corey Dickerson, hit a slow grounder to shortstop Hanley Ramirez, who gloved on the run but threw wide to first for an error, ending the perfect game. Kershaw shook it off, and with a sparkling defensive play by reserve third baseman Miguel Rojas balancing the scales, Kershaw retired the next eight Rockies, setting up a final encounter with Dickerson.

On his 107th pitch, Dickerson swung and missed—the career-high 15th strikeout victim by Kershaw on the evening—and the ace pumped his arms in the air to exult in the much-anticipated, practically inevitable achievement: his first no-hitter.

"I haven't really thought of the ramifications of throwing one of these things, but it's definitely special company," Kershaw said that night. "I don't take for granted the history of this or what it means. I definitely understand all that."

Having his baseball brother Ellis behind the plate (and Honeycutt in the dugout) made the moment even more special.

"It's been awesome, having that steady presence, him and Honey just being around the whole time," Kershaw says. "A.J. and I, we're really good friends off the field, and obviously to have him around as long as he's been there, and just kind of share in the successes and the failures, it's cool. Not a lot of people get to say they've had the same guy back there for so many cool moments. He's definitely been there for me."

When the scoreless streak ended, after a sixth-inning home run by Chase Headley marred a 2–1, complete-game, 11-strikeout win over San Diego, Kershaw's ERA had dropped below 2.00 to stay. When the regular season ended, with a chart-topping 1.77 ERA—the lowest in MLB since Pedro Martínez in 2000—a 197 ERA+, a 1.81 fielding-independent ERA, a 0.86 WHIP, 10.8 strikeouts per nine innings, and 7.7 strikeout-walk ratio, Kershaw's superiority in the pitching categories was unmistakable.

His third NL Cy Young Award was a given, and all that remained to be answered was whether a pitcher—one who missed more than a month of the season, but whose 7.6 wins above replacement still bested any other player, on the mound or at the plate—should win the MVP award. None had done so in the senior circuit since Bob Gibson in 1968.

Perhaps no game, not even the no-hitter, argued better for Kershaw than the one he played September 24 against San Francisco. The warm night offered a Kershawcopia of delights: a behind-the-back snag of a shot up the middle to prevent two runs from scoring, a fifth-inning RBI triple to tie the game at 1–1, and, above all, eight innings of one-run, 11-strikeout ball in the 9–1 victory that clinched the NL West title.

The MVP ballot deadline came four days later. When the BBWAA announced results that November, Kershaw reigned supreme, and rather handily so. Right along with becoming the unanimous NL Cy Young winner, the Dodgers' first since Koufax, Kershaw outpointed Miami's Giancarlo Stanton, 355–298 (18–8 in first-place votes) to become the fourth Dodger pitcher to be named the league's top player, after Vance, Newcombe, and Koufax.

Once that news broke, however, Kershaw was living down more postseason heartbreak.

Kershaw opened Game 1 of the 2014 NLDS against the Cardinals, the same franchise that haunted him in 2013. For six innings revenge was his, as the Dodgers scored six runs while Kershaw allowed two seemingly harmless solo homers. But for the second year in a row, Kershaw stumbled into a quagmire from which he couldn't escape and Mattingly, with a shaky bullpen as an alternative, didn't rescue him. Five singles produced two runs, cutting the lead to 6–4. With the bases loaded, Carpenter, giving Kershaw fits again, worked the count to 2-2. Once more, one more strike was the lifeline. Instead, Carpenter launched a double to right-center, scoring all three runs to give St. Louis a 7–6 lead in a game they hung on to win, 10–9, before a dumbstruck Dodger Stadium crowd.

Four days later in St. Louis came the harrowing sequel. Through six innings, Kershaw pitched shutout ball, striking out the side in the sixth to give him nine for the game. Tending a 2–0 lead in the bottom of the seventh, Kershaw allowed two seeing-eye singles, one off second baseman Dee Gordon's glove, the second off the tip of Ramirez's glove. The next batter, Matt Adams, received an 0-1 curveball, squared up, and blasted it to right. At the worst possible moment, Adams became the first left-handed hitter in Kershaw's seven big-league years to hit a home run on his curve, an echo of Ozzie Smith and Jack Clark all in one. No one would score again, and for the second year in a row, St. Louis shattered the Dodgers' season.

After the game, Kershaw struggled to come to terms with what happened.

"I can't really put it into words right now...

"The season ended, and I was a big part of the reason why…

"They just beat me. I don't know. I don't think it's anything magic. They're just getting hits right now…"

Three months later, one night after the birth of his first child in January, Kershaw arrived in New York for the annual awards ceremony to receive his Cy Young and MVP trophies. In his speech, he described all those he encountered during a day at the ballpark, using that format to navigate all the personal thank-yous he wanted to express, from his teammates to the clubhouse assistants. In his conclusion, he spoke to the events of October.

"To Skip Schumaker, Nick Punto, Mark Ellis, and Michael Young, thank you for teaching me that this game shouldn't be played like a marathon," Kershaw said. "You know, that's all we ever hear, is 'this game is a grind, and you can never get too high or too low.' Well, these guys taught me differently. They taught me that winning is worth celebrating no matter what. So tonight, I will celebrate as I look back on the 2014 season. But they also taught me that losing hurts just as much as winning feels good, and so my last thank-you goes to the St. Louis Cardinals. Thank you for reminding me that you are never as good as you think you are."

The urgency to get back to October in 2015 was unmistakable, but Kershaw had to endure more "What's wrong?" drumbeats through April and May (4.32 ERA in his first nine starts) before once again shifting into overdrive (1.39 ERA in his last 24 starts), highlighted by his latest scoreless streak, this one 37 innings from July 3 to August 1. (Kershaw became the first pitcher with two scoreless streaks of at least that length in more than 40 years, since Luis Tiant.) For the second year in a row, Kershaw danced through the division-clinching victory over the Giants in a showstopper, striking out 13 in his first career one-hitter. In his final start of the year, a tune-up for the postseason, Kershaw reached 301 strikeouts, becoming the first big-leaguer to traverse 300 since 2002 and the first Dodger since Koufax's '65 season.

"I know it meant a lot to him, even though he lied and said it didn't," Ellis says.

Kershaw's 11.6 strikeouts per nine innings broke the franchise record for starting pitchers, and his 2.13 ERA (173 ERA+) would have earned him another NL Cy Young Award in most years—indeed, by FanGraphs' reckoning, his 8.5 wins above replacement indicated that he should have. But with teammate Zack Greinke and Chicago's Jake Arrieta each posting sub-2.00 ERAs, voters relegated Kershaw to third place. Before that, in October, everyone's attention turned to the playoffs.

Kershaw's superb first three postseason starts in 2013 could hardly have been more of a distant memory for the self-appointed baseball cognoscenti, his standout work in the first six innings of his two 2014 playoff games hardly more irrelevant. The recent playoff mishaps had devalued Kershaw's October reputation into one that, quite honestly, only a World Series appeared able to salvage. This was clear whether Kershaw battled to a hard-luck defeat, such as his 3–1 loss in Game 1 of the NLDS against the Mets, or a hard-fought victory, like the win by the same score in Game 4 of the NLDS on three days' rest. Kershaw's 2015 postseason ERA was 2.63, he struck out 19 in 13⅔ innings, he battled the eventual NL champs to a draw, but he gained…nothing.

"To get to celebrate with your teammates is something that a lot of guys don't ever to get to do at all, period," Kershaw says. "But yes, at the end of the day, you lose the last game of the season, you're going to have some disappointment…I think you enjoy the heck out of wins and celebrate that night, and if you lose, you let it hurt for a little bit and you come back the next day and get after it. I guess as a starting pitcher, that's a little bit easier.

"If you can't handle failure, baseball's not the sport for you…You're going to have your bad games, and you just need to be able to respond."

Kershaw's will to respond could not have been stronger in 2016. Avoiding the awkward opening weeks of the previous two years, the 28-year-old Kershaw took his command to jaw-dropping precision as he reached the 10th anniversary of his signing with the Dodgers. In his first 15 starts through June 20, Kershaw not only had a 1.57 ERA while averaging 7⅔ innings per game, he was on pace to nearly double the MLB record for strikeout-walk ratio: 141 strikeouts and only seven walks, an incomprehensible 20.1 K/BB.

Behind the scenes, however, Kershaw was quietly battling lower back pain, which overcame him June 26 at Pittsburgh. Though he pitched six innings, he allowed four runs in his second loss of the season, and it became untenable for him to continue without treatment. For the second time in his career, he went on the disabled list, this time with a disc herniation. Kershaw avoided surgery, but the Dodgers were left to play the next 63 games without him.

Considering that Los Angeles was eight games out of first place when this happened, anyone banking on October gratification confronted a dismal forecast. But the Dodgers rallied without their injured superstar, and when he returned September 9, they were four games ahead in the NL West. Kershaw needed little time to round back into form, making three consecutive appearances in September without allowing an earned run and pronouncing himself fit for the playoffs.

The script changed for Kershaw in the 2016 postseason. He was not at his best opening the NLDS against the Nationals, allowing three runs in five innings, but came away a victor. In Game 4, on three days' rest, Kershaw exited after 6⅔ innings with a 5–2 lead and the bases loaded. The bullpen gave up the lead, but the Dodgers came back and won anyway, and the teams moved on to Washington for another winner-take-all Game 5.

An almost rhetorical pregame question about Kershaw's availability if needed that night produced an "absolutely not" response from Dodger manager Dave Roberts. But in a situation that directly recalled Hershiser in Game 4 of the 1988 NLDS at New York, a moment arose when no one, including Kershaw, could have imagined him not coming in. As Kenley Jansen wore down in his valiant third inning of relief trying to protect a 4–3 lead, Kershaw hustled down to the bullpen. He had thrown 110 pitches only 48 hours earlier, 211 pitches in the past six days. But he entered the game with one out, the tying run on second base, the winning run on first base, and NL OPS champ Daniel Murphy—16-for-32 in the 2016 and 2017 postseasons against the Dodgers—at the plate.

After a fastball on the upper edge of the strike zone was taken for ball one, Kershaw came back at 94 mph in nearly the same location. Murphy mistimed it in the worst way, popping out to second. After that, the next batter was pinch hitter Wilmer Difo, a nearly anonymous substitute except for a name that mimicked Willem Dafoe, one of Hollywood's top portrayers of on-screen villains.

Kershaw fanned Difo on five pitches—two fastballs, two sliders, and, for the big finish, the old Public Enemy numero uno. For the first time in his life, Kershaw walked off the mound to a series-ending bear hug as the Dodgers advanced to the next round of the playoffs.

"I'm exhausted," Kershaw said in the celebration. "We're all exhausted after every game, even if you're sitting on the bench. These games are such grinds that it's such a relief when they're over and you win. And it's a little bit of an adrenaline rush right there. I'm still a little bit amped up right now, but I'm sure I'll sleep good tonight."

Kershaw's valiant moment of glory marked what might have been a turning point in his postseason image, soon augmented by his seven innings of shutout ball against the Cubs three nights later in the Dodgers' 1–0 victory in Game 2 of the NLCS at Wrigley Field. But when he took the mound for the Dodgers in a do-or-die Game 6, Kershaw was all but spent, unable to command his curveball and taking a 5–0 loss.

"You look back and just kind of think of the season as a whole," Kershaw said, "and it's tough to swallow tonight, obviously, but I'd much rather be in this situation and fail then not get to be in this situation at all.

"I felt good tonight, 100 percent. I just got beat."

And so Kershaw and the Dodgers arrived in 2017. Over the first half of the season, Kershaw seemed very much his old self, except for a surprising attack of homeritis (or maybe not so surprising, given that teams collectively hit 412 more home runs than in any previous year in history). On June 19 against the Mets, a seventh-inning shot by Jose Reyes was the fourth homer of the game and 17th of the season given up by Kershaw, both career highs. (He would go on to allow 23 in the regular season, matching his total for 2015 and 2016 combined.)

At the All-Star break, Kershaw's ERA was 2.18 (189 ERA+, second in the NL) with a league-leading 159 strikeouts in 132⅓ innings. For the second summer in a row, however, a back ailment interrupted his year—he left a July 23 start after two shutout innings—potentially derailing a Dodger team trouncing the field with 69 wins in its first 100 games. But Kershaw's absence barely slowed the Dodgers, who topped their 2013 counterparts by going 43–7 in a 50-game stretch, including 24–6 in the first 30 games of Kershaw's diversion to the disabled list.

Kershaw returned to action September 1 with six two-hit, no-walk shutout innings, and finished the campaign with a 2.31 ERA and a 180 ERA+ to lead the NL, along with 202 strikeouts in his 175 innings and a league-leading 6.7 strikeout-walk ratio. With Los Angeles wrapping up its fifth straight division title with a 104–58 record (despite losing 16 of 17 games during one late-summer stretch), all eyes were once again on how the Dodgers—and particularly Kershaw—would weather October.

Steps were taken to vanquish the remaining negativity, however overwrought, surrounding Kershaw's postseason record, which more folks inside and outside the organization realized could be partially chalked up to his unsteady support system on the pitching staff—the reliance on Kershaw at all costs, as if he were pitching in the Koufax era. The Dodgers acquired Yu Darvish—the winning pitcher in the 2009 World Baseball Classic title game at Dodger Stadium for Japan, before becoming the Texas Rangers' ace—to join Rich Hill and Alex Wood in the team's playoff rotation, forestalling a need for Kershaw to start on three days' rest in the playoffs as he had the previous four seasons.

Los Angeles also found set-up relievers it was willing—even eager—to turn to in times of trouble. In Game 1 of the NLDS against Arizona, Kershaw was in control, taking a 7–2 lead into the seventh inning. When he gave up his third and fourth homers of the game, manager Dave Roberts jumped in to grab him, and the Dodgers cruised thereafter, 9–4. That game raised Kershaw's career postseason ERA in the seventh inning to (this is no typo) 27.00, and the message was clear: enjoy Kershaw's brilliance, but don't exhaust it. In NLCS Game 1 against the Cubs, with the game tied at 2–2, Kershaw went out for a pinch hitter after five innings—unthinkable in previous years. The Dodgers won 5–2.

With only 187 pitches thrown over the previous 18 days of October, a rested Kershaw threw six tight innings in the Game 5 clinching opportunity at Wrigley Field (the site of the unpleasant 2016 finale), allowing a solo homer and three other baserunners, as the Dodgers romped 11–1 behind Kiké Hernandez's three home runs. Kershaw exulted in his NL pennant, and a generation of Dodger fans who had never known such heights were energized right behind him. Smiling through the postgame interviews, Kershaw—imposingly adult in maturity and giddily childlike in desire—welcomed the reality that with time off for winning behavior, he would be back on the mound for the Dodgers' next and biggest moment. It was the final climb, and conditions at base camp were intense.

In the first World Series game for the Dodgers since 1988 and the hottest World Series game on record (first-pitch temperature: 103 degrees), against the top offense he had ever faced in the playoffs, Kershaw presented his biggest nationwide audience with his most dominant playoff start, throwing seven innings of one-run ball against the Astros in which he allowed three hits and no walks while striking out 11—the first World Series pitcher of any stripe to fan at least 11 with no walks since Newcombe in 1949. This was Kershaw incarnate, the one everybody had expected all along. After Los Angeles and Houston went on to split the first four games of the Series, Kershaw returned to the mound in Houston for Game 5, and with the Dodgers scoring three runs in the first inning and another in the top of the fourth, there before Kershaw stood the most pristine opportunity to seal his legacy.

Kershaw had faced the minimum nine hitters in three shutout innings. Backed by the stout (if tiring) Dodger bullpen, he needed at most four more effective frames.

Maybe even three.

Maybe even only two.

Again, there was no warning. To start the bottom of the fourth, Kershaw's command vanished. He walked George Springer, and after a deep fly out by Alex Bregman, the suddenly struggling lefty allowed a single to José Altuve, an RBI double to Carlos Correa, and a stunning, three-run, game-tying homer by Yuli Gurriel—the eighth round-tripper allowed by Kershaw in the playoffs and 31st of the calendar year.

NL Rookie of the Year Cody Bellinger countered with a three-run homer to give Kershaw a second chance at glory, but with two out in the bottom of the fifth, he walked Springer and Bregman, forcing his exit from the game in favor of Kenta Maeda, who had been unscored upon in the postseason as a right-handed relief specialist. Altuve blasted Maeda's eighth pitch for a three-run homer, and once again, ultimate playoff salvation eluded Kershaw, who was unable to hold two leads or stop the bleeding when he needed to. The Dodgers lost one of the most unfathomable, unforgettable games in World Series history, 13–12 in 10 innings. So close to returning home with a 3–2 Series lead for what would have likely been a coronation, the Dodgers were practically shattered, Kershaw among the wreckage.

"You want to be good every time you go out there, and this postseason I felt like I threw the ball pretty well," Kershaw said. "But yeah, that was tough, no doubt. So it's something that I'll live with."

Picking up the pieces, the Dodgers returned to Los Angeles now as underdogs, but their comeback, 3–1 victory in Game 6 set the stage for an all-hands-on-deck Game 7. "I can go 27 innings," Kershaw stated plainly, putting Game 5 far behind him. "Whatever they need." Hyperbole aside, some first-guessed that if the Dodgers were going to pitch Kershaw at all, they should start him, even on two days' rest. But Los Angeles had Darvish, whose Game 3 beatdown didn't change the fact that he had been acquired specifically to help Kershaw pitch the Dodgers to a title. Yet for the second game in a row, Darvish couldn't survive past the second inning, and when Kershaw entered at the top of the third, the Dodgers already trailed 5–0.

Kershaw pitched superbly over his four shutout innings of relief, amplifying the drumbeat that he should have started Game 7. In a weird way, the longstanding narrative questioning his postseason mettle crashed into the broader one that despite everything, this remained the best pitcher in baseball, a collision that left almost no one satisfied outside of Houston.

The 2017 season brought Kershaw closer than ever to his dream of winning the World Series, brought his admirers closer than ever to their dream of validation, once and for all. In the end, the Dodgers pushed across only one run despite 12 baserunners, losing Game 7 by a 5–1 score, and a team and a pitcher that had gone further than any from Los Angeles since 1988 fell one game short.

"Maybe one of these days I won't fail, we won't fail, and we'll win one of these things," Kershaw said. "It's hard. You go through this much effort to win that many games against this many good teams and it's…I mean, I hope to get to this point again."

Kershaw has had playoff moments spectacular and devastating, lucky and unlucky. His legacy stands to be greater than Koufax's on one level, but without a World Series victory, there would be that touch of Newcombe and Sutton, the greatest Dodger pitchers to go winless in the postseason. In his thirties, would the ultimate vindication come for Kershaw? What can he do to keep sane while wondering?

"You try to think about all the individual stuff you do, it's impossible," Kershaw says. "You just try to block that out, forget about last year. Just come in, try to win, and whether you do or not, forget about it and pitch again five days later.

"Just understanding how short a career is, even if you have a long period, even if you have a 15-year career, it's still 15 years of your entire life. To just understand that baseball is kind of a moment in your lifetime helps me enjoy it, helps me not to have any bad days in the field."

The future will tell its own story. The mystery and wonder will carry on.

No matter what happens, there will always remain the memory of seeing Kershaw, the greatest pitcher of his generation, potentially every generation, with the best adjusted ERA for a starter in history, as the flagbearer of a tradition arcing across two cities and beyond seven decades. In all of sports, Clayton Kershaw embodied one of the greatest, most reliable joys there is: the sight of a Dodger, dressed in white and blue on a pristine field at Dodger Stadium, taking the mound.

Acknowledgments

FOR MY PREVIOUS BOOK, *100 Things Dodgers Fans Should Know & Do Before They Die*, I conducted a few valuable interviews, though that project was largely research-based. But when envisioning *Brothers in Arms*, I realized I wanted to learn as much as I could directly from the pitchers about whom I was writing and the people who toiled alongside them: teammates, coaches, managers, general managers, owners, reporters, and broadcasters. My foremost thanks go to each and every one who took the time to speak with me. Not only did the conversations give the book life, each was a pleasure in and of itself, and I will cherish the sound of their voices lingering in my mind. Special thanks to those who helped connect me with this pantheon of greats, most notably Steve Brener and Peter O'Malley.

When an interview wasn't available, that meant going back to the historical record. Along with every author whose name is credited—gratefully, I should say—in the bibliography, there's an anonymous person who contributed to the preservation of articles in the archives of the *Brooklyn Eagle*, *Los Angeles Times*, *The New York Times*, and *Sports Illustrated* (my four primary sources), as well as other places. Time traveling through those pieces and bringing those worlds back to the present encompassed so much of the fun of writing *Brothers in Arms*. In addition, I wouldn't have been able to write this book without Baseball-Reference.com—and even if I had, it wouldn't have been nearly as easy to do nor as informative to produce. If Baseball Reference did nothing else besides putting annual and career statistics in context, adjusted for park and era, it would be a godsend, and yet it does so much more. When the machines take over the planet, I hope they make Baseball Reference king. (FanGraphs received many loving searches as well.)

For creating the opportunity and offering me encouragement to write this book in the first place, I'd like to thank Adam Motin and Josh Williams of Triumph Books, as well as my literary agent, Jeff Gerecke. It's been one of my greatest joys to be a published author, and they've made it possible. I also owe a huge debt to Joe Davis for contributing the foreword. His warmth and kindness while stepping into the most pressure-packed broadcasting legacy imaginable should be a lesson to us all, and I feel fortunate I can say "I knew him when" in the early years of what will certainly be a robust career.

I wanted to tell this story of the Dodger pitching tradition with meaning and authority, and that of course meant seeking help with all my blind spots. Ken Arneson, Alex Belth, Eric Enders, Jay Jaffe, Mark Langill, Craig Minami, Mike Petriello, Craig Phillips, Robert Schweppe, Brent Shyer, Sam Sokol, Eric Stephen, Bob Timmermann, Josh Wilker, and Toby Zwikel all offered valuable suggestions and (thank goodness) corrections. I'm indebted to them and just grateful to call them friends, really. I also want to thank Chuck Culpepper, Chantal Dolan, Steven Gaydos, Scott Grogin, Laura Hardy, Rick Kissell, Molly Knight, Chris Leavell, Ken Levine, Stu Levine, Brian Lowry, Cynthia Littleton, AJ Marechal, Mitch Metcalf, Gary Miereanu, Stuart Oldham, Davidson Pattiz, Mike Schneider, Christine Shaw, Bill Shaikin, Tanya Trumbull, Andy Wallenstein, Ray Ydoyaga, and Jean Yoo for their friendship, support, encouragement, and occasional therapy.

In December 2013, the Dodgers themselves hired me to oversee their editorial content, a job that everyone logically assumed would be the last I would ever need or want, and I hardly had reason to contradict them. But I have always bounced between sports and entertainment in my writing and editing career, and when an opportunity came up for me to join Showtime in 2017, I took Branch Rickey's advice and released myself from baseball too early rather than possibly too late. Nevertheless,

ACKNOWLEDGMENTS 373

I want to thank everyone with the Dodgers—including but not limited to Cat Belanger, Erik Braverman, Yvonne Carrasco, Jon Chapper, Steve Cilladi, Tom Darin, Erin Edwards, Keira Emerson, Steve Ethier, Julian Gooden, Ellen Harrigan, Nancy Bea Hefley, Joe Jareck, Desiree Juarez, Stan Kasten, Matt Mesa, Greg Morrison, Cary Osborne, Jesus Quinonez, Cheryl Rampy, Antonio Gandara Rivera, Jess Rosales, Lon Rosen, Dieter Ruehle, Alanna Rizzo, Corey Schimmel, David Siegel, Janet Marie Smith, Jon SooHoo, Daisuke Sugiura, Alex Tamin, Greg Taylor, Erick Vasquez, Shelley Wagner, Erica Weston, Nichol Whiteman, Bob Wolfe, Ross Yoshida, and Michael Young—for one of the most special experiences anyone could ever have. Frankly, I'd also like to thank Dodger Stadium itself for being the most incredible place to call my office. I'll always miss the opportunity to spend a midday break gazing out onto that field, not to mention having my own parking spot!

Thanks to everyone who has read my work on the Dodgers over the years, online (especially the Dodger Thoughts crew) and in print. I've never stopped being thrilled that anyone pays any attention at all. Thank you for all the companionship and feedback. Just be nice on Twitter, okay?

To my parents, Wally and Sheila, to my siblings and their spouses, Greg and Beth, Robyn and Gwin, and to all my extended family, thanks for all your love (which I send right back to you) and for always, always being there for me.

Finally, there's the fearsome foursome. The home crew. I'll be honest with you—they didn't help me on this book at all. Nope, not a bit. Well, except for the fact that they are my reason for living. In one respect, I couldn't wait for this book to be done, because it meant that the long streak of nights and weekends, holed up away from those four people in what passes for our home office, would abate. If you don't see another book from me right away, the explanation will be simple—my daughter and two sons are racing through time, and I want to feel like I can join my wife in spending time with them undistracted before it's too late. In any case, I'm proud of this book, thankful for all who helped me with it, but without Dana, Lilah, Casey, and Dash, it wouldn't be nearly the same. Love you guys.

Interviews

Fred Claire
Eric Enders
Carl Erskine
Orel Hershiser
Rick Honeycutt
Burt Hooton
Charlie Hough
Jaime Jarrín
Tommy John
Clayton Kershaw

Molly Knight
Mark Langill
Tommy Lasorda
Ross Newhan
Peter O'Malley
Claude Osteen
Chan Ho Park
Joe Posnanski
Ross Porter
Jerry Reuss

Eno Sarris
Mike Scioscia
Bill Singer
John Thorn
Jeff Torborg
Ismael Valdez
Fernando Valenzuela
Steve Yeager

Bibliography

Pregame: The Ancestors
Thorn, John. "Jim Creighton." *Society of American Baseball Research Baseball Biography Project* (sabr.org/bioproject).
Ward, Geoffrey C. and Ken Burns. *Baseball: An Illustrated History*. New York: Alfred A. Knopf 2010.
Faber, Charles F. "Bob Caruthers." *SABR Baseball Biography Project*.
Nemec, David. "Brickyard Kennedy." *SABR Baseball Biography Project*.
Enders, Eric. "Nap Rucker." *SABR Baseball Biography Project*.
Bennett, John. "Jeff Pfeffer." *SABR Baseball Biography Project*.
Mansch, Larry. "Rube Marquard." *SABR Baseball Biography Project*.
Honig, Donald. *The Man in the Dugout: Fifteen Big League Managers Speak Their Minds*. Lincoln: University of Nebraska Press 1977.
Faber, Charles F. "Burleigh Grimes." *SABR Baseball Biography Project*.
James, Bill. *The New Bill James Historical Baseball Abstract*. New York: The Free Press 2001.
Kavanagh, Jack and Norman L. Macht. *Uncle Robbie*. Cleveland: SABR 1999.
"Dazzy Vance." Baseball Hall of Fame website (baseballhall.org).
Smith, Red. *To Absent Friends*. New York: Atheneum 1982.
Stout, Glenn and Richard A. Johnson. *The Dodgers: 120 Years of Dodgers Baseball*. New York: Houghton Mifflin 2004.
Cohen, Alan. "Van Lingle Mungo." *SABR Baseball Biography Project*.
Chadwick, Bruce and David M. Spindel. *The Dodgers: Memories and Memorabilia From Brooklyn to L.A.* New York: Abbeville 1993.
McCue, Andy. "Branch Rickey." *SABR Baseball Biography Project*.
Farrington, Dick. "Branch Rickey, Defending Farms, Says Stark Necessity Forced System." *The Sporting News* 1 December 1932.

Part One: The Kings of Brooklyn
Durocher, Leo. "Durocher Says: Branca Fooled Cards—And Me Too!" *Brooklyn Eagle* 15 September 1946.
Burr, Harold C. "Tense Eighth Spoils Branca Bid for Fame." *Brooklyn Eagle* 19 July 1947.
Golenbock, Peter. *Bums: An Oral History of the Brooklyn Dodgers*. Chicago: Contemporary 2000.
Prager, Joshua Harris. "Was the '51 Giants Comeback a Miracle, or Did They Simply Steal the Pennant?" *The Wall Street Journal* 31 January 2001.
Noble, Marty. "Branca, Pitcher of 'Shot Heard 'Round the World' Fame, Dies." MLB.com 23 November 2016.
Corbett, Warren. "Preacher Roe." *SABR Baseball Biography Project*.
Kahn, Roger. *The Boys of Summer*. New York: Harper & Row 1971.
Young, Dick. "The Outlawed Spitball Was My Money Pitch." *Sports Illustrated* 4 July 1955.
McGowen, Roscoe. "'Supreme Artistry' of Roe's Performance on Mound Hailed By Team-Mates." *New York Times* 7 October 1949.

Golenbock, Peter. *Bums: An Oral History of the Brooklyn Dodgers.* Chicago: Contemporary 2000.
McGowan, Roscoe. "Brooks' Injured Campanella May Be Replaced by Walker in 2d Game Today." *New York Times* 2 October 1951.
McGowan, Roscoe. "Phils Beat Dodgers for Flag." *New York Times* 2 October 1950.
Holmes, Tommy. "Is Newcombe Ailment Case of Imaginitis?" *Brooklyn Eagle* 14 September 1951.
Shapiro, Michael. *The Last Good Season: Brooklyn, the Dodgers, and Their Final Pennant Race Together.* New York: Doubleday 2003.
Creamer, Robert. "Subject: Don Newcombe." *Sports Illustrated* 22 August 1955.
Rampersad, Arnold. *Jackie Robinson: A Biography.* New York: Knopf 1997.
"Henrich Stole Leaf From Stengel's Book." *Brooklyn Eagle* 6 October 1949.
Schweppe, Robert. "Q&A: Don Newcombe."*Walter O'Malley: The Official Website* (walteromalley.com).
Holmes, Tommy. "It Just Wasn't Meant For Dodgers to Win." *Brooklyn Eagle* 4 October 1951.
Campanella, Roy. *It's Good To Be Alive.* Boston: Little, Brown 1959.
James, Bill. *The New Bill James Historical Baseball Abstract.* New York: The Free Press 2001.
Prince, Carl E. *Brooklyn's Dodgers: The Bums, the Borough, and the Best of Baseball, 1947–1957.* New York: Oxford University Press 1997.
McGowen, Roscoe. "Brooks Disappointed, Not Discouraged by Defeat and Showing of Newcombe." *New York Times* 29 September 1955.
Drebinger, John. "Dodgers Triumph, 5 to 3." *New York Times* 3 October 1955.
D'Antonio, Michael. *Forever Blue: The True Story of Walter O'Malley, Baseball's Most Controversial Owner, and the Dodgers of Brooklyn and Los Angeles.* New York: Riverhead 2009.
Gross, Milton. "The Long Ride Home." *New York Post* 11 October 1956.
Young, A.S. Doc. "Don Newcombe Vs. The Booze." *Los Angeles Sentinel* 4 February 1982.
Welch, Bob and George Vecsey. *Five O'Clock Comes Early: A Young Man's Battle with Alcoholism.* New York: Quill 1986.
Young, Dick. "Walter Alston's School for Boys." *Sports Illustrated* 2 May 1955.
Creamer, Robert. "The Year, the Moment and Johnny Podres." *Sports Illustrated* 2 January 1956.
Bennett, Bob and John Bennett and Robert S. Bennett. *Johnny Podres: Brooklyn's Only Yankee Killer.* Bloomington: Rooftop 2007.
McCarver, Tim with Danny Peary. *Tim McCarver's Baseball for Brain Surgeons and Other Fans.* New York: Villard 1998.
Finch, Frank. "Podres Passes Up Final Games." *Los Angeles Times* 27 September 1961.
———. "Cards Slam Back Door on Dodgers." *Los Angeles Times* 1 October 1962.
Hafner, Dan. "Stunned Dodgers Can't Believe It." *Los Angeles Times* 1 October 1962.
Murray, Jim. "Break Up the Dodgers!" *Los Angeles Times* 4 October 1963.
Associated Press. "'I Said I Was Tired ... Why Kid Yourself? ... We Had Perranoski.'" *Los Angeles Times* 4 October 1963.
Drysdale, Don and Bob Verdi. *Once a Bum, Always a Dodger: My Life in Baseball from Brooklyn to Los Angeles.* New York: St. Martin's 1990.
Koppett, Leonard. "Witherbee's Hero Does It Again." *New York Times* 4 October 1963.
"Joy in Flatbush." *New York Times* 4 October 1963.

Part Two: The Two Emperors

Osborne, Cary. "Nickname Game: Dodgers Beat Out Kings in 1932 Vote." *Dodger Insider* 13 November 2014.
Holmes, Thomas. "Brooklyn Baseball Club Will Officially Nickname Them 'Dodgers.'" *Brooklyn Daily Eagle* 23 January 1932.
Koufax, Sandy with Ed Linn. *Koufax.* New York: Viking 1966.
Leavy, Jane. *Sandy Koufax: A Lefty's Legacy.* New York: Harper 2002.
"Tomahawks Unbeaten in C.C. 200 Court Play." *Brooklyn Eagle* 13 February 1951.

BIBLIOGRAPHY

Anderson, Dave. "Koufax, Boro Sandlot Star, Newest Dodger." *Brooklyn Eagle* 15 December 1954.
United Press International. "Sister Taught Sandy How to Pitch." *Los Angeles Times* 12 October 1966.
Weisman, Jon. "When Sandy Koufax Knew." *Dodger Insider* 6 March 2014.
Murphy, Jimmy. "Jimmy Murphy's Column." *Brooklyn Eagle* 17 August 1954.
Osborne, Cary. "The Scouting Report on Kershaw, Koufax and Clemente." *Dodger Insider* 4 December 2014.
Anderson, Dave. "Sandy Koufax and the Sistine Chapel." *New York Times* 28 January 1979.
Associated Press. "New Pitching Prospect for Dodgers." *New York Times* 14 December 1954.
Drebinger, John. "Dodgers Split with Pirates." *New York Times* 7 July 1955.
Union Oil Company of California. "Sandy Koufax." *The 1961 Dodger Family—Union Oil Brochure*.
McGowen, Roscoe. "Dodgers Win: Koufax Is Victor." *New York Times* 28 August 1955.
McGowen, Roscoe. "Brooklyn-Bred 'Bonus Baby' Is Coming of Age." *New York Times* 29 August 1955.
McGowen, Roscoe. "Koufax Blanks Pittsburgh; Brooks Need 7 for Pennant." *New York Times* 4 September 1955.
Hoffman, Jeane. "Spirit of Flatbush Reigns in Hollywood." *Los Angeles Times* 8 June 1958.
Finch, Frank. "'Koufax Case' Baffles Alston." *Los Angeles Times* 3 May 1959.
Wolf, Al. "How O'Malley Saved Koufax." *Los Angeles Times* 24 September 1966.
Florence, Mal. "'Best Game and Luckiest I Ever Pitched,' Says Koufax." *Los Angeles Times* 1 September 1959.
Finch, Frank. "Koufax Fans 18 for Record." *Los Angeles Times* 1 September 1959.
Florence, Mal. "Koufax's Name Linked with Baseball Greats." *Los Angeles Times* 2 September 1959.
Finch, Frank. "Koufax Battles Control Problem." *Los Angeles Times* 13 March 1960.
Page, Don. "Sandy Is Dandy." *Los Angeles Times* 11 June 1960.
"Man With Golden Charm." *New York Times* 3 October 1963.
Delsohn, Steve. *True Blue: The Dramatic History of the Los Angeles Dodgers, Told by the Men Who Lived It*. New York: HarperCollins 2001.
Finch, Frank. "Sherry and Koufax Fined." *Los Angeles Times* 21 March 1961.
Maule, Tex. "The Young Pitchers Take Command." *Sports Illustrated* 26 June 1961.
"Koufax Says He May Be Holdout." *Los Angeles Times* 9 February 1962.
Finch, Frank. "Sandy Impressive in First Effort." *Los Angeles Times* 1 March 1963.
Hafner, Dan. "Koufax Lost to Dodgers for Two Weeks." *Los Angeles Times* 19 July 1962.
Murray, Jim. "A Finger of Fate." *Los Angeles Times* 7 September 1962.
Associated Press. "Koufax Fears He May Be Out for Year." *Los Angeles Times* 25 August 1962.
Brody, Tom C. "A Miller-Hiller-Haller-Holler-Lujah Twist." *Sports Illustrated* 17 September 1962.
Finch, Frank. "Sandy's Finger, Arm OK—and How!!" *Los Angeles Times* 12 May 1963.
———. "Sandy Sizzles, Bombers Fizzle, 5–2." *Los Angeles Times* 3 October 1963.
Koppett, Leonard. "Koufax Stopped Throwing Curve When Elbow Began to Tighten in Mid-Game." *New York Times* 3 October 1963.
Angell, Roger. "Four Taverns in the Town." *The New Yorker* 26 October 1963.
Povich, Shirley. "Yanks Agog at Sandy: 'How'd He Lose Five?'...Yogi." *Los Angeles Times* 3 October 1963.
Finch, Frank. "Sandy Signs for $70,000 as Salary Stalemate Ends." *Los Angeles Times* 29 February 1964.
Finch, Frank. "Nobody's Perfect—Sandy Walks One!" *Los Angeles Times* 5 June 1964.
Associated Press. "Sandy Finds Flaw." *Los Angeles Times* 5 June 1964.
Finch, Frank. "Koufax Flies Home With Ailing Elbow." *Los Angeles Times* 2 April 1965.
Jares, Joe. "Sandy Makes a Pitch for Posterity." *Sports Illustrated* 2 August 1965.
Maher, Charles. "Even Koufax Admits Game 'Nearly Perfect.'" *Los Angeles Times* 10 September 1965.
"Los Angeles Dodgers 1, Chicago Cubs 0." Retrosheet.org.
Crowe, Jerry. "Pitcher Perfect: 25 Years Ago Tonight, Koufax Mowed Down All 27 Cubs to Make His Fourth No-Hitter Even More Special." *Los Angeles Times* 9 September 1990.
Finch, Frank. "It's All Over!" *Los Angeles Times* 3 October 1965.

Zimmerman, Paul. "Weary Koufax Still Calmest in Midst of Victory Celebration." *Los Angeles Times* 3 October 1965.
Angell, Roger. "The Odd Couple." *The New Yorker* 30 October 1965.
Littwin, Mike. "Koufax: 'It Was Time To Go Get a Job.'" *Los Angeles Times* 25 March 1979.
"Koufax and Drysdale Sign Pacts—as Movie Actors." *Los Angeles Times* 18 March 1966.
Maher, Charles. "Dodgers Paying Stiff Price Now for Big Holdout." *Los Angeles Times* 6 May 1966.
Finch, Frank. "Koufax: The Dodgers Goldflinger: Sandy to Lure Million Fans in 30-Win Bid." *Los Angeles Times* 1 July 1966.
Maher, Charles. "Koufax Packs 'em in as Author, Too." *Los Angeles Times* 7 September 1966.
United Press International. "Cy Young Award Goes to Koufax (Who Else?)" *Los Angeles Times* 2 November 1966.
Associated Press. "Clemente Barely Tops Koufax in MVP Vote." *Los Angeles Times* 17 November 1966.
Maher, Charles. "Koufax Quits Because of Ailing Arm." *Los Angeles Times* 19 November 1966.
Murray, Jim. "Baseball the Loser." *Los Angeles Times* 24 November 1966.
Finch, Frank. "Koufax Signs $1 Million Pact as Commentator." *Los Angeles Times* 30 December 1966.
Roseboro, John with Bill Libby. *Glory Days with the Dodgers: And Other Days with Others*. New York: Atheneum 1978.
Newhan, Ross. "Koufax Rejoins Dodgers, Keeps His Private Life." *Los Angeles Times* 26 January 1979.
Verducci, Tom. "The Left Arm of God." *Sports Illustrated* 12 July 1999.
Smith, Claire. "At Age 49, Koufax Still Stops Show on Mound." *Hartford Courant* 7 April 1985.
Shirley, Bill. "Still Elegant After All These Years." *Los Angeles Times* 4 March 1986.
Weisman, Jon. "Sandy Koufax Brings Dodger Fans the Happiest of Answers." *Dodger Thoughts* 28 February 2010.
Drysdale, Don with Bob Verdi. *Once a Bum, Always a Dodger: My Life in Baseball From Brooklyn to Los Angeles*. New York: St. Martin's 1990.
McGowen, Roscoe. "Drysdale of Dodgers Scatters Nine Hits in Posting Triumph Over Phillies." *New York Times* 24 April 1956.
Snider, Duke with Bill Gilbert. *The Duke of Flatbush*. New York: Kensington 1988.
Horn, Huston. "Ex–Bad Boy's Big Year." *Sports Illustrated* 20 August 1962.
Alston, Walter with Si Burick. *Alston and the Dodgers*. New York: Doubleday 1966.
Neyer, Rob. *Rob Neyer's Big Book of Baseball Legends*. New York: Fireside 2008.
"Buzzie and Big D Go At It In L.A." *Sports Illustrated* 29 August 1966.
Weisman, Jon. "Remembering '65: Marichal Threatens Drysdale, Drysdale Blows Bubbles." *Dodger Insider* 20 May 2015.
Finch, Frank. "Marichal Warns Big D; Drysdale 'Prepared.'" *Los Angeles Times* 2 May 1965.

Part Three: The Post-Koufax Generation

DiGiovanna, Mike. "Sutton Finally Gets Hall Pass." *Los Angeles Times* 6 January 1998.
Boswell, Thomas. "Injustice Corrected." *Los Angeles Times* 11 January 1998.
Chass, Murray. "Choose One: Koufax or Sutton?" *New York Times* 11 January 1998.
Fimrite, Ron. "'God May Be a Football Fan.'" *Sports Illustrated* 12 July 1982.
Downey, Mike. "324 Wins Mean No Ribbing Here." *Los Angeles Times* 7 January 1998.
Littwin, Mike. "The Dodger 'Dean' Is Still an Obsessed Pitcher." *Los Angeles Times* 27 June 1980.
Newhan, Ross. "Sutton Is Accused of Rough Stuff as Dodgers Lose, 4–2." *Los Angeles Times* 20 May 1974.
Finch, Frank. "Scouts' Sales Talk Landed Don Sutton." *Los Angeles Times* 7 July 1966.
Mann, Jack. "And There Were the Dodgers in Third Place." *Sports Illustrated* 27 June 1966.
Finch, Frank. "Astros' Staub Nips Dodgers Again, 4–2." *Los Angeles Times* 15 April 1966.
Finch, Frank. "Dodgers Belt Roberts, Win One for Sutton." *Los Angeles Times* 19 April 1966.
Finch, Frank. "Sutton Slings, Swats Dodgers to 5–0 Romp." *Los Angeles Times* 12 May 1966.

Murray, Jim. "Sutton Finds His Location." *Los Angeles Times* 2 August 1998.
Finch, Frank. "Sutton Hurt as Dodgers Whip Giants." *Los Angeles Times* 6 September 1966.
Hafner, Dan. "Dodgers Open Tonight; Sutton Cut." *Los Angeles Times* 10 April 1968.
———. "Mets End Dodger Winning Streak." *Los Angeles Times*. 11 June 1968.
———. "Dodger Happiness Is Sutton 1-Hitter." *Los Angeles Times* 2 May 1969.
Newhan, Ross. "Giants Hang On With 2–1 Win Over Sutton, Dodgers." *Los Angeles Times* 27 September 1969.
Wiebusch, John. "Parker's Single in 10th Gives Sutton 1–0 Win." *Los Angeles Times* 18 July 1969.
Wiebusch, John. Dodgers' Pitching Gives Alston 'Pain in Neck;' Cards Win, 11–8." *Los Angeles Times* 18 August 1970.
Newhan, Ross. "Hard-Headedness Helped Put Sutton Into the Big Leagues." *Los Angeles Times* 23 March 1971.
———. "Sutton's Injury Dampens 3–0 Win Over Mets." *Los Angeles Times* 6 June 1971.
———. "Sutton Finally Wins One, Shuts Out Braves." *Los Angeles Times* 13 May 1971.
———. "Sutton Just Misses No-Hitter in 4–0 Victory Over Astros." *Los Angeles Times* 20 June 1971.
Rapoport, Ron. "Sutton Ends Hitch, Beats Cards, 4–2." *Los Angeles Times* 9 August 1971.
Weisman, Jon. "Don Sutton's Better-Than-Fernando 1972 season." *Dodger Insider* 16 May 2014.
Newhan, Ross. "Five Dodgers Make NL All-Star Squad; Russell Left Off." *Los Angeles Times* 19 July 1973.
———. "Sutton Gets 6th Shutout; Padres Succumb, 6–0." *Los Angeles Times* 7 August 1972.
———. "Dodgers Clinch Second Place; Aaron 0-for-4." *Los Angeles Times* 26 September 1973.
———. "Sutton Puzzles Sutton But Phillies Solve Him." *Los Angeles Times* 5 May 1974.
———. "His Slump Is Serious but Sutton Isn't Critical." *Los Angeles Times* 18 June 1974.
Prugh, Jeff. "Mike Marshall 'Missing'... but Sutton Didn't Need Him." *Los Angeles Times* 6 October 1974.
Murray, Jim. "Sutton's Masterpiece Gets the Quiet Awe It Deserves." *Los Angeles Times* 6 October 1974.
Prugh, Jeff. "Signs Were Right for Flag Raising; 'Four Games to Go!'" *Los Angeles Times* 10 October 1974.
Prugh, Jeff. "Sutton Adds One-Hitter to Collection." *Los Angeles Times* 16 April 1975.
Newhan, Ross. "Sutton May Have to Wait Until Next Year for Trade." *Los Angeles Times* 13 June 1976.
———. "Sutton, Seaver Trade Studied." *Los Angeles Times* 29 March 1976.
———. "Sutton Allows Nothing and Gets Nothing." *Los Angeles Times* 18 September 1976.
———. "Sutton Finds 20 Reasons to Throw a Party." *Los Angeles Times* 23 September 1976.
Delsohn, Steve. *True Blue: The Dramatic History of the Los Angeles Dodgers, Told by the Men Who Lived It.* New York: HarperCollins 2001.
"Sutton and Lasorda on Alaskan Junket." *Los Angeles Times* 16 February 1967.
Newhan, Ross. "Little D's Big Day." *Los Angeles Times* 26 July 1998.
"TV Deal Puts Sutton Closer to Dodgers." *Los Angeles Times* 8 October 1976.
Newhan, Ross. "Sutton Finds Million Reasons to Stay." *Los Angeles Times* 20 November 1976.
Merry, Don. "Unhappy? Sutton Won't Deny It." *Los Angeles Times* 17 March 1977.
Newhan, Ross. "Sutton Follows a Blowup With Fifth One-Hitter, 7–0." *Los Angeles Times* 19 August 1977.
———. "Sutton Paints Dodger Win by the Numbers." *Los Angeles Times* 30 June 1978.
———. "Little D Starts Measuring Up to Big D Tonight." *Los Angeles Times* 7 April 1978.
Ostler, Scott. "'I'll Sue, Says Sutton After His Ejection in St. Louis." *Los Angeles Times* 15 July 1978.
"Sutton Gets Off With Warning, Pitches Tonight." *Los Angeles Times* 18 July 1978.
Ostler, Scott. "No. 200 Nice but Sutton Has Other Goals in Mind." *Los Angeles Times* 19 July 1978.
———. "Suddenly, the Hugging Turns to Punching." *Los Angeles Times* 21 August 1978.
Boswell, Thomas. "Dodger Incident Smacks of Schoolyard Scuffle." *Washington Post* 26 August 1978.
Newhan, Ross. "Sutton: From L.A. Jeers to Bronx Cheers." *Los Angeles Times* 13 October 1978.

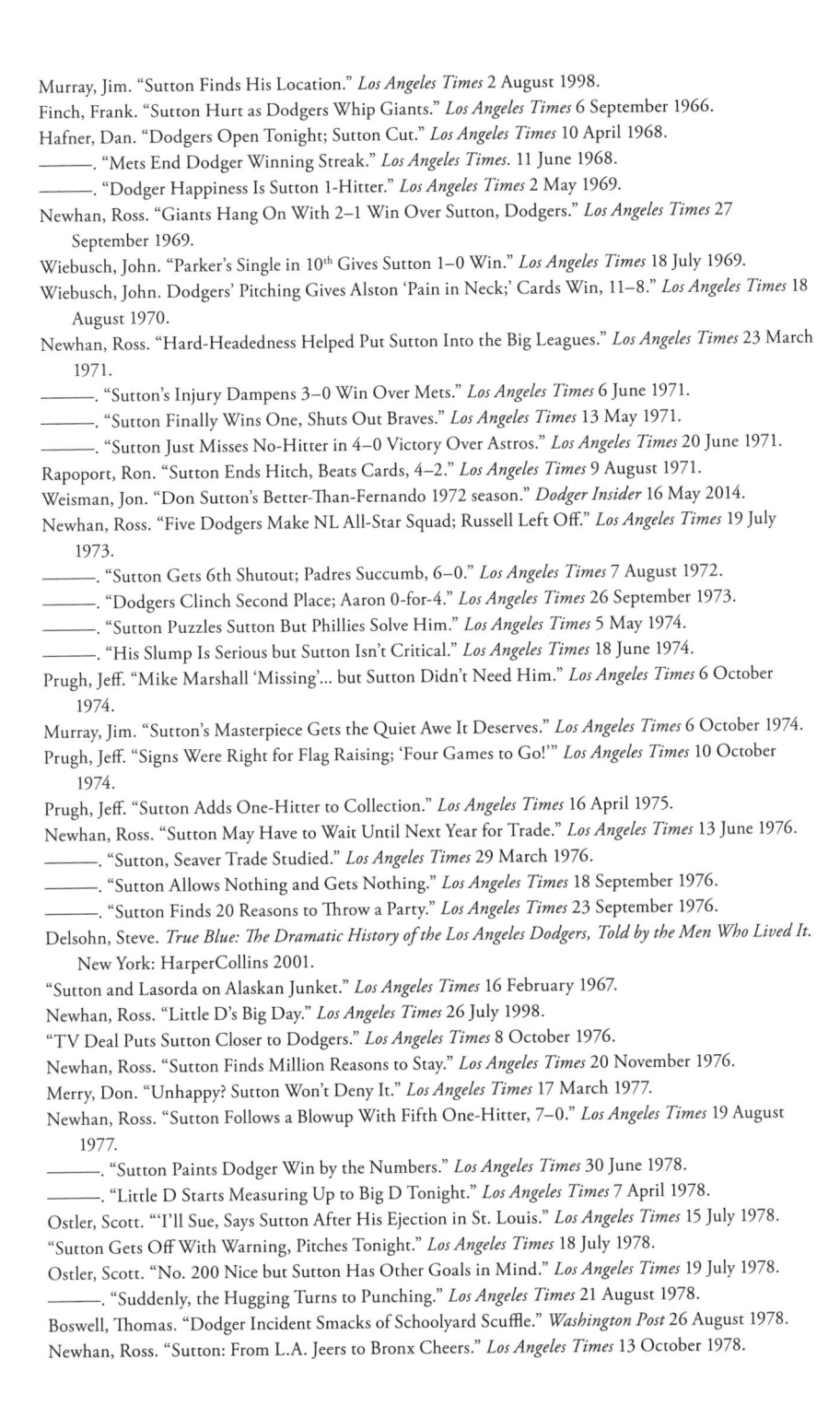

Ostler, Scott. "Dodgers Agree Yankees Great." *Los Angeles Times* 18 October 1978.
"Sutton: 'I Don't Have to Put Up With It.'" *Los Angeles Times* 7 June 1979.
Littwin, Mike. "Sutton Retires a Record, Then Talks About Retiring," *Los Angeles Times* 6 August 1979.
Hamilton, Tom. "Sutton Making His Pitch for Broadcasting Career." *Los Angeles Times* 9 August 1979.
"1979 National League Championship Series Game 1." NBC Sports 2 October 1979.
Hall, John. "Sutton's Reappearing Act Dodgertown Comedy Hit." *Los Angeles Times* 9 March 1980.
Associated Press. "Sutton Is Set to Don Pinstripes." *Los Angeles Times* 15 March 1980.
Hoffer, Richard. "Yank Deal Falls Through; Sutton Still a Dodger." *Los Angeles Times* 16 March 2016.
Littwin, Mike. "Sutton Trade Rumors Revived." *Los Angeles Times* 5 March 1980.
———. "Smith Goes on Disabled List…" *Los Angeles Times* 26 August 1980.
———. "As Astros Hit the Wall, the Dodgers Clear It—Again." *Los Angeles Times* 6 October 1980.
———. "Sutton Isn't Shutting Out the Dodgers Just Yet." *Los Angeles Times* 18 October 1980.
Heisler, Mark. "Winfield, Sutton Are 10s in Draft; Tug Is a Zero." *Los Angeles Times* 14 November 1980.
Newhan, Ross. "Sutton Moves Up a Notch, Signs with the Astros." *Los Angeles Times* 4 December 1980.
Heisler, Mark. "Dodger Offense Explodes for Two Hits." *Los Angeles Times* 28 September 1981.
Heisler, Mark. "The Astros Lose Sutton, Game, 6–1." *Los Angeles Times* 3 October 1981.
McManis, Sam. "Don Sutton Comes Full Circle." *Los Angeles Times* 20 March 1988.
Claire, Fred with Steve Springer. *My 30 Years in Dodger Blue*. Chicago: Sports Publishing LLC 2004.
McManis, Sam. "Dodgers Hand Sutton His Walking Papers and Call Up Martinez." *Los Angeles Times* 11 August 1988.
McManis, Sam. "Against Claire's Wishes, Sutton Talks to Astros." *Los Angeles Times* 10 August 1988.
Newhan, Ross. "Little D's Big Day." *Los Angeles Times* 26 July 1998.

Part Four: The Modern Classicists
"Connected With…Tommy Lasorda." SportsNet LA 3 May 2014.
Weisman, Jon. "Tales of Tommy Lasorda." *Dodger Insider* 3 May 2014.
James, Bill. *The Bill James Guide to Baseball Managers From 1870 to Today*. New York: Scribner 1997.
Jaffe, Chris. *Evaluating Baseball's Managers*. Jefferson, NC: McFarland 2010.
Fimrite, Ron. "The Week That Wasn't." *Sports Illustrated* 17 April 1972.
Rapoport, Ron. "Tommy John: He's No Longer the Villain in Dick Allen Trade." *Los Angeles Times* 14 August 1973.
Newhan, Ross. "Golf—It Helped Make John a Better Pitcher." *Los Angeles Times* 23 April 1974.
Prugh, Jeff. "John Keeps His Spirits Up Despite Pain." *Los Angeles Times* 22 July 1974.
Newhan, Ross. "Tommy John: Portrait in Blue." *Los Angeles Times* 3 October 1974.
Prugh, Jeff. "Tommy John Works for Day That May Never Come." *Los Angeles Times* 17 July 1975.
Newhan, Ross. "Tommy John Passes a Test Perfectly." *Los Angeles Times* 24 September 1975.
Murray, Jim. "The Bionic Pitcher." *Los Angeles Times* 7 November 1975.
Newhan, Ross. "Tommy John's Back, a Successful Loser." *Los Angeles Times* 17 April 1976.
———. "The Anatomy of a Trade." *Los Angeles Times* 10 December 1972.
Murray, Jim. "Ho-Ho-Ho! Santa Leaves Baseball Holding Bag." *Los Angeles Times* 25 December 1975.
Miller, Marvin. *A Whole Different Ball Game: The Sport and Business of Baseball*. New York: Birch Lane 1991.
Chass, Murray. "Messersmith Awaits Third-Strike Call in Pitch for Freedom." *New York Times* 20 February 1976.
Littwin, Mike. "Candelaria Burns the Dodgers Again." *Los Angeles Times* 29 August 1979.
Golanty, Eric. "Andy Messersmith." *SABR Baseball Biography Project*.
Associated Press. "Cubs Think Hooton Could Win 20." *Los Angeles Times* 17 March 1972.
United Press International. "Cubs' Hooton Pitches No-Hitter Against Phils." *Los Angeles Times* 17 April 1972.

BIBLIOGRAPHY

Welch, Bob and George Vecsey. *Five O'Clock Comes Early: A Young Man's Battle with Alcoholism.* New York: Quill 1986.
Sabathia, CC. "My Toughest Out." *The Players' Tribune* 7 March 2016.
Angell, Roger. *Five Seasons: A Baseball Companion.* New York: Simon and Schuster 1977.
"Another Koufax? Veterans See Curveball as Welch's Next Big Challenge." *Los Angeles Times* 4 April 1979.
Reuss, Jerry. *Bring in the Right-Hander: My Twenty-Two Years in the Major Leagues.* Lincoln: University of Nebraska Press 2014.

Part Five: El Toro and the Bulldog

Montemayor, Robert. "From Mexico with Mystery: Like Everybody Else, Fernando Valenzuela Wonders How Long His Amazing Roll Can Last." *Los Angeles Times* 24 April 1981.
Heisler, Mark. "Valenzuela Making a Pitch to Start." *Los Angeles Times* 4 March 1981.
Weisman, Jon, editor. *2015 Los Angeles Dodgers Yearbook.* New York: Professional Sports Publications 2015.
Ostler, Scott. "There's a Fan Named Gordo." *Los Angeles Times* 8 September 1979.
Littwin, Mike. "Teen-Age Beer-Drinker Is Now Dodger Stopper." *Los Angeles Times* 3 October 1980.
Heisler, Mark. "Guerrero Wins Series MVP and Job." *Los Angeles Times* 6 April 1981.
———. "Did They Tell Him Batting Practice Was Over?" *Los Angeles Times* 10 April 1981.
———. "Valenzuela Keeps the Lid on the Astros, 1–0." *Los Angeles Times* 23 April 1981.
———. "Suddenly, Life Will Never Be the Same for Valenzuela." *Los Angeles Times* 26 April 1981.
Ostler, Scott. "Fernandomania." *Los Angeles Times* 27 April 1981.
Greenberg, Alan. "On Day Off, He Takes Pounding." *Los Angeles Times* 27 May 1981.
Weisman, Jon. "Thirty Years Later, Fernando Valenzuela's Legacy is His Tenacity." *Dodger Thoughts* 9 April 2011.
United Press International. "Valenzuela's Salad Night." *Los Angeles Times* 10 January 1982.
Edes, Gordon. "Valenzuela Reaches Back for a Gem." *Los Angeles Times* 24 May 1984.
———. "Valenzuela, Gooden Draw; Strawberry Settles It in 13th." *Los Angeles Times* 7 September 1985.
Ostler, Scott. "Cardinals Baffled by Fernando; Translation: He Wins." *Los Angeles Times* 10 October 1985.
McManis, Sam. "Valenzuela Disabled by Injured Left Shoulder." *Los Angeles Times* 1 August 1988.
———. "Injuries Are Adding Up for Dodgers." *Los Angeles Times* 2 October 1988.
Plaschke, Bill. "Fernando Pitches One for the First Time as He Stymies Cardinals, 6–0." *Los Angeles Times* 30 June 1990.
———. "His Feat Is No-No Big Deal to Valenzuela." *Los Angeles Times* 1 July 1990.
———. "Waive Adios to Fernando." *Los Angeles Times* 29 March 1991.
Hershiser, Orel with Jerry B. Jenkins. *Out of the Blue.* Brentwood, TN: Wolgemuth & Hyatt 1989.
Weisman, Jon. "Orel Hershiser Still the Gem You Remember." *Dodger Thoughts* 2 April 2011.
Simon, Mark. "Inside Hershiser's Scoreless Streak." ESPN.com 30 September 2013.
Kaplan, Jim. "These Dodger Kids Are On The Ball." *Sports Illustrated* 30 July 1984.
Wulf, Steve. "Deep Roots." *Sports Illustrated* 19 December 1988.

Part Six: The International Rotation

Baxter, Kevin. "Avila Led the Charge in MLB's Latin Revolution." ESPN.com 2 October 2006.
McManis, Sam. "A Dandy Dominican." *Los Angeles Times* 26 February 1988.
———. "Hershiser Gets Win, Assist as Dodgers Sweep Past Padres." *Los Angeles Times* 20 June 1988.
Downey, Mike. "Kid Pitcher Gives Dodgers a Bit of a Flashback in His First Start." *Los Angeles Times* 14 August 1988.
McManis, Sam. "Dodgers Hand Sutton His Walking Papers and Call Up Martínez." *Los Angeles Times* 11 August 1988.

Newhan, Ross. "Danny Jackson Pitches Cincinnati Past Dodgers, 5–2." *Los Angeles Times* 10 September 1988.
Edes, Gordon. "Martínez Sharp in B Game, Morgan Struggles." *Los Angeles Times* 24 March 1989.
Crowe, Jerry. "In 13 Innings, Astros Finish 4-Game Sweep." *Los Angeles Times* 5 June 1989.
———. "Delay or Not, Dodgers Get Their Sweep." *Los Angeles Times* 6 June 1989.
———. "Glavine, Braves Put Dodgers to Sleep, 3–0." *Los Angeles Times* 7 June 1989.
Plaschke, Bill. "Martínez Shuts Out Braves, 5–0." *Los Angeles Times* 16 September 1989.
———. "Martínez Strikes Out 18, Ties Koufax." *Los Angeles Times* 5 June 1990.
Dillman, Lisa. "Not a Thing Goes Right for Dodgers." *Los Angeles Times* 26 August 1992.
King, Norm. "Pedro Martínez." *SABR Baseball Biography Project.*
Plaschke, Bill. "Pedro Martínez will get first start." *Los Angeles Times* 25 September 1992.
Weisman, Jon. *100 Things Dodgers Fans Should Know & Do Before They Die.* Chicago: Triumph Books 2009.
Nightengale, Bob. "Hernandez Has Game of His Life." *Los Angeles Times* 9 July 1995.
Piazza, Mike with Lonnie Wheeler. *Long Shot.* New York: Simon & Schuster 2013.
Nightengale, Bob. "Martínez Says No to All Hitters." *Los Angeles Times* 15 July 1995.
———. "Martínez's Pain Leads to Park's Joy." *Los Angeles Times* 7 April 1996.
Klein, Gary. "Dodgers Thrown for Two Losses." *Los Angeles Times* 15 June 1998.
Reid, Jason. "Martínez Injury a Serious Concern." *Los Angeles Times* 16 June 1998.
Gutierrez, Paul. "Farewell to Some Arms for Dodgers." *Los Angeles Times* 29 March 2001.
Hudson, Maryann. "Pitcher From South Korea Signs Deal With Dodgers." *Los Angeles Times* 12 January 1994.
———. "Foreign Mission: Park Hopes to Become First Korean in Majors." *Los Angeles Times* 28 February 1994.
———. "Park Takes a Bow During His Debut." *Los Angeles Times* 8 March 1994.
———. "Dreifort, Park Are Major Players." *Los Angeles Times* 1 April 1994.
Springer, Steve. "Park Is Sent to San Antonio." *Los Angeles Times* 21 April 1994.
———. "Piazza Is Only Doubt in Rout." *Los Angeles Times* 21 July 1997
Reid, Jason. "Park Is Finishing the Season in High Gear." *Los Angeles Times* 23 September 1998.
———. "In Grand Style--Twice!" *Los Angeles Times* 24 April 1999.
———. "Dodgers Rev Up After Kick-Start." *Los Angeles Times* 6 June 1999.
Reid, Jason with Chris Foster and Bill Plaschke. "Johnson Kicks In His Support for Park." *Los Angeles Times* 6 June 1999.
Reid, Jason. "Park Is Still Feeling Groovy." *Los Angeles Times* 30 August 2000.
Adande, J.A. "Shouldn't They at Least Make Effort to Keep Park?" *Los Angeles Times* 10 November 2001.
Nightengale, Bob. "Karros, Valdes in Altercation." *Los Angeles Times* 28 April 1997.
———. "Even a Little Support Means a Lot to Valdes." *Los Angeles Times* 16 May 1997.
Reid, Jason. "Weaponless, Valdes Hits Rock Bottom." *Los Angeles Times* 20 September 1998.
———. "Malone Values Valdes' Efforts." *Los Angeles Times* 3 August 1999.
———. "It's Not Rocket Science, but Valdes Is Tough to Figure." *Los Angeles Times* 19 September 1999.
———. "Bullpen Fails Valdes, Dodgers." *Los Angeles Times* 1 June 1998.
———. "Costs Prompt Trade Deficit." *Los Angeles Times* 13 December 1999.
———. "Valdes Is Given a Six-Game Suspension for Hitting Batter." *Los Angeles Times* 9 September 2000.
Whiting, Robert. "Contract Loophole Opened Door for Nomo's Jump." *Japan Times* 10 October 2010.
Nightengale, Bob. "Umpire Watches Dodgers' Nomo Pitch, Sees a Problem." *Los Angeles Times* 29 March 1995.
———. "Dodgers' Asian Armistice." *Los Angeles Times* 22 April 1995.
———. "East Meets West for Pitcher Nomo." *Los Angeles Times* 14 February 1995.
———. "Hey Dude, Nomo Hangs Up Two Perfect Innings." *Los Angeles Times* 9 April 1995.

BIBLIOGRAPHY

———. "Nomo Set to Start at the Top." *Los Angeles Times* 18 April 1995.
———. "Nomo Debut Great, Dodger Finish Isn't." *Los Angeles Times* 18 April 1995.
Baker, Chris. "Spotlight Gets in Nomo's Eyes in Home Debut." *Los Angeles Times* 13 May 1995.
Nightengale, Bob. "The Man, the Mania: Nomo Does No Wrong." *Los Angeles Times* 30 June 1995.
———. "Nomomania Grips L.A. and Japan." *Los Angeles Times* 4 July 1995.
Jameson, Sam. "Japanese Fans Say 'Tornado' Is Their Hero." *Los Angeles Times* 12 July 1995.
Nightengale, Bob. "Nomo Comes Close to No-No." *Los Angeles Times* 18 September 1996.
Springer, Steve. "Nomo's Decline Picks Up Speed." *Los Angeles Times* 9 September 1997.
———. "Nomo Faces Elbow Surgery." *Los Angeles Times* 7 October 1997.
Plaschke, Bill. "You Can Stick a Forkball in Nomomania: It's Done." *Los Angeles Times* 31 May 1998.

Part Seven: The Hired Hands
Chass, Murray. "Dodger General Manager Resigns After Confronting Fan." *New York Times* 20 April 2001.
James, Bill and Rob Neyer. *The Neyer/James Guide to Pitchers: An Historical Compendium of Pitching, Pitchers, and Pitches*. New York: Fireside 2004.
Verducci, Tom. "Nasty Stuff." *Sports Illustrated* 29 March 1999.
Reid, Jason. "Brown Weathers Frustration With Strong Outing." *Los Angeles Times* 20 September 1999.
———. "Pitcher Not So Perfect." *Los Angeles Times* 20 July 1999.
———. "Brown's Season Is Over Early." *Los Angeles Times* 17 September 2002.
———. "Dreifort, Brown Watch Begins Again." *Los Angeles Times* 13 February 2003.
Kepner, Tyler. "High Velocity, Some Anxiety." *New York Times* 29 February 2004.
Mitchell, George J. *Report to the Commissioner of Baseball of an Independent Investigation into the Illegal Use of Steroids and Other Performance Enhancing Substances by Players in Major League Baseball*. Office of the Commissioner of Baseball 13 December 2007.
Hernandez, Dylan, Ross Newhan, and Paul Pringle. "Dodgers Deeply Implicated." *Los Angeles Times* 14 December 2007.
Reid, Jason. "Brown Is Open to a Trade." *Los Angeles Times* 3 December 2003.
Reid, Jason and Ross Newhan. "Yankees Give Brown His Ticket to Bronx Zoo." *Los Angeles Times* 13 December 2003.
Perry, Dayn. "Should Kevin Brown Be in the Hall of Fame?" *FanGraphs* 3 December 2010.
Hernandez, Dylan. "It Was Mutual Admiration Between Zack Greinke and Dodgers Brass." *Los Angeles Times* 12 December 2012.
Moura, Pedro. "Talented Scout." *Dodger Insider Magazine* September 2014.
Rosenthal, Ken. "Halos Will Have to Pay Up to Keep Trout." *FoxSports.com* 11 August 2013.
Knight, Molly. *The Best Team Money Can Buy*. New York: Simon & Schuster 2015.

Part Eight: The Bullpen Aces
Wolinsky, Russell. "Hugh Casey." *SABR Baseball Biography Project*.
Tusa C., Alfonso L. "Clem Labine." *SABR Baseball Biography Project*.
Musial, Stan as told to Bob Broeg. *The Man's Own Story*. New York: Doubleday 1964.
McGowen, Roscoe. "Dodger Starter Is Kept a Secret." *New York Times* 27 September 1941.
Henson, Steve. "Clem Labine, 80; Former Dodgers Relief Pitcher Played in 5 World Series." *Los Angeles Times* 3 March 2007.
Wolf, Al. "'Greatest Team, It Never Quit,' Says Walt Alston." *Los Angeles Times* 9 October 1959.
Jacobson, Steve. *The Pitching Staff*. New York: Crowell 1975.
"Angels Acquire Brewer in Trade With Dodgers." *Los Angeles Times* 18 July 1975.
"Jim Brewer, Ex-Dodger Reliever, Dies From Injuries in Head-On Crash." *Los Angeles Times* 17 November 1987.
Finch, Frank. "Regan Takes Over as No. 1 Dodger Fireman." *Los Angeles Times* 24 June 1966.

———. "Sandy Foiled Again, Homers Come Too Late in 5–1 Win." *Los Angeles Times* 2 August 1966.
Associated Press. "Marshall Not Sure He'll Join Dodgers." *Los Angeles Times* 7 December 1973.
Newhan, Ross. "Cy Young: Award Goes to Marshall." *Los Angeles Times* 7 November 1974.
"It's Back to School for Injured Marshall." *Los Angeles Times* 3 September 1975.
Newhan, Ross. "O'Malley Gives Campanis the Word: Trade Marshall." *Los Angeles Times* 15 June 1976.
Heisler, Mark. "Howe Undergoes Drug Cure." *Los Angeles Times* 15 January 1983.
Edes, Gordon. "Kuhn Suspends Howe for Entire '84 Season." *Los Angeles Times* 16 December 1983.
Associated Press. "Steve Howe, 48, Pitcher Who Battled Addiction, Dies." 29 April 2006.
Crowe, Jerry. "Tom Niedenfuer Remembers but Doesn't Dwell on Fateful Pitches." *Los Angeles Times* 10 October 2010.
Newhan, Ross. "They Get a Shortstop and Two Relief Pitchers." *Los Angeles Times* 12 December 1987.
Reid, Jason. "Gagne Move Goes Against the Grain." *Los Angeles Times* 24 March 2002.
Weisman, Jon. "Rousing!" *Dodger Thoughts* 18 June 2004.
Habib, Daniel G. "As Scary as He Looks." *Sports Illustrated* 2 June 2003.
Ortiz, Jorge L. "Dodgers' Saito Living His Unlikely American Dream." *USA Today* 10 September 2007.
Hernandez, Dylan. "So Over His Past; Broxton's Not Interested in Reliving Playoff Failures as a Dodger." *Los Angeles Times* 9 October 2012.
Video: "Watch Dodgers Closer Kenley Jansen Explain How He Throws a Cutter." *Los Angeles Times* 4 April 2016.
Brown, Tim. "The Night Kenley Jansen Went from a Good Pitcher to a Great One." *Yahoo! Sports* 20 June 2017.
Swydan, Paul. "Kenley Jansen Is Marvelous." *FanGraphs* 23 October 2017.

Part Nine: The Magnificent

Verducci, Tom. "Real Men Have Curves." *Sports Illustrated* 29 May 2017.
Rosenthal, Ken. "How One of Clayton Kershaw's Most Devastating Pitches Was Born at Wrigley Field." *FoxSports.com* 15 November 2016.
Simers, T.J. "The Kid Needed Help from the Old Man but Didn't Get It." *Los Angeles Times* 16 October 2009.
Hernandez, Dylan. "Dodgers' Clayton Kershaw Keeps the Faith." *Los Angeles Times* 28 February 2010.
Keri, Jonah. "The Growing Legend of Clayton Kershaw." *Grantland* 8 May 2013.
Associated Press. "Clayton Kershaw Tosses 4-hit Shutout as Dodgers Nip Barry Zito, Giants." *ESPN.com* 15 September 2010.
Hernandez, Dylan. "Clayton Kershaw Joins Elite Dodgers Company by Winning Cy Young Award." *Los Angeles Times* 17 November 2011.
Weisman, Jon. "Opening Day Blast." *Sports on Earth* 2 April 2013.
Hershiser, Orel. "'He Takes No One for Granted.'" *Dodger Insider Magazine* April 2015.
Honeycutt, Rick. "'Driven to Go Past What Most People Will Accept.'" *Dodger Insider Magazine* April 2015.
McCalvy, Adam. "Trouble with the Curve: Kershaw Can't Follow Script." MLB.com 23 October 2016.
Weisman, Jon, editor. *2016 Los Angeles Dodgers Yearbook*. New York: Professional Sports Publications 2016.
Down, Bobby. "Clayton Kershaw and the 7th Inning Threshold." *Baseline Times* 19 October 2017.
Peter, Josh. "Dodgers' Clayton Kershaw vows to press on: 'Maybe one of these days, we won't fail.'" *USA Today* 2 November 2017.